Dutton's Dirty Diggers

Bertha P. Dutton

DUTTON'S DIRTY DIGGERS

Bertha P. Dutton *and the* Senior Girl Scout
Archaeological Camps *in the* American Southwest,
1947–1957

CATHERINE S. FOWLER

with Contributions by
Jo Tice Bloom, Susan S. Martin, and Mary Anne Stein

THE UNIVERSITY OF UTAH PRESS
Salt Lake City

The Defiance House Man colophon is a registered trademark
of The University of Utah Press. It is based on a four-foot-tall
Ancient Puebloan pictograph (late PIII) near Glen Canyon, Utah.

Cataloging-in-Publication information on this title
is available from the Library of Congress.

Errata and further information on this and other titles available online at
UofUpress.com

Printed and bound in the United States of America.

To Dutton's Dirty Diggers,
and all Girl Scouts, past and present. May you
always be curious and care about the wonderful world
and people around you.

Contents

Publisher's Note

In some cases, editorial discretion has been used to provide consistency and clarity across the primary sources.

All dates are Common Era (CE) unless otherwise stated.

Abbreviations

The following abbreviations appear in the book.

AAUW: American Association of University Women
AC: Archaeological Conservatory
ARMS: Archaeological Resources Management System (see also MIAC/LA)
ARPA: Archaeological Resources Protection Act
BIA: Bureau of Indian Affairs
DDD: Dutton's Dirty Diggers
GBASPA: Galisteo Basin Archaeological Sites Protection Act
GBP: Galisteo Basin Preserve
GSUSA: Girl Scouts of the United States of America
GS Rep: GSUSA Representative
LAA: Laboratory of Anthropology Archives (see also MIAC/LA, MIAC/LAA)
MIAC/LA: Museum of Indian Arts and Culture/Laboratory of Anthropology
MIAC/LAA: Museum of Indian Arts and Culture/Laboratory of Anthropology Archives
MoIFA: Museum of International Folk Art
MNM: Museum of New Mexico
NPS: National Park Service
NAGPRA: Native American Graves Protection and Repatriation Act
OAS: New Mexico Office of Archaeological Studies
SAR: School of American Research/School for Advanced Research
UNM: University of New Mexico

Name Changes

The following names have changed since the Girl Scout Archaeological Mobile and Dig Camps in the 1940s and 1950s. Some agencies administrating historical properties also have changed since that time. In order to maintain consistency with the young women's experience and quoted documents, the new names are placed in parentheses on first mention in the book and listed below.

Old	New
Anasazi	Ancestral Pueblo
Aztec National Monument	Aztec Ruins National Monument
Chaco Canyon National Monument	Chaco Culture National Historical Park
Chaparral Girl Scout Council	Girl Scouts of Chaparral Council
Coronado State Park	Coronado Historic Site
Jemez State Park/Monument	Jemez Historic Site
Kuaua	Coronado Historic Site
Museum of Fine Arts	New Mexico Museum of Art
Museum of Navajo Ceremonial Art	Wheelwright Museum of the American Indian
New Mexico Assoc. on Indian Affairs	Southwestern Association of Indian Affairs
Pecos State Monument	Pecos National Historical Park
San Juan Pueblo	Ohkay Owingey
Santa Fe Fiesta Market	Santa Fe Indian Market
School of American Research (SAR)	School for Advanced Research (SAR)
Sitgreaves National Forest	Apache-Sitgreaves National Forest

Preface

As we age, I suspect we all look back to special experiences in our lives that we consider seminal for charting our paths to the present. Such memories, valid or idealized, frequently involve recalling not only times, but places, events, and specific persons who made these experiences stand out and gave us direction. For me, as well as for the primary contributors to this story, one such set of special experiences came through membership in the Girl Scouts of the United States of America and particularly through a program of archaeological camps offered by a dynamic woman, Dr. Bertha Pauline Dutton, in the American Southwest, often referred to as "the Land of Enchantment." Through Girl Scouts in general, we were already familiar with the principles of Scouting, camping and outdoor living, our local environments, and commitments to friends and leaders with whom we had shared fun, adventure, and confidences. But in our Senior Girl Scout years and through Bertha Dutton's program, we learned yet more about comradeship and leadership while following her through a new region of the country well-known for its beauty, vitality, and deep history, but largely unknown to us. We were introduced to it not only by our leader, but by other men and particularly women, and through direct experience. Those we met had made satisfying and exciting careers in fields that we knew little about at the time, let alone considered for our futures. In this book, we introduce you to the program, our leader and mentor, some of our experiences, and the impacts that it all had on us at an important time in our lives—our teenage years. This is but one view, a positive one, but it is the only one we can document. The history and memories recorded here are our perspectives on something that we felt was significant and unique.

As with any such undertaking, this book has a complex history. Most of those quoted here were directly tied to the "Senior Girl Scout Archaeological Mobile

Camps in the American Southwest" as Scout participants. Our leader and mentor, Dr. Bertha Dutton, was a well-known anthropologist, curator at the Museum of New Mexico in Santa Fe, and not herself a Girl Scout. Known to us as "Bert," Dutton took groups of girls on Mobile Camps through the American Southwest for 11 summers (1947 to 1957) and also provided many of the veteran participants with actual archaeological excavation experience during an additional six of those years (1951 to 1956). By following Bert on these adventures we became "Dutton's Dirty Diggers" (DDDs), a label we have proudly carried through the rest or our lives. Each DDD took part in one or more sessions that were jointly sponsored by the Girl Scouts of the United States of America (GSUSA) and the Museum of New Mexico (MNM), Santa Fe. Others directly involved were a small staff, Girl Scout representatives, and administrators who kept the operations running.

The task of pulling the story of this program together has been a joint effort. It all started after a series of fortuitous circumstances brought us together after each of us realizing our interest in Bert and the program had not waned after all these years. The core group included, in addition to the primary author, Jo Tice Bloom, Susan S. Martin, Mary Anne Stein, and Diana (Diane) Bird. Bloom, Martin, Stein, and Fowler were all participants ("Dutton's Dirty Diggers") in the program. Bird became an honorary DDD as curator of the Bertha Pauline Dutton Collection as Archivist at the Museum of Indian Arts and Culture/Laboratory of Anthropology Archives (hereafter MIAC/LAA or "the Lab Archives"), a division of the Museum of New Mexico, Santa Fe. Bird relived many of the experiences with us by listening to us and through her untiring assistance with the Dutton Archive through the years.

The other four of us came to the project somewhat independently over a decade and a half ago. Once we met, we realized that we each had experiences through the program that illustrated its value and were perhaps worth telling. Although we had participated in the camps in different years (with little overlap), we all felt the impact of Bert as a role model at that important time in our lives when we were thinking about the future and directions we might take. Each of us went on to higher education, choosing careers not directly mirroring Bert's, but paralleling in many ways the example she set in motivation and independence. Once together, we expanded our connections to other DDDs and non-Diggers whom we knew, receiving welcomed advice, support, and additional contributions of materials to the Dutton Archive (see Acknowledgements).

As a DDD in 1956 and 1957, I (Fowler), like the others, had stayed in touch with Bert (in my case casually) through the years by visits to Santa Fe, as well as seeing her at professional meetings and at other gatherings. But her memorial service in Santa Fe in 1994 served as a pointed reminder to me of my personal debt to her for introducing me on those trips to anthropology, to vibrant Native American and Hispanic histories, cultures, and arts, plus the striking landscapes of the Southwest. Another reminder came in 2001 in a note in the newsletter *New Mexico Archaeology*, by DDD Elizabeth Galligan, reminiscing about Bert and the benefits of the program for her and others she knew. There was yet another in 2003 when former DDDs living and visiting in the Santa Fe area, with the help of Diane Bird, put together a small exhibit on the "Dig" at Pueblo Largo (part of the program) for the lobby of the Lab building. For it, they used archival photographs and notes from what was by then a growing collection of Dutton materials in the archives and contributed more of their own materials to it.

All of these reminders seemed to be saying that something more should be said and written about Bert, the program, and its impacts on the young women who had been part of it. The opportunity came for me in 2004 when a session was proposed for the annual meeting of the Society for American Archaeology titled "Unconventional Scholars: Making Archaeology Happen." The title immediately brought to mind Bert and the Senior Girl Scout program as a good example of how professionals and museums can reach out to the public, including a nontraditional audience, with their educational messages. So in January 2004, I visited the Lab Archives and, with Diane's help, went through the large Bertha P. Dutton Collection (99BPD.xx) for materials on the Senior Girl Scout Archaeological Mobile Camps, ultimately writing a preliminary paper on the program's history (Fowler 2004, 2010).

The exhibit in the Lab lobby generated yet more interest in Dutton and the Girl Scout activities, including additional offers of materials to the Archives by former DDDs and others. Bird was excited to meet former Diggers and receive the donations, but soon realized that the already large Dutton Collection (29+ cartons) could not be properly utilized for research on the Girl Scouts or any other of Dutton's many activities by using the simple box inventory then available. It needed a proper catalog, but with her time already overcommitted, she could not see her way clear to tackle the very large job without help. In 2005, Jo Tice Bloom, historian and New Mexico resident, presented a paper to the Arizona-New Mexico historical societies meeting based on her DDD experiences in 1948 as chronicled in letters written that summer to her parents (Bloom 2007; 2011). Diane already knew Jo from previous Historical Society of New Mexico meetings and was impressed by the paper. She discovered that Jo also had archival experience, had remained active in Girl Scouting in New Mexico as an adult, and had remained in touch with Bert. Diane enlisted Jo to begin the laborious task of a preliminary inventory and ordering of the Dutton Collection, especially focusing on the Girl Scout materials, but also separating out other subjects. Bloom started work that fall and continued at several intervals over the next four years until health issues intervened (unfortunately, she passed away in June, 2019). The collection is now better housed with more detailed inventories available, but is not yet fully cataloged to archival standards or generally available (thus its number: 99BPD.xx).

In the summer of 2007, I spent a month as a William Y. and Nettie K. Adams summer scholar at the School for Advanced Research in Santa Fe, working toward a larger project on Bert and the Senior Girl Scout program. (Nettie Kesseler [Adams] also had been a DDD in 1951 and 1952). While Jo continued working on the main body of the Dutton Collection, I sorted a recent addition to it by Caroline Olin, Bert's long-time friend, and it was then that Jo and I met and decided to work together on the story. That summer I also met Susan Martin and Mary Anne Stein, both DDDs from 1954 to 1956, through Diane and another mutual friend, archaeologist Alexander J. Lindsay, Jr. of the Museum of Northern Arizona, Flagstaff. Sue had maintained close ties to Bert and Caroline, and had helped with the donation of the original Dutton Collection as well as the Olin Collection that I was working on that summer. Both she and Mary Anne offered assistance to Diane, Jo, and me with any questions about the Girl Scout materials—especially by identifying photographs, developing rosters of participants, donating materials, and other matters (see particularly Appendix A and Appendix C for specific additional contributions by Martin, Bloom, and Stein; and Acknowledgements).

The following summer (2008) all of us got together for a round of photo identification and discussion at the Lab. Other DDDs, including Gillian Wethey McHugh (DDD 1952–1954), another long-time friend of Bert's and also of Sue's, and Jo's sister, Cyndy Tice (DDD 1953), were part of that gathering. That summer another Digger veteran who had remained close to Bert, Vorsila Bohrer (DDD 1947–1949, 1951, 1955), contributed additional materials, as did Anne Rushmer McClelland (DDD 1947–1949), Kate Swift (who had been a Girl Scout Representative to the program in 1953), and Sue and Mary Anne. Interests in the project, as well as potential source materials, were now expanding!

Sources

The materials that follow are thus gleaned from a variety of sources, many of them recording the direct experiences of the DDDs, as provided in letters to parents, articles for hometown newspapers, an internal newsletter (*The Sipapu*, distributed among DDDs for three years, 1953–1955), scrapbooks (especially those compiled by girls attending the Pueblo Largo Dig sessions from 1951 through 1956), and later reminiscences or other materials communicated directly to us or donated to the MIAC/LAA. Also utilized were the administrative and other files in the Lab and Museum of New Mexico, the Fray Angélico Chávez History Library of the Palace of the Governors/New Mexico History Museum. In addition, Jo Bloom and Diane Bird visited the Girl Scouts of the United States of America National Archive in New York City in 2009 and retrieved documents related to the program (see Manuscript Sources and Additional Photograph Credits).

Bertha Dutton wrote summary articles about several of the archaeological camp sessions (especially in the earlier years) for *El Palacio*, a Museum of New Mexico publication, and *Teocentli*, an informal newsletter circulated among archaeologists. In these reports, she often included itineraries, listed names of campers and staff, and summarized her impressions of the success of the year's sessions for the campers and herself. There is also a large photographic record, some professional, but most personal as donated by the girls. And there are important files in the Archives of the School for Advanced Research (Edgar L. Hewett materials, other administrative holdings). Bertha Dutton (Dutton 1983; 1985; 1987; 1990) also gave several taped oral interviews, all of which contain information on the program.

Dutton was a scholar, publishing papers in professional anthropology journals as well as scholarly and popular books. Her work with the Senior Girl Scouts is sometimes referenced in these publications as it was an important part of her career and philosophy of public education. But by far the largest collection of materials relating to her and this program is contained in the Dutton Collection in the MIAC/LAA. This book is not intended to cover Dutton's career, which is indeed vast and very important to documenting the lives of women in archaeology. She made important contributions above and beyond our focus here. We do, however, refer to some of her other interests, work, and specialties (e.g., Mesoamerican archaeology) as they are indeed important to the story.

Additional Reading

There is a very large professional and popular literature on the peoples, cultures, and places of the American Southwest. Given that, it is very hard in a book of this nature to know where to start, let alone stop, in citing sources, especially for those who would like to know more about this fascinating region. For those who have not experienced the region directly and might feel challenged by what appears to be a plethora of place names, designations for Native American groups, tribes, and nations, as well as other cultural and historical references, we recommend that you consult the various websites for each group; for the U.S. National Parks, Monuments, and Historic Sites; and the State Historic Sites (please note that some place names have changed since the Diggers visited, and a list of old and new names is provided in the front section of this book). For those who wish to learn more about regional archaeology, its methods, and some of the current thinking and views, we also recommend the School for Advanced Research's Popular Archaeology series covering several Southwest areas (Downum 2012; Fish and Fish 2007; Nelson and Hegmon 2010; Noble 2000, 2004, 2006, 2008, 2014; Powers 2005; Reed and Brown 2018). They are nontechnical but highly informative about the history and places that are discussed. Davis (2008) also provides a good account about how excavation camps were organized about a decade before the Girl Scout "Digs" at Pueblo Largo and the comradery that often develops on such projects.

Catherine S. (Kay Sweeney) Fowler
Reno, Nevada, July 1, 2019

Acknowledgments

Many individuals and institutions were important in the development of this story, and they all deserve sincere thanks and appreciation for their many kindnesses and good advice. Bruce Bernstein, who earlier was Director of the Museum of Indian Arts and Culture/Laboratory of Anthropology (MIAC/LA), first alerted me to the institution's receipt of the Bertha P. Dutton Collection, as he knew of my participation in Dutton's program. Shelby Tisdale, who later was MIAC/LA Director, provided news in 2006 of the acquisition of Caroline Olin's papers, which gave me the incentive to begin working with the Dutton materials in earnest. The School for Advanced Research kindly hosted me on their beautiful campus as a William Y. Adams and Nettie K. Adams summer scholar in 2007 so that I could really begin the work. I thank then-Director James Brooks, Nancy Owen Lewis, and Laura Holt for making my stay so pleasant (I had just retired from teaching after 38 years—and can't think of a better retirement present). James Ferris facilitated an interview with Caroline Olin that summer, and later donation of the Kate Swift materials through Lucy Lippard. Willow Roberts Powers helped me formulate various approaches to the book, also starting that summer, and provided critical comment on ideas and drafts for several years thereafter. Others who kindly answered questions, identified photographs, and provided access to their personal materials included Dutton's Dirty Diggers Nettie Kesseler Adams, Jo Tice Bloom, Vorsila Bohrer, Susan Martin, Rebecca Adams Mills, Mary Anne Stein, Cyndy Tice, and Gillian Wethey. Richard Ford, Robert Powers, Polly and Curtis Schaafsma, and Mollie and H. Wolcott "Wolky" Toll willingly shared their knowledge and personal stories of the people, places, and archaeology of the region, and listened to my endless ramblings about those Girl Scout years. Mollie facilitated my later contacts with Vorsila Bohrer, and Wolky was made an honorary Dutton's Dirty Digger for arranging our visits to Pueblo Largo (see Epilogue).

Informal reviewers of earlier manuscript drafts (some multiple times), who provided critical feedback at various stages of development, were Jo and John Bloom, Don Fowler, Mark Fowler, Susan Martin, Nancy Parezo, and Mary Anne Stein. Formal reviews with very helpful comments and suggestions were made by Ann Robertson, well-known historian of Girl Scouting, and Dr. Barbara Mills, Regents Professor of Anthropology, University of Arizona. Diane Bird, Archivist at MIAC/LA, put up with my long and short visits to read, check, and recheck materials over 15 years—always showing her good humor, patience, and long-term commitment to the project and her institution. We shared many good times (especially lunches) during this period. Nancy Parezo not only listened to my endless issues with doing archival research in fits and starts due to the distances between Reno and Santa Fe, but also provided me files on Dutton from regional newspapers and helped me with photographs. To all, I am more than grateful.

Additional thanks go to various institutions for access to their holdings, including manuscripts and photographs (see also Manuscript Sources and Additional Photograph Credits): Division of Anthropology, American Museum of Natural History; The Fray Angélico Chávez History Library and the Photo Archives, Palace of the Governors, New Mexico History Museum, Santa Fe; Girl Scouts of the USA National Archive, New York City; Library, Maxwell Museum of Anthropology, University of New Mexico; MIAC/LA, Santa Fe, for granting me Research Associate status to work on the project; and School of American Research (now School for Advanced Research), Santa Fe.

Very special thanks go to my contributing authors: Jo Tice Bloom, Susan Martin, and Mary Anne Stein. Each provided the primary data for Appendices A, B, and C, but also many other contributions throughout. Getting to know them, hear their perspectives, and collect their feedback through a project too long in the completion, has been a joy. Maps were very carefully prepared, as always, by Patricia DeBunch of Eetza Research Associates, Reno, Nevada. Patti also helped me down to the wire with glitches in technical matters with photographs. Don Fowler has put up with endless versions of the manuscript and in recent years, with my one-tract mind in trying to finish it—finally. Also, as always, Reba Rauch, and the staff and contractors (copy editor Anya Martin) of the University of Utah Press did yeoman service as facilitators all along the way. I thank them all for their patience and kindness.

1

Introduction

In five years' time the Diggers have grown into a notable family. Of course we really were not diggers, but since our primary interest was in the diggings of archaeologists in the Southwest past and present, that soon became a name which the members of the Senior Girl Scout Archaeological Mobile Camps chose for themselves. In fact, so often dusty and dirty from hours of travel and hiking, and with water not always too plentiful, they went even farther and called themselves *Dutton's Dirty Diggers*. From 1947 on, our expeditions have been the "Digs," and each year the Digger family has increased.

—Dutton (1951a:354)

The Scene: The American Southwest

On July 6, 1947, seven eager teenage girls assembled with their duffel bags at Hyde Memorial State Park on the northeastern edge of Santa Fe, New Mexico, anticipating what would turn out to be a unique experience in directed learning in one of the most scenic and culturally diverse regions of the country, the American Southwest.

They were Senior Girl Scouts from several states, already veteran campers, and part of a unique experiment in a Girl Scout camping program designed to give girls an experience beyond the local level. Few knew what was really in store for them over the next two weeks of on-the-trail living. All they knew is that they would be following a leader, Bertha Dutton (after 1952, Dr. Bertha Dutton), Curator of Ethnology at the Museum of New Mexico and Associate in Archaeology at the School of American Research (now School for Advanced Research, both in Santa Fe). Better known as "Bert," the name she preferred, Dutton was small in stature—barely five feet tall—but she was mighty in ideas and determination. There was never any doubt in anyone's mind that she was in charge. Within a very short time, she would totally engage the seven girls' minds and hearts, so that before long, they were more than willing to "follow Bert" wherever she chose to lead them.

These seven girls, along with some 285 (plus) others who came after them, would follow Bert through the Southwest during the 11-year life of the program.[1] And many would be forever changed by the experience. Nicknamed "Dutton's Dirty Diggers," many were eager to come back to the Southwest for more than one camp—one came for nine—to see and learn more and have more adventures. Several Diggers would continue to follow Bert by taking academic degrees in her field (anthropology) or closely related ones. Many would become teachers, especially in high schools, and some in colleges and universities. Several would seek postgraduate degrees in a variety of disciplines, including anthropology, history, education, biology, biochemistry, health sciences, and law. They would credit those summer experiences with helping them establish career aims and successes hardly imagined in the late 1940s through 1950s by most young women. Whatever the impacts, they would always remember their summers in the Land of Enchantment and credit the woman who truly introduced them to it and her approach to "learning while doing." This is their story, and her story, and above all, the story of a successful venture that to our knowledge was unique in its impact: the Senior Girl Scout Archaeological Mobile Camp Program in the American Southwest, 1947 to 1957.[2]

Certainly Bert, and likely also the Girl Scouts of the United States of America had little hint that first summer that the program would develop as it did, be as successful as it became, last as long as it did, or have such an impact on the young women

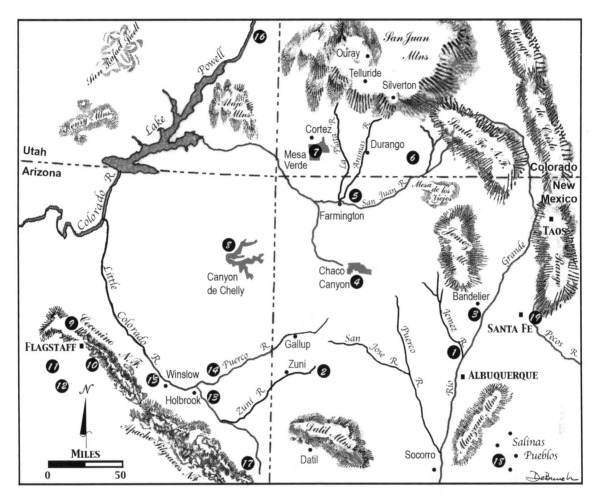

Figure 1.1. National Parks and Monuments of the northern Southwest. Map by Patricia DeBunch. (1) Coronado [State] Historic Site; (2) El Morro National Monument; (3) Bandelier National Monument; (4) Chaco Culture National Historical Park; (5) Aztec Ruins National Monument; (6) Chimney Rock National Monument; (7) Mesa Verde National Park; (8) Canyon de Chelly National Monument; (9) Wupatki National Monument/Sunset Crater Volcano National Monument; (10) Walnut Canyon National Monument; (11) Tuzigoot National Monument; (12) Montezuma Castle National Monument; (13) Petrified Forest National Park; (14) the Painted Desert; (15) Meteor Crater (private); (16); Arches National Park; (17) Kinishba Ruins (Fort Apache Indian Reservation); (18) Salinas Pueblo Missions National Monument; (19) Pecos National Historical Park.

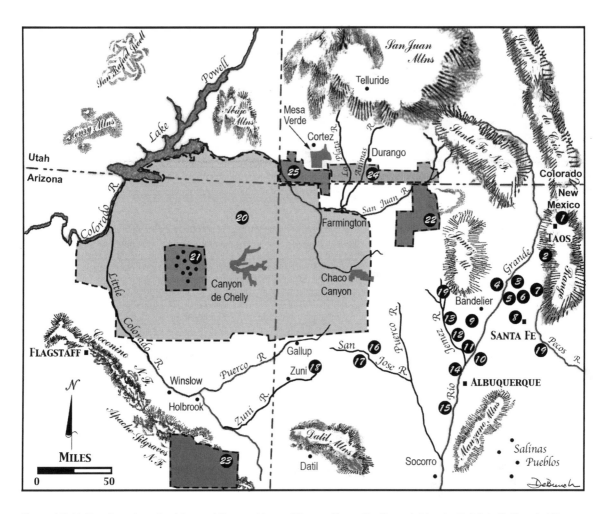

Figure 1.2. Native American Pueblos and Reservations of the northern Southwest. Map by Patricia DeBunch. Rio Grande and Other Pueblos – Tiwa languages/dialects: Taos (1); Picuris (2); Sandia (14); Isleta (15). Tewa languages/dialects: San Juan (Ohkay Owingeh) (3); Santa Clara (4); San Ildefonso (5); Pojoaque (6); Nambé (7); Tesuque (8); Third Mesa Hopi (21). Towa languages: Jemez (19); Old Pecos (19); Jemez River, some Salinas Pueblos, others no longer inhabited. Keres languages/dialects: Cochiti (9); Santo Domingo (10); San Filipe (11); Santa Ana (12); Zia (13); Laguna (16); Acoma (17). Zuni language: Zuni (18). Hopi language/dialects: Hopi Pueblos (21). Athabascan Languages/dialects: Navajo Nation (20); Jicarilla Apache Nation (22); Fort Apache Nation (23). Uto-Aztecan Languages: Southern Ute Reservation (24); Ute Mountain Reservation (25); Hopi Pueblos (21).

who participated. Seemingly the place was right (the American Southwest), as was the timing (the immediate postwar era), as were the participants—the Girl Scouts of the United States of America (hereafter GSUSA), Bertha Dutton, the Museum of New Mexico (hereafter MNM), and the Senior Girl Scouts. All contributed to the overall success and persistence of what began quite simply (Chapter 2).

The initial idea was to offer a two-week field tour taking in some of the spectacular scenic wonders of the northern Southwest while camping each night at or near National and State Parks and Monuments with major archaeological and historic sites—such as Chaco Canyon, Mesa Verde, Aztec [Ruins], Pecos, El Morro, Wupatki, and others (Figure 1.1). The tours would also visit some of the Native American Pueblo villages in the Rio Grande Valley as well as Acoma, Laguna, Zuni in western New Mexico, and the Hopi villages in northern Arizona. Homesteads (or "outfits") on the sprawling Navajo Reservation, trading posts, and Hispanic villages would likewise be on the itinerary, as would several of the museums and historic sites in Santa Fe (Figure 1.2). There would be ample time to learn at least some things about the region's complex ethnic and cultural heritage and deep history as well as the natural features of the landscape—flora, fauna, geology—all from a battery of experts. It would be far more than a mere tour. It would be a practical introduction to anthropology, history, and science in situ. Its educational orientation and content would not differ greatly from tours offered to some college and university students in the region at the time, or still offered today by organizations such as the Archaeological Conservancy, School for Advanced Research, Crow Canyon Archaeological Center, several museums and organizations, and a few private companies. All follow a long, although little known, tradition (Chapter 2). As the years went by, Dutton's plan would become more ambitious, ultimately including two-week archaeological excavation camps with the Girl Scouts as the Dig crews (Chapter 5).

The Girl Scouts of the United States of America and Bert shared overall aims for the betterment of young women, an increasing theme in the postwar period. The Girl Scout organization had a long history of supporting girls and young women to gain knowledge and responsibility in order to make them good citizens and useful to their communities. As a museum anthropologist used to interacting with the public,

Bert had the skills to provide both instructive and exciting learning experiences. She was also an excellent role model for those aspiring to a career, or undecided about what paths they might take in the future. The young women proved to be eager learners, with Bert providing them ample information backed by direct experiences in intriguing and captivating places in a region that she knew well and with people she deeply respected. The fortuitous combination helped the young participants discover new and fascinating things about their country, its people, its history, and themselves. And Bert, especially, opened their eyes to the importance of seeing— the landscape, other ways of living, the past and the present. Best of all, as one veteran Dutton's Dirty Digger remarked some 50 years later, "she taught us to be bold" (Cohen 2006).

The Times: Postwar Years

The period immediately following World War II was a difficult and often confusing time for women in the United States. Many had gone to work during the war due to the shortage of men, and/or to feed their families with husbands absent, and through the experience they had gained a new feeling of independence and self-worth. Certainly some struggled if they had not worked outside the home before, but they learned many new skills and took pride in their overall accomplishments. In other words, there was more to the famous poster of "Rosie the Riveter" and what she represented than met the eye.

With the return of service men and the end of war's hard times came a new era for women in the workforce. Not nearly as many were needed in the vital positions that they had filled. Some of those lucky enough to have their husbands come home may have rejoiced as things returned to the way they had been. They could again become stay-at-home moms and concentrate on raising their children. Others, including those now widowed or single, were not as lucky, and often felt frustrated by losing their positions to men, along with the sense of independence and responsibility that they had gained.

But the female workforce was slowly transforming in postwar years. Some of the change was due to growing consumerism and the need for more family income to enjoy the benefits of the new lifestyle in the suburbs. But there were also more women motivated toward careers, or at least going to college to increase their skills and potential marketability. At least some of this impetus likely was coming from their mothers who had lived through those difficult years and were now encouraging all of their children, and especially their daughters, to get more education to be able to support themselves when and if the need arose. Many more were also finishing high school and seeing the opportunities that college represented.

However, upon moving into higher education, women found little encouragement to go into nontraditional fields, especially those that were male dominated. They were more often guided into the pursuits deemed appropriate for women, including secretarial training, nursing (if they had an interest in science), primary and less often secondary teaching, social work, and a few others. They saw few female role models among the accountants, bankers, school principals, engineers, professors, lawyers, or physicians their families knew. The media, including radio, films, and now television, which was beginning to gain a foothold in US households, most often portrayed women as stay-at-home wives and mothers. There was no STEM emphasis as today to give women—or others underserved—either the information or the incentive to go into now familiar scientific or technical fields (Shetterly 2016).[3] They would have to discover the less well known fields—such as anthropology, marine biology, astronomy, or many others—by accident or diligent inquiry. Among the male professorial ranks the fallback position for not wanting to invest time in women, even those with obvious talent and brains, remained,: "you will just quit and get married before you finish." Men married, but it seemed to have been assumed by many that women were not capable of multitasking a career and family. In addition, women already working were often in half-time positions or positions that offered few incentives or possibilities for advancement. And there was also a wide gap in pay—a battle that continues to the present (Hill 2015, 2017; Parezo 1993b; Rossiter 1982; Vagins 2018).[4] But change was coming, and young women were looking for more and more ways to be part of it.

The Girl Scouts of the United States of America

The GSUSA was 35 years old in 1947 when the seven girls arrived in Santa Fe for the first Archaeological Mobile Camp. By this time, the GSUSA had a firm footing throughout the country, having reached an official membership of 1,000,000 just two years before (GSUSA 1962:33). Girl Scouting in the United States was created in 1912 by Juliette Gordon Low at the of urging Sir Robert Baden-Powell, based on the programs he developed for boys (Boy Scouts) and girls (Girl Guides) in the United Kingdom. His work, in turn, had been heavily influenced by Ernest Thompson Seton's Woodcraft Indians youth program, started in the USA in 1902.

The first two decades of the twentieth century, when these programs began, were a period of social reform and foment in the United States. Progressives were transforming local, state, and federal governments. Social reform was a major pre-occupation of women as they worked for passage of laws preventing the sale of con-taminated foods and drugs. The new labor unions were struggling to secure decent working conditions for their workers. In the middle of all this was the Women's Suffrage Movement, which would successfully secure the vote for women in 1920. Juliette Low's dream was to develop more capable and independent girls and young women in order to make them good citizens who would take active roles in bettering themselves and their communities. In many ways, her dream reflected the purposes of the various reform movements, and the plan received support from some of them.

Low, or "Daisy" as she was known, first published her program in a book titled *How Girls Can Help Their Country* in 1913, and then five years later, in *Scouting for Girls*. In these she put forth her plans in basic handbooks for the leaders and girls to follow. Leaders were to be average women in local communities. Originally the girls were to be 10 to 18 years of age, but later, the age requirements were altered to include younger girls. Although the first book was based on Baden-Powell's British Girl Guide handbook (*How Girls Can Help the Empire*), the American edition and the second book added several more ideas, including presenting the girls with profi-ciency badge requirements. The badges focused on the development of skills neces-sary to carry out Low's goals through specific sets of requirements to be met before each badge was awarded. Most of these emphasized citizenship, homemaking, personal health, childcare, and camping (Cordery 2012; GSUSA 1954c; Wadsworth 2012). Early handbooks also had a military cast, emphasizing military-like uniforms, marching, drills, and organizational patterns (platoons, patrols, etc.; Girl Scouts, Inc. 1925). No special attention seemed to be given to integrating real or imagined

Indigenous traditions, symbolism, or attire into badge requirements, ceremonies, or other activities as was the case with the Woodcraft Indians, Boy Scouts of America, Camp Fire Girls, or some of the other early youth programs and camps that also emerged during this period (Salomon 1928).

In addition to proficiency badges, camping was an essential part of Girl Scouting from the beginning, as Low and others felt that outdoor activities were crucial to the girls' development. The summer of 1912 saw the first Girl Scout camping trip to one of the islands off the Georgia coast. Today folklore about this trip still generates laughter, as the girls (and their leaders) apparently forgot to bring food! This experience began a long tradition of camping adventures for the Girl Scouts, many to be related as memories around countless evening campfires down through the years.

The training Low had in mind was in diverse activities after school hours and in the summers that would also give the Scouts experience working together and learning to share a sense of responsibility and accomplishment. She firmly believed that girls and young women could do anything if they had the proper education and mindset—and Girl Scouting was to be an important part of providing both. Low's rule of thumb was "if it isn't right, the girls won't take to it and it won't last" (Culmer 1962:8). The first 35 years of scouting, and ultimately, the Girl Scout Archaeological Mobile Camp Program, seemed to fit that rule very well—although no one could have predicted in 1947 that the girls would take to it as they did, or that it would last for 11 years.

As the Girl Scout movement grew, a more formal hierarchical organization developed. The first national office was located in Washington, D.C. in 1913. In 1916 it was moved to New York City where it remains. In the early days, local councils developed slowly, chartered by the national organization; many troops, however, operated as "lone troops" with a direct relationship to National headquarters. Standards, including knowledge of the *Girl Scout Promise* and *Girl Scout Laws*,[5] badge requirements, specific awards and achievement levels, needed to be maintained for all. In order to carry out these specific services more efficiently, regional headquarters were soon established (Wikipedia 2018). By the 1940s, there were 12 regions, each with overarching councils and staffs. The regional offices were set up to maintain national standards and programs as well as develop local camps and some of their own offerings. Local programs could focus on activities most appropriate to the geographic region or its specific history. In 1947, New Mexico was part of Region IX, called the "Cactus Region," including New Mexico, Texas, and Oklahoma, with headquarters in Dallas.

With the creation of more age-related units within Scouting (Brownies, Intermediates, Seniors) as well as local interests, some specific foci emerged. These were especially applicable to high school or Senior Girl Scouts, ages 14 to 18. In 1934, along the coastlines and around lakes, Mariner Girl Scout troops were formed, some with their own ratings, uniforms, and pins. Wing Girl Scouts developed in 1941 with the start of World War II for those girls specifically interested in aviation and flying (Wikipedia 2018). Both of these groups offered exciting alternatives for the older girls seeking more focused and adventurous activities.

During World War II, Girl Scouts (and especially Senior Scouts) emphasized service on the Home Front. They served as hospital aides, grew victory gardens, become bicycle couriers, helped train women in home survival skills, packed Junior Red Cross boxes, took part in sky watch teams, and much more (GSUSA 1962:32; GSUSA 2020). On the international front, Girl Scouts sponsored "Clothes for Friendship," a drive that provided more than 150,000 children in Europe and Asia with clothing. Membership in the World Association of Girl Guides and Girl Scouts, originally founded in 1928, was also spreading, so that within a few years of the end of the war, it included 50 countries (Culmer 1962:8–9).

As a result of wartime service, and the Mariner and Wing Scout programs, older girls were looking for yet more specialized programs. Many felt "grown-up" by participating in the wartime jobs (GSUSA 1962:12). They had already explored and accumulated several of the badges of their choice, including those requiring advanced camping skills. Some regions responded by starting more extensive outdoor programs—longer hiking and camping trips, such as along the Appalachian Trail, or horseback trail rides, or mountaineering adventures to new areas. Some of these opportunities were open to girls nationally where practical. But leaders, especially on the local level, were not always aware of these possibilities, and especially of those beyond their region. The focus was still largely local, with locally maintained camps available in most areas, including those operated during summer days ("day camps") as well as camps where the Scouts stayed overnight for a week or more. These were primarily at sites owned and operated by local Girl Scout councils. But the interests of some Senior Girl Scouts were waning, especially those who had attended these camps several times and found less appeal in remaining choices of badges. Regional and national leadership started looking for additional opportunities to keep the young women engaged and involved.

Thus, in late 1946, when Ursula (Sue) Little, National Community Advisor for the Girl Scouts but working through Region IX's Dallas office, heard a radio interview with Ed Ferdon of the Museum of New Mexico about an archaeological touring trip through northern New Mexico that he was planning for his Santa Fe Boy Scout troop, she was very interested. She immediately thought that such a trip would be a great opportunity for Senior Girl Scouts (Dutton 1983). Little contacted Ferdon about the idea, asked if he thought it might work for Senior Girl Scouts, and whom she should contact to discuss it. Ferdon agreed that it could work, and suggested that she speak with his boss, Dr. Sylvanus Griswold Morley, Director of the Museum of New Mexico in Santa Fe. Morley immediately saw the potential and how it might fit with the Museum's mission of public education. He suggested that Little meet with Bertha Dutton, the person on his staff with the best potential to lead such a trip. He said that it would be up to Bert to agree—he was not "assigning" her to do it. For Bert, there apparently was no question: it sounded like a fine idea.

Bertha Dutton

In the fall of 1946 when Bert and Sue Little first met, Bert had been in Santa Fe and at the Museum of New Mexico for 10 years. She was on her way to becoming a well-known figure in the town as well as in northern New Mexico generally. She was part of a community and region that, although much less populated than it is today, had already seen its share of unique personalities, and especially women. Several powerful, and for the most part, wealthy, well-educated women had arrived in the area in the late 1800s and early 1900s. Some of them had made and were still making significant contributions to the arts and literature, staking claims to and championing different causes and special interests (especially Native American rights), as well as founding and supporting important institutions. Some were involved in all three.[6] Together they provided a feeling that the region was one where women could do their own thing and go their own way, especially if they had the funds—but also the will—to take a different path.

Bertha Dutton was in some ways like her predecessors (several were still contributing when she arrived), but in other ways not like them. She did not come from a wealthy background or start out with a proper education at a fine school; but she was independently minded, strong-willed, and definitely motivated to make her own way. She was in many ways a pioneer in her chosen field—anthropology. Although not among the first generation of women to make contributions to anthropology in the region, she was among the first women to gain full-time employment associated with her degree. She was also among the first to pursue archaeology as a specialty within anthropology—although her primary employment was as Curator of Ethnology, part of cultural anthropology, another specialty within the broader discipline. Archaeology in the Southwest, as well as elsewhere in the United States at this time, was heavily dominated by men. Most of the women involved by the 1930s and 1940s were the wives of archaeologists, and few were given credit for their contributions to what were quite clearly joint enterprises—surveying, excavating, and writing reports on archaeological sites (Cordell 1993; Mathien 1992, 2003). In addition to being Curator of Ethnology at the MNM—a job Bert created for herself—she was Associate in Archaeology at the SAR (now School for Advanced Research; also SAR), a nonsalaried position, but quite appropriate considering that she surveyed and excavated archaeological sites in Mexico and Guatemala as well as locally.

Many people in Santa Fe knew Bert, or "Bertie" as she was called by her close friends. She was often seen on Santa Fe's downtown plaza talking with friends or acquaintances, or driving her beloved Model A Ford. She claimed that it was the first in Santa Fe, and it was always kept in mint condition. In her later years, she sported a jaunty beret—usually red. Some Santa Feans knew her primarily through her employment, and yet others as a good citizen, active in various civic organizations and other activities. Diminutive and jovial as she was, her piercing blue eyes could and did quickly reveal her serious side as well as her iron will. She devoted much of her time to educating the public about the lifeways of the Indigenous people of the region and their histories through her museum work, research, and popular writing. She firmly believed that sound information led to better and more nuanced and genuine crosscultural understanding—a strong message of anthropology to which she was fully committed.

Bertha Pauline Dutton was born in Algona, Iowa, on March 29, 1903, the daughter of Orrin Judd Dutton and Fannie Stewart Dutton. She was raised in Iowa, Kansas, and Nebraska on farms and in small towns. As an only child, Bert "sort of developed as I grew up into mother's girl and father's boy," learning to climb trees, race, drive horses, "and do all sorts of things that little girls aren't supposed to do" (Dutton 1985a:11). She started school in a one-room school house, transferred to other rural schools as her family moved to new situations, and finally finished high school (and some college courses) in Broken Bow, Nebraska (Figure 1.3). She credited several of her teachers along the way with sparking her interest in learning, especially about nature and ancient history (Bohrer 1979:5). She studied English and business in a local branch college while working several jobs, including in a bank and for the Board of Education of the Lincoln County (Nebraska) Schools. Already showing her fierce independence when she turned 21, she cut off her long hair and adopted a short, neatly trimmed cut, her signature for the rest of her life. She said of the decision: "I was free then, and I've been free ever since" (Kessinger 1980). Her various jobs sharpened her administrative skills but left her feeling unfulfilled, as she soon realized that she was in a dead-end situation, especially being a woman (Bohrer 1979:4–6). Besides, as she said later, "I couldn't stand the humdrum nature of being a business clerk" (Babcock et al. 1986:1).

Figure 1.3. Bertha Dutton, high school graduation, Broken Bow, NE, 1923. Courtesy of Susan S. Martin Collection.

In the fall of 1930, Bert was struck by a car while exiting a city bus. The accident left her incapacitated for more than a year. Time convalescing gave her a chance to read extensively in her favorite subject, ancient history. During this period, she was introduced to archaeology. In the fall of 1932, a settlement from the accident allowed her to buy a 1928 Model A Ford and to think about going to college full time. She chose the University of New Mexico (hereafter UNM), with a planned major in archaeology, because they responded enthusiastically to her inquiries. At that point, there were approximately 1,100 students at UNM, and over half of them had or were taking courses in anthropology and archaeology, largely due to reputation of a dynamic teacher, Dr. Edgar Lee Hewett (Bohrer 1979:8; Fowler 2004).

Hewett, also Director of SAR and MNM, both in Santa Fe, had founded the Department of Archaeology and Anthropology at UNM in 1928, and was then its Chair. He had instituted popular summer field training programs in archaeology in the Jemez Mountains and at Chaco Canyon in northwestern New Mexico. In addition, he started summer field schools through the Archaeological Institute of America in Mesoamerica and South America. All of these were open to women—making UNM particularly appealing to Dutton. Hewett had always advocated educating women in the same fields as men, and anthropology and archaeology were no exceptions (Joiner 1992; Mathien 1992).

Members of the UNM department faculty at the time Bert entered as a student in 1933 included ethnologist Clyde Kluckhohn, whom she later described as "fresh out of Oxford, holey sox, baggy pants" (Dutton 1983). He would become very well known for his work among the Navajo people. Others included Mamie Tanquist (cultural anthropology), Marjorie Ferguson (later Marjorie Tichy Lambert, local archaeology), Donald Brand (cultural geography), and Florence Hawley (Ellis), a new PhD from the University of Chicago (Southwest archaeology and ethnology).[7] Faculty in other UNM departments that rounded out the program and from whom Dutton would learn much about local history, natural history, and anthropology included Lansing Bloom (history), Edward Castetter (biology), and Stuart Northrop (geology). All added depth to the experiences of the students, including through the summer field schools that also hosted distinguished visiting faculty each year (Bohrer 1979).

Bert's first year as a student at UNM was not easy, as she was roughly 10 years older than many of the students and she had chosen to live in a dormitory. But given her outgoing personality and maturity, she fit in well, and was soon counseling students who were homesick or needed tutoring. Among the homesick was a young woman from Laguna Pueblo (Miriam Marmon)[8] whom she befriended, and who took Bert home to meet her parents (Walter and Susie Marmon) and siblings and to spend the Christmas holidays. Bert developed a lasting friendship and kinship with the Marmon family. One of her first publications was coauthored with Miriam (Dutton and Marmon 1936).

At the end of her first year, Bert became department secretary working for Hewett, largely due to her previous work experience and need for income (her

settlement monies were running out). In addition to balancing the demands of the job, which included keeping Hewett organized and moving (since he was running several organizations at once), she continued taking courses toward her degree. Bert was "on the ground," so to speak, for many of Hewett's national and international plans and schemes (D. Fowler 2000), and she remained his devoted ally throughout their years together. She also took part in Hewett's Jemez and Chaco field schools in 1933, first as his secretary but later as a member of the archaeological survey crew in the Jemez Mountains. She enrolled in the Chaco Canyon field school in 1934 to get experience in site excavation (Joiner 1992; Mathien 1992).[9]

In 1935, Bert completed her bachelor's degree with a major in archaeology and minors in ethnology and geology. Still Hewett's secretary, she decided to skip the "cap and gown falderal" of commencement and attend instead UNM's South American field school, sailing to Bolivia, Ecuador, and Peru for six weeks. She also

Figure 1.4. Fannie Dutton, Orrin J. ("Judd") Dutton, Bill Chauvenet, Bertha Dutton, Ray Ghert, Ed Ferdon, and Bob Coffin showing off Navajo blankets, 1934. Catalogue No. 2011.8.0. Courtesy of the Maxwell Museum of Anthropology, University of New Mexico.

Figure 1.5.
University of New
Mexico students
and faculty aboard
ship to Guatemala,
1937. Left to right,
back row: Carol
Bloom, Barbara
Moore, Mary R.
Van Stone, John
Corbett, Mrs.
Hewett, Dr. Edgar
Lee Hewett, Ed
Ferdon. Left
to right, front
row: Dorothy
Luhrs, Hulda
Hobbs, Bertha
Dutton, Neola
Eyer. Courtesy of
Susan S. Martin
Collection.

spent part of the summer back at the Chaco Canyon field school (Figure 1.4). After a year of graduate work, in the summer of 1936 and as an SAR scholar, she attended the Department's Mexico Field School where she fell in love with Mexico's engaging and spectacular archaeology (Bohrer 1979:10). All of these trips were at least partly arranged through Hewett's activities, and he was part of the expeditions.

Through these field schools Bert first met those whom she later would call "the outdoor people," men and women who were always warm, cooperative, interested in nature and all of its aspects, as was she, and a sharp contrast to the people in the business world whom she found dull and discriminatory on most counts—and especially gender (Dutton 1985a:7). She remained steadfast friends with many she met on these schools, a number of whom would become people of importance in her worlds of Southwest and Mesoamerican anthropology and archaeology. These

Figure 1.6. Visiting the Alibates Site, West Texas, 1935. Left to right: Hulda Hobbs, Jean Cady, Marjorie Ferguson (Tichy Lambert), Bertha Dutton. Courtesy of Susan S. Martin Collection.

relationships remained throughout her life and served her well, including during the Girl Scout years when many of them lectured to her girls and welcomed them to their archaeological excavations or "digs."

In the fall of 1936, Bert joined the MNM staff in Santa Fe as Assistant to the Director. The Director was Hewett—wearing the additional administrative hat to the one as Chair of the Department at UNM. Colleagues at the Museum at the time included Edwin Ferdon, who had been a fellow student of Bert's at UNM and also served as Hewett's driver. In later years, Ferdon would hold several other positions in the Museum system, so that they would be long-term colleagues. Marjorie Ferguson (then Tichy, later Lambert), who had been her teacher at UNM and at the Chaco field school, also transferred to the Museum as Curator of Archaeology. Paul A.F. Walter, founding editor of the Museum's journal, *El Palacio*, had been involved at UNM largely through Hewett, and she also knew him there.[10] In addition to her

full-time job as Hewett's assistant, Bert earned her Master's degree in 1937, with a thesis based on her excavation of the Chaco Canyon Pueblo site of Łeyit Kin, or "Way Down Deep Place," as it was known in the Navajo language (she had by then learned to speak a little Navajo [Dutton 1938]). She also went on the Guatemala field school that year, again with Hewett, Ferdon, and others she knew from UNM (Figure 1.5). In 1938, she and Hulda Hobbs, another lifelong friend, jointly excavated a site at Tajumulco, Guatemala (Dutton 1939; Figure 1.6).

In 1938, Bert suggested to Hewett that the Museum needed a Hall of Ethnology to match the exhibits on archaeology. He agreed, adding a Department of Ethnology and making her the curator. Of this, as well as other situations, she would remark, "You have to invent your job in so many places" (Babcock et al. 1986:2). In so doing, she initially added that duty to her work as Assistant to the Director, but later it became her primary task. As part of her new position, she also designed the furniture, cases, and exhibits, as well as cataloging, photographing and storing

Figure 1.8. Chaco Canyon, ca. 1939. Marjorie Ferguson Tichy (Lambert) on left, Bertha Dutton on right. Courtesy of Susan S. Martin Collection.

hundreds if not thousands of ethnographic artifacts. The Hall of Ethnology officially opened on July 1, 1941 in the old Santa Fe Armory (Bohrer 1979:10–11; Figure 1.7). In addition, Bert was becoming deeply involved with local Santa Fe institutions, such as the annual Santa Fe Fiesta and its Fiesta Market (now Indian Market), and the Gallup Inter-Tribal Ceremonial, serving on various organizing committees and as a judge for Native American arts (pottery, textiles, and other media).

Taking a page from Hewett's book on multitasking, for the next 20 years (1939–1959), Bert was both Associate in Archaeology at the SAR and Curator of Ethnology at the MNM. Marjorie Tichy Lambert remained the Museum's Curator of Archaeology. Bert and Marj were key people as the Museum system's outreach and educational program expanded (Figure 1.8). Bert, being single and with fewer home obligations, lectured extensively around the state at branch museums and to various service clubs. She was a very popular lecturer, as she was able to relate to the general public easily and pass on to them her enthusiasm for anthropology and the state's history.

Throughout her life she felt that anthropology and archaeology had great stories to tell and that it was the duty of professionals to tell these stories to the public—a major point on which she and Hewett fully agreed (Dutton 1985a).

During the fall and spring of the years 1945 to 1946, while on sabbatical leave (with pay) arranged by Hewett, Bert attended Columbia University in New York City. During that time, she completed all of the requirements for the doctorate in anthropology—except for her dissertation.[11] While she was in New York, Hewett died, and thus Bert lost both her mentor and good friend, and, as she saw him, "the finest man on earth" (Dutton 1985a:9). She and Hewett had hoped that she would write her dissertation on the *kiva* murals of Kuaua (then Coronado State Monument; now Coronado Historic Site, near Bernalillo), but her newly formed dissertation committee felt that the project was too ambitious. The mural project was shelved until much later, eventually to be published as *Sun Father's Way* (Dutton 1963a). In 1950, with a grant from the SAR, Bert was able to work in southern Mexico and Yucatan, and she completed her dissertation in 1952 under the title *The Toltecs and Their Influence on the Culture of Chichen Itza* (Dutton 1952d). She remained actively involved in Mesoamerican archaeology throughout her career and traveled there for fieldwork, conferences, and consultations on numerous occasions.

Thus, in late 1946, when Bert became involved with the Girl Scouts, she was actively engaged in her curatorial job and in research in New Mexico and Mesoamerica. She had not been a Girl Scout in her early years in the Midwest, nor is there any indication that she knew much of their activities at the time. (Bert remarked later, that since she had played mostly with the neighbor boys while growing up, she knew very little about young girls and their interests [Dutton 1985a]). But once involved, as with everything else she did, Bert became fully engaged, and the activities required for the program that she created would consume a major part of her time over the next 11 years—to her benefit as well as the lives of some 292 plus Senior Girl Scouts from throughout the United States.

2

Getting Started

The 1947 Camp

Nature is the only place where blue and green go together—the deep blue sky against the green pine needles. The huge, towering pines and hemlocks, tangled growth—Northwoods and yet is not. Oh boy! We had lunch there.... It is strange how one can feel at home in any Girl Scout camp—bound by common songs and customs and interests.

—Vorsila Bohrer (1947a)

The Meeting

Sue Little of the GSUSA (working through Region IX) arrived in downtown Santa Fe one cold spring morning in 1947. She went to the headquarters of the MNM and introduced herself to the Director, Dr. Sylvanus Griswold Morley, and spoke with him about the idea for a Senior Girl Scout tour through the Southwest. After a short time, she was ushered to Bertha Dutton's office. Bert described her meeting with Little as follows (Dutton 1955a:35):

I was working at my desk, one March morning in 1947, when there was a knock on the office door, and, at my invitation, Sue Little entered.... It was explained to me that the girls organization was having difficulty in keeping older girls interested in the scouting program. It had been found that these more mature members seldom wished to return to the same established Scout camp for more than two summers. There seemed to be a need for some other type of camp. 'Why,' asked Sue Little, after outlining something of her hopes and aspirations, 'couldn't we work up a trip for Senior Girl Scouts to places of archaeological importance in New Mexico and the nearby states—a trip where we'd camp out as we moved along?'

Thinking back to several archaeological camps in which I had been privileged to participate, particularly the field schools initiated by the late Dr. Edgar L. Hewett and his associates, I saw the merit of Miss Little's suggestion, and immediately became enthusiastic about a possible program. We got out maps of New Mexico, Colorado, and Arizona, and had soon blocked out a route which appeared so attractive that we both wanted to start on it right away.

Bert was also enthusiastic about such a trip because the Museum's program of archaeological field research had "come to a sudden standstill" with the beginning of WWII and had not been reactivated. "I most wanted to revisit [sites] and see new places which I wanted to investigate. Then I commenced to get a notion of how fascinating it would be to show some of these wondrous monuments of prehistoric times to a group of live-minded young women" (Dutton 1955a:36). The idea sounded like a double plus for both Bert and the GSUSA.

After Sue left, Bert continued to work on the details, and before long, presented a plan to the officials of the Museum and to its "mother" institution—the SAR.[1] The Boards approved and were particularly enthusiastic about bringing Senior Girl Scouts from all over the United States to the Southwest to show them not only the spectacular scenery, but also "acquaint them with the basic principles of anthropology" and expressions of past and present cultures "first hand" (Dutton 1955a:35). After all, there had been a long history of touring the Southwest's treasures based out of Santa Fe prior to WWII, including the famous Fred Harvey/Santa Fe Railway's

"Indian Detours," now seemingly on the wane (Thomas 1978).[2] These efforts had been good for promoting the local region as a tourist destination while helping the economy. Although not on that scale, these trips could not hurt and would also fit with the Museum's outreach program. It had long been a goal of both institutions to help develop a more nuanced understanding of the region and the aims of science through public education.

Bert spent time that spring working with Region IX officers (especially Eunice Prien) and Sue Little and perhaps others from the national Girl Scout headquarters in "shaping up a Mobile Camp program for this summer" (Dutton 1947b:5).[3] The plan was to explore and develop a feasible route for a 10-day to two-week camping trip for 10 to 15 Scouts. Included in the itinerary would be visits to national and state parks and monuments, major archaeological sites preserved therein as well as elsewhere, contemporary Pueblos and other Native American communities, and major points of scenic, historical, and scientific interest—all designed to produce a sound overview of the ancient and contemporary history of the region. At the same time, the girls were to learn about the "many phases of *conservation*: conservation of antiquities, of the land itself, of the products of the land, of health, and so on. There will be many opportunities to point out the values of anthropology" (Dutton 1947b:5).

Trial Runs

From June 2 to 9, Bert and Ed Ferdon, in an MNM car, explored a possible route in north-central and western New Mexico, northern and eastern Arizona, southwestern Colorado, and southeastern Utah, totaling nearly 1,350 miles. At that time, most of the national and state monuments and parks, like Chaco Canyon, El Morro, Canyon de Chelly, Aztec, Mesa Verde, and Coronado (Kuaua), as well as other potential stops such as Monument Valley, the Pueblo villages and additional Native American communities, were mostly on unimproved roads, a factor to consider in plotting any route and timing for a trip. While en route, they scouted specific camp sites, spoke with National Park Service (hereafter NPS) officials about their plans and warned them of impending visits. They also determined where they could secure supplies (water, gas, groceries, mail), looked into emergency services in several locales, and attended to other details required for a trip to go smoothly and produce the fewest inadvertent adventures. Experience with Hewett's field schools, plus Bert's and Ed's own travels to many places in the Southwest, Mexico and Mesoamerica, had taught them the importance of preplanning. Bert also took the opportunity on this trip to check into the postwar development of Native crafts and industries in various places—not only for potential shopping opportunities if the girls were interested, but also for her own information; and she looked into matters of health care and the employment situation for the Native peoples (Dutton 1947b:5). As part of her position at the MNM, she needed to stay informed about conditions and issues in the region, so that she could help if the opportunity or need arose.

In mid-June, Ferdon took his Boy Scout troop on the full route, including the farthest extensions into Mesa Verde, Colorado, and Monument Valley, Utah. His group kept to the same basic itinerary, roads, and camp spots, and found that it worked pretty well, including giving the group enough time for good visits to the places of interest, some hiking, and time to complete necessary camp chores. The rest of the logistical preplanning had paid off as well, although it does not appear that Ferdon or any other Boy Scout leader repeated the trip beyond that year. Ferdon continued to work at the MNM for many more years, but apparently was unable to interest the Boy Scouts in additional trips or other training programs.[4]

Based on Ed's feedback, along with some rethinking of the plan, Bert decided that going into Monument Valley made the trip too long and too rushed. Taking out the Monument Valley excursion would shorten the mileage for the Senior Girl Scout Mobile Camp by roughly 200 miles, thereby providing more slack in an already tight schedule. In subsequent years, separate excursion routes were developed for northern, southern, and central loops with several variations, so that yet more of the Southwest country and its many treasures could be seen and explored. This accommodated other interests expressed by the girls and enhanced the experiences for those who returned for another season's camp or camps (see Chapters 3, 4).

Learning While Doing: Edgar Lee Hewett's Field School Camps

From the beginning of the program, Bert had in mind a learning model similar to the one developed by Edgar Lee Hewett for his UNM field schools at Battleship Rock in Jemez Canyon and for the Chaco Canyon field school,[5] as well as at least in part the popular "Indian Detours" trips for tourists developed by the Fred Harvey Company/ Santa Fe Railway. As noted, Bert had attended the Jemez field school as Hewett's secretary and an undergraduate at UNM. She also had visited it a few times after that. And she had been on the Chaco Canyon field school as a graduate student and excavated the site of Łeyit Kin there for her Master's thesis. She knew how both worked and the benefits of these experiences. Tours to other sites of particular interest in the vicinity were part of these summer field schools, as they were for similar field school programs at other Southwest universities. These experiences helped students contextualize what they were learning through their field school experiences as well as created new and often permanent social bonds among them (Gifford and Morris 1985:397–99). In 1933, Hewett (1933:58) described his vision for such programs as follows:

> There has long been criticism of the fact that college education has become too much campus-bound, a matter of study from books and in classrooms. At Battleship Rock camp, there has been a partial breaking away from these traditions and a substitution instead, of education in the open, where students study under a minimum of restrictions the subject of *man and nature* [emphasis added], the methods by which every civilization has been built in the process of humanity's adjustment to its environment.
>
> Students at the Jemez camp learn by doing and observing at first hand. In company with experienced archaeologists, anthropologists, ethnologists, biologists, and geologists, they explore the small world of which their camp is the center, study its resources capable of supporting human life, the dependence of that life upon the natural elements, and the means by which the Indians who have inhabited that region since long before the coming of the White Man, have adjusted themselves to these conditions and achieved a satisfactory life. It is the

kind of learning which enlarges the vision and gives a view of the meanings of
life which cannot be obtained in any other way.

Although Bert did not actually write about her plan for what would become
the Senior Girl Scout Archaeological Mobile Camp Program until 1950, when she
did so it is quite clear that she was drawing heavily from Hewett's philosophy on
the importance of outdoor experience in education—including the one-week trip to
prominent archaeological sites, present-day Pueblos, and other Indigenous peoples
(Watkins 1928).[6]

Dutton's general theme was also "Man and Nature in the Southwest." The major
difference was that the Girl Scouts would not be taking part in an actual archaeological site excavation—at least not yet. She summarized the approach as follows
(Dutton 1950a:367):

Not only is archaeology stressed, but all of the disciplines of anthropology,
and such related subjects as botany, biology, art (particularly that of the original Americans), Southwest history, Spanish, etc. The importance of conservation of natural resources is brought to attention, and consideration is given
to Southwestern industries and businesses. Traveling some 1,200 miles during
each camp, to places of archaeologic, historic, scenic, and industrial importance, the girls are given a broad view of the cultural backgrounds of the region,
and of the vocational opportunities offered.

Over the years the plan would become more ambitious, but the overall orientation would remain the same. This appears to have been a particularly good fit for
the goals of the Girl Scout movement in the postwar years as well. Although still
heavy on homemaking skills and helping others, there was the stress on camping and other outdoor activities and regional education. In this situation, the girls
would learn not only what the various disciplines had to teach about the Southwest
region, but they would also develop an overall context for what they were learning
through the outdoor touring combined with lectures. And they would learn to share,
become independent yet work together in teams, and bond—many beyond the life

of the camps—also Girl Scout themes. Bert and the GSUSA seem to fit together much like hand in glove.

Thus, clearly from the start considerable thought was given to the overall educational value of the Mobile Camp experience. The 1947 session was not to be merely a sightseeing trip, nor one geared primarily to "fun in the sun." Bert was a scholar and very serious about public education in anthropology and science in general. She saw the trips as a form of "Applied Anthropology"—and her duty as a person firmly committed to the overall goal of anthropology to improve mutual cultural understanding (Dutton 1983).[7] But she also did not intend to be the sole source of knowledge for the girls. From the beginning she enlisted other well-known authorities on relevant topics as speakers—similar to the "guest faculty" Hewett and others employed for the field schools each summer, but with less of a time commitment (a lecture or two versus a full summer session). More needed to be taught to the girls who would be participating as few would be local or have much knowledge of the region's geography and complex and lengthy history. Nor would they have sufficient background to be able to understand the context for what they would be seeing or hearing. There was a deep human story as well as an important environmental one to tell. And there were rich contemporary cultures to introduce. There would have to be introductory lectures on many of these topics, illustrated by visits to local museums and other venues to see the cultural products and arts produced in the past and present in order to prepare the girls to gain the most from their experiences.

In addition to the planning that all of this would take, there was also the need not to overwhelm the participants with the educational components of the trip. Bert was used to interacting with the public through her position in the museum—in exhibits, lectures and tours of the museum. And she could count on her museum colleagues and others to put on their "public hats"—challenge thought but neither oversimplify nor overwhelm. More lectures by her or others at places that they would visit would fill in and remind campers of topics covered in introductory sessions. There would also be a naturalist staff member on the first trip (and subsequently) to identify and discuss changing vegetation, animals and birds, and other topics of interest. Bert knew the geology reasonably well, as she had minored in geology at UNM. But would it all work as planned, and would it attract and hold the girls' interest?

The list of those involved in lecturing to the Senior Girl Scouts that first year as well as in later years reads like a "who's who" of Southwest archaeologists, anthropologists, historians, conservationists, and agency employees (Chapters 2 to 5; Appendix E). Bert expected the girls to take good notes on all lectures and experiences. Many diligently complied, accumulating several pages of notes in their required notebooks.[8] They specifically learned the basic archaeological sequence for the northern Southwest, its dating, and central characteristics (sidebar 2.1). Most of the larger and smaller ruins they would be seeing in national and state parks would be from the later periods (900–1200) in what had been a long continuum of occupation and adaptation by Ancestral Pueblo (then called Anasazi) farming peoples in a not always friendly desert environment. They also needed to know the basic aspects of the ethnography of the contemporary Pueblo, Navajo, Apache, and Ute peoples, including their cultural similarities and differences. The girls would recognize obvious parallels between the archaeological sites they visited and contemporary Pueblo villages in the Rio Grande Valley, at Zuni, Laguna, and Acoma, and the Hopi villages. But there was far more to their stories than superficial resemblances. The same was true of the non-Pueblo peoples, including the Navajo, who in the late 1940s were primarily tending flocks of sheep, planting small fields of corn and other crops, and living in dispersed family homesteads or "outfits" on their sprawling reservation in northwestern New Mexico and northeastern Arizona. The Apache and Ute peoples, who once had been warriors, raiders, and traders locally and on the western Great Plains, were on their own reservations (see Figure 1.2) and trying to support themselves in a variety of ways. Similarly, superficial observations of the architecture, food, and other features in and around Santa Fe would only begin to help them bring into perspective the significance of Spanish, Mexican, and American settlement in the region, and the influences that these had on Indigenous life ways as these new peoples also adopted new ways of living.

In the late 1940s through 1950s, the broad outlines for the chronology of peoples in the Southwest was roughly as follows: 10,000–5,000 BC, Paleoindian hunter-gatherers; 5,000 BC–CE 1, Archaic hunter-gatherers with late transition to Anasazi (now known as Ancestral Pueblo); CE 1–600, Ancestral Pueblo Basketmakers (three stages): pithouse dwellings, introduction of corn, beans, and squash gardening; 600–present, Ancestral to present-day Pueblos (four or five stages): development of larger villages; 1150–early 1200s, migrations from northernmost villages settlement in present-day and other locations; 1300–1450, Navajo and Apache arrival; 1540, Coronado's first expedition; 1598, first Spanish settlement in NM; 1610, Santa Fe founded; 1680, Pueblo Revolt; 1692, Spanish return to northern NM; 1846, U.S Army under General Kearny occupies NM.[9]

Of course, in addition to all the notetaking and the educational orientation of the trips, there would be plenty of time for sightseeing and "fun in the sun"—what else could be expected of a group of teenage girls—and it is clear that Bert enjoyed being part of it all, including a bit of tomfoolery now and then. She loved the Southwest and was always happy and proud to show it off, including its obvious esthetic values. And her enthusiasm for the region was contagious. As she wrote to Anne Rushmer, one of the 1947 campers a year later (B. Dutton to A. Rushmer, July 28, 1948, MIAC/LAA):[10]

One of the things I've always liked apart from the great open spaces of the Southwest is the quiet and peacefulness of it all. I love to sit, or better, to lie and listen to the natural noises of the desert, the rustle of the trees, or the murmur of a mountain stream. I want the girls to enjoy that great quietness, of the Chaco, Mesa Verde, Canyon de Chelly, etc.... my favorite places—places which I think have everything—beauty, quietness, ruins, fossils, Indians, and so on.

Figure 2.1. Lila Luckie (TX) and Vorsila Bohrer (IL), Senior Girl Scouts on first Archaeological Mobile Camp, 1947. Photograph by Anne Rushmer. LA08.ARM.100-101 #43. Courtesy of MIAC/LAA.

Thus, there was clearly a dual purpose in Bert's approach: the camps were to be serious learning experiences as well as infect the campers with the magic of the Southwest as an enchanting place. Juliette Low's dictum was right: "If it isn't right, the girls won't take to it and it won't last." The persistence of the program and the return of many girls over the years, as well as its short and long term effects on them, amply demonstrate its impacts and value (Chapter 10).

The 1947 Senior Girl Scout Archaeological Mobile Camp

Bert summarized the activities of the first camp in an article titled "Girl Scout Archaeological Expedition" (Dutton 1947a), and in two shorter synopses (one prior to the trip and one after) for her archaeological colleagues in the newsletter *Teocentli* (Dutton 1947b; 1947c). She added some additional reflections in her history of the early years of the project later (Dutton 1955a) and in interviews (Dutton 1983; 1985a; 1990). However, in none of these does she dwell on details. She provides a basic overview of the route, itinerary with the names of speakers and their topics, and her feelings as to the trip's overall success. She does not cover "adventures," such as numerous flat tires, camping problems, or other personal experiences for this first "expedition." Fortunately, one of the campers, Vorsila Bohrer, provides some of this detail in her diary and a later reminiscence (Bohrer 1947a, 1954; Figure 2.1); and there are a few other notes in Bert's correspondence with other campers that year and later reflecting back on that first trip. The only known photographs are those taken by camper Anne Rushmer and now part of the Bertha Dutton Collection (13ARM.001–100; 99BPD.xx). These materials add to the story, but for other details, we can only read between the lines of accounts of later trips for more of a feel of the comradery and other insights the participants likely shared. There are also more photos and other materials documenting these later trips (Chapters 3, 4). For the 1947 trip, we follow Bert's narrative (largely Dutton 1947a) with Bohrer's additions, but also include some further descriptions of places visited and their significance to help those less familiar with the region.

Campers and Crew

The campers that first session included seven girls, two from Texas, two from New Mexico, and one each from Arizona, Illinois, and Oklahoma (Dutton 1947a; see Appendix A for names and camps attended). Throughout the life of the program, Bert kept track of the "states of origin" of the campers, ultimately achieving a nearly complete tally of the United States (plus England). In addition to Bert, who was on loan from the MNM and SAR as director, the staff included two representatives of Region IX and the GSUSA (hereafter GS Rep/s), Sue Little and Nyla Harvey. Not much is known about either woman's background, other than that Little had a home

in Albuquerque and was National Community Advisor, apparently working at least part time out of the Region IX office, and that Harvey was from El Paso. They apparently knew each other, likely through the Region IX office, and both seem to have been Girl Scout professionals. Velma Whipple, or "Whip," the nickname by which she would be known (all leaders and most girls had nicknames; see Appendix A) was from Prospect Heights, IL, and a high school biology teacher and scout leader. She would serve as the naturalist on the crew and was very familiar with the Southwest landscape, its plants, and especially its birds. Little seems to have known her as well as Whip seems to have grown up in Albuquerque and her family still owned property there. Whip was also well known to camper Vorsila Bohrer and had many friends in the Albuquerque area.[11] Vic Malone of Santa Fe was the driver. He had been a driver for the Santa Fe Indian School and may have owned the vehicle used—or leased it. According to Bert (1990:8) in an oral interview, the vehicle was a "stretched out Chevy [nicknamed "the Clipper" by the girls] about that far off the ground" [hand gesture of a few inches] that would hold 15 passengers. "Every time he saw a rock in the road he'd stop and get out and throw the rock out of the road and we'd go on to Zuni or wherever else we were going. So it didn't suit me well." Once the group was on the road, the Clipper pulled a small trailer for the gear. Bohrer (1954:1) says that "Vic drove the Clipper, a long, low-slung, light blue auto," not very well adapted to the road conditions (Figure 2.2). The cost of the 14-day trip that summer was $60 per camper, covering all but transportation to and from Santa Fe.

The 1947 Itinerary

The group met in Santa Fe on July 6 and set up camp in Hyde Memorial State Park in the foothills northeast of the city. The arrival day (Saturday) and the next were spent getting acquainted, practicing skills, checking camping gear, packing and repack-ing, and developing a *kaper chart*, Girl Scout-speak for a roster of duties to be per-formed on the trail and by whom—fire building, cooking, cleanup, lunches, latrine duty, and more. They also attended worship services of their choice on Sunday and held a *Scouts' Own*—a special interdenominational way for Girl Scouts to acknowl-edge ideological values. This was normally developed by the girls themselves as part of their camp experiences.[12]

On Monday, there were orientation visits to various places in Santa Fe, with talks at each on specific topics. The first stop was the Auditorium at the Museum of Fine Arts (now New Mexico Museum of Art) where MNM Director Morley intro-duced the girls to the city and its history, and shared with them some of his personal experiences in archaeology in the Four Corners region some 40 years previous.[13] His talk was followed by tours of the Museum's archaeological and historical exhibi-tions and collections conducted by Bert's colleague Marjorie Tichy, plus the Hall of Ethnology by Bert (Dutton 1947a:192). The next stop was the Federal Building for talks by a member of the Soil Conservation Service on the effects on Southwest soils of overgrazing and erosion, a major issue affecting Southwest landscapes (Dunmire

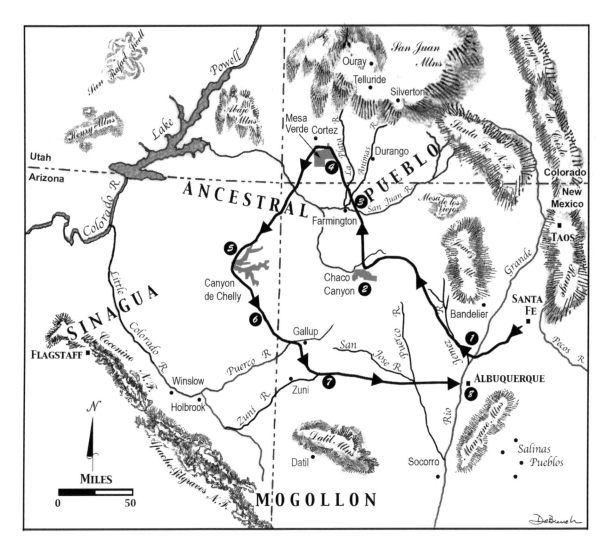

Figure 2.3. Route of the first Archaeological Mobile Camp, 1947. Map by Patricia DeBunch. (1) Coronado [State] Historic Site; (2) Chaco [Canyon] Culture National Historical Park; (3) Aztec Ruins National Monument; (4) Mesa Verde National Park; (5) Canyon de Chelly National Monument; (6) Wide Ruins Trading Post; (7) El Morro National Monument; (8) Albuquerque.

2013). After lunch, they visited National Park Service headquarters and heard from personnel about their activities in the region, the difference between parks and monuments, and a bit on some of the places that they would be visiting. Natt Dodge, noted Southwest naturalist, who published several popular guides to Southwest flora and fauna, was one of the speakers there. Next, the group visited the Museum of Navajo Ceremonial Art (now the Wheelwright Museum of the American Indian) to hear about Navajo sand paintings; and then the Laboratory of Anthropology (Lab or LA) where Kenneth Chapman spoke on Rio Grande Pueblo pottery and showed them baskets, textiles, jewelry, beadwork, and other Indigenous arts, illustrating his lecture with specimens from the extensive Lab collections.

After that very full day, the campers and staff adjourned to their Hyde Park camp to prepare dinner. There was no professional cook that first year; Harvey and Little, with assistance from the girls, prepared the meals. The girls also did the required *kapers* to keep the camp running. That evening they had a campfire presentation by U.S. Forest Service Ranger Newnham on regional forests and their conservation. There had been a lot to take in on their first day, and the campers were undoubtedly glad to roll into their bed rolls or sleeping bags for the night. In addition, given that most were from much lower altitudes, they were adjusting to Santa Fe's 7,000 feet (2,194 m) elevation—as Bert and Little had planned.

July 8 found them packed into the Chevy, with duffel bags and cooking gear in the trailer, and officially on their way out of Santa Fe (Figure 2.3).[14] Their first stop was Coronado State Monument (now Coronado Historic Site) near Bernalillo and the famous Kuaua Pueblo, a fourteenth to sixteenth century Pueblo community. It was likely one of several Rio Grande Pueblos occupied when the Spanish explorer Francisco Vásquez de Coronado and his expedition first entered the area in 1540, but was abandoned soon thereafter. Bert had visited this site and its excavations while a student at UNM, and she would later write a major work on the impressive painted murals found in one of its *kivas*, or ceremonial chambers (Dutton 1963a). However, she deferred to the site custodian John Sinclair, who gave the girls a tour of the museum, the reconstructed *kiva* with its elaborate wall paintings, and the rest

Figure 2.4. Pueblo Bonito, Chaco Canyon, 1947. Photograph by Anne Rushmer. LA08.ARM.001-101 #25. Courtesy of MIAC/LAA.

of the site. Bert then spoke to the girls on the overall position of this place in the early history of the upper Rio Grande Valley.[15]

The group boarded their vehicle for the drive north from Bernalillo on NM Highway 888, ate *nosebag* or sack lunches at San Ysidro, and then traveled toward the trading post at Nageezi, the turnoff to Chaco Canyon National Monument (now Chaco Culture National Historical Park) and their first camp on the trail. The drive to northeast was through pinyon and juniper covered mesas and was very beautiful—the clouds unusually so—wrote Bohrer in her diary (1947a). They pitched their tents in the rain that night, "Rambler" (Bohrer) wrote, although on other nights of bad rain, they sometimes crowded into a single wall tent—a tight squeeze. Otherwise, Army surplus pup tents—two girls to a tent—were the norm. They preferred to sleep in the open if the weather cooperated.

Although Bert does not say where the group camped at Chaco during their two-night stay, they may have camped near the University of New Mexico's field station on the south side of the canyon across from Pueblo Bonito.[16] At least they went there that night to hear a talk by William Kelly of Harvard University on Navajo culture. The next morning, NPS Ranger William Guillet took the group through Pueblo Bonito (Figure 2.4), the largest and most impressive site of several in the canyon, with its five-story back wall and perhaps as many as 700 rooms, including multiple kivas. This ancient structure was built in several phases between roughly 900 and 1130, and is one of many large and small Ancestral Pueblos in the canyon. By 1947, several well-known archaeologists had excavated in Pueblo Bonito as well as the several other large Pueblos there (Lister and Lister 1981). Its carefully dressed stone masonry that had changed at several points during its construction remains very impressive. Its

Figure 2.5. Senior Girl Scouts listening to NPS Ranger at the base of Threatening Rock, Chaco Canyon, 1947. Bertha Dutton Photos, Girl Scouts (File 6-No.6). Dutton Folder 3.038-.048. National Park Service. Courtesy of MIAC/LAA.

interconnected rooms proved exciting to explore, as did seeing the many kivas—they were told the count was 32 for the building (Bohrer 1947a). The site yielded thousands of turquoise beads, finely painted Black-on-white pottery, and many other significant artifacts, and the site and its material remains still excite and provide new and different interpretations (Clark and Mills 2018; Crown et al. 2016).

After walking through Pueblo Bonito and discussing its complicated construction, Guillet took the group past Threatening Rock[17] and to see the petroglyph panels and several smaller sites located at the base of the steep north cliff (Figure 2.5). Gordon Vivian, who was working for the NPS on long-term site stabilization that summer, then continued the tour by taking the group to Chetro Ketl, another very impressive site east of Pueblo Bonito. Bert had excavated there briefly while a student at UNM in 1934. From there the group went back to the UNM field station for a lunch break and tour of sites being excavated that season by UNM students and crews. Later that afternoon they continued to explore the canyon as far as Mesa Fajada, a tall rock formation at the eastern edge of the canyon. Bert then took them to Kin Kletso (Yellow House), another large site. After viewing the site they climbed the cliff to the top of the mesa by means of one of the ancient stairways cut into the sandstone cliff.

Chaco Canyon National Monument, and all of its Ancestral Pueblos and other features, are now within Chaco Culture National Historical Park, also listed as a UNESCO World Heritage Site. Many questions remain about the Chacoan region and its archaeology, and especially the function of its spectacular "Great Houses" and their place in the cultural history of the region and Ancestral Pueblo life (Lekson 1999 [2015]; Noble 2004; 2014; Van Dyke 2007). But it was in 1947, and remains today, one of the most impressive places in the United States—even if not well understood. For the Girl Scouts, visiting it and the other sites made for another very full day. But there was still dinner to prepare, camp chores to do, and likely a campfire with the UNM crew still to come before turning in for the night.

On July 10, the group drove north to Aztec National Monument (now Aztec Ruins National Monument), another very important site in the San Juan River Basin

near the town of Aztec, New Mexico. This site not only features some five well-preserved Ancestral Pueblos dating from roughly 950–1300, but also a fully reconstructed Great Kiva—a very cool as well as impressive place to get out of the sun in the middle of July. This large (63 feet [19.2 m] diameter) sacred ceremonial chamber can be entered by visitors who can readily appreciate the ingenuity that it took Ancestral Pueblo people to build it, and especially to support the building's massive log roof. The main Pueblo open to the public, called Aztec West, and the Great Kiva were excavated by famous Southwest archaeologist Earl Morris who for many years was also the caretaker of the site and supervised its stabilization and reconstruction (Lister 2018; Figure 2.6; Figure 2.7). In the late 1940s and 1950s, when the Girl Scouts visited, the site was known to have relationships to those in Chaco Canyon because of similarities in architecture, pottery, and some of the other materials found there.

Figure 2.6. Interior view of reconstructed Great Kiva at Aztec National Monument, NM. Photograph before 1957. SWPC (Southwest Post Card Company). In possession of C.S. Fowler.

Figure 2.7. Ruin, Aztec National Monument, 1947. Photograph by Anne Rushmer. LA08.ARM.001-101 #17. Courtesy of MIAC/LAA.

Today more has been learned through restudy of all of these sites, although many questions as to what these similarities signify remain open to interpretation. Aztec and other large sites in the region are now referred to as a "Chacoan Outliers," known to have been part of a large network linked to Chaco Canyon through travel routes or "roads," and likely involved in important trade, ceremonial, and other activities.[18] After a tour through Aztec's museum, the girls watched with fascination as a Navajo woman at the museum demonstrated carding, spinning, and weaving on her upright rug loom. They had seen the finished product and learned a bit about designs on their visit to the Laboratory of Anthropology, but here was a chance to see the full process (Bohrer 1947a).

After visiting Aztec, the group headed for Mesa Verde National Park in southwestern Colorado, being first amazed at the scenery and the "breathtaking views" as the Clipper labored up the winding, steep grade to the top of the mesa. They spent three days touring many of the ancient and spectacular cliff houses in the steep,

Figure 2.8. Square Tower House, Mesa Verde National Park, 1947. Photograph by Anne Rushmer. LA08.ARM.001-101 #12. Courtesy of MIAC/LAA.

wooded canyons. Among them were Cliff Palace, Balcony House (accessible only by ladders and a long climb up the sandstone cliff face), Long House, Spruce Tree House, and more (Figure 2.8, Figure 2.9, Figure 2.10). Most of these sites were built and likely occupied between the late 1100s and 1280 based on their tree-ring records (Varien 2010:20–21). They also viewed the excavations at earlier Basketmaker and Pueblo period sites on the mesa top, places that were part of archaeologist Deric O'Bryan's work that summer. O'Bryan guided the group around the sites and spoke

Figure 2.9. Senior
Girl Scouts
descending ladder
at Balcony House,
Mesa Verde
National Park,
1947. Photograph
by Bertha Dutton.
Bertha Dutton
Photos, Girl Scouts
(File 6). Courtesy
of MIAC/LAA.

"enthusiastically" with the group about the Basketmaker-to-Pueblo transition (500–900), viewed in the 1940s as when people moved from underground pithouse dwellings to aboveground structures, and began cultivating crops of corn, beans, and squash more intensively.[19] The Scouts were also able to view the unique depictions of this and later sequences of living changes in the region through the classic dioramas in the Mesa Verde Museum.[20] And they saw many examples of the artifacts that had been excavated from these sites through the years.

Bohrer (1954:2–3) says the following about one of three "impressive" evening programs given by National Park Service Ranger Don Watson at Mesa Verde and other happenings:

Figure 2.10. Viewing New Fire House [Temple], led by Ranger Jim, Mesa Verde National Park, 1947. Ranger Jim, Skipper Reynolds, Barbara O'Boyle, Ursula Little, Nyla Harvey, Vorsila Bohrer. Photograph by Anne Rushmer. LA08.ARM.001-101 #15. Courtesy of MIAC/LAA.

As we assembled in the campfire amphitheater, the silhouettes of the mesas against the skyline grew sharper with the setting sun, and a few bats began to dip to and fro. This was only to be surpassed by the cheerful blaze of the campfire for Mr. [Don] Watson.[21] And it was at Mesa Verde that we celebrated Vic's birthday. My little notebook records gifts of candy kisses, peanut brittle, a toy gun, tent stakes, and a grasshopper.

On July 14, the expedition proceeded west to Cortez, Colorado, with stops at trading posts along the way. On these stops Bert pointed out the differences in the items made for sale by the Ute and Navajo peoples (baskets, rugs, pottery), and the Scouts were able to buy those pieces they could not resist. Bert was there to advise on purchases and negotiate appropriate prices, or to tell the eager buyers to wait until a later stop for better examples or values. In later years, part of the application form for Mobile Camps included a checklist of what types of Southwest arts and crafts the camper would be interested in seeing and purchasing. Bert knew most of the traders in the region and specifically included scouting trading posts for arts and crafts inventories in what became her yearly pre-camp reconnaissance. Purchasing Indigenous arts grew more important through time, as many of the girls were impressed by the spectacular Pueblo pottery, Navajo rugs and baskets, and the paintings, and began collections of Southwestern Indigenous art. Rambler bought a small Navajo rug on the 1947 trip (Bohrer 1947a).

Next on the agenda was a two-day visit to Canyon de Chelly National Monument just east of Chinle, Arizona. But the first task was to find a place to camp, given that there was a major rainstorm that day, with as Bohrer (1954:3) says: "adobe colored water reach[ing] the running board of the car. Bert waded out (barefoot) to inquire about a place to sleep…and we passed the night in the Chinle Indian School with the rain pattering on the tin roof. My adobe hacienda and such was a bit irritating" (Bohrer 1947b). They did the same the next two nights, courtesy of the Indian Service. The first day the girls began exploring parts of the Canyon's main stem, plus Canyon del Muerto, each with several spectacular Ancestral Puebloan sites, including the famous White House, a site built into the red cliff face, with a white veneer that literally glows. As Bohrer (1954:3) remarked:

> We had blue skies to contrast with the reddish sandstone of the canyon walls. I still remain impressed from such an inspiring example with the large amount of beauty contained within such an inanimate thing as rock. Exploring the ruins was great fun, but the damp, finely layered sandstone proved treacherous footholds and in some instances a long slide was saved by only a shirt tail.

Given that the Monument is on the Navajo Reservation, Navajo families were living in the canyons (and remain today, especially in summer) in their traditional homes, tending their sheep, cattle and horses, and growing gardens of corn, beans and squash—all of which could be viewed from the canyon rim as well as the floor. Custodian of the Monument Meredith Guillet and Ranger Scotty Benson "spent long

Figure 2.11. Three Turkey Ruin, near Canyon de Chelly National Monument, 1947. Photograph by Anne Rushmer. LA08.ARM.001-101 #41. Courtesy of MIAC/LAA.

hours in conducting the group," including a trip the last day past Spider Rock and a trek to and through Three Turkey Canyon to Three Turkey Ruins, a special and important site outside the Monument with particularly well-preserved architecture (Figure 2.11). It is normally off limits to visitors so this was a special privilege extended to Bert and the girls (Dutton 1947a:193; Colton 1939).

After Canyon de Chelly, the group headed for Gallup, with more stops at trading posts along the way. A special detour included the post at Wide Ruins, Arizona, run by Bill and Sallie Lippincott. They were famous traders to the Navajo people who were partly responsible for the development of the local Navajo rug style named for the post and featuring vegetable dyes. Sally opened the "back room" with its stacks of rugs and blankets, and rows of beautiful silver jewelry, some taken in as "pawn" from Navajo customers, to be redeemed when their wool or lamb crops were ready to sell. Sally and Bert told the girls about author Alberta Hannum's charming book, *Spin a Silver Dollar,* based on life at the post and illustrated by Beatien Yazz ("Little No Shirt") or Jimmie Toddy, who went on to become a very well-known Navajo artist (Dutton 1947a:193; Wagner 1997).

July 18 found the group camping at El Morro National Monument (also known as Inscription Rock), the "billboard" of the central New Mexico-Arizona border area, after following a very rutted road in—"a long four miles indeed" (Bohrer 1947a). Here travelers over millennia had left their marks and signatures—petroglyphs, elaborate Spanish inscriptions from the 1700s, names and dates of early American explorers and travelers, and many more—all having been attracted by the large spring at the base of the tall sandstone outcropping. That evening after Custodian Bates Wilson and Ranger Bill Scott welcomed the expedition, Harvard anthropologist Evon Vogt, who was raised on a ranch at nearby Ramah, provided a campfire talk on his studies of the changes occurring in Navajo lifeways by the return of their WWII veterans. "Then, taking out his guitar, Mr. Vogt entertained the girls with Spanish songs" (Dutton 1947a:194).[22]

The following day, the girls spent time looking at the inscriptions on the rock face, some deeply etched, and also climbed to the top to see the foundations of two ancient Pueblos. Later in the day, the group continued eastward to Acoma, also known as Sky City, where the girls had their first chance to see a fully inhabited Pueblo village, this in one of the most beautiful settings in the Southwest—atop a high mesa with a commanding view of the entire region. In addition to the multi-storied homes of the people, the eighteenth century Spanish mission church with its interior paintings was available to see. And women were selling bread and their beautiful finely painted pottery. Bohrer (1954:3–4) says of the trip up the mesa to Acoma:

As we were pushing the car up to Acoma [a very steep grade], we had the most beautiful view of Mt. Taylor. When we got to the top of that same incline and around the curve, we had a panorama view of Acoma and Enchanted Mesa. The slanting yellow rays of the sun were illuminating the two mesas and throwing storm clouds in dramatic poses behind them.

This view still amazes visitors to Acoma today, although now they park below at a beautiful tribal visitor center/museum and are bussed to the top of the mesa for a guided tour of the village and the church by members of the community.

The final camp of the expedition that night was near Enchanted Mesa. Bohrer (1954:3–4) continues her thoughts:

As we made camp near Enchanted Mesa, a chill wind came up. We gratefully warmed our fingers and insides on Skip's [Reynolds] hot puffy Navajo fried bread which she learned to make at the International Camp held at Toadlena, New Mexico. Soon the white, feather-like clouds that were scattered overhead began to glow with the pink and then deeper orange shades until the whole sky vibrated warmth and color. Who could ask for a more fitting close for the evening.

The following day, July 19, was their last together. A final stop at Laguna Pueblo, not far from Acoma, to see the church and go to the trading post where Bert had special friends,[23] completed the tour and they were on to Albuquerque (or Santa Fe) and the end of the first year's archaeological expedition. We can be sure that as the girls cleaned up and prepared to catch their trains and busses there were many tearful "good-byes," exchanges of addresses, and promises made to write and stay in touch, which indeed many did, including with Bert in the years to come (Chapter 4). The girls were likely tired, but they certainly had a unique and rewarding experience "learning while doing," as was Bert's aim. They had seen some very spectacular scenery and some amazing archaeological sites, including ones that tourists rarely if ever see, been introduced to the sciences of archaeology and anthropology in the field by several famous participants, and learned much about the fascinating early and later history of this region—and done it all with good companions. As Bohrer (1954:4) remarked, "in two weeks we had become a close knit working group and felt as if we wanted to keep right on traveling." Their learning had been through direct experience—"learning while doing." It all was a lot to digest while "following Bert" for 1,100 miles.

Bert, and several of the campers, felt that the first year's Senior Girl Scout Archaeological Expedition was a success, although as Bert reminisced later: "I had no idea that anything permanent was going to come of it" (Dutton 1985a:17). But five of the seven campers vowed to come back for the next summer if there were another Mobile Camp. They had not seen enough nor learned enough about this unique region of the United States, and were eager to come back for more. As Bohrer (1954:4) later summed up, "The success of that first year's experiment started a chain reaction that brings more and more Scouts to the Southwest for more and better Girl Scout Archaeological Mobile Camps. It [also] has borne fruit in the first Archaeological Excavation Camps—something undreamed of by those first Mobile Campers in 1947."

3

The Archaeological Mobile Camps Refined and Developed

1948–1951

Digger Song

Oh we're so happy we took this trip
In the land where there aren't any chiggers.
We hunt for potsherds all day long
For we are Dutton's Dirty Diggers.

–Jo Tice [Bloom], 1948

The success of the 1947 archaeological expedition showed that Bert might be on the right track with an idea that was appealing and valuable to young women. They seemed willing to follow her wherever she wanted to lead them, especially to some of her favorite places and ones that she felt were important to their learning about the Southwest and the nature and processes of science. In the 10 years to follow, there would be 20 more Mobile Camps with nearly 300 girls in all becoming "Dutton's Dirty Diggers." What started as a simple idea to engage a group of teenage girls through a unique "on-the-trail" experience soon blossomed into a full-fledged program that garnered attention regionally and nationally.

The first camp had been an experiment—definitely successful—but in need of some refinement if there were to be another.[1] For that to happen, the success of the first year had to remain in the minds of Region IX as well as GSUSA officials. Unfortunately, early that fall, Sue Little, the camp's primary advocate, left Region IX's Dallas office for a position in California, and the new person in her slot, somewhat overwhelmed by all that was going on in the Region, put the camp on a back burner. However, that fall one of the 1947 campers (Lila Luckie) gave a glowing report on the camp at a regional conference in Houston, including its merits for Senior Scouts. This was backed up by her mother who was a regional official and very enthusiastic. They got enough attention that the officials moved it forward in priority, and another session was scheduled for the summer of 1948 (Dutton 1955a:37; 1985:9).

The years 1949 through 1951 were both formative and crucial to the future success of the camps, in that they allowed Bert to refine her approach and fix the problems that had occurred during the first year. They also gave the sponsors time to further explore their roles and to get the word out that there was something significant happening in the summers in the Southwest for Senior Girl Scouts. Later years would see some additional changes, especially in administration, that were necessary but not always easy or beneficial to the program (Chapters 6, 7).

Documentation on the Mobile Camps is richer for the years 1948 through 1951 than for 1947, thus allowing us to say more about several topics. Bert continued to do annual summaries for these years in *El Palacio*, and these contain full itineraries and lists of participants (campers, staff, and speakers).[2] The Laboratory of Anthropology Archives (hereafter LAA), including those of the MNM, has flyers advertising the camps and more official and personal correspondence giving information on such matters as organization, camper requirements, costs, and itineraries. There is also a scrapbook for 1948, as well as additional photographs, diaries, and other reminiscences by camp participants. Together these documents provide a richer picture of activities for these years and the impacts. In the account of 1948, parts of camper Jo Tice's "letters home" and Evelyn Stobie's later reminiscence are included. Vorsila Bohrer (1948a; 1948b; 1949) also kept daily diaries providing additional details. Tice's chronicle of the trip captures some of the on-the-spot views of a wide-eyed 15-year-old, who had no idea of the adventures that lay in store for her while "following Bert" through the Land of Enchantment. Her letters, as well as Stobie's comments (written seven years later), Bohrer's, and those by others who went in subsequent years (Chapters 4, 5), reflect some of what the girls were absorbing out of the information that Bert and other speakers and guides were trying to provide. They also show some of the impact of Bert's persona on these girls, something that would make many campers personal fans and friends of Bert's throughout their lives. It was during these years that Bert began to devote more and more of her time and energy to the Girl Scout effort, and when it truly became a significant part of her life.

Organization and Management: 1948–1951

Administration and Personnel

As already noted, the Mobile Camp program was initiated through Region IX of the GSUSA and, until 1952, was primarily administered through their office in Dallas.[3] This effort fits with the GSUSA emphasis on local innovation and governance that was set in place at the beginning of the Girl Scout movement. Eunice Prien, Executive Director of Region IX, and Bert apparently corresponded on various aspects of the program beginning in 1947 and continuing into the spring of 1948—although there are no letters between them in the Dutton Papers or in other files of the LAA or the MNM administrative archives. Camps in 1948 through 1951 were advertised by the Dallas office through flyers sent to GS Councils largely within the region (Texas, Oklahoma, New Mexico) but with some beyond.[4] Camper applications were processed by the Region IX office. This office apparently also collected the camper fees, and redistributed funds to the MNM.[5] It also appears that Prien had approval authority over the annual budget and staff suggestions, both of which came from Bert, and recruited some of the official GS representatives who accompanied each camp.[6] Prien seems to have been the first person Bert asked about policy matters, but Prien, in turn, seems to have forwarded some queries to GSUSA officials at the organization's national headquarters when undecided about them. Prien also participated in 1949's Camp II being listed as both a "camper" and as a GS Rep.[7]

From the beginning, the MNM was an equal partner in the program with Region IX and the GSUSA. The Museum's cooperation was vital, especially in "loaning" Bert to direct the program and, most importantly, paying her salary. Neither Region IX or the GSUSA could have afforded to totally fund the program at a reasonable price for the campers had this not been the case. The Museum allowed Bert time released from her duties as Curator of Ethnology to do the necessary preseason reconnaissance as well as to conduct the actual camping trips. Although MNM paid her salary, it did not cover her expenses for either activity. In 1948, an additional sponsor is also listed: the SAR where Bert was Research Associate in Archaeology and had additional duties. At that time, and throughout most of the life of the program, the MNM and SAR were sister institutions (actually SAR was the "mother") and their governing boards had several overlapping duties and personnel, as noted previously (Chapters 1, 2). In her summary for 1949, Dutton (1949a:278) wrote that "the School of American Research and the Museum of New Mexico grants me the time necessary for planning each year's program and for personally directing the expeditions; they furnish a car for the preparatory trips and pay the expenses therefor" [the car, her salary]. The Museum did furnish a car for this purpose, while GSUSA supplied money for the actual field expenses of the pre-camp trips ($25 in 1951—perhaps a little less, earlier). In 1950, SAR was not listed as an official cosponsor on the applicant flyer, although Bert's affiliation there is still noted, and her involvement with the organization continued for many years thereafter.[8] Members of the governing bodies of both MNM and SAR remained actively interested in and supportive of Bert's Girl Scout program throughout its existence. It was common for both institutions to cosponsor projects including public education and research. But the Museum often took the lead in this type of public outreach as it was part of its mission, while the SAR focused more on research and scholarly publication.

Although Bert was officially the director of the camps, and seemingly got along with Prien pretty well, she did not always see "eye to eye" with her or some of the official GS Reps who went on the trips. As Bert wrote to Anne Rushmer, one of the older 1947 and 1948 campers with whom she had an active correspondence over several years: "But first and foremost, I am going to be boss this season, and direct the whole setup" (Bert's emphasis; Dutton to Rushmer, Feb. 2, 1949, MIAC/LAA). It seems that she had a bit of trouble with one of the GS Reps in 1948 acting too much like a director, at least in her view. Bert had her agenda and way of doing things, coupled with a strong personality. She was not averse to putting her foot down, especially if she felt that her goals were not being met. Camps were to be run her way, at least as far as she was concerned.

On the other hand, GS Reps and other Scouting professionals sometimes also had strong personalities and strong opinions about what they felt was the backing of precedent and tried-and-true traditions in organizing and running programs for girls. The function of the GS Reps on the archaeological Mobile Camps was apparently first to make sure that official Girl Scout goals and standards of practice were maintained, and secondarily to oversee the girls' conduct. Standards included the division of girls into *patrols*, organizing *kapers*, holding *Scouts' Own*, plus promoting singing, nightly campfires, dress codes, and more. From the Scouting perspective, the purpose of most of these was to place more responsibility on the girls, democratize decision-making, and help the girls to learn to work together efficiently. Bert not only needed to learn about the goals of scouting and the terminology, but also to evaluate how these could and would function in a Mobile Camp setting with its particularly tight scheduling and occasional road delays. The least useful from her perspective seemed to be the *patrol system* (the division of girls within a troop into subunits of six to eight members who meet separately, plan programs, and take a larger role in what happens within the main body of the troop). *Patrols* worked fairly well during the initial orientation sessions—to make sure that the girls from different states were on the same page as to how routine camping activities were to be accomplished (setting up/packing tents, testing skills such as fire building, axe handling, latrine care, kitchen duties, etc.). They worked for planning *Scouts' Own* (observed nearly every Sunday while on the road) or campfires—the frequency of the latter being limited by nightly chores and locations of camps. But beyond these times, the trips were already carefully planned and timed, so that there was little room for democratic decision-making once on the road. Bert also could see *patrols* possibly leading to the formation of cliques: e.g., the same set of girls always taking the lead, or wanting to always ride and camp together. She was much more in favor of them "mixing it up" when it came to most things, but also making sure that they stuck to their assigned tasks to aid camp efficiency. Assigning tasks by developing *kaper charts* early each session actually increased efficiency, as everyone knew their assignments ahead of time and when each had to be completed.

Dress and camping gear for on-the-trail camps needed some modification from Bert's perspective, especially given the changeable weather conditions (intense sunlight, cold nights, heavy summer monsoons) and weight and bulk limits for the vehicles. These needed to fit the situation, even if not official Girl Scout issue—practical walking/hiking shoes, sturdy heat/cold/rain/cactus spine protective outerwear, brimmed hats; compact sleeping bags/bedrolls, small day packs, all fitting within prescribed weight limits (Appendix B). Singing (definitely popular) initially displeased her, as it seemed to distract the girls' observations from what they were seeing and also caused them to pay less attention to what was being taught. After the second year Bert also complained to Anne Rushmer that the girls were singing too much, especially in the cars when they should be paying more attention to the landscape, the people, and what was being said (Dutton to Rushmer, July 28, 1948, MIAC/LAA). She did not realize how much singing was a part of Girl Scout tradition, with many special songs and unique words developed by the girls through the years. It was also Girl Scout tradition to exchange songs with other Scouts, and this required practicing them. She would realize how important singing was as the years went by, and she came to enjoy the creativity of the songs. She specifically enjoyed those composed on and for the Southwest camps—including those focused on her, the staff, and activities (Appendix C). She was not known to sing along on the trips, but she did print the text of one song in a yearly summary (Dutton (1951a:358–59).

The GS Reps and other officials had to adjust to Bert's requirements that camps be genuine learning experiences (complete with lectures, note-taking, periodic verbal quizzes) and still run as efficiently as possible due to the on-the-road scheduling requirements. At the same time, Bert had to learn about Scouting and its traditions and how well they could work in certain situations, as most were basically compatible with providing a good camping experience with a little modification for this situation. Each side had to give a little for the overall success of this program, which they did quite successfully until other matters intervened in the final years (Chapter 6).

Fees and Requirements

The fee charged the participants for the 1948 through 1951 sessions was $70 per camp—up from $60 in 1947—which basically covered transportation for the roughly 1,200 mile tours (vehicle rental, insurance, gas, repairs), food (basic supplies as well as fresh produce/meat purchased along the way), the cook's salary (beginning in 1948), and incidental expenses, such as entry fees to some places. Apparently neither the MNM nor Region IX charged any fee for administering the program. Although there are no copies of draft or final budgets in the archives, at that base rate during 1948 to 1951 the fees for each Mobile Camp would provide $1,120.00. Estimated expenses would be roughly $500–550/session for vehicles, $550 for food and cook's salary, leaving $25–75 for fees and incidentals.[9] The budget was tight, but sufficient, and apparently every effort was made to keep costs low. Bert occasionally indicates in correspondence that she is working hard to stay within budget, especially by buying nonperishable supplies in bulk in Santa Fe before leaving or elsewhere on the trail.

Participants had other expenses. The $70 camper fee did not include transportation or other expenses to and from Santa Fe in any year of the program. This could be quite a burden for some girls. In some cases, local GS councils assisted with various fees, including personal transportation and especially participant fees, by offering "camperships." And Bert solicited local organizations in Santa Fe to pay for some participants (see Spreading the Word, below). Campers remember parents driving them to Santa Fe and/or picking them up. Some traveled unaccompanied or with another camper by plane, train, and/or bus, and had pleasant adventures along the way. Girls were encouraged to travel in uniform, which resulted in many comments and kindnesses from other travelers. Most learned quickly that the famous "Santa Fe Railway" did not actually go to Santa Fe—only to Lamy—so taking the train (or plane) usually meant going to Albuquerque first. They then transferred to a bus to Santa Fe or had someone pick them up and drive them there. Camps early in this period ended in Albuquerque or Santa Fe in order to accommodate the girls' needs for exit transportation.

All girls attending in the late 1940s and early 1950s needed to be a minimum of 16 years old (or of junior standing in high school), be registered Senior Girl Scouts, and have the skills and knowledge that went along with that rank. By 1949, likely through experience by Bert and the staff, camping skills were more clearly spelled out in the flyers advertising the program. Bert (Dutton 1949a:279) emphasized them in her summary for 1949:

> Each girl must be endorsed whole-heartedly by her troop leader…local council, or troop committee chairman. All candidates must give evidence of excellent physical condition…know how to take care of her health…and enjoy living out of doors regardless of the weather…. The purpose of the camps is not to teach anyone how to camp. All…must have experience in primitive camping, and demonstrated skills in building fires, cooking, clean-up, establishing a camp and the various tool crafts.

Bert also expected that they know and practice the Girl Scout code (*Laws, Promise*), be familiar with typical camp routines, such as the duties associated with camp chores (*kapers*), and be eager to volunteer to do whatever "would increase the efficiency of each expedition" (Dutton 1949a:281). Typical *kapers* included cook's helpers, washing dishes, packing lunches, collecting fire wood, and more (Chapter 2). The flyers listed what participants needed to bring in the way of personal clothing, gear and supplies (all secured in a duffel bag not exceeding 50 lb [22.7 kg]), and also had information for parents about the itinerary, mail stops and addresses (usually four to five en route), required health information, spending money suggestions, and other matters. From 1948 to 1951, as the program expanded, flyers became multipage and more informative—perhaps again in part to weed out the underprepared. By 1950, the flyer was 10 pages long and spelled out yet more precisely specific camper knowledge and skill requirements (Appendix B). Some editions also included a checklist of Southwest art/craft items that girls might be interested in purchasing, to give Bert the opportunity to plan specific stops at trading posts and artists' homes as well as to properly advise girls on the best buys.[10] Successful applicants were notified by mail roughly two months ahead of camp starting dates. By 1950, they were given the names and addresses of girls who had attended before to write for additional information, and/or of those who would be attending with them for making joint travel arrangements—or just as friendly gestures (Bohrer file, 99BPD.xx).

Naming the Program

One additional organizational matter needed some attention in these developmental years: what to call the program. Although apparently not a major concern, a good name was needed, especially when it came to advertising the camps more widely. In 1947, Bert referred to the camp as the "archaeological expedition" (Dutton 1947a). Region IX's flyer for 1948 was titled a wordy "The Trail of the Archaeological Mobile Camp Designed for Senior Girl Scouts," and a year later, it was shortened to "Senior Girl Scout Archaeological Mobile Camps 1950." The camps often were referred to as the "on-the-trail" camps by Bert, a name she preferred at least for reference. In later years, sometimes the title on the flyers also included the names of the primary cosponsor—the Museum of New Mexico. But the label "Senior Girl Scout Archaeological Mobile Camp(s)," seemed to be the most reliable referent by 1950 and thereafter—or more simply, "the Mobiles" or "the Digs." Beginning in 1951 when an actual excavation camp became part of the program, "the Dig" title was reserved for that session (Chapter 5).

Fixing Some Problems

Although Bert felt that the 1947 session was successful, she recognized that there had been some problems, and she felt that certain refinements were needed to make a more successful session.[11] In early 1948, she focused on improvements to smooth out operations, especially during the actual field camps. These included alterations in the route and itinerary, policies on meals and beverages, transportation type and the related issue of optimal participant numbers, and safety. Other issues such as age limits, sponsor responsibilities, and authority also needed to be addressed, especially if the program were to expand—as it soon did. Discussions on these last points began in 1948, but the issues were not resolved until 1949 and 1950.

Routes and Itineraries

The first change Bert made for the 1948 session was to alter the route, the places visited, and the itinerary at the stops.[12] She did this largely for two reasons: first, to reduce the pressure of going too far and too fast; and second, to hold the interest of the 1947 campers who wanted to return for a second year. Although she and Ed

Ferdon had made a careful reconnaissance of the route before the 1947 trip, including estimating the times for each stop, it turned out that they were probably trying to do too much to allow for a smooth and comfortable trip while camping each night. This camp was not quite like a typical archaeological field school, which usually had a permanent location, or at best, a location where participants stayed for days or a week. As any traveler knows, moving each day is time-consuming and tiring. In 1948 and thereafter, 16 Girl Scouts and five crew would have to be up, fed, packed, and on the road early enough to reach a destination each evening in time to establish a camp, eat, do the necessary chores, and still get some sleep. These morning and evening activities added three or more hours daily to the travel and stop times—on a good day. There were the added complications of the road conditions in the region at any given time (many dirt roads, access sometimes compromised by the weather, and vehicle issues). These varied from year to year, so that Bert felt it imperative to continue to conduct the annual reconnaissance of each year's trip(s)—especially to see specific road and camping conditions—and again to keep careful track of the time needed for each stop along the way. She always planned for three to five mail stops per trip, and these needed to be at places with good service, and if possible, in proximity to spots where the girls could rest over the lunch break or immediately after—a Girl Scout tradition. On her 1948 reconnaissance (as well as thereafter), she personally camped at and visited all the spots to check facilities, and she carefully chose alternatives, in case there were problems (as there had been at Canyon de Chelly in 1947 due to rain). She shortened the 1948 route by about 100 miles, and also decreased the number of daily stops to add more time at each. Nonetheless, routes would still average roughly 1,100–1,200 miles each year. Distances are long in the Southwest, made even longer with so much to see and talk about.

The second reason for reconsidering the route and itinerary grew as a result of the enthusiasm of several of the 1947 girls to return for another season (five of the seven girls said they planned on coming back for 1948—three actually did). Varying the destinations would give them new places to see and new things to learn. There were always alternative places and scenic attractions to visit and stops to see different and ongoing excavations. With Bert's connections to the archaeological world in the Southwest, she knew who would be digging where and when in any given year so that visits could be added to their sites. For the 1948 trip, Bert developed a "central" route that preserved part of the 1947 itinerary (visiting Santa Fe museums and agencies, Kuaua and Chaco Canyon), but routing the group west to various places in Arizona as far as Flagstaff and the Verde Valley. The group then returned to New Mexico via present State Route 260 and the Mogollon Rim. This allowed the campers to learn about two additional archaeological traditions in the Southwest, the Sinagua in northern Arizona and the Mogollon in east-central Arizona and New Mexico, in addition to the Anasazi [now Ancestral Pueblo] who were well-represented in the areas that the campers had seen in 1947 (see Figure 3.2).[13] In the years to follow, as more and more girls returned and the goals of the program became more ambitious, Bert developed routes and itineraries with northern, central, and southern/southeastern foci so that girls attending multiple camps would learn even more about *Man and Nature in the Southwest*—that is, cultural diversity and human environmental adaptations, important anthropological lessons. In 1948, the emphasis continued to be visiting archaeological sites, including those preserved as parks and monuments as well as ones under excavation. But from that trip onward, the living cultural traditions of the region were given more attention, thus providing a better balance and broader view of the region's complex cultures and histories.

Meals and Beverages

Another change in 1948 concerned policies on meals and beverages. In 1947, with Sue Little and Nyla Harvey in charge of meals and the girls sharing cooking duties, things did not go too well, and some girls apparently got sick (Stein 2008b). Bert insisted that beginning in 1948, there needed to be a full-time qualified cook on all Mobile Camps or she would not continue to lead them (Dutton 1990:8). She felt that the girls were too busy all day long with strenuous activities to have to focus afterwards on meal preparation. She knew from working on archeological sites that an experienced camp cook was not only essential to good health, but also fostered good harmony. After all, it is an old saw that an army travels best on a stomach full of good food (but not too full while on bumpy roads!). The cook was the only paid staff member throughout the life of the program (other than Bert as director).[14] Cooks were usually local to New Mexico and carefully screened by Bert who also oversaw the menus. The food was wholesome and nutritious, including pancakes, French toast, eggs, and bacon for breakfast, as well as various types of salads, casseroles, and meats (occasionally steak), and even food with a regional flair—sopaipillas, enchiladas, chile, and more. Nosebag lunches prepared ahead of the day's travel became the norm as it had taken too long in 1947 to stop at lunchtime, make the lunches, and rest. Lunches included sandwiches, juice, and a piece of fruit. Knowledge of how to cook for a group and in a Dutch oven was a requirement. Some of the cooks returned for several sessions and were very popular with the campers (see Appendix A: Staff). Campers assisted the cooks by building fires, some food preparation work, and washing up and packing pans and dishes, also as part of their normal camp *kapers*. They also helped prepare and pack the lunches (night before or in the morning—depending on the daily schedule) and were responsible for making sure that they were loaded into the vehicles. On her yearly reconnaissance, Bert scouted places to buy fresh produce and supplies—although they carried a number of staples purchased in Santa Fe ahead of each session.

The beverage policy also changed. Carbonated drinks, common to stops in 1947, were no longer allowed, but stops could include juices and milkshakes or malts when available and time allowed. Most of these stops were at trading posts, other supply points, or mail stops along the trail. Certainly from 1948 on, what became known as the "tea ritual" was also instituted. This usually involved mandatory weak hot tea with dinner, but sometimes also at lunch or a stop during the day. All travelers were to participate. Bert considered weak tea to be a fine thirst quencher in the hot and dry Southwest, something she learned from Hewett, who had in turn learned about the supposed benefits of hot tea from colleagues in Europe who worked in the deserts of the Middle East. Not everyone appreciated this ritual, but most participated—up to a point. Stops for milkshakes sometimes included Bert's favorite "milk nickel" ice cream bars—always a bigger hit!

Transportation and Number of Participants

Cars, a trailer to haul baggage, and the number of girls and staff who could be accommodated were related in Bert's mind. In 1947, as noted, transportation was in a single vehicle (a "stretched out Chevy" plus trailer) with a single driver—who brought

Figure 3.1. Jack Stacy and Bertha Dutton, Camp II, 1953. Photograph by Kate Swift (99BPD.xx, K. Swift Collection). Courtesy of MIAC/LAA.

along his 12-year-old son as a "helper" (Stein 2008b). Bert learned quickly that this vehicle was a bad choice and basically unworkable for the route, although it accommodated the needs of the number of campers and staff for that year. Beginning in 1948, with more participants expected, three more appropriate vehicles plus a trailer made up the caravan, with a "chief of transportation" to drive one and manage the others—including fixing the numerous flat tires and other broken parts, overheated radiators, and more. The vehicles also needed to be able to navigate the roads at the time: largely dirt rather than paved. Bert's philosophy on roads seemed be "never take a paved road when a dirt one will do." And besides, many of the best sights and sites were accessed only by dirt roads at the time. The same plan as to vehicles was followed thereafter, a much better solution in case of breakdowns or other problems—someone could go for help if needed!

The transportation chief—Jack Stacy—was the only male on the trips that year and thereafter (Figure 3.1). An old friend of Bert, Jack owned and ran his own tour company (The Santa Fe Cab and Transfer Company), and had been a driver for Fred Harvey's Indian Detours (Thomas 1978). Thus he knew most of the routes and also the places along the way to get repairs (especially flats). The vehicles in 1948 and for several years thereafter included a nine-passenger Cadillac, a Chevrolet station wagon, and a seven-passenger Oldsmobile, leased through Stacy's company. Jack was a beloved non-salaried volunteer, and he remained with the Mobile Camp program throughout its life. The girls composed several songs in his honor (Appendix C).

Bert felt that three vehicles better accommodated a proper number of campers, staff, and gear. She also felt that a good optimal number of campers was 16—small enough for her to get to know each of them and large enough to promote new friend-ships. Five staff were also optimal, allowing for three drivers (including herself and Jack plus one other adult), plus two others who could also pitch in (the cook, natu-ralist, or GS Rep sometimes drove). Multiple vehicles also encouraged the campers to ride with different girls and staff, promoting a more "harmonious" situation, and a better learning experience for all. It discouraged separation into cliques based on age, place of origin, "best buddies," or other factors. Again, Bert's instructions were to "mix it up."

Safety

From the beginning, it is likely that all the sponsors considered safety issues for on-the-trail expeditions. The GSUSA, used to running camps and other excur-sions, would have been particularly familiar with this issue. However, 1948 is the first year that there is specific evidence for it in the records. One step included mak-ing sure that at least one adult was certified in First Aid in case of accidents, infec-tions, insect bites, severe sunburn, dehydration, or other calamities (Jack Stacy was certified, as were some GS Reps). A second was a required physician's statement as to the camper's general fitness for the expedition as well as details on any health issues that might require adult monitoring. And the third was to encourage the par-ents of all campers to sign up for special illness/accident insurance for a minimal charge ($0.30/week accident, $0.50/week illness), a form for which was included in the registration packet. Bert also made potential medical needs a routine part of her annual reconnaissance, including checking on locations of emergency facilities and getting the contact information for clinics and physicians along the routes.[15] The issue of actual liability would resurface in later years (Chapter 7).

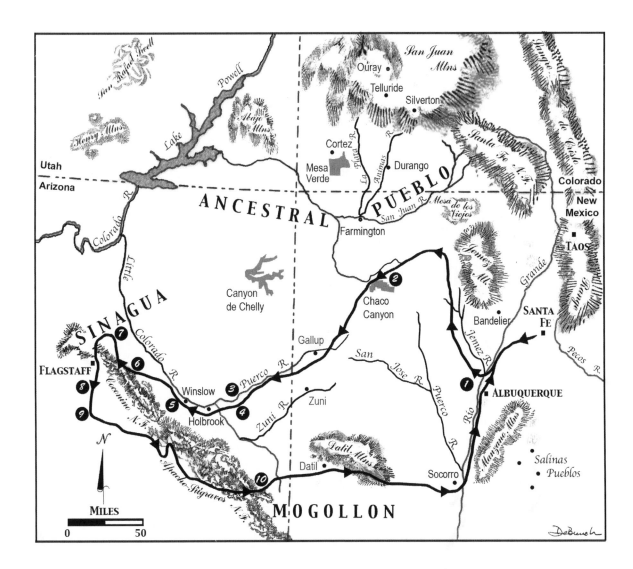

Figure 3.2. Route of the second Archaeological Mobile Camp, 1948. Map by Patricia DeBunch. (1) Coronado [State] Historic Site; (2) Chaco Culture National Historical Park; (3) Painted Desert; (4) Petrified Forest National Park; (5) Meteor Crater; (6) Walnut Canyon National Monument; (7) Wupatki National Monument; (8) Tuzigoot National Monument; (9) Montezuma Castle National Monument/Montezuma Well; (10) Kinishba Ruins.

Figure 3.3. Mobile
Campers in dress
uniforms and
ready for first day
in Santa Fe, 1948.
Photograph by
Jo Tice [Bloom].
99BPD.xx,
Scrapbook, 1948.
Courtesy of MIAC/
LAA.

The 1948 Mobile Camp

Jo Tice [Bloom's] Letters Home

These and other changes in the camper experience are well reflected in Jo Tice's letters home, sent during the 1948 trip. The following selected quotes and photographs provide a rough itinerary of the trip as well as a firsthand account as seen by a 15-year-old Midwesterner about the new world she found in the Southwest. The letters and photographs recount her many learning experiences, adventures in on-the-trail living, and her memories and enthusiasm for that special two weeks (July 10–24) in 1948 (see also Bloom 2007, 2012; Dutton 1948b). The route that year initiated what would become known as the "central route" that included crossing into Arizona as far as Flagstaff (Figure 3.2).

> [Saturday, July 10, on arriving at Hyde Memorial State Park:] Gosh! New Mexico is Amazing!! The mountains come right up out of the plains. [Sunday they spent

Figure 3.4. Chetro Ketl, Chaco Canyon, in process of stabilization. Photograph by Anne Rushmer. LA.08.ARM.001-101 #55. Courtesy of MIAC/LAA.

practicing skills—pitching pup tents, developing axe skills, packing compactly, preparing a *kaper chart*, and more]. Great laughter ensued when we discovered that the New Jersey girls didn't know how to make a 'cat hole' latrine. In New Jersey camps, we learned, you couldn't dig holes! [Monday] The cars haven't arrived yet so I'll review the morning's activities. When we got up, half the girls started getting ready. After breakfast we changed to our uniforms and went down to wait. We took several pictures [Figure 3.3]. Later—lunch at last!!! This morning when we arrived in Santa Fe, we went to the Museum of New Mexico where Bert met us. She introduced us to Mrs. Marjorie Tichy who took us thru the Hall of Archaeology. She gave us the history of the Pueblo Indians. First there was civilization about 10,000 yrs. ago. Then came the Basketmakers. Basketmakers III started making pottery. After this came the Pueblos of Chaco. Then the present-day Indians.[16]

Then we went to the Hall of Ethnology where Bert lectured us. At 11:30 Dr. Sylvanus Morley spoke to us for a short while. Then we ate and went to town. Bert told me I was going to be on a 'man-on-the-street' radio program with Luckie, Joan, Whip, and Pete [Dorothy Peterson, GS Rep]. Then we got into Mrs. Luckie's Jeep, Bert's Model A Ford, Whip's coupe and Pete's car and headed for the Laboratory of Anthropology. There we went into the auditorium where we heard Dr. Kenneth Chapman who lectured us on Indian pottery. It was very interesting. The Zuni Pueblo is the only one now making good pottery.[17] At 3:00 we left for the radio program. It was swell and we had loads of fun. When we got back the rest of the girls were at the National Park Service Region III headquarters, listening to a lecture by Mr. Natt Dodge on Natural History and Mr. Charlie Steen on national parks and monuments.[18] We got back to camp. We repacked our duffels, and left out quite a bit.

Tuesday: we're on our way!!! We left Hyde Park at 8:30 am after packing the Olds station wagon (seats 6), the Chevy (6) and the Cadillac (9). I rode in the Cadillac. Right now we are stopped for the flat the Olds had. Food!!! We're at Coronado State Monument. We went into the Kuaua ruins. We got to go down in a restored *kiva*. It was the Painted Kiva. Originally there were 85 layers of plaster, 17 painted. It was cool and stuffy.

[After two days at Chaco Canyon and tours of Pueblo Bonito, Chetro Ketl (Figure 3.4) and Basketmaker III sites, some led by Gordon Vivian, they were on the road again.] What roads they have here in Arizona! This morning we pulled out on time. Jack Stacy had taken the tires to Holbrook, so we stopped for 20 minutes. At 11 we arrived at the Meteorite Museum. D. H. H. Nininger gave us a short talk and a demonstration. Then we headed for Meteor Crater [impact crater, roughly 50,000 years old and 3600 feet (1097 m) diameter, 360 feet (110 m) deep]. After lunch we headed for Flagstaff…and arrived at Dr. Watson Smith's excavations [at Wupatki; see below]. We walked around for a while; then headed for a campsite…After dinner we walked over to see the other camp and Mr. Smith showed us around and answered our questions. We turned in about 9:30.

Figure 3.5. North Room Block of Wupatki Pueblo with large amphitheater or kiva in foreground, Wupatki National Monument, AZ, 1948. Photograph by Jo Tice [Bloom]. 99BPD.xx, Scrapbook, 1948. Courtesy of MIAC/LAA.

Figure 3.6. Navajo hogan, Wupatki National Monument, 1948. Photograph by Jo Tice [Bloom]. 99BPD.xx, Scrapbook, 1948. Courtesy of MIAC/LAA.

Figure 3.7. Tent
camp at Oak Creek
Canyon, 1948.
Photograph by
Jo Tice [Bloom].
99BPD.xx,
Scrapbook, 1948.
Courtesy of MIAC/
LAA

Figure 3.7. Tent camp at Oak Creek Canyon, 1948. Photograph by Jo Tice [Bloom]. 99BPD.xx, Scrapbook, 1948. Courtesy of MIAC/LAA

This morning we visited Wupatki National Monument. We saw the Citadel and Wupatki ruins [Figure 3.5]. We also visited a Navajo *hogan* and summer camp [Figure 3.6].[19] Then we headed for Sunset Crater [the eruption of] which [in 1068–1080] caused the Indian farmers to come and settle. In one square mile in Wupatki, there are 200 ruins.... We saw Ice Cave which has ice the year 'round. On the way out, Jack took the wrong turn and got to the museum before we did. Bert and Whip went through Schultz Pass which was beautiful, even if it did rain. Then Whip missed Bert's turn and ended up in Flagstaff. Finally we all got together at the Museum of Northern Arizona. Now we are camped across the road. Later tonight we pitched our tents for rain. We fixed ours up real swell.

Wupatki Pueblo was built in the early 1100s and soon became the largest village in the Sinagua area. Its builders had various points of origin and brought with them markers of their home regions (architectural styles and forms, pottery types and designs, and other material clues). Changes in climate in their homelands, including widespread droughts, were reducing yields of crops (corn, beans, and squash). The mulch created by the ash layers from the eruptions of Sunset Crater helped to hold soil moisture, thus making the area attractive. Construction at Wupatki ceased in the early 1200s, and people again moved on to other locations. Wupatki Pueblo has both an amphitheater and ball court similar to those of Hohakam areas near Phoenix and Tucson. Ball courts were used in those areas to play a ceremonial ball game also known in Mexico (Downum 2012: Downum et al 2012).

We left Flagstaff after lunch and headed for Oak Creek Canyon. It is beautiful. The red sandstone cliffs, the green pines, the mountain creek running below. It was simply gorgeous. We camped about five miles from the highway on Beaver Creek. It is a beautiful spot. We camped under the trees by the creek. Farther down was a swell swimming and washing spot, so we all went down there. The water was wonderful. We had loads of fun. After dinner we pitched our tents again and had a sing.... Finally we crawled into bed. Most everyone couldn't sleep for the mosquitoes, but I slept like a log [Figure 3.7].

[After touring Tuzigoot National Monument and another camp providing swimming, they stopped at Camp Verde for mail and then began to motor up the Mogollon Rim]. We waited for Jack to come back with the station wagon and lunch. After lunch we went into Sitgreaves National Forest [now

Figure 3.8. Dutton
illustrates tentative
dating of site
by potsherds
recovered from
surface, 1951.
95PLE.034©.
Courtesy of MIAC/
LAA.

Figure 3.8. Dutton illustrates tentative dating of site by potsherds recovered from surface, 1951. 95PLE.034©. Courtesy of MIAC/LAA.

Apache-Sitgreaves National Forest]. In the early PM, we stopped along the Mogollon Rim and noticed that the Caddie hadn't been with us. Finally it arrived after I helped Jack fix the twisted spring, raising the total delays [today] to five flats [due to] blowouts, lost tread; one muffler broken, one twisted spring. [They learned that 20 fires had broken out, so the ranger had to cut his lecture short, and they spent the evening viewing elk].

...When we reached the Tonto Rim, we waited for the Chevy and the Caddie. When they arrived we found out that they had another flat and a broken muffler. Later when we turned to go to the Rynch Ranch, the station wagon had a flat. We got water and went on. Then we hit an electrical storm and downpour. The station wagon began to leak on all of us. Soon we met a new resident who was having trouble, so we helped him up the hill. Later he couldn't get around a log, so we helped him again. Then we had lunch in the rain. Finally we got to the Fort Apache Indian Reservation. About 11 miles from the turnoff we had another flat. We left six girls, the driver, and the station wagon and went on to Kinishba. At 7:30 the Caddie came back to get us. [The next day] we explored Kinishba ruins, and one girl found a tarantula to take back to New Jersey...I saw three deer, three burros, two rabbits, numerous chipmunks, sheep and several squirrels.

Kinishba Ruins, located on the Fort Apache Indian Reservation, includes several significant masonry pueblos. The largest has roughly 600 rooms, and features communal courtyards or plazas and ceremonial rooms, including *kivas*. It was built and occupied primarily during the twelfth to the fourteenth centuries, and has architectural features and ceramics suggesting occupation by Mogollon as well as Ancestral Pueblo peoples. It was excavated and partially restored under the direction of Dr. Byron Cummings of the University of Arizona between 1931 and 1940, using university students, local Apache men, and Civilian Conservation Corps workers. Today it is administered by the White Mountain Apache Tribe. It was made a National Historic Landmark in 1964.

[On our last day] we reached Isleta after having two flats and losing Bert. We ate [lunch] on the Continental Divide and slept at the Isleta Indian School. We had a wonderful meal and showers. [The next morning] we went through the Isleta pueblo. All the buildings are one-story and they have one kiva. It was very interesting.

[On to Albuquerque where the group began departing:] The rest of us went out to Roosevelt Park for lunch. We all went wild. I was to meet family friends there, so the rest left after we ate. As they left they sang our song:

> Oh we're so happy we took this trip
> In the land where there aren't any chiggers.
> We hunt for potsherds all day long
> For we are Dutton's Dirty Diggers.

I burst out crying. It was a wonderful ~~trip and I~~ enjoyed every moment of it. The gals were swell.

Jo Tice Bloom's (2007:3) postscript to her account of the 1948 trip provides one of her many memories:

When I think back about those magical two weeks, the most vivid memory is of the moonlit night in Chaco Canyon. We had explored Pueblo Bonito, Chetro Ketl and other sites with Bert and the ranger. Pearl [Kendricks] had cooked a tasty, filling dinner, as always. We had sung around the campfire and slipped into our sleeping bags under the moonlight and stars. Then we heard the pounding of horses' hooves come closer and closer. Suddenly silhouetted against the clear sky, were Navajo riders, cantering along to the trading post whose lights shone nearby. Magical! Mystical! Memorable! Thank you Bert [Figure 3.8].

Evelyn Stobie's Memories

Unlike Jo Tice's account, which was written at the time of the trip, Evelyn "Les" Stobie's (1955) views of the 1948 camp were written as a remembrance seven years later. By then she was in her mid-twenties, had been to college, and had moved to Portland, Oregon from Missouri. She ultimately went on five Mobile Camps and four Pueblo Largo Digs, and served one year as a driver and naturalist. Her account is reflective of the experience and poetic about the country seen during that special summer in 1948.

Perhaps it is that every eastern child dreams of going to the West someday. I was no different! Was it really like the movies? Was it all hot and dry? Did the Indians all live in teepees? In 1948 I had the opportunity to see the West for the first time.

Camp opened that year at Hyde [Memorial] State Park in the Sangre de Cristo Mountains. I believe I just sat with my mouth open when I saw the trees and the lush vegetation. <u>This</u> was the arid Southwest? No one had said anything about trees.

As with all camps, the first few days were spent getting acquainted, practicing skills, writing books of notes in the Santa Fe museums, and exploring—especially the latter. This was a whole new world!

How well I remember the hike up to the falls the ranger had told us about [above Hyde State Park]. We climbed over rocks, under trees, around logs, and through masses of vegetation. The whole time Whip was giving a discourse on the local flora, we were saying to each other, "Where is the water? This creek looks pretty dry to me."

Panting (from the altitude, we told ourselves), we finally got to the location of the falls. Yep, it was the location all right—but the water didn't know about it. All there was was a puny trickle down the rock face of the small cliff. Ah well, we had a nice walk!

Then came the first day on the road. Great stretches of sand and rock and suitable vegetation gave the 'western' atmosphere to much of the land. And everywhere there was sun!

Chaco Canyon gave me the first introduction to Indian ruins on a grand scale. Where were all those cliff dwellings I had heard about? These were all sprawled on the canyon floor. Could it be that I had been misinformed? I did not stop to ponder long—there was too much to see and do. The ruin of Pueblo Bonito occupied considerable time. What type of people had lived there who had constructed such a great place and lasting edifices? Why had they taken such pains to fit the stones of their walls into patterns and then plaster those same walls with mud? What type of life had they led? What happened to the people? Archaeology dull and dry? Far from it.

Since it was first seen in the 1860s, many people—archaeologists and visitors alike—have marveled at the aesthetics of the construction of

Pueblo Bonito and other Chacoan sites. Monumental walls, obviously preplanned to reach several stories, interlocking rooms with doorways leading from one to another, complicated roof construction so that each room's ceiling would support the floor(s) of the room(s) above; and the beautifully dressed, fitted, and banded stone masonry, all reflecting superior workmanship and engineering (Lekson 2014).

Everywhere there were potsherds. Potsherds in bags. Potsherds in duffels. You never saw so many potsherds before going to the West, there I was madly collecting them like a child collects shiny pebbles. Maybe it was because they were "history." There is a certain fascination about holding several hundred years of history in the palm of your hand.

Bert frequently stopped at less well-known sites to have the girls collect a "grab bag" of potsherds from the surface. She would then demonstrate how a surface collection of sherds was the quickest way to assess the age range of the site (Figure 3.8). Girls were allowed to keep a few of the sherds from some sites; others were taken to the MNM for the collections. The girls were not allowed to collect, let alone keep, anything from National Park or Monument lands—as the statement in this paragraph seems to imply. Today rules are even stricter for all sites: The NPS motto of "take only pictures, leave only footprints" applies to all.

The Painted Desert—area of indescribable beauty, desolation, and mystery. When holding a piece of petrified wood, you aren't fooling around with hundreds of years of history—you are holding untold eons of geologic time. What a paradox it was to have to haul in wood to cook hamburgers while surrounded by tons of wood.

Figure 3.9. Cooks prepare a meal from chuck box, at Bibo Ranch, Los Pilares, NM, 1951. Bertha Dutton Photos, Girl Scouts (File 6, No. 1). Courtesy of MIAC/LAA.

At the western end of the route we visited Wupatki—a settlement born of volcanic violence, but empty because of the steady and relentless wind and sun of Mother Nature. In the midst of the gaunt black lava and cinders is this warm red sandstone village of Wupatki. A gem on the vast backdrop of nature.

Zane Gray must have felt the beauty of Oak Creek Canyon as we did when we first looked down into its rainbow depths. He wrote "Call of the Canyon;" we can only cherish within ourselves the sweep of this earth cut. Best of all, tho', was the water. Cool, wonderful, sparkling, refreshing water. How good it felt to just sit and soak—not only ourselves but our clothes. Playing 'Ring Around the Rosy' in [three and a half] feet of warm water beneath a full moon had certain charm, too.

God must have loved the Southwest, for he gave it so much—mountains, forests, canyons, meadows, friendly towns, and the vast reaches of deserts. It is not only a beautiful and strange land where I learned so much of archaeology and geology and biology, but it is a place where I met some of the finest people in the world—FOR WE ARE THE DIGGERS—AND WE SAY 'THE FINEST IN THE U.S.A'

Spreading the Word: 1949–1951

The success of the 1948 trip generated more enthusiasm for additional Southwest Mobile Camps, and Bert and Region IX were soon ready to move forward for another summer. The "fixes" put into place in 1948 smoothed operations for all concerned—except for the ever-present flat tires. Six campers again indicated that they wanted to come back for more. The enthusiasm of these returnees seems to have prompted Bert to begin thinking of the camps as more of a "program" for young women than as single experiences—although these were still important, as not everyone was going to return. As a program, the camps might make a real difference in the campers' future lives and possible career choices, as several were now about to enter college. If it were to have an impact, then it was even more important to let people know what the camps were about in order to continue to attract the best participants.

In 1949, 1950, and 1951, the operations became even smoother, as Bert, the Girl Scout organization(s), the MNM, and other participants, including the girls, "learned while doing." It is clear that some of the key players in recruiting new campers were the girls themselves. Veterans of the 1947 and 1948 camps were spreading the word through newspaper interviews, as it was an important requirement of being awarded a "wider op" that participants tell local people about your experiences and what you had learned. They also were speaking at venues such as local, regional, and national Girl Scout gatherings. Bert, Region IX officials, and GSUSA national headquarters stepped up activities to promote the sessions. Bert lectured about the trips to numerous New Mexico organizations, including PTAs, civic organizations, and museum society groups. Demand began to increase, so that there soon were waiting lists, and the single camp was replaced by two camps per summer in these years. Visits to Santa Fe by regional and national GS representatives increased—seemingly to strategize—as can be seen in Bert's personal correspondence. Bert encouraged even more local groups to sponsor camperships to allow girls without sufficient funds to attend—and was quite successful at it. She requested additional help from the Santa Fe Girl Scout Council. Although the local council apparently had not been an overt sponsor earlier, they had been arranging housing and hosting for visiting Region IX and GSUSA representatives (including GS Reps going on Mobile Camps) when possible, sometimes in the summers at the Santa Fe Indian School (Bohrer 1948a; 1949). The council, along with regional headquarters, now helped solicit camper sponsorships and other contributions for the program. Local Santa Fe businesses were coming forth as well. And the GSUSA began promoting the trips more widely through distribution of Region IX's flyers to other regional offices and councils.

Bert apparently continued to correspond in 1949 and 1950 with Eunice Prien in a manner that suggests that she now had a bigger plan in mind. As former campers began "aging out" of the Senior Scout program at 18 years old, but still wanted to go on more Mobiles, she asked for various rulings having to do with the upper age limits and whether campers could attend if they were married. Bert saw the camps as a good chance to keep young women older than 18 in school and also as lifelong participants in Scouting—valuable to them as well as the GSUSA.

Bert received positive answers to the age limit and marital status questions in early 1949, and the flyer that year included the phrase "for Senior Girl Scouts and Girl Scout Adults." The solution was for the girls to "register as Girl Scout Associates." Bert was pleased with the lack of an upper age limit, saying that "there is, then, the opportunity for the older girls to enjoy camping privileges and other kindred interests. Each year the routes differ...so that all the campers can look forward to new experiences and different places, even though many of the camp faces are familiar" (Dutton 1950a:366). Bert was also becoming attached to some of the girls who had returned, corresponding with them, and beginning to think of them as her "Digger family" (Chapter 4).

Bert was also seeing the larger impacts that the camps were having, especially on the returnees. The camps were a good opportunity for the young women to continue to explore their interests—and potential career choices—in academic fields that went beyond the traditional choices available to young women in those times (secretarial training, teaching, nursing, and so on), just as she had. The camps emphasized the sciences and academic disciplines/fields such as archaeology, anthropology, biology, geology, geography, history, Spanish, folklore, and more. She wanted these young women to explore their passions and also to think about alternative paths to follow in life, especially if their first choice did not work out as they had planned.[20] This did not mean that they should not marry and have children—or that they should all become anthropologists—but additional choices provided additional options. In 1949 she wrote (Dutton 1949a:285):

> It is particularly satisfying to observe how much knowledge girls who have gone on one trip and returned for a second or a third have retained from the preceding camps. The routes differ from year to year, so that a continuous program is offered. One of our campers has commented: 'Two Digs and I am not satisfied. I like this country too much! I will never forget all you have done for me.' And another: 'The educational part created new and lasting interests. I never before realized that this whole new field of southwestern culture—past and present—existed'.... If a girl returns for the third season, we feel that we are indeed accomplishing the goals of this project, and that she is getting the utmost benefits from our program.

Bert was indeed realizing a more personal goal when in the fall of 1949, two veteran campers registered at two western universities majoring in anthropology.[21] They would be the first of many that she would see attend college in a variety of fields and whose careers she would continue to follow closely (Chapter 10). She added, "regardless of what these young women do in the future, I am certain of this: They will be better citizens as a result of their travels in the Southwest, and by reason of the knowledge of mankind and his works that these camps afford" (Dutton 1949a:285).

Bert reinforced the focus and purpose of the camps in her "Message from Dr. Dutton" that accompanied the Region IX flyer advertising the 1950 camps. The focus, "Man and Nature in the Southwest," had not changed, nor had the method (on-the-trail experience) profiling "centers of great archaeological importance...Pueblo and Navajo Indian territory...[and] the greatest wonders of nature":

En route, a program constituting <u>a study of human life in its out-of-door set-</u><u>ting</u> will be conducted, and with the natural world for its laboratory, and with both ancient and living communities for its books. This camp will introduce to the young citizens of the United States, the anthropological background of the Southwest, and will serve to widen and sharpen their perspective of the science of man from the standpoint of general education and culture [Dutton's emphasis].

As the program began to expand, and became better known, more people provided funds and in-kind matches for program needs. Donations in 1949 by individuals and local civic groups beyond camperships included a full set of two-person pup tents, other camping gear, and food preparation and serving equipment (meal trays, silverware, cups, etc.). All of these became part of the permanent equipment for the field operations and would be carefully cleaned, repaired as necessary, and stored in Santa Fe for upcoming sessions. One girl's father made a chuck box with donated lumber to fit into the back of the station wagon (Figure 3.9). This piece of equipment facilitated cooking operations in 1949 and for several more years thereafter (Dutton 1949a:281). A women's auxiliary group had a benefit bridge party and turned over $14.60 to purchase a 20 gallon water tank to allow for dry camps (Dutton 1949a:281). It was still in use in the mid-1950s. Several newspaper stories in Santa Fe, Albuquerque, and elsewhere generated yet more enthusiasm and more donations—none very large but all welcomed.

The 1949 to 1951 Mobile Camps

Beginning in 1949, all camps were able to start and end at Bert's new home: El Rancho del Cielo, with its small Southwest-style adobe home and an outbuilding, located on what was then undeveloped pinyon-juniper covered land off Arroyo Chamiso Road south of Santa Fe. This site was large enough for the girls to spread out and camp for the two-to-three nights needed for orientation and the visits to the Santa Fe museums—which by now had become routine—and also the last night of each session. There was room for a permanent campfire circle, a firepit for cooking, a large picnic table, and latrine facilities. It was a much better alternative than Hyde Park, which had served its purpose for the first two years, but was basically a public facility with all its associated vulnerabilities. Arriving campers could easily be taken to Bert's *ranchito*, as she called it, and also could be released at the end of a trip(s) without the problems of trying to drop individuals at various venues in Albuquerque or Santa Fe in order to make bus, plane, or train schedules. The ranchito also provided a place for more properly concluding camps, with the required cleaning, repairing, and storing of equipment. Importantly it was a more relaxing and private atmosphere for properly saying goodbyes. The girls could get rid of the top layer of dirt, repack their gear, exchange addresses, and have a final campfire together. It also allowed for a smoother exit to see more of the city and surrounding areas, either by themselves, with others, or with parents who might have come to pick them up.[22] The end of the camps often coincided with summer dances held in the Rio Grande Pueblos, with the Intertribal Ceremonials in Gallup, or in later years—when there were yet more camps at later dates—Santa Fe Fiesta and Indian Market. These late summer/early fall events were major yearly tourist attractions.

Having a permanent home base also eased Bert's burden, as she no longer had to ask the Museum to find places to store donated equipment. She and the other adult leaders could more easily observe and assess the skill levels of the campers, and correct deficiencies which had become apparent in 1948—such skills as pitching, taking down, and storing pup tents, proper axe handling, campfire safety, and more. They all could spend more time getting acquainted—the staff with the girls and the girls with each other—and developing *kaper* charts. The staff could check duffels (50 lb [22.7 kg] limit, including sleeping bag). Excess baggage, including traveling clothes, could be safely stored in Bert's outbuilding until camp ended. There was also more time and a proper site for evening lectures, barbeques, and campfire sings—overall a much better working arrangement.

The route for the two 1949 camps was yet another alternative to the mostly northern 1947 and central 1948 routes, combining a little of each (Figure 3.10). It added a component for east-central New Mexico, focusing initially on the area to the south and east of Santa Fe, including the turquoise mines at Cerrillos, the

COLORADO

MANCOS
DURANGO
PAGOSA SPRINGS
MESA VERDE
DeBunch
SHIPROCK
CEDAR HILL
CHAMA
AZTEC
SAN CRISTOBAL
BLOOMFIELD
ARROYO HONDO
TAOS PUEBLOS
TAOS
ABIQUIU
RANCHOS de TAOS
River
CHACO
CUBA
LA VENTANA
BANDELIER
JEMEZ SPRINGS
SANTA FE
NEW MEXICO
JEMEZ
SAN YSIDRO
KUAUA
GALISTEO
BERNALILLO
SANTO DOMINGO
ALBUQUERQUE
TIJERAS
CHILILÍ
Grande
TAJIQUE
TORREON
MANZANO
Rio
QUARAI
MOUNTAIN AIR
ABO
GRAN QUIVERA
SOCORRO

Figure 3.10. Route map of Mobile Camp II, 1949. Based on sketch map by Vorsila Bohrer, 1949. Redrafted by Patricia DeBunch.

Hispanic villages near the Manzano Mountains, and the sites of the historic east-ern [Salinas] Pueblos and their seventeenth century Spanish Missions (Quarai, Abó, and Gran Quivera, all National Monuments and State Historic Sites; sidebar Chapter 4; Appendix D). Campers for the first session then went north, by way of San Juan Pueblo (now Ohkay Owingey), visiting several Pueblo homes and being able to purchase art directly from potters. The next stop was Chimney Rock National Monument in Colorado[23] where they visited its important sites, and then on to Mesa Verde National Park where they spent three days. They looped back through Shiprock, New Mexico to Aztec Ruins National Monument, Jemez State Park (now Jemez Historic Site), and Bandelier National Monument (see sidebar 4.3 for informa-tion on these sites).

This itinerary included much more emphasis on the living and late historic tra-ditions of the Southwest with the stops at Hispanic villages (including Abiquiú, where they met the famous painter Georgia O'Keeffe), the old Spanish missions, and then Pueblos, including San Juan, Santo Domingo, and Zia. The returnees requested to see dances and other ceremonies and festivals open to the public, and Bert did her best to comply for both camps. Camp II reversed the route, again to enable the campers to see Pueblo ceremonies, which are timed to their own ritual calendars, as well as other regional events. Highlights were the Corn Dance at Zia and spending a night at San Juan Pueblo, where the girls saw a hoop dance performance by a young boy, all arranged by a San Juan Girl Scout on the trip (Louise Cata) and her family. This group also spent a day at the annual Pecos Conference of Southwestern archae-ologists and ethnologists, held that year at the Laboratory of Anthropology in Santa Fe. This provided the Scouts with another opportunity to meet prominent attendees and for the conferees to learn firsthand about Bert's program (see Woodbury 1993 for the significance of these annual events). Vorsila "Rambler" Bohrer kept both a diary of the trip as well as a detailed set of notes as to what she learned, including from various speakers at the conference (Bohrer 1949).

Each session in 1949 covered approximately 1,100 miles—a slight reduction that added comfort and time. Bert (1949a:284) stated for the record that there was another unrelated benefit: "no flat tires occurred en route. After some 13 or 14 flats last year (even though we started out with all new rubber), this is something of which we may be proud." (The group was not as lucky in 1950. Flat tires were back, along with two broken axles and other mechanical problems.) Feedback from the girls was very positive, with remarks like, "I've had more fun here than I ever had anywhere. I hope all the trips will be as successful." And, "Why do I keep coming back? Because we learn about six times as much as any regular tourist would, live with the swellest bunch you could find anywhere; we have a chance to prove we can take camping about as tough as it is dished out." And, "What had been a rubble pile to me before held a fascinating story of real people" (Region IX flyer 1950:2; 99BPD.xx).

Region IX's flyer for the 1950 trip contains a good account of a day on the road, written by an anonymous camper under the title "Our Day":

Pearl [Kendrick], our pearl-of-a-cook, taps the fire-builders who have hung a white cloth on their tent poles, in the brisk early dawn—usually 5:30! Half an hour later cooks and lunch makers show up and there is a gentle busy hum around the chuck box kitchen fitted into the back of the station wagon. Six-thirty to seven o'clock breakfast may be bacon and eggs, flapjacks or French toast, plus the standbys of hot cereal, coffee, and hot chocolate. Early risers, especially staff—and always Jack—will have been tapping the coffee pot long before Grace. Then the bustle of breaking camp. "Water boys" are filling the canvas bags that hang on the cars, checking the 20 gallon trailer tank and making sure individual canteens are filled.

Eight to 8:30 and we're off to see new sights and to learn more than we dreamed possible. Will it be an Indian dance today? A fabulous climb to cliff dwellings? Meeting and chatting with experts and watching them work? Noon and "Bert" has timed things so that we have a spectacular view while we eat our poke lunches, with milk from thermos jugs. Some take a cat nap. Others use their lunch orange for a brief game of ball.

An unbelievably good dinner follows the afternoon trip and there is always a vast quantity of weak tea—because it prevents thirst the next day. We settle in, wash out socks, jot down notes of the day and chat with Bert, discover new friends, sing songs Girl Scouts know wherever they're from.... Some go off to bed. And some nights we reminisce about troops and dream of international camps we hope to attend, or have a Ranger visitor. Quiet, stars, sometimes a drizzle—but in or out of pup tents we are snuggled in sleeping bags for morning, and Pearl's tap comes early.

The two camps in 1950 were focused along the central route as in 1948. In addition to the established Santa Fe venues, they made several stops as far west as Flagstaff, Arizona. During both sessions participants were able to visit Acoma, Laguna, and Zuni pueblos, as well as El Morro National Monument. They saw ongoing excavations near Flagstaff, exhibits at the Museum of Northern Arizona, heard presentations there, and visited sites in Walnut Canyon.

Walnut Canyon, like Wupatki, today is considered to be part of the Sinagua (Spanish "without water") archaeological tradition in affiliation. It includes some 80 rock-walled houses built under limestone ledges (which form the ceilings) that were occupied primarily between AD 1225 and 1250. Other Sinagua sites in the area date roughly between AD 1100 and 1250. In this biologically diverse location, the people depended on the waters in the canyon to grow their crops, but also were able to gather a wide variety of local plants and hunt animals for their food. The area has been a National Monument since 1915, and today, as well as in the early 1950s, many of the dwellings can be seen from a loop trail that descends into the canyon.

Girls in both camps also witnessed Hopi *katsina* dances (either at Old Oraibi or Shungopavi)—a special privilege. And they spent two days in Canyon de Chelly viewing White House, Mummy Cave, and several smaller archaeological sites. They then spent another two days at Chaco Canyon, before they headed back to Santa Fe via Coronado State Monument and Kuaua. Bert noted that Camp I that year "was a particularly important camp by reason of having two Negro girls, an Indian girl, and a set of identical twins," none of whom caused heads to turn during their journeys

(Dutton 1950a:370). Again, Bert and others had worked to make sure that all girls had a chance to have this experience, with monetary support if necessary. Bert specifically wanted local Indigenous girls to have the opportunity to attend, both for their benefit and for that of the other campers from all over the USA. Over the years, most of these girls came from the Girl Scout troop centered at the Santa Fe Indian School and led by Bertha Talahytewa, a teacher at the school. Rosita Sandoval from San Felipe Pueblo attended two Mobile Camps (1952, 1953) and the Pueblo Largo Dig Camp (1954).

Camper Marty Harlan wrote a glowing review of Camp II that year concluding as follows (Harlan 89LA5.063 [1950]):

> It came as a distinct shock to me when I realized that during 14 days of vacation, I learned so much...Before we were through we were thumping pottery with an expert's finger, recognizing grass covered rubble as an ex-Pueblo, and understanding the scientific jargon that labels stuff in museums. No small items were our shaping into excellent physical trim, and gaining 20 of the best friends we ever had. If all knowledge could be administered as painlessly as that which I soaked up, we would be a race of sages. Besides having an invaluable acquaintance with peoples who originally settled this continent, I find I have the wildly beautiful New Mexico landscape under my skin.... It doesn't matter to me where they go [in 1951], I intend to be there ready, with wanderlust and duffle.

In fact by 1950, as Bert added in her 1950 summary, the camps had become so popular with all Scouts and the number of girls not accepted so large "as to make it apparent that three expeditions might be in order for 1951" (Dutton 1950a:366). That did not materialize for Mobile Camps until 1955, although in 1951, the first excavation camp was added (Chapter 5).

The itineraries for the two Mobile Camps in 1951 followed another route, ultimately referred to as the southern route, and for that year we have Bert's reconnaissance report filed with the Director of the MNM, Boas Long (89LA5.063). In it Bert details all of her stops, conversations with potential hosts, vehicle mileage, her check on road conditions, and much more. Of particular note that year would be overnight

Figure 3.11. Agnes
Morley Cleaveland
speaking to a
mobile camp
group, at her ranch
near Datil, NM,
1954. 95PLE033.
Courtesy of MIAC/
LAA.

stops at the ranch of Agnes Morley Cleaveland, writer of the famous book *No Life for a Lady*[24] and an old friend of Bert's, who hosted the girls and spoke with them about ranch history and her personal experiences (Figure 3.11). Bert arranged for camping and lectures at Harvard University's field camp at Quemado and Chicago's Field Museum of Natural History's camp at Reserve (Appendix D). In addition to camping stops, the girls took site tours and heard about Mogollon culture history from the well-known excavators (Appendix E). The caravan ultimately crossed the Mogollon Rim and the Sitgreaves National Forest, as did the 1948 group—but in reverse. They stayed in the cool forest for three days, visiting additional archaeological and historic sites. Then they went on to Walnut Canyon and Flagstaff, and headed back to New Mexico with various stops along the way, including Fort Wingate where they stayed in the Bureau of Indian Affairs (BIA) vocational school, a welcomed spot with real beds and showers! They hiked in Canyon de Chelly to its famous sites and saw yet more excavations in process. On the return they visited Laguna Pueblo (Camp I) and attended a Green Corn Dance at Santo Domingo (Camp II) before finishing in Santa Fe.

The year 1951 also saw the first of what became Camp III, the excavation camp, or "the Dig." Several of the returning girls had been asking Bert if they could really "get their hands dirty" now that they had seen so many sites, including several under excavation. Could they please have a "dig of their own"? So in early 1951, Bert began looking for a place where this might be possible. She and the Museum were able to make arrangements with a private landowner to begin excavating an Ancestral Pueblo in the Galisteo Basin southeast of Santa Fe. She planned to offer this opportunity to girls who had been on at least one Mobile trip (though preferably more), were mature, and showed the best promise of working hard and getting the most out of an actual excavation experience. This extra opportunity would be offered after the two Mobile Camps for 1951 (Chapter 5).

4

Archaeological Mobile Camps Continue

1952–1957

A Leader

Five-foot-two, hair steel gray,
Navajo boots, eyes searching far away.
Searching for a ruin on a mesa top,
she doesn't have to search for a cool place to stop.
Adopted by Laguna, tops with us she's rated.
She tells us of the calendar by which the Pueblo's dated.
About the Pueblo people, she's a walking book of knowledge.
Six weeks with her is like a year of college.
"It should only take you '30' what you do in '45.'"
Down an arroyo full speed—a breathtaking dive.
She'll go off without you, like she says she will.
And I can't imagine her in anything with a frill.
I'd know her in the winter, washed of all the dirt;
for even on Fifth Avenue, she'd still be our BERT!

–"Jeff" [Judith Franklin], 1954

By 1952, almost all of the issues involving on-the-trail camps had been resolved so that they were running smoothly. Bert had settled on a schedule that included her preseason reconnaissance plus two Mobiles per summer (and the newly-added excavation camp)—quite enough given her curatorial duties and research schedule. She was now devoting a full eight weeks each summer to the field program, plus more time during the rest of the year to promotional tasks, correspondence, budgets, lining up speakers, visits, and more. She continued to build relationships with the campers, and they remained eager to stay in touch with several planning to return. They were fascinated by the Southwest landscape and the region's deep history, pleased by the positive learning atmosphere that Bert had created, and very happy to have her as their leader and mentor. As camper Martha "Marty" Harlan (89LA5.063) wrote, "despite PhDs and scientific eminence, Bert could out-hike, out-drive, and out-joke the whole bunch of us. She tipped us valuable tricks of the trade, that even long hours in scouting had not taught us—drinking hot tea at night, for instance, which makes water no more necessary the next day than it is to a Sahara camel, and how to sling up a pup tent single handed." The girls were her devoted fans and continued to say so, not only to her directly but also to others at regional and national Girl Scout venues. Bert's policy of varying the routes showed returnees that there was always more to see, do, and learn in the Southwest, and always more fun and adventures to be had with each new season.

The Digger Family

From the beginning of the program, Bert received letters and postcards from the girls who had been on Mobile Camps. She started keeping track of many of the girls—especially those who returned—and their lives. By the end of the 1951 season (including the first excavation camp), one girl had been on five camps, two girls on four, three on three, and four more on two. These figures rose steadily, with some accepting volunteer staff positions, so that through the last camp in 1957, Evelyn "Les" Stobie had returned for 10 sessions as either a camper or staff member; Gwenyth "Que" Morris for seven; Vorsila "Rambler" Bohrer and Carolyn "Casey" Kline for six; Sue "Skip" Martin, Eloise "Patches" Moore, Sandra "Sandy" Reimers, and Gillian "Gill" Wethey for five; Jeanne Ellis, Martha Ann "Marti" "Bubbles" Emery, Elizabeth

"Bets" Galligan, and Claire "Squeaky" Yeagley for four. Twenty-two returned for three camps, and 47 for two. Several staff members who had not been Scout participants also returned for more than one season and session (see Appendix A).

The most frequent returnees stayed particularly close to Bert, but many who participated in only one Mobile Camp also wrote thanking her for the experience and letting her know how things were going for them—such things as school plans and/or progress, engagements, weddings, and later, births of children, moves, and new jobs. By the end of 1951, Bert knew of campers and ex-campers then attending 26 different colleges and universities (Dutton 1951a:368). By 1957, these figures were even higher, with some of the earliest campers now college graduates and seeking postgraduate degrees. Some were also married. The idea of keeping them involved beyond age 18 had worked as they were still Girl Scout Associates (Chapter 10).

Some girls (and staff members) who lived in Santa Fe, Albuquerque, and adjoining areas and states visited Bert often, either at the museum or at her home. Others who were scattered across the country visited whenever they were in the neighborhood. Some moved from distant places to Santa Fe or other nearby spots permanently, as they had fallen in love with the country, its multicultural and art traditions, and its general ambiance. Others established second homes in the area and visited periodically. In later years, Bert kept a guest book for visitors to sign. All soon became part of what Bert called her "Digger family," and she looked upon ex-Diggers as her "daughters," telling people in later years that although she had never married, she had over 200 daughters.

Although she did not have time to write to everyone who sent her letters and cards—especially as the years went by and the numbers increased—she did correspond with several campers on a regular basis.[1] And whether she wrote or not, she kept track of everyone's accomplishments, often spreading the word to girls she did write or see as to how the others were doing, where they were, and what was going on in their lives. Unfortunately, the Dutton Collection does not contain very many of the letters Bert received, although there are references in some of her reports and other sources that indicate who among the girls she had heard from recently.

In 1953, when several campers started a newsletter,[2] sanctioned and christened by Bert as *The Sipapu*, she contributed a column titled "Dutton to Diggers" that summarized the news for everyone. In 1954, she also began sending a Christmas letter with news of her year plus recent word of the Digger alumna. Both of these efforts show her devotion to those who continued to stay in touch with her, as well as their desire to keep her in their lives. Many continued writing and visiting her long after the program ended in 1957, and their friendships with her and each other were deep and rewarding. Many wrote to each other as well, several continuously for years thereafter. Sixty plus gathered in Santa Fe for her eightieth birthday, and some remained close to her until her death in 1994. Several gathered again to pay tribute to her at her memorial service (Chapter 9).

Once it became clear that the Southwest Senior Girl Scout undertaking would continue and grow, Bert started keeping better track of the numbers of campers and their states of origin. She often recorded these figures (along with other information) in her yearly summaries of Girl Scout activities in *El Palacio* and *Teocentli*. By the end of 1951, she reported that 89 girls had gone through the program representing 14 states—from New York to California (Dutton 1951a:354). By 1957, the count was roughly 292 girls from 41 states plus England.[3] Her goal of representative campers from all 48 states was not quite reached, but she came close! And as noted earlier, she tried to have at least one Pueblo, Navajo, or Hispanic girl on each Mobile, and this goal was met, except in the beginning. At least one Native girl also participated in an excavation camp (Appendix A; Chapters 3, 5).

Mobiles from 1952 to 1957

Given the previous five years of experience with the Mobiles, Bert was able to say in her summary for 1952 that "the superstructure [for the year] went up rapidly, and its outlines were most pleasing" (Dutton 1952a:342). Of course, flexibility for the routes and itineraries for any given year was still the byword, as these depended on Bert's yearly reconnaissance of road and campground conditions, as well as her knowledge of who would be doing what and where that season—especially excavating. Since she was well "plugged in" to the broadly based archaeological community working in the Southwest (several of whom were from Eastern universities and museums as well as local institutions), she had a good idea about who would have open excavations early on in any given year. And given her position as Curator of Ethnology at the MNM, she was well positioned to track the dates of other events of interest that would be occurring, such as the Inter-Tribal Ceremonials in Gallup, the Santa Fe Fiesta, Indian Market, and various craft fairs. She likewise knew the general outlines and timing of open ceremonies and other activities for the Pueblos—such as their Saint's days or other feast day celebrations—and rodeos, fairs, or additional planned events in both Native and Hispanic communities. Her annual reconnaissance would then fix the tentative schedule for a given year to provide the best and most varied experiences for the campers.

By the end of 1951, the travel routes for the Mobiles (now dubbed "northern," "central," and "southern") were generally established—although the exact routes, especially to campgrounds and excavations, were changeable. In any given year multiple camps followed the same chosen route, although not always visiting the same stops or in the same order. The northern route typically covered New Mexico north of Santa Fe as well as southern Colorado and always included two to three nights and days at Mesa Verde. It featured stops at Aztec, Bandelier, usually Chimney Rock, one or more of the northern Rio Grande Pueblos, and parts of the Navajo, Ute, and occasionally the Jicarilla Apache reservations. Hispanic villages near Chimayo and their resident weavers and carvers were often visited either when leaving Santa Fe or on the return trip. This route plus alternatives was taken by Mobiles in 1952 and 1955 (three that year;[4] see Appendix D).

The central route basically paralleled US Hwy 40, zig-zagging to include visits to one or more of the central Rio Grande Pueblos, Coronado State Monument (Kuaua), three nights and two or three days in Chaco Canyon, sometimes stops or overnights in Canyon de Chelly, El Morro, and Zuni Pueblo, and continuing as far west as Flagstaff. There were stops at Meteor Crater, Petrified Forest, and the Painted Desert, either while travelling west or returning east. That route, which formed the basis of the Mobile Camps for 1953 and 1956, normally included time at the Museum of Northern Arizona while in Flagstaff (often for one of the fairs focusing on Hopi or Navajo artists), and at Wupatki National Monument and Sunset Crater immediately to the north. It usually included Walnut Canyon National Monument south of Flagstaff. The campers then returned via the Hopi Mesas, often witnessing a *katsina* dance, and finally visiting either Acoma or Laguna Pueblos (see Appendix D).

The southern route usually veered to the southeast from Santa Fe to include the Spanish mission churches of Abó, Quarai, and/or Grand Quivira, and then the group traversed central New Mexico by way of Socorro and Datil, with an overnight stop at the Agnes Morley Cleaveland's ranch. It then continued across the Mogollon Rim with various stops to see excavations in east-central Arizona and spend some time in Oak Creek Canyon. Depending on the number of stops, the caravan might loop back through Walnut Canyon National Monument, the Painted Desert, Petrified Forest, and/or Canyon de Chelly, and then go on to Zuni Pueblo and El Morro National Monument. The Mobiles in 1954 followed this route (see Appendix D).

The Mobile Camps of 1957, the last year, followed parts of the northern route combined with the southern for the last round, likely because of several factors (Chapter 7). Bert led only Camp I that year, with Jan Fleming, who had been on three previous camps as a GS Rep, leading Camp II. But as usual, by mixing the itinerary, there was no lack of alternative places and people to visit and events to witness.

Bert made sure that all Mobile Campers spent quality time in at least one of the large and spectacular Ancestral Pueblo archaeological site areas—most by then either National Monuments or Parks: Chaco Canyon, Mesa Verde, Wupatki, Aztec, and Bandelier. Also high on the list were Chimney Rock, Canyon de Chelly, and Walnut Canyon. The sixteenth-to-seventeenth-century mission sites of Abó, Quarai, and Grand Quivira, and Pecos[5] helped to illustrate the Spanish period, as did visits to the Hispanic arts and crafts villages north of Santa Fe. The Museum of Northern Arizona was a featured stop for the central route, as was El Morro National Monument for the central and southern. In 1952 and 1955, on the northern route, the camps went into Utah as far as Arches National Monument and Dead Horse Point (1952), and Durango, Ouray, and Silverton, Colorado (1955). These were the only two years that the Mobiles ventured that far north. The Colorado cities helped to illustrate the regional geology and extensive mining history. The southern route always stayed north of the low desert country of southern New Mexico and Arizona, thus avoiding high summer temperatures that would have made camping—and campers—miserable. Whenever possible, rest stops for lunch included some "down time," something all appreciated.

The list of archaeologists who hosted and spoke to Bert's camps in orientation sessions or at their own digs from 1952 through 1957 continued to read like a "who's who" of well-known Southwestern specialists, and the sites visited like a textbook list of significant places. But archaeologists were not Bert's only targets for tour guides and speakers. Well-known National and State Park personnel, museum people, biologists, ethnologists, historians, and others were scheduled each year, sometimes speaking or guiding her campers two or three times each summer. Bert did not hesitate to ask anyone and everyone to speak to her girls (Appendix E). (As far as we know, no one ever refused.) Given that she was respected in Indigenous communities in the region, and especially among members of the Rio Grande Pueblos, Hopi, Zuni, Laguna, Acoma, and other people with whom she had frequent contact, she could arrange with their officials for her girls to visit and meet people on appropriate occasions. She carefully schooled the campers on protocols and ways of showing proper respect in dress and behavior for these occasions, including any dances that they were privileged to attend. Several Native authorities gave Bert's girls permission to take photographs in their communities when appropriate, at a time when photography on any occasion was rarely allowed.

From 1952 through 1957, Bert continued to start and end all trips at Rancho del Cielo. Each Mobile started with the orientation routines begun in the earlier years: the gathering of the campers on Saturday; an additional day for getting acquainted, reviewing skills, getting organized (*kapers*), and if desired, attending a worship service of their choice and/or *Scouts' Own*. Monday included stops and lectures at local museums (MNM, Lab, and, after it opened in 1954, the Museum of International Folk Art [hereafter MoIFA]), National Park Service headquarters, and Museum of Navajo Ceremonial Art). This orientation and its accompanying lectures set the stage for the new campers and refreshed the memories of the veterans. Tuesday was then the first day of on-the-trail travel, and 10 days later (usually Friday), campers were back at Rancho del Cielo for one last night and the official close for the session—with cleanup, gear repair, storage, and personal packing—completed by Saturday noon. Excavation camps, given that all attendees were veterans of Mobile Camps, required less orientation time, as getting to work quickly was the priority (Chapter 5).

Selected Camp Memories, 1953 to 1957

Unlike the years 1947 through 1951 (and 1952) when personal accounts by campers of their experiences are few, there are several memories available for 1953 to 1957, and more photographs (none for 1952). Some accounts were published in *The Sipapu* (1953–1955); others are contained in diaries or letters written home.[6] The following are selected examples—some longer, some shorter to avoid too much redundancy. Again, the impacts of the camps on the young participants are varied but striking. Some focus on what they were learning about the deep history of the region; others marvel at the scenery; some remark as to cultural experiences with Native peoples; and some relate activities with staff and fellow campers (after all, they are teenagers!). But each girl carried home some unique memories, many lasting a lifetime.

1953: Camp I, Gillian Wethey (The Sipapu I:1:3–5, MIAC/LAA)

[July 3]…first to the Museum of Northern Arizona [patio, Flagstaff] for the Hopi Arts and Crafts Show, where we stand spellbound before the silversmith, who meticulously handles tiny fragments of silver. Each of these is welded to its background, which is cut with perfect symmetry, and shaped by very simple tools with the utmost precision of hand and eye to the required use of earring or pin, belt buckle, or *concho*.

The weaver sits beyond, cross-legged before his tall, upright loom, his hands so dexterous that the shuttle and batten, warp and weft, seem to be one continuous movement of color and glowing design. The basket maker appears almost unconscious of the work of her hands, which move rhythmically from the choice of a willow strand to the cunning inclusion of it into the pattern of the framework which she weaves. Occasionally, she pauses to sell the delicate sweet rolls of *piki* [wafer bread] to the many who enjoy its original texture and flavor.

Last of all the potter sits enigmatically looking before her, her wise lined face with its dark frame of hair unexpectedly lighting up at times in answer to a friendly smile. Her fingers shape and mold the vessel in their care to a complete roundness, and only cease when their owner is startled to sudden movement by the intrusion of a lizard, who seems as intrigued by her work as the spectators! [After Flagstaff] we travel by way of Sunset Crater (which we climb energetically) and Wupatki [Figure 4.1], our program brings us on the afternoon of Sunday July 5, to Moencopi School. Here an unexpected experience awaits us—a visit to one

of the *kivas* of this Hopi village.[7] We walk silently on our way, past fertile, waffle-like fields, and beneath tall green trees, and then through the utterly quiet and seemingly deserted village, to the semi-subterranean *kiva*. Descending by means of a wooden ladder, we find the rectangular ceremonial chamber cool and dim, lit only by the hatchway through which we climbed. Almost in the center of the chamber stands a great iron stove. At one end there is a slightly raised platform, and from hugely rounded *vigas* hang clusters of prayer feathers. On all four sides are benches built against the walls, and beneath them are compartments where ceremonial materials are placed for safekeeping. All of us are aware, I think, that the *kiva* has much atmosphere. With Mr. Dickerson, principal of the school, who has so kindly arranged this visit for us, we sit quietly looking, discussing with him the objects around us, and sensing all the while, the hidden reality of the occasions when these symbols can come into their own…

We reluctantly leave Moenkopi, and head for Canyon de Chelly…. The cottonwoods of Chinle where we camp are restful and cool, and here unexpected

Figure 4.2. White House Ruin from below, Canyon de Chelly National Monument, Camp II, 1953. Photograph by Kate Smith. 99BPD.xx, K. Swift Collection. Courtesy of MIAC/ LAA.

flashes of purple and red through the trees show us Navajo travelers, either riding easily on nodding ponies or walking with long graceful strides, the women's flowing skirts which brush the grass accentuating the sinuous rhythm of their movements. [In Canyon de Chelly] we spend a day we will not soon forget. Here gigantic walls tower above the canyon floor, offering treasures to the seeker. History is in the dwellings of the cliffs; fascination in startling brightness of White House [Figure 4.2] and in the swirling lines of age-old rock formations; the beauty, and infinite spaciousness, in vistas from Antelope House and Mummy Cave to which we climb. There is living culture too, where Navajo people build their *hogans* and graze their flocks on the fertile islands of green at the base of precipitous walls.... climbing at the day's end, up the steep trail which will lead us out of the canyon we turn for many a last look back, to where gigantic sentinels of rock stand monumental to the littleness of man (Figure 4.3). Centuries, it seems, have molded them from the eternal winds; and flooded by the clear light of day, they rise in glory, the great cliffs illumined to a fiery sunburned gold.

Figure 4.3. Girl Scouts hiking out of Canyon de Chelly, Camp II, 1953. Photograph by Kate Swift. 99BPD.xx, K. Swift Collection. Courtesy of MIAC/ LAA.

Yet before us lies the charm of Window Rock [Figure 4.4], where rain reaches us and leaves trailing smoky clouds behind it, which seem to be almost a continuation of our campfire, until they part to reveal a glorious sky of stars...Chaco Canyon where more history awaits us in the great ruins of Pueblo Bonito and further afield along the canyon floor—all of which give us pictures we will remember for many a long day to come [Figure 4.5]. Surely Chaco is a fitting finale to such a journey, which now draws to a close as we reach El Rancho del Cielo once more.

1953: Memories of Camp II (Anonymous The Sipapu I:1:1, 6)

Although the summer's second crop of Diggers slept on the same rocks and ant-hills as the girls on the first expedition, Camp II was hardly repetitious. Some unique experiences and memories....

The mixed *katsina* dance that we just happened to see at Zuni...Sitting on a kiva roof entranced in the magnificent array of masked dancers in the plaza below. Windblown sand smarting in our eyes and gritting between our teeth passing almost unnoticed as we lost ourselves in the kaleidoscope of brilliant rhythmic patterns of waving feathers and pinon sprigs, swaying masks, tossing, knotted buckskin; silver and turquoise flashing against brown skin—all timed to the emotionally overpowering beat blended from the thud of the drum, the chanting of many voices, the shuffle of moccasined feet, and the rattle of the gourds.... The *Koyemsi* [ceremonial clowns] with their clever beanbag game, their horseplay, and their jokes—which were only pantomime to us.... The sun, dropping below the horizon, slanting its red rays in under the cloud whose sprinkles spotted our shirts and patted down the dust....

The evening at Canyon de Chelly that 14 of us sardined into the Cadillac, and set off, with four more girls bouncing along in the caboose, to find the [Navajo] Squaw Dance we had heard about.... In the dis-

Figure 4.4. Kate Swift, Girl Scout Representative, in front of Window Rock, Navajo Nation, Camp II, 1953. 99BPD.xx, K. Swift Collection. Courtesy of MIAC/ LAA.

tance, the dark silhouettes of the assembled revelers and their transportations—horses, wagons, trucks—against the glow of the fire. The thrill of being made welcome and following the example of the Navajo girls—that is, pulling and coaxing the boys into the fire-lit circle which constituted the dance floor to join the line of couples doing a modified walk to the rhythm of the chant.... The shock we received when the singers broke from Navajo into the intelligible phrase, "Along the Navajo Trail." The friendliness of the star-silvered world as we drove away....

Figure 4.5. NPS Ranger talking to Girl Scouts, Pueblo Bonito, Chaco Canyon, Camp II, 1953. Photograph by Kate Swift. 99BPD.xx, K. Swift Collection. Courtesy of MIAC/LAA.

These memories and many others—the black on orange pattern of firelight and shadow on the walls of the cave we slept in at Window Rock, the dignity of the Navajo Tribal Council meeting, the rain-wet rocks of Canyon de Chelly glowing and polished red in the light of the reappearing sun—have been filed, in an easily accessible cranial corner, in the hope that we may add to our already rich store next summer.

1953: Camp II, Cyndy Tice (letters home)

Dear Folks,[8]
The girls are real nice and swell campers, of course. The weather is very hot and dry as expected, but I wasn't cold or even cool during the night.... We also have an English counselor, Jill [Gillian "Gill" Wethey].[9] She's the nurse. Dr. Dutton is a real person [!].

We're staying in Santa Fe until Tues. morning. Today we're getting used to the weather (I'm doing fine). Pardon the absence but the photographer came

[Figure 4.6] and tonight we have U of C Southwest Indian specialists here to talk and Scouts Own.

Today (Monday) was briefing day. First stop was the Lab of the Museum where the world's authority on pottery talked to us on the same and then took us down to the files (3,000 pots) and showed us examples. One of the most interesting things he told us was how to identify the pots as to Pueblos and period. Of course, we're real experts!

The next stop was the Park Service where we were told such things as how to estimate alt. by vegetation, and what to do in case of rattler bites, black widow bites, flash floods, or being lost. We also got a lecture on Southwest Indian history there too. The great drought that made the Indians leave today's ruins in 1300 and the Great Indian Revolt (against the Spanish) in 1680 were some of its highlights. After lunch we took a tour of the Arch[aeology] Museum and learned Santa Fe history, for instance, it has the oldest public building and the oldest church in the USA there. We leave tomorrow and have learned how to roll the tents the way Jack likes them, to drink tea every night and as little as possible water the next day to keep from being thirsty and drinking too much water. Bert was whooping [characteristic call] for dinner. . . .

[Tuesday] Well, we're really seeing Indian country now. Our first stop was an old Indian mission church established in 1699 [San Jose, Laguna Pueblo]. It was pretty, and typical. After driving through mesas all morning we stopped at Enchanted Mesa for lunch, and hear[d] the interesting story of the destruction of the one way up and how the people [Acoma] starved to death on top. A little way from there we stopped at Acoma Pueblo, the sky city. It was built on top of a 300-feet [tall] mesa with one rock path, and toe and holds, and one steep sand road. The Indians carry everything, including graveyard dirt and rafter logs, up one of the paths. . . . Tonight (Wed) we are in the Zuni (modern) Pueblo. We are really seeing Indian life here. We visited a jewelry craftswoman and saw some women baking bread in outdoor ovens. The main thing there is hot showers and water for clothes washings, and mattresses to sleep on in the school gym, where

Figure 4.6. Cooking
in Dutch oven,
fireplace, Rancho
del Cielo, Camp I,
1953. Left to right:
unknown, Rosita
Sandoval, Mrs. M.W.
Woodward, cook.
Photograph by
Betty Theil. 99BPD.
xx, Scrapbook,
1953. Courtesy of
MIAC/LAA.

we are staying. All the girls and staff are swell, in fact I can't decide who I like better than anyone else. There are all swell campers and Scout laws to the fullest. It is still early but I'll fall asleep if I write any longer!

I'm in Flagstaff now seeing the Indian Ceremonial Dances. They should be good and our seats are swell. Since we were Dutton's Dirty Diggers from all over the country we got in early and for half price.... The slowness and monotony of the work was very surprising. After the museum visit we saw the opening parade for the Pow-Wow in which all the dancers marched in full dress. The band (Indians) just started, so excuse me. The band just stopped and applauded itself so I'll tell you about the atmosphere around here. The Indians who have been making things to sell for months are camped in teepees, lean-tos, and wall tents all over the fields around the Rodeo Stadium, and their horses are corralled in the part of the arena that isn't being used by the dancers, and Indians surround four huge council fires which will be used by the dancers. Real cowboys, some still with this afternoon's rodeo numbers pinned to their shirts, are sauntering or riding around about. Except for the dudes programs, the grand states, it's as real as ever. Buying a cowboy hat which I found quite a convenience. The weather here continues hot and with occasions sprinkles of rain.

1954: Camp I, Casey [Caroline] Kline (The Sipapu II:1:5–6, MIAC/LAA)

Dear Mert,

Hi! Boy have I had fun! I've been following Bert! Just having a grand ol' time being a Dirty Digger—and I mean dirty!

Our camp started on the nineteenth of June [Saturday], at El Rancho del Cielo. Kids were there from all sections of the U.S.—East, North, South, and West. Tuesday came like a whiz, and with excitement settling down to a dull roar, we all jumped in the cars ready to follow Bert. Our first stop was at Paa-Ko [ruins] where Bert told us to find potsherds. All of us looked a little dumbfounded, so she explained then what they were.

That night at Abó, while jumping into our bedrolls, some headlights put us in the spotlight. Jack with his 22 (I didn't think he had one) went out and shot (he didn't really, but it makes a good story) the varmints down. Anyway, they left, and our first night out [we] slept peacefully in knee-deep sand [Figure 4.7].

The Salinas Pueblos and associated Spanish Missions (Abó, Quarai, and Gran Quivira) are today protected as Salinas Pueblo Missions National Monument in east-central New Mexico near Mountainair. Pueblos here before the Spanish arrived served as major trading centers with Indigenous people from the Plains as well as others. A major item of trade was local salt—hence the name. The Spanish constructed mission churches beginning in early 1600s, the remains of which still stand. The area was abandoned by Pueblo peoples and the Spanish by the mid to late 1600s due to a severe drought and raids from Apaches and Comanches.

We spent our second night under nice tall, cool pine trees on Mrs. Agnes Cleaveland's ranch in Datil. She told us tales of the old West and how she came to write No Life for a Lady [Figure 3.11].

Almost to the Mogollon Rim, Bert spied a parked truck filled with melons. She stopped, and Gill (dignified Englishwoman) went into the bar to find the melon-man. She found him—I don't know how—and we bought about a dozen melons which came to a happy ending like all our food.

On the Mogollon we met the Rain and the Mud. "Never say die" was our cry as the Caddie and trailer got stuck for four hours in the Mud. We slipped and slid all the way on the Mogollon, but it was fun and we saw some beautiful country. At high altitudes we soon were riding in the clouds. The Texas girls had never been in a cloud before, so they had to get out and touch one. I guess the great state of Texas doesn't have low clouds—or maybe no high mountains.

Boy, did that first week go fast! But the second week went faster—We went to Flagstaff, Walnut Canyon, and then came upon the Petrified Forest. This Forest is quite different from any usual one being that all the trees are lying down and are stone. We also stopped and looked at the Painted Desert under our legs which supposedly made it look more colorful. I guess it made it look redder because of all the blood running through our eyeballs.

We went on a highway, for a change, until Bert got an Indian named Joe to take us out to the Manuelito Area. We had some crazy time going through those gullies singing "Tennashay" to the car so it would be sure to make every hill. At Fort Wingate a lady showed us beds (strange desert animal) and then some showers. When we saw those we went completely wild! So we cooked dinner,

Figure 4.7. Viewing ruins of the mission church at Abó, Salinas Pueblos, 1954. Photograph by Laura Gilpin. 99BPD.xx. Courtesy of MIAC/LAA.

washed up, and went to a square dance down at the main hall of the Indian School [vocational school]. That was really rip-roaring!

At El Morro National Monument we saw the [Richard and Nathalie] Woodburys' diggings on top of Inscription Rock, and then it was Friday, our last traveling day. We stopped at Laguna Pueblo, and then non-stopped to the ranch. On the way we met a sandstorm—quite exciting especially for the Easterners. That night we had our last campfire which was nice even without the fire. After the program and after saying goodbye to all our early-bird leavers, we went to bed thinking about the wonderful times we had on Mobile I. Well, I gotta' go now *Au Revoir* or *Auf Wiederseh'n* (since I don't speak Spanish)

1954: Camp II, Carla Fritsche (The Sipapu II:1:7-8)

On July 13, a unique group of campers—each of the 16 girls was from a different state—started on their never-to-be-forgotten Mobile Camp. Because four of the campers were from the South, some very "lively" discussions were inevitable.

Several times these discussions nearly got out of hand, threatening to become a second Civil War.

Through observation and participation we learned the value of cultures. Our New Mexico camper [Emily Garcia] taught us the traditional Corn Dance and Chant which is a necessary part of each year's harvest festivities at her Pueblo [Santo Domingo]. At a Squaw Dance[10] near Thoreau, we saw the Navajos as they stood in front of the sick man's house, trying earnestly to cure him by chanting.... As the fire's light flickered on their intent faces, we began to understand other peoples and their way of life.

At our farewell campfire the night before our departure, we were reluctant to say goodbye; for during those two weeks our group had become very closely knit; we had made lasting friendships. But sad as we were to go, we were eager to tell others of our wonderful experiences so that they might share in our opportunity of a lifetime.

1955: Camp II, Mary Anne Stein (Stein 1955–56; 2008b)

July 16: [After a plane flight from Amarillo, TX, lunch and shopping] we finally got out to the ranch (Bert's home) in a rain and changed clothes. We were divided into four groups (*patrols*): A, B, C, and D, and are that way for *kapers*. After everyone came—some real crazy kids—we ate supper, HAMBURGERS, and then met to hear "Bert" tell us about it (the Mobile Camp). We like her lots. She is short, gray haired and dresses like a man. We have a very nice set-up, not too primitive and just right...the "Ranch" is very pretty...

July 17: I woke up at 5:00 a.m. and pretty soon all of us were up. We had EGGS, BACON, and TOAST, and I was on cleanup and all (fun). We have a Hopi girl on the trip [Bertha Mae Talahytewa]. She is more fun! Everyone went to church (a few), and the rest of us wrote letters. After lunch which was FRIED CHICKEN, RICE, GRAVY, and SALAD, we played "lemmy sticks" [a game learned at GS "All States" in 1954] and then came "Court of Honor" and then *Patrol* meetings. We planned the *Scouts' Own* and have planned a lot. *Kapers* aren't too good as of yet, but should improve.... After dinner (CREAMED CHICKEN on TOAST), we laughed a lot and then had *Scouts' Own* (fair), and a talk by Mr. Wendorf, an archaeologist who told us oodles![11] It was very helpful and taught us a lot about their work. We all took lots of notes and are frantically working on hometown newspaper reports.

July 19: We got up at 5:00 a.m. and really ginned!! We left Santa Fe and had our first "digging" [excavation] near Tesuque at a place where a highway is going to be built and we saw the men at work.[12] The room outlines were evident. After the excavation came Tesuque Pueblo, and Bert talked to us about the Pueblo life and all. We met the Governor (of the Pueblo) and saw an 1863 cane given to them by Abraham Lincoln.[13] We ate lunch (SANDWICHES AND MILK) at "Te'ewi" and then came the digging place (site, to surface collect—no shovels ever involved) on a mesa top. Pottery was everywhere and we picked up all we could till our sacks were huge. We sorted it and had some of all kinds.

Pottery types in the Southwest can be keyed by several methods that involve identifying paste, temper, surface paint or slip, decoration (pattern, color, glaze), and more. Through the years most of these features and their combinations have led to naming many wares. They have been correlated to time periods using other dating techniques (such as tree-ring dates from site excavations) to give regional chronologies. Most Southwest archaeologists have a good working knowledge of at least 50-100 known types and their approximate periods of manufacture (see also sidebar Chapter 3).

July 20: I'm in the "country wagon" and I'm next to Bert. A very high position and so I may not have it again (desirable to sit next to Bert so are able to learn more)...We are about to make a Digger song to "Desert Silvery Blue." We then entered the Jicarilla Apache country and after, the Navajo checkerboard area.[14]

We stopped at several trading posts and saw "Huerfano Peak." and "Three Sisters Buttes." Paula bought a rug and we got pictures of a *hogan* and Bert riding a little bicycle. She said it helped to have short legs!

July 21: We woke up without Cricket's (GS Rep) help, and soon ate breakfast of HAM OMLET and COCOA and TOAST. We packed and laughed and we heard a lecture and then walked through the Aztec Ruins and museum [Figure 4.8].

At Farmington we stopped at a trading post and I got a saddle blanket for $6.00. Others bought things also. We go on to Mesa Verde.... Stopped at a Methodist Indian school to buy oranges and had sandwiches. Also a stop for "milk nickels" (Bert's term for chocolate covered ice cream bars on a stick). We had a low tire and became lost once and that was this morning's adventure. Bert is disappearing in a cloud of dust ahead. She really goes in her Suburban. We laughed a lot over her. Paula and I have been discussing our troops now and she has been copying songs from me. At Mancos we stopped to fix a flat so were late to Mesa Verde. The drive up the canyon was super, like an aerial view, and you could see mountains, valleys, plains, deserts, mesas, and ridges. Simply Super!! We sang lots along the way and copied oodles of songs [Appendix C].

July 22 [Mesa Verde]: We got up at around 6 am and at 6:45. We slept very well but it was hard to get up. We had BACON, TOAST, CEREAL, and EGGS. At 8 we left for the Mesa Verde Museum. It was very good and I bought a book there on Mesa Verde Indians. Then we loaded in and went on the Mesa Top Caravan. We saw the development of the *Kiva* and homes and all. It was very good and we drove some and walked some. The views of the cross canyons are very good and we went to the Sun Temple and saw the symbol, walked around on top. It was good and we learned about it.... We set out at 1 pm for the walk and climb to Balcony House. The ladders made me dizzy and I almost fainted. We took pictures, got in the cars, and went to see the Palace [Cliff Palace]. We had an excellent Ranger, took pictures, and laughed a lot. We're gonna start washing our hair. Cheryl used all the hot water up so Gwennie and I really had a time and

Figure 4.8. Girl Scouts of Camp II at West Ruin, Aztec National Monument, 1955. Photograph by Mary Anne Stein. 99BPD.xx, M.A. Stein Collection. Courtesy of MIAC/ LAA.

laughed till we nearly died. We rolled up our hair and walked back talking and laughing all the way. We ate STEAK, SALAD, RICE, TEA, and all.

July 23...After lunch we went to visit more ruins, the Far View to be exact. We got in a horrible rain and it was a long time before I dried out. We were soaked. After thoroughly getting all three cars stuck, we had a "question and answer" period and some did not do too well. We all decided we better stay on the ball!! We returned to camp and had time to mess around before supper and we washed clothes and all. Then we worked on the party for Elaine [birthday] and it was a howl! Cricket [GS Rep] caught some and bawled them out. We scurried to bed...finally we quit laughing....

July 27: Cricket woke us at 5 min. to 6:00 a.m., and we rolled out fairly quickly and soon were on the ball. After the patrol meeting yesterday we are doing better. We finally finished and got loaded and set off around 8:00. More singing and finally got over a bad road to Antonito, Colorado. Bert and Cricket have been discussing National Scouts and all. We are very happy. We stopped at "Houri" [Howiri] ruins where there are billions of potsherds![15] Two hours were spent hunting stuff and Bets [Galligan] found a perfect bead and Beth [Nash] an arrowhead. Then on to Bandelier National Monument.

We set up camp in the rain for the third night in a row. At supper we had STEAK, RICE, GRAVY, SALAD, BEETS, and FIGS! IT WAS SUPER!! Went to a picture showing in the Ranger office, just for us. We came back to camp and saw many skunks. This livened up the bed preparations immensely. One went through Cricket's tent and around our tent...Riot!

> Bandelier National Monument is located on the Pajarito Plateau on the eastern slope of the Jemez Mountains. The archaeological sites here are in a deep canyon (Frijoles Canyon). Those that can be visited are pueblos in the canyon bottom, such as circular Tyouni ruin and Rainbow House. Another, once called Ceremonial Cave and now known as Alcove House, lies well above the canyon bottom. In 1955 it was still reached only by ladders. Sites along the canyon's north wall include ground-level rooms and others carved into the volcanic tuff ("cavate" dwellings). Ancestral Pueblo occupation in the canyon is principally from 1150-1600, roughly the time of the Spanish *entrada* (Powers 2005). Close to the Monument is Jemez Historic Site, featuring the ruins of Gíusewa, a Pueblo established around 1500, with its Spanish Mission Church, San José de los Jémez, founded around 1631 and abandoned near 1640.

July 28: [After breakfast] we went on a hike with Bert to Tyouni and the cliffs around. There was much ladder climbing, and we went to Ceremonial Cave and all. We enjoyed it and Rambler [Bohrer] caught a lizard which she carried in her handkerchief. Then Bert led us on a hike down the canyon. It was rough. We saw the upper and lower falls, and then climbed to the lower. She explained the

Figure 4.9. Drying out camp gear after rain, Rancho del Cielo, Camp II, 1955. Photograph by Mary Anne Stein. 99BPD.xx, M.A. Stein Collection. Courtesy of MIAC/LAA.

Figure 4.10. All dressed up and ready to travel home, Camp II, 1955. Photograph by Mary Anne Stein. 99BPD.xx, M.A. Stein Collection. Courtesy of MIAC/LAA.

geology and we picked up pumice, and then went back to the museum to finish up. Then we played baseball (real ball borrowed from some campers) with a log for a bat near a *kiva* and kept losing it [ball] there. It was a riot! Everyone got cut and bashed to pieces, but more fun! We went to the john [restroom] to talk…almost everyone was on the roof and we sat there knowing we'd get caught and watching for lights. We had a riot! We laughed and laughed over it and finally went in groups on scouting trips to see if Bert was back in camp, then went to camp and to bed.

July 29: We are going over the Sangre de Cristo Mts. and rollercoaster hills. We stopped at Chimayo to buy blankets [from Hispanic weavers] and later at Cordova to visit George Lopez to get wood carvings (I got a sow and piglets, and a carved box), also a couple of doves to hang on soft white leather cords. Then came Taos Valley, Tres Ritos, and Las Vegas and Pecos ruins,[16] only church of adobe here. Then after busily writing songs, we got home (Bert's "ranch") and set up camp and ate in the rain [Figure 4.9]. We then sang the songs, made travel arrangements and had campfire for hours. Then came to bed, finally, out in the open. Bertha [Talahytewa] sang us to sleep. Mobile '55's last night is over.

July 30: We got up early and soon had eaten and drawn for *kapers* to leave camp. We had tent duty, checking, rolling, and marking for repairs to be done off-season. We washed, had lunch, and soon everyone was leaving [Figure 4.10]. It was simply awful!

1955: Camp III, Marty Gerber [The Sipapu III: 13–4, MIAC/LAA]

Dear Mother,
Here's the letter I promised to write, but I just haven't had time. So I thought I'd better mail this before I arrive home.

My first exploration in New Mexico was unpacking my duffle in the train station to find my raincoat. I was already wearing my jacket. Who said New Mexico is hot and dry? As we rode the bus from Albuquerque to Santa Fe, we saw numerous flooded areas.

Our camp was unique in many ways. First, we were invited to go swimming the first Sunday in a newly completed pool near Bert's. Also the camp was an experiment to discover if more girls could share this wonderful experience by offering another camp under Bert's direction, but with someone else leading the girls from one *kiva* to the next. Rambler [Bohrer], an early Digger who chose botany and archaeology as a career, served as actively in charge of our camp. With Rambler in the lead, we toured many ruins in New Mexico, highlighted by our trip to Aztec, thanks to Jack. If it hadn't been for Jack's mechanical skill, we might still be sitting in Gallina country with a bad starter.

Of course, it rained every day, but our most astonishing experience was at Mesa Verde. Danny [Linda Danforth] and I were sitting peacefully in our tent when we noticed our duffels floating around us. Scrambling for higher ground, the Diggers were able to salvage everything. Final toll was four soaked sleeping bags.

From there, we left for the breathtaking Rockies, where, of course, it rained. One highlight was an impressive *Scouts' Own* which took place in a flower-clad valley nestled among the snow-capped peaks.

After filing up to Chimney Rock we left for Bandelier where we were introduced to Miss Gretchen Yoffa [GSUSA Camping Division] who accompanied us for the remainder of our trip. At Bandelier, we took a four-mile hike in the morning to see the ruins and another four-mile hike in the afternoon to view the roaring waterfalls and intriguing geological structure. As we returned, everyone looked at us to study the resulting ruins.

Camp was over too soon, and our final farewells having been said, we departed for all parts of the country. Imagine the surprise of the porter who, upon entering my roomette, discovered that I had turned on the heater instead of the air conditioner, for, after two weeks of pouring rain and subzero temperatures, I was indeed, your Dirty Digger, "Chilli."

1956: Camp I, Kay Sweeney [Fowler]

June 30: We [Elaine Johnson and I] made it to Santa Fe just fine [by bus], and had fun talking on the way to Denver to some cute soldiers. They asked us about

Figure 4.11. Horno (oven) at Isleta Pueblo, Camp I, 1957. Photograph by Kay Sweeney [Fowler]. Courtesy of the author.

our uniforms, and we asked them about theirs. They left at Denver and we transferred to another bus for New Mexico. When we got to Santa Fe, bus station was right across the street from the place we met up with our ride [at Montezuma Hotel]. We went out to the ranch and got our tents up. Bert talked to us about what we would be seeing along the way, archaeology and all, and told us to take lots of notes, and to stay away from the cholla cactus. If it gets on you, you have to take it off with a stick, not your hand. She said we have to always be ready and packed early when we travel—move fast, be punctual! She is really nice, though.

On Sunday some of us went to the Cathedral for mass, and it was really something! People were there in Mexican clothes, with long dresses and mantillas and men with sombreros and silver conchos on their pants, and there was Mexican music after mass.

July 3: We started traveling today. Bert is nice, but she wants us to pay attention to what we are seeing—lots of desert, but it is tan instead of gray like home and some of the mountains are flat. But a big one we passed, named "Sandia" isn't flat—it's a regular mountain with forest. But I like it all and am learning a lot, especially about Indians. Our first stop was at Kuaua…Then we mounted up and went on to Chaco Canyon and camped for the night [spent two days]. This is a wonderful place. The ruins here are like big apartment houses, only made of sandstone, not bricks. It takes a while to see them, as they are the same color as the cliffs in the canyon.… The biggest is Pueblo Bonito and it is five stories high, shaped like a giant "D" with hundreds of rooms, all connected by doorways and you can see the roofs above some of the rooms. The big beams are called *vigas*, and small ones crossing them are *latillas*, and these are original and 900 years old! It has lots of *kivas* (ceremonial rooms) of all sizes, and big ones in the plaza in front. The ranger took us on a hike past "threatening rock" which is behind it. It is a huge rock that fell quite a long time ago onto the village [January 22, 1941]. Another ranger had been waiting to see it fall (had his camera ready), but he missed it. We also saw ancient steps up the cliff to the top where there is another big ruin.… On the other side of the canyon is a giant *kiva* called Casa Rinconada. This one is as big as our school gym, and perfectly round. It is all made of sandstone pieces carefully fit together, with foot drums on the floor and benches for sitting inside along the walls, and a place on one side for the priests to be. We made a song about it.[17]

July 6: …We went to Canyon de Chelly and hiked down to a cliff ruin called White House. It is beautiful, and looks like it is painted white against the super high red cliffs. It was a hard climb back up out of the canyon, but it was nice and cool down in the canyon. This is the most beautiful place I have seen yet. It is all red cliffs with white sand in the bottom and big green cottonwood trees. Navajos live in the canyon and they have sheep and grow corn and beans in fields that you can see from up on the edge of the canyon. It is hundreds of feet deep, and is so quiet you can hear people talking way down there. There is a tall skinny rock in the canyon called Spider Rock, and Bert told us that Spider Woman lives on top of it. She taught women how to weave, and she catches bad kids and takes them up to her nest on top!

July 8: We went to Hopi villages and camped on the floor at the Hopi day school [Toreva Springs] and got showers and Corkey [cook] got to cook on the stove again.... We got up early to see a *Katchina* dance at a Hopi village the next day. Bert told us to be real quiet, don't take notes or pictures, and stay back. She said they were "Pretty Katchinas" and they were dancing and singing for rain. They were all dressed the same, and had on big painted masks and pine branches around their necks. They danced in a line, one behind the other, and had turtle shell rattles tied to their legs that made this neat sound. After the dancers left, men came out and made fun of the tourists. One had cameras around his neck. Another one had a towel wrapped around his chest with two oranges stuffed in it and he was strutting around and laughing. Bert went to eat with them in the middle, and said she got a TV dinner! She said the men were clowns. It was fun, but it was hot. Indians were sitting on top of the houses all around....

The next day we stopped at the oldest Hopi village called Old Oraibi and went to a very old man's house, the Chief of the village. He made *katsina* dolls and sang us a song and two girls bought dolls. Bert said that he was a famous man [it likely was Tewaquaptewa (see Simmons 1942)].

The next day I was riding with Bert, and she asked our car "Where are we?" and I said "Navajo country" (because I saw a *hogan*). She said "good, you're paying attention," and I was happy.

July 12: We went to Zuni Pueblo and walked all around and visited a house and saw a woman grinding corn. I took lots of pictures of the village. Hope this camera works.[18] We camped at Zuni Day School, and after dinner, Bert sat us down and asked us what we wanted to be. We all went around the table, and I said "a veterinarian." Bert said that was good, but it's always good to have another plan in mind if the first one doesn't work out.[19]

July 13: We went west to El Morro rock where all kinds of travelers, Indians, Spanish, government explorers, ranchers, carved their names. The Spanish were the best, with very fancy writing. Then we hiked on top of it and saw a dig by some friends of Bert's [Richard and Nathalie Woodbury]. We found an eagle feather up there, and passed it around. It sure was special....

On the last day we hit a big sandstorm on the way to Albuquerque and had to stay at a café along the road until it quit. We couldn't see anything at all there was so much sand and dust blowing. We were late getting back to Bert's ranch, but it all worked out o.k. In the morning, after we packed up everything, cleaned up, and said "goodbye" to everybody, we all cried a lot.

1956 Camp II: Rebecca Adams (letter home; excerpts; R. Mills Files 2017)

[Went by train to Lamy and] after a short bus ride we arrived in Santa Fe, collected baggage, and met a crowd of other archaeology-pals, and were on our way to Rancho del Cielo, Dr. Bertha Dutton's ("Bert's") ranch. We changed into our jeans, etc., and I was lucky enough to tent with someone—Ellen Martin— who'd already put up a pup tent! Once our gear was all settled, and we'd met everyone, dinner was served—and what a discovery we made! We have a COOK! Although we do help her. After dinner, Jan [Fleming] gave us some info on the camp, we introduced ourselves, and then we met "Bert." Bert told us that some things—such as punctuality—are very necessary on the trip, and generally told us about our trip. What a wonderful person she is! Afterwards, we sat around a campfire, sang a bit, and numbered off in patrols. Bets Galligan is patrol three's (my patrol) leader—ein, schwei, drei, horse 'n goggle! Then to bed.

...Before I forget, I must describe the country. For some reason, the sky seems much larger and much more beautiful here than in any other place. Sunsets, striking cloud effects, and gorgeous night scenes, with a full moon are frequent ever since I've been here. The country is sandy—reddish in color— and dotted with yucca and small cedar trees (bushes, really). Mesas and black mountains stand in the distance. Almost all architecture is modeled off Indian homes—Pueblos—in Santa Fe. Thus the country—with the houses and buildings fitting into their surroundings—seems wide and uninhabited. It is beautiful in a different way.

Four girls chose to remember Camp II 1956 in song (R. Mills Files, 2017):

Many a State Tune (tune: "Sixteen Tons")
Written by Carol Hammer, Karen Rieley, Lois Richard, Patty Sowers

Chorus—sung after each verse:
24 girls from many a state
Many an accent and many a shape
We've had loads of fun and we'd like to come back
By taxi cab or railroad track.

Verses:
Our trip began on a Tues. morn.
A plan for many a mile was born
But soon our chariot began to fail
And this was a lag in a well started trail.

But we weren't stopped because we're Scouts
And we came to Kuaua after long hard bouts
The moon shone on us and kept us awake
But we weren't sorry it gave us an ache (I mean a heart ache).

Chaco was once a populated place
And now it's full of ruins and space
The ruins offered much besides a snake
Kivas, rain and many little lakes.

Our dinner was delayed at Window Rock

'Cause of a knee with an insect shock
Next day we went on to Canyon de Chelly
Which made it a perfectly beautiful day.

The Niman[20] dances impressed us all
Besides making very heavy raindrops fall
The early waking hours created a stir,
And made that whole durn village purr (I really mean purr).

Our next accommodations were good but wet
The cooks like the kitchen, that you can bet
The museum [MNM] kept us all entranced
And surely enjoyed the songs for to dance.

The following helped make this camp a success
Jan, Ginny, Marge, Lori and Jack, no less
We like them all a lot, they're really swell
Without them camping would surely be nil.

Bert we decided that this is enough
Thanks for the time spent on roads that were rough
We can't explain our feelings toward you
We'll remember this camp our whole life through.

1957: Camp I, Kay Sweeney [C. Fowler] Diary excerpts, Scrapbook

July 2: We went at Santo Domingo Pueblo today, and the governor showed us his cane with Abraham Lincoln's name on it. We sat on the floor of his house, and he passed it around for all of us to see it up close. Then we went to Isleta Pueblo and walked around and saw the church. We bought some bread that had

Figure 4.12. Cliff Palace, Mesa Verde National Park, Camp I, 1957. Photograph by Kay Sweeney [Fowler]. Courtesy of the author.

just come out of the *horno* [round earthen oven] from the woman who had just made it that morning [Figure 4.11]. It sure smelled good. We had it for lunch and it tasted really good too.

We went to Pottery Mound next, and it sure was hot.[21] It was burning our feet through our shoes! We got to see them peeling paintings off the walls of a *kiva*, like at Kuaua last year. We took turns going down there, and we could see the paint and it was neat. The people working were under a tarp, and they could only stay for 15 minutes before they had to come out and get water and rest in the shade of another tarp. We camped that night at a ranch in the pines at Datil, and heard the story of the ranch from a woman who lived there,[22] and saw where a horse was tied to a tree by the reins and broke away—and the reins are now sticking out of the tree way up high now, because it grew up around them!

July 4: We went to see some excavations at Vernon [Arizona], where they were digging in pithouses.[23] The archaeologist talked to us, and showed us where the firepit was, and the storage room outside of the house, and other things. We camped that night up in the pines at a forest camp. We had lots of sparklers tonight to celebrate the Fourth of July....

July 9: We are at Mesa Verde today, yesterday and tomorrow, and it is very beautiful—high up on a green mesa and you can see Shiprock way off to the south. Ruins are under the cliffs in the canyons and all over the mesas, and lots more old villages and a neat museum where we saw some miniature exhibits of all the early periods of life here.[24] We are camping in the trees and it is nice and cool. We went to Cliff Palace and some pithouses today [Figure 4.12], and to Spruce Tree House, another ruin in the canyon. We will go to Sun Temple tomorrow, and also to Balcony House.

July 10: ...The climb in and out of Balcony House was scary. We had to go up ladders and then hold on to ropes as we climbed up the rock to the top. Sun Temple was easy, and so was Far View Ruin, and the view from there is great. Dinner tonight was a turkey and dressing cooked in a Dutch oven. But our cook put sagebrush leaves in the dressing which wasn't the right kind of sage. It was very strong and made the whole thing taste bad!

Bert is not going to do camps next year, and so we all put in some money to buy her a present. Jan bought a red Hopi pot with black designs on it at the Mesa Verde store.

Figure 4.13. "Baby" gives out, northern Arizona, Camp I, 1957. Photograph by Kay Sweeney [Fowler]. Courtesy of the author.

[We gave her the pot when we returned to Rancho del Cielo.] We all thanked her for a great trip, and sang our songs around the campfire for a long time before crawling into bed.[25]

July 14: Before getting on the bus to go home, another girl and I went to the Montezuma Hotel. They let us take a bath for free. The bathtub had sand all over the bottom when we finished. We were really Dirty Diggers!

Other girls likely remembered other aspects of the camps than these, but we all carried away wonderful memories of places, people, fun, fellowship, and adventure from those summers in the Southwest. There were never any serious accidents or injuries on the Mobile Camps, and no one was left behind—in spite of threats by Bert and the GS Reps to do so. All survived two weeks of sometimes rough camping, hiking, variable weather conditions, altitude changes, camp meals, and drinking tea (although some downed far less than others). By having achieved the rank of "Senior" Girl Scouts, all should have been prepared to meet such challenges, and most proved that they were. Also contributing to the overall success and safety of the program were the many precautions taken by all of the adults along on the trips. They made sure that, apart from some vehicle breakdowns, problems with the weather, and a few other minor occurrences, inadvertent adventures were more positive than negative. And who could have asked for more to see, in what was for many, an entirely new and one of the most beautiful and intriguing parts of the United States. Those who continued to come back year after year to be reinfected by the "Southwest bug" were testimony to the region, Bert's overall plan, and considerations of logistics, safety and other aspects of on-the-trail living by her and the GSUSA. The girls (and the staff) were ultimately the beneficiaries.

5

"A Dig of Our Own"

The Pueblo Largo Excavation Camps, 1951–1957

On a hill far away, stands an old rocky room,
the emblem of suffering and pain.
Still I love that old room,
with its boulders and rocks,
we'll dig till we hit that old floor.
Oh I'll cherish the old rocky room,
till my shovel at last I lay down.
I will cling to the old pick and trowel
and exchange them some day for a bed!

—Camp III, 1951

By the end of the third, and especially the fourth, seasons of the Mobile Camp program, repeat campers began asking to become "real Diggers," to participate in an actual archaeological excavation (Dutton 1951a:364). By then they had seen a variety of stabilized and partially reconstructed sites, large and small, over much of the Southwest—north, south, and central. They had visited sites being excavated, seen crews in action, and heard from the people in charge of the excavations about what they hoped to learn from digging in these particular places. They had seen that digging was dirty, sweaty, hard work, but at the same time, fascinating, rewarding, and obviously fun. They had absorbed the numerous lectures by Bert and others, and begun to ask good questions about the region's deep history. Some were intrigued by the obvious parallels between the ancient sites and the modern Pueblo villages along the Rio Grande, on the Hopi mesas, and at Laguna, Acoma, and Zuni. They had also heard stories from the Pueblo people about migrations by their ancestors from distant places to present locations. And they had heard theories about possible reasons for these migrations—the Great Drought of the late 1200s, raids by Navajo and Apache people, the Spanish *entrada*, and more.

So now Mobile Camp veterans, several of whom were now in their late teens and early twenties and in college, were anxious to do more than just watch and listen from the sidelines to the slow unraveling of the story of the Southwest. They wanted to be participants and partners in the process, especially with "a dig of our own." In 1951, Bert arranged for that to happen by offering an additional camp session, an opportunity for a crew of carefully selected girls to excavate a site in the Galisteo Basin south of Santa Fe called Pueblo Largo.

The Galisteo Basin

The genesis of Bert's interest in excavating in the Galisteo Basin began in roughly 1940, when, in her Model A Ford, she began spending weekends and holidays exploring that area south of Santa Fe. She looked for the sites described by the pioneer historian Adolph Bandelier in the 1880s, as well as by archaeologist Nels Nelson, the first to actually conduct excavations in the area. Nelson had spent roughly seven months in the Galisteo Basin in 1912, mapping and partly excavating sites (a few rooms to several in each), including eight medium-to-large Pueblos: San Cristóbal, Largo, Colorado, Shé, Blanco, Galisteo, San Lazaro, and San Marcos (Figure 5.1). His work was sponsored by the American Museum of Natural History in New York (Nelson 1914).

On her weekend jaunts, Bert located Nelson's sites plus others recorded by Bandelier and other archaeologists, and collected samples of pottery from

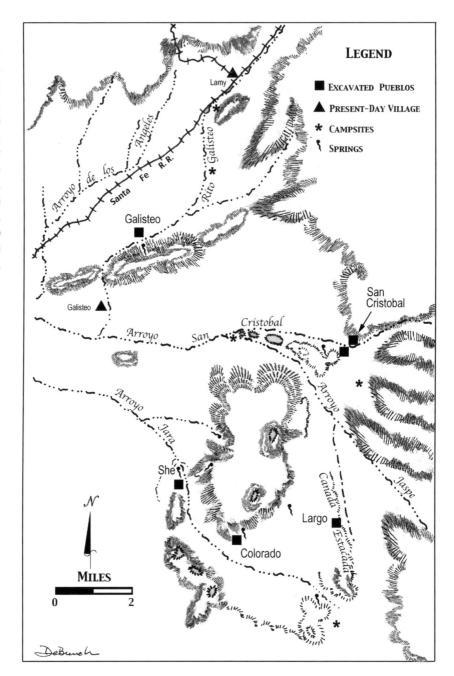

Figure 5.1 Nels Nelson's map of principal Ancestral Puebloan sites in southern Galisteo Basin (after Nelson 1914). Courtesy of the Division of Anthropology, American Museum of Natural History, New York. Map redrawn by Patricia DeBunch.

LEGEND

■ EXCAVATED PUEBLOS
▲ PRESENT-DAY VILLAGE
✳ CAMPSITES
⌇ SPRINGS

throughout the Basin. She hoped to establish a preliminary chronology for the area as well as make some suggestions as to which present-day Pueblos in the Rio Grande Valley and elsewhere might show historical affiliations to them.[1]

Being true to what she had been telling her Scouts about the importance of having a purpose or reason for digging a site other than idle curiosity, Bert thought that some very useful information could come from Galisteo Basin excavations. She had begun to question the hypothesis current at the time that the area was occupied, at least post 1275, by people migrating from the Mesa Verde area in southwestern Colorado. This idea was based on similarities in the area's Galisteo Black-on-white pottery to that from Mesa Verde and the San Juan Basin—the latter area thought to be a logical stopping place for people moving from the once verdant Mesa Verde country to set up new homes near permanent water as a result of the Great Drought (roughly 1280–1300). Bert had good working relationships with fellow MNM/LA and UNM archaeologists, a small group at the time, and they were all discussing these ideas; but she felt that the issue was not resolved for the Galisteo Basin. The area was as yet poorly known, as most of the sites had only been "tested" rather than more fully excavated, and their architecture and artifacts needed to be more thoroughly analyzed. An alternative hypothesis was that these sites were home to peoples who had always been local to the area. Yet another was that the people had come into the region from another direction, perhaps from the south, east, or west—or all directions. Thus, when the request came from the girls for "a dig of our own," Bert was willing to consider the possibility of combining her interests with the "minds and muscles of a group of Senior Scouts and excavate a site in the Galisteo Basin" (Dutton 1951a:364).

During the winter of 1950–51, Dutton explored the idea of a two-week excavation camp as part of the Senior Girl Scout program. This would be a way of capping the program of Mobile Camps with a different, more scientifically oriented experience. It would also make the Girl Scout program equivalent to a college course in archaeology: "three Mobile trips [one each year, different routes] and one archaeological dig to provide them with the equal of a summer course in college archaeology" (99BPD. xx M.A. Stein letter, Aug. 26, 1955). She began looking for a site reasonably close to Santa Fe for logistical and safety reasons, and one that had been and would be

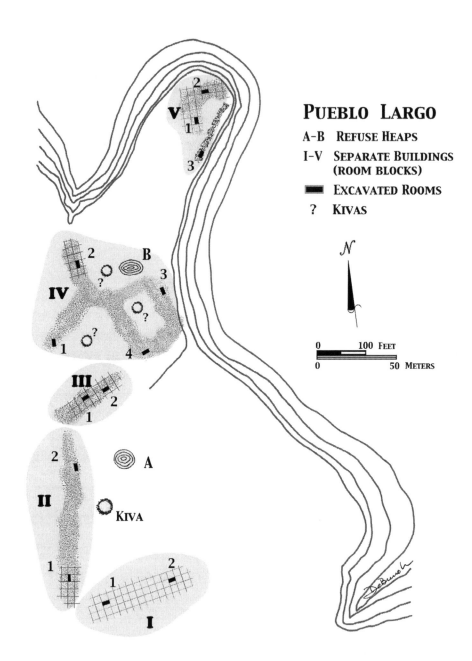

Figure 5.3. Nels Nelson's map of room blocks and other features, Pueblo Largo (after Nelson 1914). Courtesy of the Division of Anthropology, American Museum of Natural History, New York. Map redrawn by Patricia DeBunch.

PUEBLO LARGO

A–B REFUSE HEAPS
I–V SEPARATE BUILDINGS (ROOM BLOCKS)
▬ EXCAVATED ROOMS
? KIVAS

N

0   100 FEET
0   50 METERS

Figure 5.2. View of Estacado Creek looking southeast from Pueblo Largo, 1955. Photograph by Mary Anne Stein. 99BPD.xx, M.A. Stein/S.S. Martin Collection. Courtesy of MIAC/LAA.

protected from vandalism once excavations began. It also had to be one that would merit what she hoped would be several years' attention, and likely to shed light on the Mesa Verde connection and/or other hypotheses. She settled on Pueblo Largo, one of the medium-sized villages tested by Nelson in 1912, and one securely located on an 8,000-acre private ranch. She and the MNM successfully negotiated with the owners of the land, Sawyer Cattle Company of San Angelo, Texas, to work at the site and set up a field camp on the ranch.

Pueblo Largo (LA 183) is located on a juniper-studded sandstone mesa on the eastern side of the Galisteo Basin some 30 miles south of Santa Fe. The mesa provides spectacular views of the Sangre de Cristo Mountains to the north as well as the valley below, with its ribbon of green marking the intermittent flows of Estacado Creek (Figure 5.2). The mesa and surrounding area is a combination of yellow and red sandstone cliffs, and parts of the Pueblo are precariously perched on its eastern edge. Several of Nelson's other sites are located within a few miles, as are rock art panels and other places suggesting a long period of people living in the area. The site is within the known territory of the Southern Tewa (also known as Tano) people, present-day occupants of several Rio Grande villages (see Figure 1.2).

In 1912, Nelson (1914:68–73) mapped Pueblo Largo, estimating that it had 489 ground-floor rooms clustered in five areas (Figure 5.3). He excavated one to three rooms in each of the five areas (labeled as Buildings I–V [V with two parts]), and partially exposed a large semi-subterranean *kiva* or ceremonial chamber in the central plaza between Buildings I and III. He designated two "refuse heaps" or mounds as A and B, but did not examine them further. Bert visited with Nelson and his wife Ethel while in New York City studying for her doctorate at Columbia University during the school year of 1945–46. She discussed this site (and others in the Basin) with him and looked at the collections he had made from the region. These artifacts were stored at the American Museum of Natural History in New York where Nelson was still affiliated. Nelson also served on Bert's oral examination committee for her doctoral degree that year (Dutton 1989:97).

Getting Started

In the spring of 1951, and using Nelson's map as a starting point, Bert visited Pueblo Largo and relocated the rooms he had excavated. She also worked out a strategy for excavating additional rooms and areas. She then scouted a place to establish the field camp (pup tent village, lab tent, mess tent and table, firepit, latrine), settling on a large, open area adjacent to the site. Water would be the biggest problem as there was only one small spring (inactive) reasonably close to the site. A ranch well with a stock tank was located off the mesa in the valley below, but access was over a very rough dirt road that wound down the mesa. This problem was ultimately solved by hauling a water tank (water buffalo) holding 650 gallons from Lamy up to the camp (Figure 5.4).

The plan was to run the camp like any other archaeological field school, such as UNM's Chaco Canyon school, with which Bert was very familiar. The girls were to be divided into teams partly based on the GS *patrol system*, but with Bert choosing her most experienced Mobile Camp veterans as leaders. Each team was assigned rooms or other areas to excavate (*kiva*, refuse mounds, exploratory trenches, etc.). Girls would rotate to different teams to gain experience at all excavation tasks. Team leaders were to take notes on the excavations in their areas, especially during the

Digs in 1951 to 1953. All artifacts and notes were to become part of the permanent record for the site and cataloged into the collections of the MNM according to standard procedures.[2]

Note-taking responsibility apparently changed during the years 1954 to 1956, so that each girl was to keep her own notebook on her part(s) of the excavation—supposedly giving all more experience. Then the team leaders were to pool these periodically toward summaries while the excavations were in progress (Figure 5.5).[3] The notes from all years are of varied quality, although some include line drawings of artifacts, wall profiles and other features, and architectural measurements (for example, Holien 1953; Nash 1955; Reimers 1955; Skidmore 1954). The collections from later years also have fared better and their documentation is more complete. As the girls gained more experience (many of them now veterans of Mobiles plus three or more excavation sessions), team leaders functioned much as do "crew chiefs" at today's archaeological site excavations, and each also recorded the progress of her team.[4]

In 1951, as well as subsequent years of the Pueblo Largo excavation camps, Bert continued to use Nelson's numbering system as the overall site control. She kept his building or Room Block designations (I–V) as well as his other feature designations (his Refuse Heaps [Refuse Mounds] A, B, *Kiva*, etc.). She then added new room numbers and other feature numbers to his system as needed (e.g., V-4, for room #4 in Room Block V).[5] The locations within rooms where significant artifacts (ground stone, bone tools, beads, whole pots or concentrations of pottery sherds, and more) were to be recorded by depth and distance from walls. These artifacts were given catalog numbers to match those in the notes.[6] Nearly all excavated material (especially from room floors) was screened for artifacts according to standard procedures of the day.[7] Other tasks for the girls, including regular *kapers*, plus the new duties of washing and cataloging artifacts in the lab tent, were to keep pace with camp life in general and the excavations in particular.

As the years went by, Bert apparently assumed less responsibility for day-to-day operations at the site due to an increase in her museum duties (Chapter 8). She visited periodically to answer questions if crew leaders were uncertain as to how to proceed.[8] She felt that the girls in charge of crews had enough experience to continue without

Figure 5.4. Pueblo
Largo excavation's
water supply, 1951.
Two unidentified
Diggers plus
Bertha Dutton and
Huston Thompson.
95PLE.034(a).
Courtesy of MIAC/
LAA.

her, or to wait for her to visit before taking any drastic steps or excavating something that they did not understand. When Bert was not actually on the site, her assistant, the GS Rep, the cook, and the crew leaders—all of them now adults—made sure that the operation continued to run smoothly. Bert summarized the progress and some of the findings for most years in her annual summaries of the Girl Scout program (Dutton 1951a; 1952a; 1953a; 1954b; 1955a). Issues of *The Sipapu* from 1953 to 1956 contain additional summaries and commentaries by the Diggers. There are also scrapbooks for all of the Dig years in the collections of the Dutton Collection (99BPD.xx). These contain a wealth of candid comments, photographs, poems, transcribed songs, cartoons, and other memorabilia, including in some cases, a worn-out glove (added by Bert), a broken trowel, a fake pot sherd, and more. The scrapbooks were sent to Bert as mementos after each year's Dig was completed. It is quite unusual to have these types of references for an archaeological excavation, but they sometimes provide important and useful information and pictures on the course of the excavation

Figure 5.5. Caroline "Casey" Kline, a team leader, taking notes, 1955 or 1956. Photograph by Mary Anne Stein. 99BPD.xx, M.A. Stein/S.S. Martin Collection). Courtesy of MIAC/LAA.

as well as the girls' experiences and perspectives. The following accounts by season were put together largely from these scrapbooks, along with Bert's summaries and other resources in her collection (see also Chapter 8).

The Dig Sessions

The 1951 Season

On August 18, 1951, 13 Diggers and four adults, including Bert, assembled at El Rancho del Cielo for Camp III, the first Pueblo Largo Dig camp. Given that the

Figure 5.6. Aggie
Sims, Assistant
Director, posing
beside MNM station
wagon, Pueblo
Largo, 1951. 99BPD.
xx, Scrapbook, 1951.
Courtesy of MIAC/
LAA.

Figure 5.6. Aggie Sims, Assistant Director, posing beside MNM station wagon, Pueblo Largo, 1951. 99BPD.xx, Scrapbook, 1951. Courtesy of MIAC/LAA.

girls chosen for the excavation crew (Appendix A) were all Mobile Camp veterans, experienced campers, enthusiastic, and generally knowledgeable about regional chronologies, Bert did not feel she needed to spend much time orienting them to either the region or the work. After a day spent at the Lab with Marjorie Lambert reviewing Galisteo Basin and other regional pottery types, Bert and the Diggers proceeded south to set up camp at the site. Agnes "Aggie" Sims, Research Associate at the School of American Research, an old friend of Bert's who was studying Galisteo Basin rock art, served as associate supervisor that first season (Figure 5.6). Ted Lovato was the cook, and Gretchen Yoffa from Girl Scout national headquarters served as GS Rep. The cost was $37.50 per participant. This covered the cook's salary, all food and supplies, plus gasoline for transportation of the girls to and from the site, and a few additional trips to town by the "shuttler" (usually the cook) for more supplies and mail. It was roughly half the fee for the Mobile Camps given that this camp was stationary, and all expenses were lower. The MNM furnished the vehicles and excavation equipment.

The first year Bert and Aggie took charge of the overall excavation, as none of the girls had any direct excavation experience. Martha "Marty" Harlan (1952)

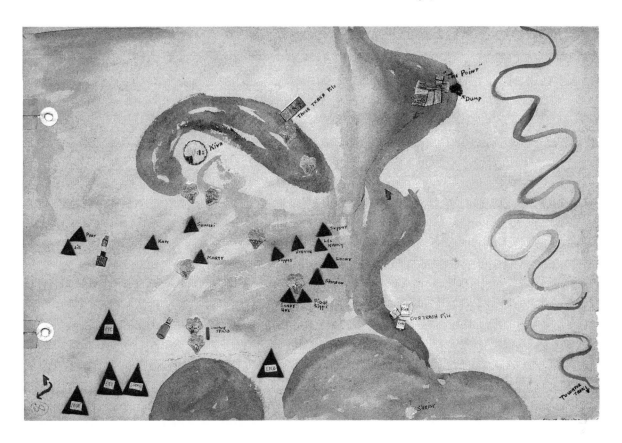

provides a spirited account of the 1951 Dig in an article in *The American Girl* magazine, a monthly publication of the GSUSA. According to Marty, after a brief tour of the site led by Aggie Sims, "Bert handed out picks and shovels on the first day in camp and put us right to work." One team started on the Refuse Mound B, just to the north of the small plaza (IV), and immediately began encountering broken pottery, bone awls and other tools, and then a burial, the first of four for the season. (By today's ethical standards, excavation of human remains would not be allowed, and excavating would cease in that area if they were encountered. If the remains were in danger of being destroyed, they might be studied in place—or removed and reinterred elsewhere after proper Tribal consultations.) A second team volunteered to dig in the depression in the center of the larger plaza in front of buildings I, II,

Figure 5.7. Layout of Pueblo Largo field camp, 1953, by Claire Yeagley. 99BPD.xx, Scrapbook, 1953. Courtesy of MIAC/LAA.

and III, identified by Nelson as a *kiva*. This was harder digging and far less rewarding in artifacts and information, and required removing "truckloads of dirt with little of interest in it besides an occasional potsherd." The third crew (on rotation) in
the lab had plenty to keep it occupied, however, as the artifacts continued to roll in.
All Diggers persevered through that first as well as subsequent days in the hot sun,
anticipating lunch and juice breaks, an evening meal cooked in Dutch ovens, and a
night under the stars (see later years for menu examples).

The camp was well planned and was soon running smoothly (Figure 5.7). The
pup tent village (two per tent) was set up in the flats between the main site and the
eastern cliff. The mess tent and other cooking facilities were to the south. The girls
built a stone slab fire hearth there of local materials for the cook's convenience and
to ensure fire safety. The lab tent was in between the pup tents and the mess tent.
Bert's, Aggie's, and Gretchen's tents were on the western and eastern margins of the
overall camp. Other common facilities, such as the water tank, the latrine (dubbed
"It" that first year, and later, when a permanent one was built on the eastern edge of
the mesa, "the loo with a view"), and trash dump, were also carefully placed, creating the overall look of an efficient and well-organized operation.

Then the rain began to fall. Late summer is monsoon season in northern New
Mexico, and the Galisteo Basin was no exception that year—although it was reported
that there had been a series of dry years leading up to 1951. The campers soon found
that the monsoonal rains, according to Marty, "plagued them nightly," often blowing through the camp and rending and tearing tents and even pulling the bigger
lab and cook tents from their ropes and pegs. Subsequent days found excavation
trenches filled with rain water, sending crews to alternative rooms while the ground
dried out. Some nights were worse than others, but all did their best to take the rain
in stride. Mornings often found belongings draped across tents to dry, even with pre-
cautionary trenching around tent perimeters.

In spite of the rains, some coming in the late afternoon and providing welcome
relief from the heat and grime of digging, lack of potable water was still an issue,
even with the 650-gallon (2,461 l) tank on site. This main water supply was to last
for the full two weeks and thus had to be used sparingly. Basin baths were the norm
for the crews and staff, and according to Marty, "all we could do was slosh off the
top layer of dust." Now the girls were truly "Dutton's Dirty Diggers!" Many couldn't

tell whether they were improving their tans—a desirable thing in those days—or the dark color was really dirt, acting as sun block. Some respite for bathing came every other night when they loaded alternating halves of the camp into the museum's pickup truck for a trip to the ranch stock tank down in the valley. There they had a "back-scrubbing, bra-washing, hair-sudsing party," from the tank's outflow pipe (Harlan 1952:7).

All soon settled into daily routines of digging and their *kapers* (cook's helpers, wood gatherers, cataloging, potsherd washing, messenger). These, like the digging crew assignments, were set up on a rotational basis so that all girls could get experience at each task. They occasionally had a day off from these alternating duties. But even these times meant that they were available to fill in on other tasks if needed—such as cutting down dead trees to add to the firewood pile. The cook, Ted Lovato, complained that the crew "ate like lumberjacks," often serving themselves breakfast two or three times. Everybody lined up for chow in the morning and evening, sometimes having to flee to the lab or mess tents to eat as the rain started coming down. Bert's dictum, as for the on-the-trail camps, was that they all should drink lots of hot tea each evening, and they closely observed "the hot tea routine." Nosebag lunches, often eaten at the excavations with juice and water, were followed by breaks to rest and recoup for the afternoon's efforts. The excavation day ran: 7:30–9:30, juice break, then 10–12, lunch, then 1–3, juice break, and 3:30–5. Lab work, if needed beyond as assigned *kapers*, continued after dinner—often by lantern light (see Figure 5.18).

In spite of the rains, good progress was made at the site, and in the roughly two weeks in 1951, the crew that called themselves "the *kiva* kids" excavated roughly one-third of the large *kiva* in the south plaza, but not to the floor. The second crew started work on a long stratigraphic trench through Refuse Mound B (north of Room Block IV), and a third completely cleared two dwelling rooms (in Room Blocks IV and V) and part of a third (in Room Block I), two with flagstone floors (see Dutton 1953a:344–46 for details). Clearing rooms "necessitated extensive pick swinging, rock toting and throwing, and diligent shoveling" (Dutton 1951a:366). Dr. Fred Wendorf, seasoned archaeologist, on visiting the site, remarked that he "had never seen any boys work as hard." By spending some of their downtime after lunch and some evenings on cataloging and other paperwork, lab processing kept pace with

Figure 5.8. Bert,
Huston Thompson,
Gretchen Yoffa,
and Vorsila Bohrer,
Pueblo Largo,
1951. 99BPD.xx,
Scrapbook, 1951.
Courtesy of MIAC/
LAA.

the excavations, and at the end of the session, all materials were ready for deposit in MNM's collections. Lab work could not go too late as the girls soon found that they needed at least some sleep to put in a full day at the end of the shovel or pick. As Marty remarked, "Lab chores, although technical, fascinated even those of us deficient in scientific talent. Even shard scrubbing was fun, for striking glaze-paint patterns often emerged on the muddy chunks of pottery.... The digging bug bit all of us one way or another" (Harlan 1952:9).

The camp and dig attracted several visitors during that season, including Professor Charles Lange, who lectured on Pueblo ethnology; a busload of Senior

Figure 5.9. "Aggie [Sims] tells a story to the Texans"; Left to right: Roberta and Rogene Faulkner, Ann Hunt, Martha "Marty" Harlan, Eloise Moore, Joan Wehrli, Pueblo Largo, 1951 (official photo; note GSUSA hats). Photograph by Larry Kafer. 99BPD.xx, Scrapbook 1951. Courtesy of MIAC/LAA.

Scouts from Lubbock, Texas and their leaders; and two MNM/SAR board members, one from Santa Fe (Henry Dendahl) and the other from Washington, D.C. (Huston Thompson; Figure 5.8). Vorsila Bohrer, a veteran of several Mobile Camps and now majoring in anthropology at the University of Arizona, was also on hand part of the session as naturalist. Bert was pleased with the overall progress of the excavations, but noted that the primary questions to be answered by digging the site—who were the people, and when and from where did they come—were not answered by the end of the session. More seasons would have to be spent, but "we have the satisfaction of work well done—and done by Senior Girl Scouts" (Dutton 1951a:366).

On August 31, they dismantled the lab, took down the big tents, razed the pup tent village, packed up equipment and specimens, and returned to El Rancho del Cielo. There was some time left in the next couple of days before departing to clean and prepare the gear for next season, and to go to Santa Fe Fiesta festivities, including the annual Fiesta Market (precursor to today's Indian Market). This was followed by the usual teary goodbyes, and exchanges of addresses, as more were going off to college that fall. Bert hoped that they would spread the word in their GS Councils at home as well as elsewhere about this unique experience. As Marty Harlan (1952:9) summed it up, "we could hardly help speculating on what might be in the rock-filled rooms yet untouched. And we were ready to take pick in hand and find out. [For the $37.50 fee] a better bargain is hard to find. Those of us who dug in the Galisteo last August are sold on that."

There are numerous photographs of the excavations in progress during that season. Larry Kafer, a professional photographer from Santa Fe, spent a day posing the crew and documenting the excavation for the Museum (Figure 5.9). That fall, several of the girls prepared a scrapbook with some of these as well as their own photos and artwork (especially Marty Harlan's cartoons) and presented it to Bert the following spring.

The 1952 Season

Bert later admitted that in the beginning she had not been fully convinced that a crew made up entirely of young women, especially ones who were "almost exclusively accustomed to town life," could fully handle all the physical labor required in a full-scale excavation. She, as well as most others working in the region at the time, hired local Hispanic or other seasoned diggers on most excavation projects, especially if large quantities of materials needed to be removed. But the 1951 season convinced her that the Senior Girl Scouts (and Scout Associates) "proved almost indefatigable, though there is no denying that they were more than ready to 'hit the sack' when nighttime came" (Dutton 1953a:343). However, they were also more

Figure 5.10. Nettie Kesseler (back row, third from left), 1951. 95PLE.034. Courtesy of MIAC/LAA.

than ready to get to work as soon as they rolled out each morning, and even volunteered for more as time got short. Her concern had been misplaced. Her plan for the 1952 excavation session, and ones thereafter, would be based on accomplishments during the previous session: complete any excavation work already in progress first, and then add new and interesting rooms and features that would add to the site's story.

The 1952 Dig session began August 18 and ended August 31. Three girls who had been on the 1951 excavation crew were back for the second year, and two who were part of the second session of the 1952 Mobile Camps stayed on to participate in the Dig—making roughly half the crew veterans. Given this situation, and after assembling briefly at El Rancho del Cielo, Bert decided to take the crew directly to Pueblo Largo, set up camp, and get to work. The field camp at the site was in the same location as before and consisted of three large wall tents for the lab, mess, and kitchen; the pup tent village for the girls (two to a tent); and individual tents for the staff. In addition to Bert, Gretchen Yoffa returned as GS Rep. Elizabeth Parker of the Pueblo, Colorado, GS Council served as cook with Esther Lucy of Los Alamos as her assistant plus camp shuttle (from Santa Fe to the site). Velma "Whip" Whipple, by then living in Albuquerque, was the naturalist. Gillian Wethey, a Girl Guide from England on a special international fellowship, was assigned as counselor-camper (see Chapter 4). She already had experience as a counselor in Oklahoma, as Nettie Kesseler (Adams), a Digger again that year, remembered her from her Tulsa camp experience (Figure 5.10; see also *Tulsa Tribune*, 6/24/52).[9] Gill [pronounced "Jill"] worked alongside the other girls, digging, troweling, and screening for artifacts, but also carried out other camp duties. She was in charge of first aid, from treating sunburns and blisters to removing cactus spines and splinters, as well as other assorted annoyances.

According to Bert's summaries, the 1952 crew of 11 concentrated on the large *kiva* in the south plaza and the Refuse Mound B in the north plaza, continuing the areas started the previous year. They also excavated some additional dwelling rooms. The *kiva* crew removed an additional quarter to one-third of fill from that structure, this time down to the floor which was partly paved with flagstones. Important finds there included a fire screen (or altar) with an oblong adobe firepit in front of it and a ventilator shaft behind (see Figure 5.13). There was also evidence of part of a plastered and painted wall (yellow and green pigment), but no mural images were seen (Dutton 1952a:349–350). Given that Bert had considerable experience with *kiva* murals at Kuaua (Coronado Historic Site), this proved to be a most intriguing find (see also Dutton 1952a:349–350). Results from Refuse Mound B where another crew continued to work yielded nine more burials, bringing the total for the two years to 13. None of these burials had grave offerings or other accompaniments that could help in identifying their specific cultural affiliations. Additional rooms in Nelson's buildings I and IV were also cleared (95PLE.031; Dutton 1952a).

Many more artifacts were recovered overall this season than in 1951, including the always numerous potsherds, plus bone and antler tools, projectile points, knives, scrapers, grinding stones, shells and other items of adornment, earthenware pipes, and a spindle whorl (suggesting the spinning of cultivated cotton or perhaps other local fibers; see Dutton [1952a] for details). As in the previous season, all were duly cataloged and deposited in the MNM collections for study after the end of the session.

On the last day, just before closing the site for the season, the crew asked to dig an additional trench through Nelson's Building V, or "The Point," on the east-ernmost extension of the mesa. They soon encountered a room with a roof par-tially intact that yielded wooden beams that could be dated by tree-ring analysis. Bert reported the following year that three of the samples of those beams sent to the University of Arizona Laboratory of Tree-Ring Research produced cutting dates between 1275 and 1299, and along with the pottery discovered from that section, sug-gested that this section of the site was very likely the oldest found thus far (Dutton 1953a:351). Further, she added that given these dates, and especially when com-bined with the preliminary analysis of materials from the other sections, this find-ing "reflected a certain degree of social stability, and no great influence from outside sources" (Dutton 1953a:351). They were beginning to make progress on answering one of the questions posed at the initiation of the excavations.

On August 31, as was inevitable, the girls packed up the camp and trans-ported all of the equipment, supplies, and artifacts to Bert's *ranchito* and then to the museum. That night, after cleaning and storing the equipment, they had their last campfire, singing songs under the stars. According to Bert, by noon following day, all duties were done, and "tanned, healthy, jean-clad campers—after bathing and doing miraculous things with curlers and cosmetics—blossomed forth as lovely, feminine creatures once more, often difficult to recognize" (Dutton 1952a:351). After more farewells and poignant moments, "by 2:00 p.m., the ranch was loud with silence," and the "director stayed on, awaiting the return of 'the Dirty Diggers' or the arrival of new recruits" (Dutton 1952a:352).

The 1953 Season

The 1953 crew included Bert as director with Kate Swift acting as assistant director, GS Rep, and shuttler. Esther Lucy from the 1952 Dig served as cook. In addition, 12 campers, dubbed by Marty Harlan (1953) as "Dutton's Dirtiest Dozen," dug at Pueblo Largo from August 17 to 31. Harlan claimed that during this third season the crew moved more dirt into the air and took fewer baths than any crew thus far—thus the nickname. In addition to all the moving dirt that they caused, there were frequent sandstorms in the afternoons, keeping those shoveling "plastered with grit." Also, water shortages struck the first few and last days, keeping bathing to a minimum.

Figure 5.11. "The Big Portage," 1953. Cartoon by Martha Harlan. 99BPD.xx, Scrapbook, 1953. Courtesy of MIAC/LAA.

The difficulty for the first few days was because after filling the water tanker at the windmill and attempting to pull it up the hill to the camp on the badly eroded road, it became mired in an arroyo. Bert was pulling it with a "weapons carrier" at the time, according to Kate Swift (1953). Given that it did not make it to the camp for two more days, what water was on hand had to be rationed, including for basin baths and washing up before meals. Simultaneously, heavy rain limited bathing trips to the cattle tank the first week to one per person due largely to access. Estacado Creek, between the camp and the tank, was often in flood that season, and thus the "short" way of driving there was impassable. The alternative was to drive the camp truck over a worse road south and around the end of the mesa to the cattle tank. During the last few days of the session the camp water tank ran dry, and in order not to risk a second incident on the road, which was flooded again (in spite of continual maintenance by the girls), the alternative was to fill five-gallon jugs at the windmill pump and haul them back up the hill. Rationing was again required.

The weather turned out to be the biggest problem that summer (Swift 1953). There were cloudbursts that soaked bedding, spectacular gully-washing hailstorms, and *chindis* (dust devils) that collapsed the lab tent and carried away pup tents. The second afternoon in camp a major wind ripped and flattened the lab tent, putting a temporary halt to cataloging, until two Diggers were able to stitch it up with binder's twine using an ice pick as an awl. A semi-flood the next day made a mud puddle of the mesa top and bogged down incoming groceries on the wrong side of the Estacado Creek in the valley. "In order to get the makings for supper into camp, the Diggers trucked within sloshing distance of the stream, which was waist-deep and swift," and then waded across and formed a bucket-brigade to pass boxes of chow across to the remainder (Swift 1953; Figure 5.11). The crew then dug the shuttle car out of harm's way in the stream and pushed it to where it was retrieved three days later after the arroyo dried. A similar fate befell some campers in the pup tent village, who, after tiring of re-digging moats around their tents for the first few days, moved to higher ground—only to have the rain stop for the duration of the dig.

In addition to weather issues, there were several encounters with local wildlife, particularly rattlesnakes. One enterprising snake was found under the bed in the cook's tent, and "promptly canned in a quart jar by dietitian Esther Lucy so she could show it to her family" (Harlan 1953; Figure 5.12). Other rattlesnakes turned up in excavation rooms and near the *kiva*, and were dispatched and made into belts by the crew. A very large tarantula was also caught and placed in a bottle for all to see. It was later released off the mesa. But, apart from these minor interruptions, digging continued as planned for the two weeks.

Bert spent the first day of the camp giving the girls the history of work at the site, and providing a site tour. The girls were divided into three teams and given their digging assignments: continuation of work on the large *kiva* in the south plaza, rooms on The Point (V), and continuing the trench through the large Refuse Mound B—"yet

Figure 5.12. The
Pueblo Largo
camp kitchen,
fully developed,
1953. 99BPD.xx,
Scrapbook, 1953.
Courtesy of MIAC/
LAA.

again." The teams stayed with those tasks for the two weeks, as they said that it had taken them at least three or four days to get into "good digging condition" working at these, and switching midterm would delay progress as the others got into shape (Swift 1953). With some girls now with two Dig sessions behind them, Bert made them team leaders, giving them more responsibility for directing the excavations in their assigned areas. As usual, all crews rotated to the lab tent for artifact processing, and most personnel spent time in the evenings there in order to have processing keep pace with the excavation schedule.

About halfway through the session, Bert used the pottery samples cataloged thus far to suggest a tentative chronology for occupation of the site from 1275 to 1475, with Room Block V being the oldest; but not all room blocks were necessarily occupied simultaneously. None of the artifacts found to date indicated that Pueblo

Figure 5.13.
Excavating the kiva
in the south plaza,
Pueblo Largo, 1953.
Photograph by
Larry Kafer (posed;
note GSUSA
hats). 99BPD.xx,
Scrapbook, 1953.
Courtesy of MIAC/
LAA.

Largo's people remained at the site beyond the early 1500s (if that), let alone into the period of Spanish explorations and eventual arrival in the region (1540s–1590s).

The crew that continued with work on the large *kiva* that season made excellent progress (Figure 5.13). They cleared most of the remaining materials down to the floor level. The floor turned out to be partially paved with long flagstones mixed with some adobe flooring, and removing some of the stones revealed what appeared to be a second paved layer beneath. The altar, discovered the previous year, remained of interest, as did the ventilator shaft (provides for outside air flow into these underground chambers). The crew then looked for a *sipapu*, a small hole in the floor usually found near the fire hearth. It commonly symbolizes the spirit entrance through

Figure 5.14.
Excavating at The
Point (Nelson's
Room Block V-b;
note screens in
use), 1953. 99BPD.
xx, Scrapbook,
1953. Courtesy of
MIAC/LAA.

which the Ancestral Pueblo people came up into this world. They found a small hole that might have been one, but it was not in line with the other floor features (as was traditional), so they doubted that this identification was correct (Figure 5.13). There was also evidence on one wall that the *kiva* may have been burned at one time, partially filled, and then possibly reused (Harlan 1953).

Attention was again focused on The Point (V), the northeast extension of the site that Bert suspected might be the pioneer settlement at Pueblo Largo, given the older Black-on-white pottery that predominated (Santa Fe Black-on-white) and a report from the University of Arizona Laboratory of Tree-Ring Research that the wooden beams recovered from in 1952 showed an initial cutting date of 1275, another at 1295, and four at 1299. But the whole area was a difficult one to excavate because it had rooms with irregular shapes, crooked walls, and missing walls due to erosion of the hillside into the canyon below (Figure 5.14). But additional rooms were cleared there, and two exploratory trenches added input toward determining more of the original outline of this part of the site.

The crew that worked on the trench through Refuse Mound B near Room Block IV also made significant progress. Additional human remains were located in this area, along with a probable dog burial and many discarded artifacts (see Harlan 1953 for details). The overall cataloged artifact count for the season was 232 and included a miniature clay bowl, three large metates, three stone balls, more than two dozen projectile points, a considerable number of worked and unworked sherds, several bone tools, and stone, bone, and shell beads (Harlan 1953).[10]

By the time the crews were ready to wrap up the season, all felt that they had a wonderful experience, in spite of the weather. There had been time in between digging and other duties to celebrate *"Scouts' Own"* on the theme of "Nature's Inspiration." With Gill's input, the whole group discussed the topic of why some girls, especially in their Senior Scout years, seemed to be ashamed of being Scouts and dropped out. There were comments on the "out of date" uniforms as one contributing factor, and several girls suggested updates on them to the GS Rep (Swift 1953). On the other hand, Gill reported the pride felt at the accomplishments of British Girl Guides and Continental Guides toward their organizations and recounted stories of heroism of Guides in the underground in France and the Low Countries during World War II. Appreciative townspeople often greeted them with cheers and tears whenever they saw them wearing their trefoil pins. Kate Swift reported that the other campers were much moved and vowed to promote scouting when they returned home. A lighter evening discussion involved the girls' reactions to the Kinsey Report on human sexuality, which had just been released (Swift 1953)![11]

When time came to break up camp on August 30, an additional *Scouts' Own* on the topic of friendship was held on a hilltop southeast of the site. Gill (Wethey 1953:6) summed up her experience as an international camper on both the Mobile Camp and Dig experiences with these words:

> Although the Scout/Guide movements in our two lands differ widely in very many respects, I found here, in these Scout projects, strong links which could service to bind in understanding the youth of many nations. The love of

adventure and the search for knowledge; the putting into practice of the qualities of resource and ingenuity, which are inherent in each one of us; and the desire for friendship, bearing fruit in combined work and play between representatives from widely differing parts of a great land—and from still farther countries across the sea. So I would like to finish, firstly, with a most sincere word of thanks to all of you who have made a stranger in a strange land feel so much at home and so much a part of your experiences and adventures; secondly, with an equally sincere invitation to all of you whose search for wider horizons may lead you eastward to the shores of Britain. You will find there, I know, the warmest of welcomes and much also, I believe in the way of culture and beauty to carry with you on your further journeyings.

All girls vowed to publicize the experiences in their hometowns and do their best to recruit new campers for the following year's Mobiles and Dig sessions. They also urged the staff (especially Kate Swift) to convince the national leadership to work harder to publicize the value of them both. Once back in Santa Fe at El Rancho del Cielo, all participated in cleaning the equipment and packing it up for the next season. The usual teary partings with promised reunions and pledges to write soon and often followed, before all went their separate ways.

Dutton's (1953a) report for this year is her most detailed summary of the excavations for the three seasons to date. She provides detail on architecture, especially room dimensions, wall heights, and floor and wall treatments for several sections of the site. She also discusses dating based on pottery types and tree-ring evidence thus far, as well as interesting artifacts recovered from each. It is clear that she is now able to make some broader statements based on the work that the all-women's crews have been doing, contributing to a better understanding about Pueblo Largo and its history.

The 1954 Season

The 1954 Dig saw "the largest crew of Dutton's excavation engineers, 19 Dirty Diggers in all, to delve into the mysteries of Pueblo Largo" (Jeff [Franklin] and Marty [Emory] 1954). Fifteen were campers, plus four staff (Bert, Director; Anita Myers, GS Rep;

Justine Martin, shuttle; Lois Corkery, cook). This year, there were enough seasoned Dig veterans that the four crews were headed by the young women as assistants to Bert, and each had a nickname: "Que's *Kiva* Crew," "Gill's Gems," "Les' Labor Leaders," and "Sandy's Sunburned Strippers." The *kiva* crew finished the large south *kiva*, exposing an unexplained wall gap from floor level up but containing two stone-lined niches in the middle of the vacant space. The horizontal and vertical ventilator shafts were cleared, including the vertical one (with a teaspoon due to the restricted space). Gill's Gems worked in the northeast area (IV) of the site, clearing the largest room thus far encountered. They found "bushels of burned corn" which they sacked and returned to the lab, along with several stone axe heads and what appeared to be a stone fetish. After completing the *kiva*, Que's crew moved to The Point (V) and began work on a large room with *vigas* (roof beams), reporting that ants had already started excavating it for them; thus they proceeded "with aerosol bombs in one hand and pickaxes in the other" (Jeff and Marty 1954). Also on The Point, the Sunburned Strippers worked on a long wall in the southern section, following it—and following it—and finally leaving completion for the next season. The Labor Leaders worked down the hill from The Point, on an exploratory trench in a depression that they learned was likely another *kiva* some 30 feet (9 m) across. Additional work on it would also have to wait until next season.

Camp adventures that season were less about rain than about heat and dust storms, the latter occurring daily at lunchtime and requiring all to sit on the edges of the lab tent to keep it from free flight. Jeff and Marty (1954) wrote: "we would sit, trying to drink our tea before the wind buried us each in her own private sand pile." Lois "Corky" Corkery, the cook, also stepped on the tail of a rattlesnake attempting to escape into the stone fireplace. The girls tore the fireplace apart and converted the snake into two hatbands with nice diamond patterns. Trips to the cattle tank for ablutions alternated again, occasionally interrupted by cowboys coming by "to water their horses." News had spread among the ranch crew that a trip to the tank was well worth the view.

But the season ended too soon as usual and found several hoping that the arroyo would flood so that they wouldn't be able to get out to go home. But it didn't work and all were left with more teary goodbyes. Some were off to college, including

Figure 5.15. Muddy Dirty Diggers, after rain, 1955. Left to right: Evelyn Harvey, Hope Owen, Caroline Gray, Sandra Reimers, Sue Martin, Mary Abbie Higley, Isabel Burns. Photo by Mary Anne Stein. 99BPD.xx, Scrapbook, 1955. Courtesy of MIAC/LAA.

Figure 5.16. Susan Martin peering out of ripped tent after horses ran through camp, 1955. Photograph by Mary Anne Stein. 99BPD.xx, M.A. Stein/S.S. Martin Collection. Courtesy of MIAC/LAA.

graduate school, and others to get married. Their Senior Scout years were coming to a close.

GS Rep Anita Myers (1954) filed a summary report on the Dig that year, suggesting that some changes be made, if possible, including getting larger sleeping tents (pup tents were too small for a permanent camp, and the girls were not resting properly after a hard day's work); that the *patrol system* was not of much use (other than planning *Scouts' Own*) given the organization of Dig crews; plus requesting acquisition of more equipment for the lab and kitchen. The Diggers also suggested that GS Councils be better informed as to what the Dig camps were all about (hard work); that additional changes of work clothes be allowed (more than two) and that the girls bring sturdy work shoes or boots; that there was no need for GS issue crew hats: cowboy or other suitable hats and jeans and Lee jackets with the official DDD patch should be the approved wear (Chapter 4). Most felt that the work was harder than they had anticipated, but that they learned how to work, and all felt that they liked the feeling of being on their own and wanted to return.

The 1955 Season

This year saw the crew size at 19 campers plus staff (Bert, director; Marie Nourse, cook; Justine "Tiney" Martin, GS Rep; and Dorothy Lourie, shuttler. Vorsila Bohrer, who had finished her MS at the University of Michigan, was there part of the time as well. She had just returned from leading Mobile Camp III (Chapter 4).[12] The Mobile Camp program was becoming a little too successful by now, and beginning to tax the staff (Chapter 6). But again, with several veterans returning to the Dig, more concentrated excavations could be carried out. The session ran from August 20 to September 3. Susan Martin (1956) and Mary Anne (1955–56, 1956, 2008) provide accounts of the Dig that season.

Martin's (1956:1) tale starts with the summation day back at Rancho del Cielo on September 3, when Bert asked:

> "Just what have we accomplished?" Martin adds: After a moment of silence, some brave soul spoke. "The first day we were initiated properly by pushing everybody through the mud to get in" [Figure 5.15]. Then bedlam broke loose. Everyone started jabbering excitedly.

Remember the horses invading camp? [Figure 5.16]. Tiney vs. the rattle-snake? Boiling gas? Sitting under the wall during the rain?

Someone suddenly collapsed in a fit of laughter, finally gasping, "wasn't it funny when everybody spent half the day running to the john??" "Yep," screamed another voice, "but how about the daily line to Dr. Tiney's green monster [First Aid tent], and that Kneeling Camel [nickname for visitor Yoffa's tent], and do you remember Casey [Kline] and her sewers?

Sandy [Reimers], standing calmly amidst all the furor, kept announcing in her best speech voice, "But I found a wall! Imagine it! I found a wall—even if it doesn't go anywhere!" Squeaky [Yeagley] attempted to squelch this by remarking, "But who else found a projectile point every day?" "You don't have a seven-sided room," yelled Casey. "No, but you don't have walls under your floor,

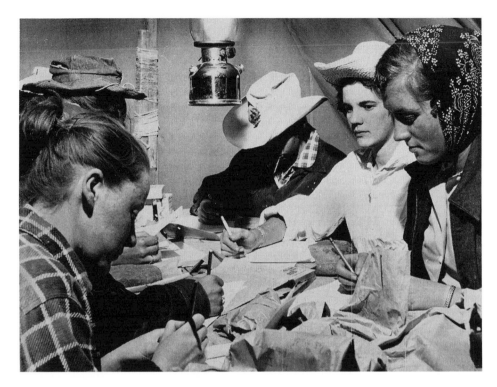

Figure 5.18. Cataloging by lantern light, 1955 or 1956. Photograph by Mary Anne Stein. 99BPD.xx, M.A. Stein/S.S. Martin Collection. Courtesy of MIAC/LAA.

either," answered Que [Morris]. Taking advantage of this first available opportunity, Bert announced firmly, "Now see here, let's get this straight."

Martin (1956:2) then continues with the more basic summary of what was accomplished that season, noting first that the area of most concern that season for excavation was the problematic Room Block V (The Point). One crew followed out V's elusive plaza walls, "finding such puzzles as a young architect's training room." Work also continued on several rooms, including ones where roofing timbers or *vigas* were located. These fragile beams required processing before they could be successfully removed for eventual shipment to the University of Arizona Laboratory of Tree-Ring Research for dating analysis (Figure 5.17). Walls appeared under one of the floors, but as usual near the last day so there was not time to follow them out. More human remains were also encountered and carefully removed (Martin 1956).

The southern section of The Point kept additional workers busy as they traced out converging walls. It seemed like endless catalog sheets were filled out that year for bone awls, manos and mano fragments, worked sherds, projectile points, etc., and sherd washing often proceeded "by Coleman lantern (or the silvery moon) and all hands came to enjoy the singing and ended up joining the scrubbing" (Martin 1956:2; Figure 5.18). Special treats on the occasional days off this year featured trips to Pueblo Colorado, just south of Pueblo Largo, and Pueblo San Cristóbal to the north. In other years, Dig crews had also hiked to some of the spectacular petroglyph sites in the Basin as a special treat—so it was not always all work and no play—but work came first.

In her diary and letters home to her parents, Mary Anne Stein gives a full account of camp activities, these backed up by her scrapbook and a valuable series of photographs (Stein 1955–56, 1956, 2008a). From Stein we get a good account of the kinds of meals cooked at the camp. With the increase in crew size, sack lunches were by now a thing of the past. Lunch break involved a full fare. Breakfasts included a choice of pancakes, oatmeal, or French toast, depending on the mornings, plus bacon and often eggs, along with coffee and cocoa. Lunch might be Spam salad, chile with sopaipillas, soup with crackers, plus a variety of desserts, including chocolate pudding. Dinner could feature chicken, steak, pork chops or Spam, with gravy, potatoes, or rice; a vegetable such as beets or peas; salad; and then dessert—often cake baked in a Dutch oven. All food was pronounced "good to very good" by the campers and staff. Juice breaks were still held mornings and afternoons, and the beverage of choice for lunch, and tea for dinner.

Stein (1955–56; 1956) reported some weather incidents, including rain with beautiful rainbows, big wind storms, and hail. Tents required mending after such events—hence the reference to "Sandy's sewers." All soon learned to keep their backs covered against sunburn—necessitating visits to Tiney's medical tent (the "Green Monster"). Another rattlesnake was dispatched, properly cured, and turned into a hatband that Stein still has (Epilogue). Bathing and clothes-washing events at the cattle tank in the valley took place, and visits by cowboys "made the wash trips nice." The crews and *patrols* (mostly still in charge of *Scouts' Own*) had meetings to

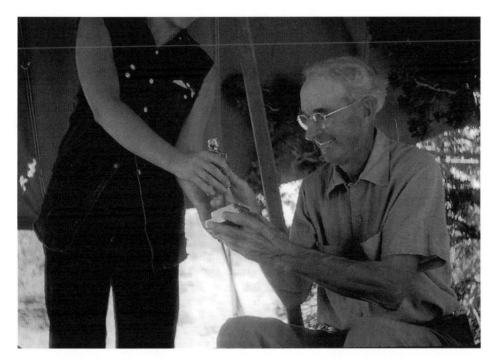

Figure 5.19. Gwynyth Morris presents GSUSA "Thanks" statue to Orrin "Daddy D" Dutton at Pueblo Largo, 1955. Photograph by Mary Anne Stein. 99BPD.xx, M.A. Stein/S.S. Martin Collection. Courtesy of MIAC/LAA.

discuss progress, and lab duties continued along with talking, laughing, and singing until all were exhausted and ready to turn in each night.

Another important event that occurred that year was a dinner and presentation honoring Bert's father, Orrin "Daddy D" Dutton, for all his work through the years on behalf of Mobile and Dig Camp Scouts. A special dinner and presentation of a statuette occurred, much to Daddy D's pleasure (Figure 5.19). He had enjoyed every minute of his association with the girls each year, and he always looked forward to their time on the *ranchito* and helping out with whatever needed to be done. Bert was more than grateful that he enjoyed it all, and that the girls chose to honor him in this way.

The 1956 Season

By 1956, Bert was devoting a good third of her time on the Girl Scout effort and was feeling the burden. She recommended to the Girl Scout officials that the 1956 Dig

Figure 5.20. Bert Dutton giving orientation to dig crew, 1955 or 1956. Photograph by Mary Anne Stein. 99BPD.xx, Scrapbook, 1955-56. Courtesy of MIAC/LAA.

session at Pueblo Largo be the last, and that she be relieved of most of the duties for the Mobile Camps as well (see Chapter 7). However, she refused to turn Pueblo Largo over to someone else to supervise, as it was the MNM and not the Girl Scouts who had primary contractual responsibility. She thus was determined to have just one more Dig session as part of the 1956 season.

The Dig (Camp III) that year (August 18–September 1) included 20 campers, a combination of veterans and new girls from that year's and past Mobiles (Figure 5.20). In addition to Bert, staff included Jan Fleming as GS Rep, and Patricia and Paul Beltz as cooks and shuttler (Paul). The only specific accounts of site work and progress for that season are contained in Stein's scrapbook (99BPD.xx), and in the notebooks turned in by several of the girls at the end of the season (primarily 95PLE.026–029).

Figure 5.21.
Excavated Room
Block V-b on
The Point, 1956.
Photograph by
Mary Anne Stein.
99BPD.xx, M.A.
Stein Collection.
Courtesy of MIAC/
LAA.

Based on these sources, work seems to have been concentrated again on The Point (V, sections A and B), where several rooms were excavated to their floors, thus adding more to the list of completed rooms and other features for the combined seasons (Figure 5.21). Although the exact count is not clear, Bert had reported the previous year that in the 10 weeks thus far they had cleared 18 of Nelson's suggested 489 rooms and fully excavated the large southern ceremonial chamber plus two other smaller ones as well as a "tower" (see 95PLE.025).[13]

Crews had trenched and screened (Figure 5.22) in several places, including central Refuse Mounds (A, B). Roof beams collected and analyzed by the University of Arizona Laboratory of Tree-Ring Research showed overall dates from 1202 to 1442, with most clustered in the late 1200s to the mid-1400s. There was no evidence of either immediate pre- or post-Spanish *entrada* occupations, suggesting that the people had left this area and moved to other sites before Spanish settlement of the region in the late 1500s. The ceramics analyzed up until that time were classified as

Figure 5.22. "Hear
no evil, see no
evil, speak no
evil": Donna Lee
Myers screening
at edge of mesa,
Pueblo Largo, 1955.
Photograph by
Mary Anne Stein.
99BP.xx, M.A.
Stein Collection.
Courtesy of MIAC/
LAA.

Galisteo Black-on-white, Rio Grande Red, and Rio Grande Yellow glaze wares, and corrugated utility ware. Dutton was suggesting a principal time span for site occupation of from 1275 to 1475, although she had some evidence for an earlier component, especially on The Point. (These dates span what is referred to in regional chronologies today as the mid Coalition Period [1150–1325] and the early part of the Classic Period [1325–1550]). She reiterated her conclusion that "for approximately two centuries there is a record of slow change at Pueblo Largo, reflecting a certain degree of social stability but no great influences from outside sources" (Dutton 1953a:351;

Figure 5.23. Claire "Squeaky" Yeagley relaxing, 1955. Photograph by Mary Anne Stein. 99BPD.xx, M.A. Stein Collection. Courtesy of MIAC/LAA.

1955a:40). In other words, she saw no clear evidence of a Mesa Verde migration or occupation in this particular site. She would return to this question—the one she had posed in the beginning of the excavation camps—in the following years (Chapter 8; Figure 5.23).

The big event for the 1956 camp and campers was the bridal shower thrown for Claire "Squeaky" Yeagley and her intended, Dan Young. Stein's scrapbook describes the event in "The Daily Digger: News of Society" for August 30, 1956 as a grand affair, held in the rain but under a tarp with all campers in attendance attired stylishly in raincoats:

The bride was devastating in her original gown by D.D.D., her eight gored underskirt was of Kotex with a billowy Modess flounce. She wore a modest bodice of pleated Modess. The veil and train was a *Kiva* gauze original. Make-up by Amy

Figure 5.24. Excavation crew at El Rancho del Cielo, 1956. 99BPD. xx. Courtesy of MIAC/LAA.

of Largo. The groom—Mr. Dan Young of Austin—was dashing in his suit of Santa Fe Black-on-white. Crewcut by Dennis of Texas....

[Those attending were] led by Dr. Bert, head of the Galisteo Health Resort for exhausted Girl Scouts. Special guests included Mr. and Mrs. Paul Beltz, noted chefs of New York, and Miss Jan Fleming. The Guests were served from an antique Largo table. The cake was a Paul-Pat original. Everyone wishes the bride and groom the best of happiness and success.

Camp closed that year with a general dismantling of most of the permanent features.[14] All in attendance were saddened that this was the last Dig, which had been rumored the previous season, but they had hoped would not become a reality. The campfire back at El Rancho del Cielo was a sad event, although the crew picture showed all with smiles, including Bert, and the cow skull and sign that marked the entrance to the Pueblo Largo field camp well in evidence (Figure 5.24).

Although the Senior Girl Scout excavation camps at Pueblo Largo officially ended in 1956, Bert intended to return fairly quickly to the site, continue the work, and then proceed to the analysis and reporting phases of the project. Producing reports of findings and interpretations is considered the appropriate outcome for excavations at any site, and Pueblo Largo was no exception. Bert's plan was to offer some of her "best girls" the opportunity to continue the work with her on those reports. But other matters intervened, and this plan was not put into action (Chapter 8). She would return to the archaeology of the Galisteo Basin within a few years, as well as to her interest in the migration issue, while continuing to make some progress on the Largo reports. But ultimately, it would be others who picked up where she left off, and analyzed pottery collections and some additional aspects of the Pueblo Largo excavations (Wilson et al. 2015; Chapter 8; Epilogue).

6

Transitions and Changes

1952–1958

Digger Farewell Song
There's a long, long road a winding
All over mountains and plains.
And the fun we've shared together
Will never be again.
Digging, working, and hiking
Singing the same old refrains.
And without us all together
Things will never be the same.

−C. Kline, E. Galligan, C. Hammer, K. Bahlinger, 1955

The early 1950s brought two important changes to the Senior Girl Scout Archaeological Mobile Camp program. First, there was the expansion of the program to include the excavation camp (1951–1956) and a third on-the-trail camp (1955). Second, there was an administrative change: switching oversight of the program from Region IX's Dallas office to the Camping Division of the GSUSA in New York City. The first change meant that Bert would be devoting yet more time to the program—eight or more weeks of field time each summer, and additional time to make all of the arrangements for each trip plus promotion during the rest of the year. The second change, although of minor impact when it first went into effect in 1951, became more important during the 1952 and 1953 seasons. It meant in the long run that Bert and the MNM would have less direct control over some aspects of the program but more control over others. Both changes coincided with additional demands placed on Bert's time due to her employment, her wish to continue her research interests in Mesoamerican archaeology, and the need to complete her doctoral dissertation.

Dutton's Non-Scout Activities: 1950s

As noted in Chapter 2, in 1938, Edgar Lee Hewett had appointed Bert as Curator of Ethnology at the MNM, tasking her with developing a Hall of Ethnology to parallel the exhibits devoted to New Mexico's archaeology and history.[1] Bert took on the new Hall, basically from the ground up, converting the former Santa Fe Armory building adjacent to the Palace of the Governors to this new purpose. The many tasks involved took roughly three years, and the Hall of Ethnology opened on July 1, 1941 (Bohrer 1979:10).

But her responsibilities to the Hall and to New Mexico ethnology did not end with the Hall's opening. Bert's contributions to the newsletter *Teocentli*, as well to *El Palacio* through 1958 (and after), chronicle her busy life at the museum. Temporary exhibits in the Hall needed to be changed on a regular basis, and she not only developed most of them, but installed them herself. She also worked on revisions of permanent exhibits periodically and continued to curate the ethnographic collections, including acquiring, cataloging, and photographing new accessions and overseeing collections care (Figure 6.1).

There were other duties connected with her employment, including preparing yearly budgets for her department and helping to lobby these plus other needs through the New Mexico legislature; giving tours of the Hall to visiting dignitaries and the interested public; answering inquiries from visitors and others (orally and by mail); and helping with the expansion and programing at the branch museums

Figure 6.1. Bertha Dutton checking Hopi baskets, Laboratory of Anthropology, 1953. Courtesy of Palace of the Governors Photo Archives (NMHM/DCA) Neg. No: 040970.

throughout the state. In addition, as any understaffed museum employee soon learns, there are a hundred and one other small tasks to be done, like running the desk during lunch, checking restroom sanitation, helping visitors find what they are seeking, and more. All of these can quickly take up much of a day. Bert was a popular lecturer, and frequently was called upon to speak at the branch museums and in other venues (e.g., civic organizations, PTA, and others), often driving for a day or more to complete each of these tasks. Given that she did not have a family, she became the Museum's "go-to person" to fulfill most of the presentation requests. She and Marjorie Lambert sometimes traveled together to venues, although Bert frequently drove alone. She often stayed with friends (old and new) to save on expenses and paired travels throughout the state with viewing archaeological and historic sites or attending Native activities—all designed to increase her knowledge of Southwest anthropology—a requirement of her job but also of great interest to her (Bohrer 1979:11).

Bert had writing duties as part of her position at the Museum of New Mexico. During the 1950s she routinely published three to five articles a year in the museum's journal *El Palacio*. Some involved the Girl Scout Mobile Camps, but many more documented activities at the museum or other topics of interest to the museum's membership (who received the journal). The journal was also available for purchase by nonmembers, and that helped to stimulate more people to join and/or be better informed. Articles covered new acquisitions, new exhibits or events scheduled or presented, or Bert's own research and other interests (e.g., Dutton 1951c, 1955b, 1958). She published in other places as well and updated several popular publications for the New Mexico Association on Indian Affairs (later the Southwestern Association of Indian Affairs) on New Mexico and Southwest Indian tribes and their cultures (e.g., Dutton, ed. 1948; Dutton 1960a). And she consistently judged arts and crafts competitions such as the Santa Fe's Fiesta Market (later Indian Market), the Gallup Inter-tribal Ceremonial, New Mexico State Fair, Arizona State Fair, and others (Bohrer 1979:13). For eight months in the fall of 1952 through early summer of 1953 she taught a course to adult learners twice a month in Taos (70 not-so-easy miles from Santa Fe) on Southwest archaeology (Dutton to Rushmer Dec 20, 1952, Dutton 1952c, 1953b).

Bert's duties for the School of American Research were less well-defined, but they included at a minimum attending to Board of Managers' interests and concerns—some of those individuals also serving on the MNM Board and being personal friends—as well as other assignments by the MNM-SAR Director. Throughout the 1950s, the Honorable Boas Long was director (see below). As Associate in Archaeology at SAR, she made additional presentations and fielded questions, especially concerning Mesoamerican and South American prehistory, her primary research specialty. And she answered other queries related to New Mexico's Native peoples and archaeology, as did Marjorie Tichy (Lambert), who also held dual positions at MNM and at SAR.

Bert's interests in Mesoamerican archaeology ran parallel to those in Southwest archaeology and ethnology, with her field studies in Mesoamerica increasing in the 1950s. In 1950, she was awarded a grant from SAR to continue her Toltec research in Mexico and spent five weeks in Mexico City, Tula Hidalgo, Guatemala, and Veracruz. She wrote up these and other materials throughout the following year—often after her day at the museum was finished. She wrote in her yearly post in *Teocentli* in December, 1950: "I've been spending about 15 hours per day, working on my Mexican report, chasing the Toltecs back and forth throughout Mexico and Central America" (Dutton 1950c). She completed this work and submitted it to her committee at Columbia as her doctoral dissertation in June of 1952. She had developed and printed all of the photographic illustrations in her darkroom at El Rancho del Cielo (Dutton 1952b). Her committee granted her the PhD that fall.

Then Bert was given a six-month sabbatical from the MNM in 1953–1954 to continue her Mesoamerican research. From November through May, with a grant from the American Association of University Women (AAUW), she and Gillian Wethey, Mobile Camp program veteran now living in Santa Fe, drove from Santa Fe through Mexico to Guatemala and back (Dutton 1954a). They spent a month at the National Museum in Guatemala, then conducted an archaeological survey and some site testing in the vicinity of Tapachula, bringing home pottery for further study. She squeezed in work on these and publications during weekends (Dutton 1956, 1958).

In addition to these and other activities, Bert was an active participant in the social and cultural life of Santa Fe, and in various professional organizations—all of

Figure 6.2. Marjorie Lambert, Bertha Dutton, and Florence Hawley Ellis, Pecos Conference, 1954, Gila Pueblo Archaeological Foundation, Globe, AZ. Courtesy of Palace of the Governors Photo Archives (NMHM/DCA) Neg. No: 013143.

which required time from her already busy schedule (Bohrer 1979). She also served as Chair of the Social Sciences Section of the Southwestern Division of the American Association for the Advancement of Science, the premier national scientific organization, from 1951 through 1953. This position obligated her to attend its regional and national meetings, along with other related professional conferences, including the annual gatherings of the Society for American Archaeology, Pecos Conference, the Mesa Redonda Conference, and others (Figure 6.2).

In 1950, Bert's father Orrin Dutton, whom many of the Girl Scouts loved and referred to as "Daddy D," came to live with her permanently in a small house at Rancho del Cielo.[2] Daddy D was an important part of Bert's life, and he helped her with many tasks around the place. He was also there while she was away on GS Mobile Camps in the summers, as well as during her other absences. In addition, Bert's home was the center of her active social life, and the place where she entertained many visiting anthropologists, museum people, and scores of other visitors, including former Dirty Diggers, and sometimes their families and friends.

Her welcome mat was nearly always out, and friends often stayed, including while she was traveling. She had become, and would remain, a permanent fixture in the Santa Fe scene. As Vorsila Bohrer—Digger, colleague, and close friend—remarked in her summary biography of Bert's career through 1978, Bert's "concerns bonded with those of Santa Fe; she could scarcely walk a block from her office without being extended a greeting" (Bohrer 1979:14).

Administrative Changes to the GSUSA Oversight

We found no clear documentation as to the motive(s) for changing the administrative oversight of the archaeological program from the office of Region IX to GSUSA national headquarters (henceforth National) in 1951.[3] The reason why it occurred may have been as simple as that the program had grown too large or complicated, and was beginning to swamp the administrative capabilities of the small regional staff. However, there are hints that the switch may have been related at least in part to changes in some of National's policies and particularly the continuing awareness that something more needed to be done to increase retention of Senior and young adult scouts in the scouting movement (Chapter 2).[4] Perhaps continuing to foster (on a national level) good, solid, and popular camping programs, such as the Southwest Archaeological Mobile Camps, could be part of a retention solution. The program had always been partly National's anyway, in that attendance was not limited to girls from Region IX and National was involved in various aspects of decision-making. But whatever the motive(s) may have been, the change added some new complications to everyone's lives—not all for the better. It certainly meant more administrative time and paperwork for all—but then both of these were likely on the rise anyway due to the steady growth of bureaucracy for all of the sponsors.

GSUSA Camping Programs: Policy Changes

Although GSUSA National was involved in the Archaeological Mobile Camps to some degree from the beginning, almost all the real work had been handled by the Region IX office in Dallas (see Chapter 3). But as the program's visibility and popularity grew, so did National's interest. It was getting a lot of press as girls promoted it in their local communities and spoke about it at regional and other gatherings. But there is also evidence that during the late 1940s and early 1950s National's policies involving camping, especially for Senior Scouts, were changing from a longstanding emphasis on local and regional initiatives to a companion program promoting more national and international opportunities.[5]

During most of its early history, the GSUSA's camping emphasis (a significant focus of its overall program) had been designed to help local Girl Scout Councils build and maintain camps for their own troops. These were primarily permanent summer camps and day camps, to promote what was called "troop camping." Some troops, especially at the Intermediate and Senior levels, also traveled outside their local areas to broaden their learning experiences on horseback, canoe, bicycle, and car trips to different places, and on major hikes, such as along the Appalachian Trail. These were referred to as "trip camps," but again they were commonly troop-based. A major function of GSUSA's Camping Division was to publish and distribute manuals and other literature on developing these troop experiences, as well as to provide consultants and advisors to help with planning (especially for permanent camps). Regional offices also helped with the organization and dissemination of information on these local activities, and developed a few of their own (as had Region IX with the archaeological program), but again, most of the actual activity took place locally.

As was noted in Chapter 2, interest and enthusiasm of experienced and older Senior Girl Scouts often waned after they learned the required skills for their ranks and went through several of these local experiences. Local councils had difficulty keeping young women engaged and involved in their teen years, and as they began to "age out" of Scouting at age 18. There were some additional opportunities, or "Wider Opps" as they were called, especially for Senior Girl Scouts, and these were available to individuals outside of the troop structure. Not all were camping oriented, and competition to attend one or more of these was high. Some local councils and troop leaders were also better than others at advertising these different programs. And there were some special troops, such as Mariner Scouts, that emphasized additional outdoor activities. But again, some councils and regions were better at developing and promoting these alternatives than were others. The Southwest

Archaeological Mobile Camps had been Region IX's shining example of a unique extra-troop opportunity for Senior Girl Scouts, although even from the beginning, it drew some participants from other regions—largely ones who just happened to hear about it, or whose mothers had deeper connections with scouting.

Apparently recognizing these problems in 1949–1950,[6] GSUSA's Camping Committee came up with recommendations to strengthen the camping program for girls at all levels, but especially to "provide opportunities for adventurous camping for girls and to stimulate particularly more camping of better quality for Seniors" (GSUSA 1953a:2). As an experiment in 1951, the GSUSA held its first *All States Encampment* in Cody, Wyoming. *All States* was not troop-oriented, but rather for individual advanced Intermediate and Senior Scouts to focus on furthering their camping skills and experience, as well as provide them an opportunity to develop other life skills. The first two *All States* (1951, 1952) were quite successful, so that in 1953, *All States* was referred to as "our best example of a nationally operated camp" meeting this "earlier recommendation" (GSUSA 1953a:2). It thus seems possible that given the growing popularity of the Senior Girl Scout Archaeological Mobile Camp program, the administrative change from Regional to National control was linked to this initiative, as the Mobile Camp program was placed under the Camping Division in 1951, along with *All States*. At the time, the other major responsibility of the Division was oversight for the GSUSA's only permanent camping facility, Rockwood, near Potomac, Maryland.[7]

Growing Pains: The Administrative Transition 1951–1953

In 1951, signaling the change in administration to GSUSA headquarters, the GS Rep on Camp I of the Mobile Camps was Gretchen Yoffa of the Camping Division in New York City. She also attended the first excavation camp, held that same year. Yoffa was there primarily to observe the operations of the program, but doubtless encouraged to come up with recommendations for alterations if she felt that they were needed.[8] National headquarters had its goals—scouting goals—as well as some different rules and procedures to consider in continuing sponsorship of the program. Although Bert and Eunice Prien had some rough spots to overcome in developing the camps from 1947 through 1951, their proximity to each other made for easier face-to-face contact, and they had been able to work through issues to the satisfaction of all parties involved. But now there potentially would be new scouting goals and procedures to consider, as well as greater communication distances. And given that the Mobile Camp program was unique, as was the excavation camp, National may not have fully understood what Bert was trying to achieve, let alone how things actually worked "Out West." Bert's purposes were more intellectually oriented, through a model in directed learning with which she was already familiar. The Dig camps were work-oriented—quantities of dirt had to be moved using proper excavation techniques, artifacts collected and cataloged, and notes taken—like any other archaeological field session. Scouting's purposes were slightly different: emphasizing the personal development of young women through shared group experiences, but also following long-held guidelines which "allow for and expect initiative, versatility, responsibility, creativeness, concern for others, all of the characteristics that we hope to help young citizens develop" (Yoffa to Long, July 30, 1955; 89LA5.064). In most ways, the two orientations were compatible and complementary, but the exact means of achieving the end products were not quite the same. Yoffa's orientation was toward seeing Scouting's goals as rules rather than recommendations. Especially when it came to the Digs, this was not always practical, as there was already a long tradition within archaeology as to how excavations should be conducted. Their goals were more scientific: obtain well-controlled data about the site and organize so as to obtain those data as efficiently as possible. It was not the same as educational touring, even with the limited lecturing it involved. And there was not a lot of room for showing "initiative, versatility, and creativeness"—although these worked within limits. The clarifications and changes that followed in succeeding years were likely more irritating than confrontational, although Bert would stand firm on certain points. She had long demonstrated her independence. And besides, she had developed the program and was very proud of what it had achieved thus far for the young women, especially in opening their eyes to alternative educational and career paths.

Initially Yoffa seemed pleased with what she saw and experienced on the 1951 trips (Camp I Mobile, Camp III, Dig) and was quite convinced of the program's benefit for Senior Scouts. The following appeared in the *Monthly Report* of the Camping Division that fall: "Miss Yoffa and her stories of artifacts, scientific expedition in the *Kivas* and housing units of the thirteenth century Indians had us jealous of the opportunities Senior Girl Scouts today have" (GSUSA 1951). But in spite of her over-all enthusiasm, some minor clashes apparently had occurred on Yoffa's first summer in the Southwest. They might have had more to do with the excavation camp than the Mobiles, but this is not certain. Some were expressed by Dutton's veteran Dirty Diggers who sensed that change was in the wind when they penned this tongue-in-cheek song at the 1951 Dig camp, sung to "Down in the Valley" (99BPD. xx, Scrapbook, 1951):

> Down in the valley, to Pueblo Largo
> Came Gretchen Yoffa—
> it was quite a show.
> She brought "minimum standards,"
> and rules galore.
> "Now let's all wear Scout socks,"
> so our feet won't get sore.
> And then there were crew hats,
> for the photos to log.
> "Have you written home lately?"
> And "wear your Scout togs."
> But Bert to the rescue,
> we all gave a cheer.
> "To hell with the rules,
> things are different out here."

Although their ditty voiced only minor complaints, before long additional issues began to surface as Yoffa and National became more involved in oversight responsibilities. Some of these included negotiating contracts (there had not been any before), outlining job specifications, discussing liability clauses, and other matters. Given the times, these may well have surfaced anyway, as both the GSUSA and the MNM were expanding and becoming increasingly watchful of all matters of concern (see below). But in the interim, until all of this could be worked out, Region IX would continue to handle the 1952 brochure and to pre-process the camper applications before sending them to Bert for a final decision. It was likely too late for National to fully take over the program for that season. But starting early in 1952, Yoffa busied herself preparing materials advertising the archaeological camps for various National GSUSA publications, like the *Girl Scout Leader, The American Girl,* and *Camp Clues.* She also suggested that information on archaeology (perhaps badge requirements?) be included in the planned revision to the new *Girl Scout Handbook,* implying that she felt that the camps and subject matter were valuable enough to make them a permanent part of the Girl Scout program (GSUSA 1952a). She was happy to report that by June, 1952, Mobile Camps I and II were filled with long waiting lists, although it appeared that the Dig Camp would be "very small this year," given that there was not a backlog of experienced campers available or applying (GSUSA 1952b). (Applicants for Dig Camp [Camp III] had to have been on at least one Mobile Camp, and had to be personally approved by Bert.) Ultimately, the 1952 Dig had 11 campers and three extra staff, including Yoffa as GS Rep. As noted in Chapter 5, its numbers increased from 11 in 1952 to 20 by 1956.

Once the archaeological program became part of the GSUSA's Camping Division, it began to assume a larger role in the "Wider Opps" program available to individual Senior Girl Scouts through the National organization. Extra publicity generated enthusiasm. In addition to Yoffa's efforts, the May issue of *The American Girl,* a monthly magazine especially designed by the GSUSA to capture the attention of maturing young women, carried an article by Martha Harlan, a veteran Mobile camper, titled *The Dig* (Chapter 5). In it, Harlan chronicled the first excavation camp at Pueblo Largo, complete with her excitement at the finds, the weather (they were plagued by rain), the scenery, the comradery, the chance to contribute to scientific research, and the fun of being on their own. She stated in this very well-written piece that although most girls her age were of course thinking about summer jobs, saving money for college, and "other matters" (boys?), that they should not miss the opportunity to go on the archaeological Mobile Camps or the Dig—the most fun and best bargain around (Harlan 1952:10). Her article was also distributed separately to GS Councils as an offprint. Two other articles by New Mexico photographer Paul Theil appeared, one in a national Boy Scout publication and the other local.

Archaeological Trip Camps

1952

July 5-19 — July 26-August 9
August 18-September 1

GIRL SCOUT NATIONAL BRANCH OFFICE
208 ARGYLE BUILDING, 3721 HALL,
Dallas 4, Texas

Start El Rancho del Cielo, Santa Fe and
Embark the second morning through
Navajo country on an
Impressive and indescribable
Odyssey, to discover
Remote ruins and relics, the

Gateway to past and present cultures,
Inspiring and instructive,
Reaching rare resources and
Led by an expert, Dr. Bertha Dutton, with

Specialists along the way, experienced staff, and
Comrades from many states, to live
Out of doors and
Use all your camping skills—
Telescoping a lifetime of adventure, under the
Sponsorship of THE MUSEUM OF NEW MEXICO
and GIRL SCOUTS OF THE U. S. A., Region IX.

Photo by Evelyn Stobie, St. Louis, Mo.

His photographs portrayed the girls digging, and his text focused on how much they were enjoying the experience (Theil 1953a; 1953b).

In 1952, Camp III (Dig) had its first international participant, Girl Guide Gillian Wethey from England (Chapter 4). Gill was in the USA on an exchange program, sponsored by the Juliette Low World Friendship Fund and arranged through Girl Guides and GSUSA. Bert lobbied National to have Wethey come to Santa Fe and the Pueblo Largo Dig as part of her U.S. experience, and she later attended mobile camps in 1953 and 1954, ultimately acting as GS Rep (Chapter 5). Wethey wrote an article for *Arizona Highways* magazine on the 1954 Mobile Camp (I) and the Pueblo Largo excavation camp, complete with photographs by Laura Gilpin, noted Southwest photographer (Wethey 1955; see Chapter 4). Like Harlan's and Theil's articles, Wethey's article broadened the popular coverage and appeal of the program as did several newspaper accounts that appeared locally and across the country. However, the latter focused on interviews with local girls who were going or had gone on the Southwest camps and were not written under the auspices of GSUSA—although girls were always encouraged to share their experiences widely if and when they went on "Wider Opps."

In 1952 the brochure advertising the archaeological program became much more attractive, likely due to National's efforts. No longer a multipage, typed, mimeographed booklet, it was now a professionally designed and

Figure 6.3. Pamphlet advertising Archaeological Mobile Camps, produced by GSUSA, 1952. MIAC/LAA.

printed triple-fold pamphlet complete with photographs (Figure 6.3).[9] This format and content remained standard for the remainder of the program, substituting only the new camp dates and itinerary each year, along with new quotes from camp veterans. Beginning with the 1953 sessions, all applications were directed to GSUSA's New York office for processing and initial approval. Yoffa reported to the Camping Division that for 1953: "Announcement of plans and qualifications for girls attending National Camping events were prepared and sent <u>for the first time</u>. The same information applied for archaeological trips, archaeological dig, and All States" (emphasis added; GSUSA 1953b). These brochures (at least 3,000 by 1955) were widely circulated to regional offices, councils, GS Associates (women older than 18) and others (Stein 1955–56).[10] All these efforts (plus the continuing local ones) resulted in yet more applications, especially for the mobiles, and longer waiting lists.

As waiting lists became longer, criteria for selection also became stricter. Local Councils remained the first level of certification to make sure that a girl met the standards for Senior Girl Scout rank in outdoor camping skills, knowledge of Scouting principles, rules and standards of conduct, and ability of get along with others. Some local councils required yet more of their Senior Scouts to qualify for "Wider opps." Even by the 1951 season, Nettie Kesseler [Adams] reported that in addition to meeting these criteria, to be endorsed by her Tulsa Council, she had to be an accomplished craftsman, have a "talent" (she was a square dance caller), speak one language other than English, know US and Oklahoma history, and "be able to bring back to Tulsa results of her experiences" (99BPD.xx, Scrapbook, 1951). There are no figures available for the number of applications forwarded by local councils to Region IX (and Bert) for approval, but indications are that increasing popularity of the camps was leading to difficulties that would soon warrant attention.

Formal Agreements and Other Matters, 1953-1955

During the spring of 1952, Yoffa apparently visited Santa Fe and had some conversations with Bert about the division of duties and responsibilities between the MNM, the GSUSA, and Bert's duties as program director. After her time at the 1952 Dig (Yoffa again acted as GS Rep), she told the Camping Division that she was having "some difficulties taking over the archaeological project.... We hope that this is a period of growing pains and realize that some of the difficulty lies in the fact that no agreement has ever been written between the Girl Scouts of the USA and the Museum of New Mexico. Some of the misunderstandings and duplications arise out of this situation" (GSUSA 1952c). Exactly what these difficulties were is not spelled out, although based on later negotiations, ultimate authority, job duties, and liability seem to have been the main points to be clarified.

On October 27, 1952, Mrs. Richard Beckhard, Director of the Camping Division, wrote to the Honorable Boas Long, Director of the MNM, basically congratulating him and the Museum on their role in that summer's successful camp activities. She stated that she had just returned from a field trip to several Regional GSUSA conferences wherein girls who had participated in either the Mobile Camps or the Dig had presented "enthusiastic and professional reports," of which he would have been proud. But she also informed him that beginning in 1953, GSUSA's Camping Division would be taking over full responsibility from the Regional office and that Miss Yoffa would now be in charge. And, she added, "I know that we will continue our fine relationships in the future. We are going to try to get even better representation [more girls from different regions?] and, with the help of Dr. Dutton, encourage girls returning to their own communities to develop similar exploratory projects suitable to their regions" (Beckhard to Long, October 27, 1952; 89LA5.063). This last clause can be read as the beginning of the marginalization of Bert and the MNM in managing the program that would soon happen; or it may merely reflect the GSUSA's attempt to again promote Regional over National development of such programs—which had always been its goal.

Long's response is worth quoting at length, as it portends some of the issues that would now surface and likely reflects Bert's view of the situation and Long's concurrence with that view (Long to Beckhard, November 18, 1952, 89LA5.063):

We, too, derive considerable satisfaction from the success of this very worthwhile project, and sincerely hope that it will continue to be popular and as rewarding as it has in the past. In this connection, we would like to say that the primary credit for the success of these archaeological mobile camps from our end goes to Dr. Dutton whose deep interest in these young women and enthusiasm for and knowledge of our Southwest leads her to expend considerable time, thought, and study in preparation for the three trips scheduled each summer.

Inasmuch as the third camp [still only two Mobile Camps at this time] is an archaeological expedition where membership is restricted to young ladies who have previously participated in one or more of the on-the-trail expeditions, these campers are naturally 'the older girls.' Our continued experience has indicated that it is also the more mature girls who receive the greatest benefits from these camps, and we are therefore particularly interested in serving the Senior Girl Scout and Girl Scout Associate of the same age level as we have been doing to date. As a venture in applied anthropology, we feel that this is a group of young citizens especially meriting our attention.

In reviewing the six years during which we have carried on this cooperative archaeological and scouting program we feel that it has operated very smoothly. We hope that the program will not become encumbered through any changes which might be brought about by moving the administration from the regional to the national offices.

With all best wishes for the continued success of this mutual program and congratulations to you for the wonderful part your organization plays in the growth and development of the young women of America, I remain

Sincerely yours,
Boas Long
Director

Long, who took over the directorship of the MNM in September, 1948, after the death of Sylvanus Griswold Morley, was no stranger to bureaucracy—or diplomacy. New Mexico born, he had been US Ambassador to Ecuador and Guatemala, had served on the boards of the MNM and SAR since 1945, and as vice-chair since 1947. Although not an anthropologist, he was very well respected for his knowledge of history and science, and skills in diplomacy (Lewis and Hagan 2007:65). He was very well liked, especially by the MNM staff (including Bert) and the Santa Fe community.

Bert noted in an earlier letter to veteran Digger Anne Rushmer, that even though he had just been appointed director, he was already "<u>doing</u> many things. He will make just the kind of administrator we need" (Dutton's emphasis; Dutton to Rushmer, Sept. 23, 1948; 99BPD.xx). This proved to be the case, and Bert and he remained on the best of terms as to the archaeological program, the museum, and personally. Long obviously knew from Bert all about conversations with Yoffa that summer and was backing her view of the situation plus his own. After all, Bert was doing this not with GSUSA pay, but released time by the MNM. He also knew that the program had run smoothly up until that time, and that it had had a positive impact on the young women who were in college or college-bound. There really was no need for significant changes at this time.

On November 11, 1952, Long received an additional letter from Eunice Prien, Region IX Director, expressing her appreciation for his and the Museum's full support of the program and to Bert as "the real underlying reason for the great satisfaction of this joint effort" (Prien to Long, Nov. 11, 1952; 89LA5.063). She was graciously bowing out and turning the reins over to the National Camping Division. He responded in kind, and with the hope that the future of the program would be "equally bright, or even brighter" (Long to Prien, Dec. 4, 1952; 98LA5.063). There is no documentation as to Prien's view of the administrative change.

Apparently in November and early December, Bert received communications from Yoffa suggesting that a formal agreement be drawn up between the MNM and the GSUSA, specifically spelling out the various responsibilities of each institution and the program director.[11] Although Yoffa's letters are no longer in the files, Bert responded on December 22 with a five-page letter containing a 24-point agreement delineating the Museum's and the program director's responsibilities, including three pages of detailed comments on actual operations and why certain practices had to continue the way they were. This latter portion of the letter seems to be Bert's response to whatever Yoffa and National were suggesting in terms of matters of authority and responsibility—things that she (or the Museum) were not willing to give up. Bert apparently worked out the wording of these 24 points with the executive secretary of the Museum's board (Albert Ely), and with the full knowledge and backing of Director Long. It basically codifies what she and the Museum had been doing successfully—on a handshake agreement—for the previous six seasons.[12]

In summary, the written agreement commits the Museum to continue to pay Bert's salary as director, give her release time up to eight weeks, and provide her support vehicles for the annual reconnaissance and transportation of campers to and from El Rancho del Cielo and during the Pueblo Largo camp. As director, Bert would continue to conduct the annual reconnaissance and the field trips (with all of the work that entails—some 10 specific points); coordinate with the contracted head of transportation for the Mobiles (Stacy); help recruit and review staff applications (especially cooks, driver-naturalists); work directly with cooks on menus and all food orders; and receive and pass on all applicants for the Dig camp. While on the Mobile Camps, the Director would also: keep watch over all aspects of the program and coordinate all staff activities; drive the lead car and inform other drivers of the route; teach anthropology and related subjects; and provide total mileage and all records to the GS Rep and authorize that person to sign bills. Post-camp duties of the Director would include arranging to store and care for all equipment; send in all financial, health records, and follow-up evaluations to National within 4 weeks; and continue with promotional and preparatory activities throughout the year for the following season.

The key issues for Bert in these negotiations, based on her extended comments on these proposals, were: 1) retaining her authority to review and recommend staff (especially cooks, driver-naturalist) and 2) review and, more importantly, approve/veto all applications for Camp III (Dig) members. With reference to staff she wrote: "As long as I am designated as the director of these camps, I feel that it is essential that I have a part in selecting all of the staff members, for no one knows better than I the desirability of having a compatible staff" (Dutton to Yoffa, Dec. 22, 1952; 89LA5.063). She was particularly anxious to hire local cooks for the Mobiles, as they needed to be good at camp cooking and quick, given travel. She also wanted to make certain that the driver-naturalist knew local species and not just general natural history information. She wanted to have a say on the GS Rep's application, but ceded actual contracting for that person and all staff to the Camping Division. With reference to the Dig crew, she requested that she actually receive all applications, and that she certify their qualifications. The Dig was a work project with definite scientific goals for each season and thus required different skills than the Mobile Camps. Bert seems to have won on both points, as an "Agreement" for 1953 was signed by Director Long (with Bert's assent) in early March, 1953 (Yoffa to Long, February 27, 1953; 89LA5.063). The 1953 camps were now legal, safe, and ready to roll.

Although a copy of the 1953 Agreement was not found in the administrative files of the Lab, there is a copy of the 1954 Agreement, and its wording is likely similar. With reference to staff, the Director (Bert) "shall recommend to the Girl Scouts of the United States of America persons to serve as cooks, driver-naturalists, and other staff members;" and with reference to the Dig camp, it states that "the minimum number of qualified Seniors and young adults...shall be agreed upon by the Museum of New Mexico and the Girl Scouts of the USA, a number adequate enough to accomplish the prescribed program for 1954 Camp III" (Agreement [1954]; 89LA5.063). The 1954 Agreement also states what the GSUSA agreed to provide in exchange: fund pay for an Assistant Director (the GS Rep) for each camp; do the formal contracting for all staff and provide job descriptions (mutually acceptable to the Museum); lease vehicles and a trailer in good condition for the Mobiles; "supply equipment, materials, and services to maintain Girl Scout standards"[13]; develop the operating budget based on camper fees (with MNM approval); and ensure that all camps are "operated in accordance with policies and standards" of the GSUSA and the MNM. The GSUSA would also provide a maximum of 16 and a minimum of 12 girls of suitable age (15 years to young adult) for each Mobile (presumably based on GSUSA's screening).[14] One additional clause was added to the Museum's duties: to provide and ensure that all drinking water for the Mobiles and the Dig Camps is safe. Lastly, there is a proviso clause for notifications of any and all cancellations (Agreement, 1954; 89LA5.063).

The Agreement also restates the purpose and place of the camps in the overall GSUSA plan in its preamble as follows (Agreement 1954; 89LA5.063):

The Girl Scouts of the United States of America wishes to bring together experienced campers to take part in a vocational and adventurous program, and, further, to give girls an opportunity in close association with one another to learn more about each other and the Southwest, which is accomplished through a program of <u>the study of Man and Nature in the Southwest</u>, presented by the Museum of New Mexico [emphasis in original]. Education is emphasized, but adventure and overall social goals are also primary—in keeping with the principles of good Scouting.

New Agreements: More Sessions and Liability

The 1953 and 1954 seasons produced some additional paperwork, likely owing to the new definitions of responsibilities,[15] but otherwise the sessions ran smoothly. National headquarters was taking the lead on several things, including budgets and processing applications (except for Camp III), two big jobs. Although these first two agreements (1953, 1954) clarified these and several other responsibilities for the program, additional issues began to surface in 1954. These were largely due to the program's increasing popularity nationally, as well as, this time, some rethinking about the camps by the MNM Board.

By March 1954, the GSUSA Camping Division began giving figures as to how many applications from candidates for the Southwest Archaeological Camping Program were being received from local councils. In that year they screened 72 applications forwarded from local councils for that season's camps and were able to place 31 for the 32 slots available (Camps I, II [16 each]), leaving only one space and difficulty in choosing among "a number of well qualified applicants. [The result would be] "a large number of girls for whom there will be no room" (GSUSA Archives: Camps and Camping, Camping Division Meeting, March 9, 1954). Some of these girls would receive information about the Senior Girl Scout Faunal Survey camp being led by faculty members of Dartmouth College.[16] Bert would ultimately choose 15 girls for the Dig Camp.

Due to an even heavier demand and the longer waiting list for 1955, Bert initially agreed to run three Mobile Camps that season along with the Pueblo Largo Dig. Stein (1955–56) reported in her diary at the end of Mobile Camp II in 1955, the Scouts were told that after passing the local council hurdle, applications went through preliminary scrutiny at National by a committee of five reviewers. In 1954, the selection

group for the 1955 camps had included Yoffa, Mobile and Dig veterans Caroline Kline
and Kate [Karen] Rieley, former GS Rep Kate Swift, plus a Miss Dunham (perhaps
a GSUSA official). The committee then spent two days going through these carefully, awarding points to each applicant based on clearly stated additional scouting
accomplishments (e.g., Trailblazer status, years as a Scout, years of camping experience, number of club memberships, ability to make friends, writing skills, and an
interest in archaeology). An additional application form was then sent out to girls
and young women who made this cut (previous program campers were automati-
cally accepted). Successful applicants filled out yet another form and were notified
if they were chosen within two months of the start of the season. At that point, they
had to submit any remaining paperwork (such as health certificates, final payments
of fees and health insurance, anything else missing from their file). Stein was told
that applicants needed to be specific about all requirements, including why they
wanted to attend, as by then "as many get turned away as get to come" (Stein 2008b).
The minutes of the GSUSA Camping Division Staff Meetings for September 30, 1954
and March 8, 1955 confirm that out of a total number of 121 candidates for the 1955
camps, 97 scored 55–75 points in the first round, out of which the committee ultimately selected 47 to attend the three planned Mobile Camps that Bert had agreed
to lead. The Camping Division initially felt that since Bert could only do three, that
GSUSA should hire another person to take a fourth trip—if a salary could be found
(GSUSA: Camps and Camping, Sept. 30 1954). As it turned out, Bert could only lead
the first two Mobile Camps and the Dig due to a conflict in her schedule (she was
already committed to head the judges committee at the annual Gallup Inter-Tribal
Ceremonial in August).[17] The salary, to be paid by the GSUSA, would then have
to go to someone to lead the third Mobile trip. This turned out to be veteran Dirty
Digger Vorsila Bohrer, who was well qualified with a BA in Anthropology from the
University of Arizona and an MS in Botany at the University of Michigan. This division of labor would, with the annual reconnaissance, keep Bert generally within
the eight weeks of released time allowed by the Museum, although even without
her direct participation in one of the Mobiles, it would lengthen the season to three
full months. That also would increase the overall time to be devoted to the program
by other Museum employees who helped the effort in various ways, including by

lecturing and with administrative time. But again, the MNM saw the program as part of its educational and outreach activities, and fully backed it and Bert. The Mobile Camps were fast becoming victims of their own success.

At the same time as the program's expansion, the MNM Board of Regents was going through a change in membership after several years of stability, and the new board was in the process of scrutinizing all MNM programs and activities as part of its responsibilities. Curious about the Girl Scout effort, the Board asked that Director Long request of the GSUSA that "an impartial representative of the Museum accompany at least two of the Mobile trips and the excavation" (Long to Yoffa, June 9, 1955; 89LA5.064). Given the lateness of the request, and that the Mobiles were already over-subscribed, with vehicles full and no cancellations in sight, Yoffa wrote back that this could not be arranged. But she did invite a representative to accompany her on her brief August visits (August 5–6, 10–12) to Mobile II (Yoffa to Long, July 20, 1955; 89LA5.064). (Bert had earlier told Long that there would be no problem with a Museum representative visiting or camping with the Dig group.) The person from the Museum to be involved was apparently Mrs. Ward Curtis, wife of a Board member. There is no indication that she ever accompanied Yoffa, however, nor is there record of an oversight report to the Board.

The 1955 sessions seemed to go well and the MNM (and the Board) remained enthusiastic about the program. Both now more formally defined the Girl Scout camps as part of the MNM's public outreach and educational effort. However, the MNM was less enthusiastic about the increased workload involved with three Mobiles plus the Dig.[18] When the time came for the Agreement for 1956 to be developed and signed, Director Long consented to have Bert plan and direct the camps, but by their mutual agreement, there would be a limit of three two-week expeditions—two Mobiles plus the Dig. In addition, given that the Museum's attorney (O. Seth) was now reading the Agreement carefully, Long requested that the

> contract concerning the camps should provide that the Girl Scouts of the U.S.A. are entirely responsible for the personal supervision of the girls, their welfare, safety, and care. The Museum or the School [SAR] will have no responsibility or duty whatsoever in connection with such matters, since their sole function

will be to make available Dr. Dutton as your camp director. We further feel that the Girl Scout organization should hold the Museum and the School harmless from any claims or suits that may arise in connection with the trips (Long to Beckhard, Nov. 1, 1955; 89LA5.065).

Liability was now obviously of concern (it had also surfaced in 1954 for the GSUSA), probably given the perceived dangers of the on-the-trail expeditions (the sometimes hazardous nature of the country covered and the vehicle miles traveled), as well as the inherent difficulties related to a full-scale excavation.[19] Long added in his letter that the Museum still intended to make the camps as "pleasant and instructive as possible...[and that] we do not feel that this, as a practical matter, will substantially alter the operation of the camps, which, thanks to good teamwork, have been so successful" (Long to Beckhard, Nov. 1, 1955; 89LA5.065). But the Museum had reassessed its position, and both it and Bert were asking for some limits.

After a brief period of negotiation that involved the GSUSA turning Long's request over to its Insurance Division, the Agreement between the two entities containing the changes requested by the Museum was forwarded to Director Long for signature (Beckhard to Long, December 12, 1955; 89LA5.065) and was signed and returned (Long to Beckhard, Jan. 31, 1956; 89LA5.065). It limited the camps for 1956 to three—two Mobiles and the Dig—and contained a clause in which the GSUSA agreed to "hold harmless" the Museum of New Mexico, the School of American Research, and the Camp Director from "any claims or suits which may arise from these causes [activities, camping, travel?] as a result of the operation of this event" (Agreement, 1956; 89LA5.065). It contained wording that justified the MNM's participation as "part of its educational and public information program" and reemphasized that the camps would be run by mutually agreed-upon standards—those of the MNM and the GSUSA. It emphasized that the duties of all employees would be covered by the attached job descriptions—some seven pages worth—which were now part of the Agreement (Appendix F). However, a provision added by the GSUSA raised the number of on-the-trail campers per camp to 24 instead of 16. This was to be on a trial basis (Beckhart to Long, December 12, 1955; 89LA5.065).

Apparently sometime during or shortly after the 1955 season, Bert and Gretchen Yoffa conferred as to what solution might work best for accommodating the number of girls still wanting to go on a trip (waiting lists were still long) while keeping the program manageable and within Bert's and the MNM's time constraints. An alternative might be to increase the number of girls attending the 1956 Mobiles. Bert checked with Jack Stacy about the feasibility of transporting more girls per Mobile trip for the 1956 season. Jack replied that he was willing to provide a fourth vehicle, either a new station wagon or a suburban, which would accommodate eight additional girls and their luggage, at the cost of $0.20 per mile. If this were to be done, they would need an additional driver, which would push the total passenger count to 30 people for each of the two camps. They were at that point paying $0.17 per mile for two vehicles, and $0.20 for the third. In early November, Bert wrote all of this in a letter to Ellen Zabotinsky, Yoffa's secretary, adding that she had spoken with other people about the advisability of increasing the size of the Mobiles, and that few favored the change. It would likely "add certain complications and would slow up our program" (Dutton to Zabotinsky, Nov. 1, 1955; 89LA5.065). However, she reluctantly agreed to the increase, on a trial basis only; she would attempt to make it work if the Girl Scout organization wanted to attempt it. They did, and the wheels were then set in motion as per the 1956 agreement between GSUSA and the MNM. But it could be a risk, and as it turned out, a danger to the entire program.

7

Bert's Final Season
and the Demise of the Program

For All We Know

For all we know, we may never meet again
We'll still be friends, makes no difference where or when
We won't say farewell until the last minute
We'll hold out our hands and hearts will be in it
When memories fail, this will only be a dream
We will still be friends, wherever we will be
So sing out tonight, as tomorrow will soon unfold
Fond memories for you and me, for all we know

—Camp III, 1956

The 1956 season would be Bert's tenth year as director of the Archaeological Mobile Camp Program in the Southwest. She had created the program and loved it and the girls and young women she had met, and it had been a great success in so many ways. But it was beginning to take its toll on her, and especially on her time. Perhaps what tipped the balance was feeling responsible for four camps in 1955, which basically committed her to the Scouting program for nearly one-third of her time, including being in the field fairly continually from June 1 through September 3, plus the additional time for program planning, advertising, assorted logistical details, and the final wrap-up and reports. The field season alone was nearly a month more than her MNM contract allowed.[1] All of this left her little time to meet her other obligations, including to her job, her father, and her research, while still getting some sleep. An added factor may have been all the discussions and negotiations surrounding the contractual arrangements and the legal complications of liabilities and formal job descriptions—a sign of the times. These were likely to continue in the future for the on-the-trail camps and the excavation camps. But for whatever reason/s, by the spring of 1956, Bert knew she had to cut back her participation in the program, although she did not wish to sever her ties with it completely, or with Scouting.

In May, 1956, Bert wrote to A.V. Wasson, president of the Board of Regents of the MNM and SAR, that she wanted "to have my responsibilities with the national Girl Scout organization lessened...by withdrawing my services therefrom on a diminishing scale." She informed the GSUSA that if "they wish to continue this program, provision should be made for someone else to step in at the end of this summer's expeditions" (Dutton to Wasson, May 21, 1956; 89LA5.065). Further, she had been handed what seemed like the perfect exit opportunity—a request from the Chairman of Region IX's Executive Committee for her to become a member-at-large of the committee to oversee the "development and execution of the scouting program in west Texas, New Mexico, and eastern Arizona" (Dutton to Wasson, May 21, 1956; 89LA5.065).[2] This was a clear way to stay involved and continue to contribute, but at a more manageable level. As a member of this committee she would need to attend two to three meetings per year in Dallas or elsewhere in the region, for which she was now seeking permission—if it be the Board's pleasure that she should act on the invitation. Apparently, the Board and Director Long agreed that Bert could join the committee and also that she should begin to turn over the reins and the directorship of the Archaeological Mobile Camp program to someone else. But it was not going to be quite as easy or immediate as all might have hoped.

Wrapping Up the 1956 Season

Although the 1956 season went ahead without major difficulties, it was not without problems. Most were due to complications caused by increasing the number of campers from 16 to 24 for each of the two Mobile Camp sessions. The Pueblo Largo Dig crew was also larger (20) that year, but this would have been Bert's choice and with her approval.[3] By the time that the camps were over and all of the post-camp duties were being completed, Bert was well aware that changes needed to be made if the program were to continue—with or without her participation. She had made up her mind as to what was needed.

Bert's summary report to Gretchen Yoffa for 1956 clearly states that the "experiment" of increasing the number of Mobile campers from 16 to 24 per session had not worked. She cited eight points that she felt were obstacles to the "former overwhelming success of the program," all due to the larger number of girls and her perception of her "decreasing lack of control" (Dutton to Yoffa, Sept. 14, 1956; 89LA5.065). The increase slowed the pace each day and the program overall, thereby exacerbating the stress on everyone. It necessitated the elimination of certain program features and privileges previously enjoyed (visits to some places, such as individual's homes and other venues, difficulty arranging for some speakers, lack of space at some desirable campgrounds). There were difficulties in hiring a cook due to the greater workload, and overhead expenses were higher due to the inability to carry sufficient basic supplies. Finally, the numbers limited personal interaction, especially leaving the director unable to get to know the campers individually (something Bert always considered a major part of the experience). Her final point was perhaps the most telling:

> Most important of all, [this has] obviously resulted in the acceptance of younger and unqualified campers in order to fill quotas; several of these younger, extremely immature girls showed promise, indicating that some two years from now they would have been prepared for the experience offered; some, even older, had utterly inadequate camping experience, skills, and background for this opportunity, and were a detriment to our camps (Dutton to Yoffa, Sept. 14, 1956; 89LA5.065).

The policy of screening Mobile Camp applicants by the national office, rather than by Bert in cooperation with regional GS officials as in the early years, was not working. She added that perhaps more thought was being given to numbers than to the quality of the applicants. The current arrangement was undermining her ability to run an effective camp for all parties concerned. And it also undermined her authority and the pleasure she had taken getting to know so many fine young women.

Under a series of recommendations for the future of the program, Bert added that "if this program, which has now completed its tenth year, is considered to have been of sufficient value as to merit continuance, then I suggest that provision be made for someone else to step in, at this time, and allow for my diminishing services. I must be released from the responsibilities which I have been carrying" (Dutton to Yoffa, Sept. 14, 1956: 89LA5.065). She would be willing to serve as a program advisor and do the annual reconnaissance, but she felt that the number of Mobile Camps needed to be held to two as in previous years, the campers limited to 16 "older, mature, girls," and that preference be given to "campers [who] have proven their interest and abilities"—not girls who could better participate in some other nationwide opportunity than one this specialized (Dutton to Yoffa, Sept. 14, 1956; 89LA5.065). These changes would bring the transportation, pace, and provisioning aspects of the program back within reasonable limits and under control (20 not 30 people), and allow the program to have a greater impact on the girls personally. She added: "One of the major features of this program has been its continuity [i.e., so many girls returning], which has made it possible for several young ladies to chart their futures thereby" (Dutton to Yoffa, Sept. 14, 1956; 89LA5.065). As to the excavation camp, she stated that it was of genuine interest to a very limited number of girls, and consequently, she felt that it should be discontinued. This had the advantage for the GSUSA that they would no longer have to have a professional archaeologist on the camping staff, thus providing more flexibility in hiring for the program in the future.

Yoffa responded that the National Camp Committee would be reviewing all of their plans for the 1957 season soon, and that they would "consider all the aspects of your recommendations for the Senior Girl Scout Archaeological Mobile

Camps"—and get back to her (Yoffa to Dutton, Sept. 20, 1956; 89LA.065). But in the meantime, since their fiscal year was closing on September 30, would she please "expedite" any of her bills and reports so that Yoffa could have them by September 28? Bert had been out of the field by then for only about 10 days. One suspects that this response from Yoffa was not well received, especially given that the agreement specified that she was to have four weeks from the end of the sessions to submit all financial records and reports to National (Agreement, 1956; 89LA5.065).

The "Special Events" unit of the Camps and Camping Committee of the GSUSA met on September 24, and after agreeing that the archaeological program had been of great value to the GSUSA program, National committed to "begin to help the Regions to develop their own programs along this line" by "getting guides out to them on how to do this and other kinds of experiments" (GSUSA Archives 1956:1). In the interim, they would try to find a new director—or choose someone who had already been on one or more of the trips to become director—and urge Dutton to go on an exploratory trip to orient her on details. Further, they would ask Bert to do the Dig plus this orientation, but "for 1958 drop the Dig but continue the trips. By 1959 try to turn this over to a local council or region," and then "begin easing out of the Archaeological" camps (GSUSA Archives 1956:1–2). They agreed that this would mean that Bert would now play more of an advisory role. There would be problems, however: a need for storage for equipment, a new starting/stopping place, size of group, and most of all, a bigger budget. The GSUSA would now have to fund salaries for the director and ideally for staff—but at least transportation for staff—and still keep the cost low enough for girls' families to be able to afford the experience. Or the GSUSA would have to find other sponsors to subsidize the program as the MNM had done for the previous 10 years.

In all likelihood, others in the GSUSA continued to discuss these matters, as it was two months later that Yoffa wrote to Bert that the National Camp Committee had met and, although fully aware that "this national event is taking more time than you should be asked to give," and having given "thoughtful and serious consideration" to her recommendations, had voted the following: "1. The Mobile camps; that each accommodate 24 girls providing a sufficient number of qualified girls make applica- tion. 2. The Excavation be operated if qualified supervisory personnel is available"

(Yoffa to Dutton, Nov. 20, 1956; 89LA5.065). Yoffa added that: "It is our greatest hope that the experimental work done by you and [us] will be taken over by councils in the future," to which end "I am now preparing a guide for councils on ways to operate similar events." She hoped that Bert would act as "a reader" for this material as "you and I know the importance of this material before embarking on a cooperative program" (Yoffa to Dutton, Nov. 20, 1956; 89LA5.065). But further, the National Camp Committee was unable to agree with Bert's recommendations as to number of participants this year because of the "tremendous impact of the 1956 Senior Girl Scout Roundup" (12 veterans of Digger camps attended),[4] which should produce enough qualified applicants. And besides, "this year no other opportunity of similar interest is being offered" (Yoffa to Dutton, Nov. 20, 1956; 89LA5.065). It was hoped that Bert would reconsider her decisions for 1957 and run the mobiles and Dig this last time. Yoffa further suggested that Jan Fleming, who had acted as GS Rep in 1956 on Camp II and Camp III (the Dig), might work as a new Director for the Mobile Camps—if Bert found her acceptable. It was obvious that the National Council either had not listened attentively to what she was saying or that they could not find a ready solution for the coming year.

Bert's response to Yoffa was quick, answered the same day her letter was received. In it she reiterated her positions taken in her September letter: she needed to be "released from much of the work which I have carried on in behalf of the Girl Scouts.... Let me state again that for the 1957 session I shall be willing to conduct the reconnaissance for the on-the-trail camps, in company with whoever your organization selects as your agent." If necessary, Bert wrote that she would try to go on the first camp to show someone how it was done; "but after that, my assistance would be in an advisory capacity" (Dutton to Yoffa, Nov. 23, 1956; 89LA5.065). She acquiesced on the numbers of campers for the mobile camps, but held firm on her position on the excavation camp. She wrote:

> It will be impossible for me to conduct another excavation camp for the Girl Scouts. Personally, and as an agent of our institution, there is too much involved at Pueblo Largo to allow anyone else stepping in there. We have obligations and unfinished studies which must be continued in due time. What we have

accomplished during the six seasons that the Senior girl Scouts have been working there, will be made a part of the reports which will be published, with full
recognization [sic] given to the Scout organization (Dutton to Yoffa, Nov. 23,
1556; 89LA5.065).

Bert had professional and personal responsibilities regarding Pueblo Largo, and
it was obvious to her that the GSUSA did not fully understand what these entailed.
Her professional ethics would not allow a site that she had begun to excavate be
turned over to just anyone. In addition, she and the museum had entered into a contract with the owners of the property, and that contract had to be fulfilled by them.
The GSUSA "considerations" had not taken either condition into sufficient account
and likely would not in the future. Also, Bert was not through with Pueblo Largo.
She had written that fall to one of the veteran Diggers that the two-week sessions
were not long enough to make real progress, and further, "I don't feel that enough
girls get enough (or give enough) for the experience to make a worthwhile expendi-
ture of time, effort, and money" (Dutton to Claire Yeagley, Sept. 21, 1956; 99BPD.xx).
She felt that a more concentrated effort was needed at the site to make real progress,
with longer sessions and perhaps "a few strong men to do the heavier excavation
work."[5]

Archaeologists faced similar problems at that time to those they do today: time,
training, and money. In the Southwest, with its many large sites (especially Pueblos),
archaeologists often continue working at one or a few adjacent sites for several
years before they feel that they understand their complexity. In the past, they often
employed seasoned Diggers to do the heavy work, including removing materials that
naturally filled Pueblo rooms after they were abandoned. Then more attention could
be paid to lower levels near floors and other key areas of the sites and to the actual
construction techniques, the placement of artifacts, and other important features
within them. Archaeological field schools offered through universities—including
those at UNM that Bert attended—had then and still have obligations to teach students proper methods and techniques of excavation. This takes time, and cannot be
accomplished in two weeks, or even over a six or eight week summer session (Gifford
and Morris 1985; Mathien 1992; Mills 2005). Bert did not necessarily have this teaching

obligation at Pueblo Largo, but she still felt the responsibility to train those girls and young women who were truly interested in archaeology. And she counted on her most experienced Diggers returning each Dig session to pass on what they had learned to newer recruits. Two weeks per summer over six summers had been nowhere near long enough to learn all that Pueblo Largo had to reveal, let alone answer the complex question posed as to whether the site provided evidence either for or against a Mesa Verdean in-migration. Bert planned to do more concentrated work at Pueblo Largo after she wrote a preliminary report on what had been learned through the excavations thus far as a guide to future work. Then she would offer some of her "best girls" the opportunity to continue the project through an analysis phase (Chapter 8). But she needed a chance to breathe and catch up with her life first.

Bert received another letter, this time from Mrs. George S. Dunham, Chairman of the National Camp Committee, again requesting that she reconsider her positions and continue the 1957 season the same as in 1956—with two Mobile Camps of 24 girls plus the Dig. In her response, Bert reiterated again her feelings that the Scouts got much more from going on the Mobile Camps than they did from the excavation project, and that "I do not feel that young ladies are being offered any less by dropping the latter from your offerings in 1957" (Dutton to Dunham, December 1, 1956; 89LA5.065). Furthermore, given that the GSUSA intended to make the 1957 camps "available to as many as 48 qualified Senior Scouts," she recommended that they stay with the two Mobile sessions and that they schedule each camp so as to leave the girls and their families time to visit Pueblo ceremonies taking place that summer (activities that could not be incorporated into the schedule given the numbers involved). She added: "In the future, when I am serving only in an advisory capacity, you may, of course, have as many camps and as many girls therein as you desire, and wherever you wish" (Dutton to Dunham, December 1, 1956; 89LA5.065). For 1957, she said that she would do the annual reconnaissance, and lead the first camp, "on a slowed-down basis which the larger number of campers requires" (December 1, 1956; 89LA5.065).

As to the Dig, Bert held firm on her decision to discontinue it, but attempted to explain more clearly what was involved and why simply finding "qualified supervisory personnel" was not an adequate solution. She wrote:

I do not know if any other archaeologist might be available or not. The point I am endeavoring to make is that the Pueblo Largo excavation project has been a serious undertaking of the Museum of New Mexico, with Senior Girl Scouts worked into our operational plans. We, the museum, will continue our studies at that site, which would preclude anyone else from working there. Therefore, if you were to continue the excavation program, you would not only need an archaeologist, but also a ruin site in which to work, with proper permits therefor, etc. (Dutton to Dunham, Dec. 1, 1956; 89LA5.065).

The permits would be something likely beyond the GSUSA's ability to obtain, and the other logistics difficult for them work out from a distance. It was better to end the Dig aspect of the program for all of Dutton's reasons and to focus instead on the Mobile Camp program, she stressed. Although Bert did not go into more detail about what was involved in running an excavation, she may have been depending on Yoffa who had been on two Digs (plus a Mobile Camp) to explain the situation. However, Yoffa clearly had not learned enough about what was involved or really at stake to explain the situation to her superiors sufficiently—or she had been over-ruled. Archaeology was a profession with standards and principles to be met and followed. One could not substitute just anyone into a leadership position without considering many factors. Bert finally put her foot down on firm ground, and she would not give in.

1957 and Beyond

With these matters settled, attention turned to finding someone to replace Bert as director of the program. Bert was leaving that choice open to the GSUSA, but the name that surfaced from National was Jan Fleming, who served as GS Rep on Camp I in 1955 and Camps II and III (Dig) in 1956 and Camp I in 1957. Fleming apparently was well trained as a Senior Scout leader, naturalist, and camper, and seemed to work efficiently on those camps.[6] She was not an anthropologist, although if the program was to be reoriented that probably would not matter. Unfortunately, we know little else about her background. Bert told Yoffa that, based on her association with

Fleming, she "seems the most promising of anyone whom I can think of who might be chosen to carry on a Mobile Camping program.... She would, of course, adapt it in accordance with her own views;" but Bert would help her as much as possible (Dutton to Yoffa, Nov. 20, 1956; 85LA5.065).

Yoffa apparently visited Jan in her home in Indiana in February 1957, and she agreed to take over the directorship and to work with Bert on a smooth transition for the 1957 Mobile Camps. She acted as assistant on the first 1957 Mobile, which Bert guided (Appendix A), and directed Camp II that year, using the same itinerary followed during Camp I. Bert seems to have been marginally involved in Camp II, although it began and ended at Rancho del Cielo. It is likely that she was also involved initially in the museum tour and an introductory lecture at the Rancho. But there is no mention of Fleming accompanying Bert on the annual reconnaissance that year.[7]

At the close of Camp I on July 13, Jan presented Bert with a Hopi Black-on-red bowl, purchased at the Mesa Verde store with contributions made by that year's campers and staff. Many of the campers most likely did not fully realize the significance of the gesture or the gift, and especially what Bert had given to Senior Girl Scouting, to all of the participants in the program through the years, and especially to many girls individually.[8] In her annual contribution to the archaeological newsletter *Teocentli*, Bert wrote simply "I completed the eleventh season of directing and conducting Archaeological Mobile Camps for Senior Girl Scouts. And with this I signed off. I no longer have the time to carry on such a program. Museum demands necessitate my full attention" (Dutton 1957b). In a note to veteran camper Anne Rushmer McClelland in early June, she said that after Camp I, "I'll begin living my life" (Dutton to McClelland, June 6, 1957; 99BPD.xx).

At the end of September 1957, Bert was in an automobile accident, while driving to a meeting in Dallas of Region IX's Advisory Committee, part of her new Girl Scout involvement. She spent 11 days in a hospital in Spur, Texas, with compound fractures of the nose and right kneecap. She spent several months recuperating in Santa Fe after that (Dutton 1957b). Although she was back to work in early 1958, her knee did not heal as quickly as she had hoped. In a note to McClelland nearly nine months after the accident, she said that she had been able to walk without a cane for only about a week, but that "my knee is still very stiff, and I wonder if it ever will be o.k. again. I think my strength is about normal again, but it's been a long siege" (Dutton to McClelland, May 18, 1958; 99BPD.xx). Thus it seems doubtful that Bert did a reconnaissance for the Mobile Camp program in 1958—if indeed she was asked.

In 1958, the Scout program was retitled "Senior Girl Scout Mobiles to the Southwest" and turned over to the new director, Jan Fleming, who was well qualified in scouting and perhaps natural history. In late March, Yoffa reported that staff jobs were pretty much filled; that all camper reservations were filled except one, which was going to a girl on the alternate list; and that three Native American girls would be participating (likely one on each of three trips). She noted that Fleming was taking the route through the National Parks, the Hopi country, canyons, etc., and that the camps would be headquartered at Jack Stacy's ranch (GSUSA Archives, 1958).

In April, Fleming wrote to W.L. Mauzy, Acting Director of the MNM, requesting speakers from his staff for three groups of Scouts, one for a date in June and two in mid- and late July (group size is not specified). She added, "We are broadening our program to include nature, wildlife, types of terrain, natural history, geology, and archaeology" and confirmed that the camp headquarters while in Santa Fe for the three camps would be at Jack Stacy's ranch (Fleming to Mauzy, April 15, 1958; 89LA5.066). Although she did not provide an itinerary for the trips, she said that that they would cover the usual 1,200 miles, and that they would be making three "archeological stops: Petrified Forest, the Flagstaff Museum [Museum of Northern Arizona], Wupatki National Monument, and present day Hopi Country."[9] She requested dates for their visits to the MNM, one each for the three planned trips. Fleming specifically asked that Marjorie Lambert be a speaker, as she was "quite pleased with her complete presentation" in past years (Fleming to Mauzy, April 15, 1958; 89LA5.066).

After some initial confusion as to how long the groups would be at the Museum, and whether Fleming was requesting speakers other than Lambert, she clarified the situation by saying that they would be going to the Laboratory of Anthropology and National Park Service headquarters in the morning, and be at the Museum—but only the Palace of the Governors—for two hours in the afternoon. As to the Hall of Ethnology (Bert's department), she said that she knew of Bert's accident and "how busy she is," and that she did not want to bother Bert. (Bert had already told Mauzy that she was prepared to do her usual one-hour presentations.) Fleming added that if girls were interested in ethnology, they could "go through that on their own" (Fleming to Mauzy, May 10, 1956; 89LA5.066). As it turned out, only Lambert and Mauzy spoke with the groups. There is no indication that either the MNM or Bert was further involved in the program that summer or in later years, or what became of it ultimately. The Museum of New Mexico's files, as well as Bert's materials, are silent beyond this point, supporting the assumption that any further cooperative agreements with the GSUSA ended with the 1957 season.

If Yoffa succeeded in writing and distributing the manual on running camps like the Southwest Archaeological Mobile Camps through the GSUSA as she had hoped— or asked Bert to review such a document—no evidence of either was found in the GSUSA Archives.[10] However, in the absence of data to the contrary, it may be that if one was created, the GSUSA was not able to convince any other Region or Council to take on this type of large-scale project. The Chaparral Girl Scout Council of northern New Mexico (now Girl Scouts of Chaparral Council) did follow through some years later with a small archaeological program at their Eliza Seligman Camp in the Jemez Mountains, run first by DDD veteran Vorsila Bohrer, who was working for the Council at that time (Chapter 10). It was a direct legacy of Dutton's efforts. As Yoffa's correspondence with Bert indicated, there would have been significant hurdles to overcome in order to continue the Mobile Camps, a major one being money for salaries and other expenses to keep down costs. And there could be "other issues." After all, Region IX and the GSUSA had been given a major gift by the MNM in providing Bert the release time to engage in the activities, plus subsidizing her salary and some additional costs. As a not-for-profit organization, the GSUSA likely would have had to enlist some other individual or institution to provide a similar subsidy and work out other problems. But perhaps the best course for the GSUSA short of this was the Camping Committee's other suggestion: going back to their longstanding policy of being more advisors than innovators and leaving initiatives to the regional and local councils—and thus easing out of archaeology. They would continue to sponsor some "Wider Opps," but these seem to have focused more on international opportunities than on local ones.

8

Continuing along the Trail

The Galisteo Basin Again

Tune: *Auld Lang Syne*
Should all good Diggers be forgot
And never brought to mind?
Should happy days be bygone days
That are left so far behind?
Let's pause a moment now and then
To think of the fun we had
The friends we made, the things we did
That will never come again.

—E. Boettcher, G. Bell, P. Pachlhofer,
M. A. Stein, B. Talahytewa, 1955 (Camp II)

Bert's life was far from relaxed for the next few years after the Senior Girl Scout program ended. But even in 1956, with the close of the Pueblo Largo excavations, it was clear that she intended to stay involved in archaeological research in the Galisteo Basin, at the least "in the hope of clarifying the Galisteo–Mesa Verde migration problem" (95PLE.005). She felt a keen obligation to complete the Pueblo Largo work as part of the museum's research program, as she had made clear to Gretchen Yoffa when she discontinued the excavation camps (Chapter 7). After all, her long-term research interests in the archaeology of the area, plus the migration hypothesis, were what led her to undertake the Pueblo Largo excavations as part of the Girl Scout archaeological program in the first place (Chapter 5).

In a letter to Claire Yeagley, veteran of three Dig camps, Bert explained what she had in mind shortly after the close of the 1956 excavation camp (Dutton to Yeagley, Sept. 21, 1956; 99BPD.xx):

> Don't think for a minute that I am giving up on Pueblo Largo. We have too much unfinished business there. So, for your private information, what I want to do is this: work up P.L. materials to date and evaluate our progress to now, so as to know better where to concentrate future efforts. Then, as part of our museum research program, hire a few strong men to do the heavier excavation work, and to work longer than the two-week period to which we have been confined. When this can be undertaken, I shall hope that some of my most select Diggers with P.L. experience may join in the work, as "captains" and lab workers, and also aid in further research. This seems much more attractive to me.

Bert was feeling the pinch that most excavators feel who attempt to run digs with short time limits—even a month or six weeks—too much to do, too little time to do it. This then leads to the old archaeological adage "more work needs to be done." Unfortunately, time and ability to do more work can easily evaporate. Although Bert made progress on her plans to continue with the Pueblo Largo excavations, and in the Galisteo Basin generally, some aspects had to be delayed and others abandoned entirely. There were a variety of reasons for this, as will be clarified below, although chief among them was access to the site: Bert was denied permission to continue any type of work at Pueblo Largo due to a change in land ownership. In the interim, until new plans could be put into place to continue her efforts with the archaeology of the region and the migration question, Bert would not be idle.

Getting Back to Business: 1957–1961

During the 11-year period that Bert conducted the Girl Scout program, she was physically absent from her MNM and SAR posts for two to four month intervals with a cumulative equivalent of three full years. Also, in 1953, she was granted a six-month sabbatical leave for research in Mexico and Guatemala through outside grant funding—the trip in which veteran Mobile and Dig Camper Gillian Wethey participated. This brought her cumulative absence to three-and-a-half years. Add another three months for the accident in the fall of 1957, and it was yet longer before she was back to office duties. Although Bert's annual Girl Scout trips counted as part of her public education work through the museum, and her Mesoamerican sabbatical for research was easily justified as part of her joint position at SAR, being away from her other responsibilities for this long was significant. Unfortunately, some tasks that were part of her workday had been left undone or only partly completed. There is no evidence that the MNM hired anyone to fill her position, even part time, during her absences.[1]

According to Bert's job definition at the MNM and the SAR, half of her time was to be devoted to administration and maintenance of the Department of Ethnology, and half of it to research. As she once stated, "I have found, as usual, that either [of these] is really a full-time assignment" (Dutton 1951d:47). Research was obviously an important part of Bert's positions at both institutions (MNM—Southwest research; SAR—Mesoamerican research), and it was counted in various ways. The work that went into exhibitions involved research, as did that for the several articles she wrote per year for the MNM's publication, *El Palacio,* and the 10 to 15 public lectures she gave, the questions she answered for the public, and her attendance at Native and other events. The administrative side included planning and installing exhibitions (anywhere from three to five smaller installations or renovations per year), cataloging and managing collections, interacting with the public, establishing budgets, attending meetings, working with legislators, and handling several other tasks. Most of these were of higher priority than her personal research specialties in Galisteo Basin and Mesoamerican archaeology. Time for these needed to be folded into her other commitments—a few hours here, a day or two there, or when specifically granted releases to work on them. If these solutions were not effective, personal research was moved to evening hours, weekends, and days off. Bert needed to get back to work on all of these activities—and did so immediately.

Less than two months after Bert had written Anne Rushmer McClelland that with the end of Mobile Camp I in July (1957), she could "begin living my life," she penned

Figure 8.1. Bertha Dutton (left) and Agnes Sims (right) view cover of *Sun Father's Way*, 1965. Courtesy of Palace of the Governors Photo Archives (NMHM/DCA) Neg. No: 119709.

the following to her: "My program keeps unmercifully filled. Have just had to work up the 50 year history of our SAR, and some job it was...never came closer to having a nervous breakdown, I'm sure, what with the endless interruptions" (Dutton to McClelland, August 23, 1957; 99BPD.xx). SAR was celebrating its fiftieth anniversary that year, and Bert, through her longstanding connection as a Research Associate, was the logical choice to write its history. In short order, she produced a thorough, detailed, and personally typed (no computers in those days!) 71-page report (Dutton 1957a) in time for the celebration in the fall of that year.[2]

With that behind her, and when she was able to be back in the office after her medical leave, Bert turned her attention to two other research projects long overdue. One was a study of the *kiva* murals at the Ancestral Pueblo site of Kuaua near Bernalillo (now Coronado Historic Site), always a favorite stop on the Girl Scout trips, where they saw replicas of multicolored paintings on the walls of one of the *kivas* (Chapters 2, 3, 4). This project had been hanging over Bert's head since her student days at UNM. Now it was reinvigorated by some funds made available for publication through the MNM, ultimately resulting in one of her favorite products (Dutton 1963a; Figure 8.1).[3] The second project involved writing up the results of her recent sabbatical in 1953–54, including her excavations at an archaeological site in Chiapas (Dutton 1958; 1961a). This then led her to expand work on the similarities and differences among material and ideological features of the ancient Southwest and some areas in ancient Mesoamerica, something that had intrigued her since completing her dissertation (Dutton 1961a; 1964a). Both projects involved significant analysis and writing time, and as usual, both took longer than anticipated. Bert seems to have worked on the two projects simultaneously—between other duties—and while still recuperating from her knee injury. The projects helped her to catch up on the literature in both regions, as she had had little time to stay current on the latest finds and interpretations while she busy with the Scout program (99BPD.xx; 13ARM.001 [Christmas Letters, 1960; 1961]).

Significant museum work kept Bert well occupied during this period as well. During those 11 years, she had been able to keep pace and refresh the exhibit program at the MNM by installing smaller exhibitions and/or rotating the contents of individual exhibit cases. But in late 1959, she was made Curator of Exhibits for the whole of the Museum of New Mexico and immediately set in motion a plan to totally revamp the Hall of Ethnology with a "nearly invisible budget"—the third total renovation since the hall opened in 1941 (Bohrer 1979:14). From early January until June 15, 1960 (opening day), she claimed that this "took almost all of my waking hours"

(99BPD.xx; 13ARM.001 [Christmas Letter 1960]). This total upgrade involved basically gutting the hall and starting from scratch with a new design. It included "full-size architectural structures, furnished with appropriate cultural materials for the Pueblos (Hopi, Zuni, and San Juan), Navaho, Papago, and Mescalero Apache"—*life groups*, in museum parlance (A.E. Dittert to D. M. Kelb, Nov. 19, 1965; 89LA6.061). She also wrote two popular booklets to accompany the new hall (Dutton 1960a; 1961b). Once the new Hall was completed, Bert and other MNM employees then "moved everything anthropological <u>not</u> on display," including all of the ethnographic and archaeological collections (150,000+ items), from the MNM storage facilities downtown to the Laboratory of Anthropology building south of the city. "It was no small task, but we got it done by the first of September, for the most part" (99BPD.xx; 13ARM.001 [Christmas Letter, 1960]). Bert also moved her office from downtown to the Lab as part of the relocation, thereby gaining needed laboratory space to study research collections.

Unfortunately, in the summer of 1960, Bert had to place her father, Orrin (Daddy D), in a care facility, as he "crumpled very rapidly, and got beyond what I could do for him" (99BPD.xx; 13ARM.001 [Christmas Letter, 1960]). She visited him frequently and he recognized her, but she wrote, "that is about all." In 1961 and 1962 she wrote to friends, including some of the former Dirty Diggers, about his condition and her visits to him. He passed away two years later. His death was very hard for her to take, and the *ranchito* was very lonely without him.

Continued Girl Scout Activities: Late 1950s-1960s

Bert continued to keep up an active work and community life after her father's passing. She had remained involved with the Girl Scouts during the late 1950s and continued to do so through the early 1960s, but to a lesser extent. She attended meetings of the Region IX Advisory Committee, which she had joined in 1956, but the auto accident curtailed her participation until she fully recovered. She continued with some activities by representing both Region IX and the Sangre de Christo Council (Santa Fe, Raton, Las Vegas) when the Chaparral Girl Scout Council was formed in May 1958 in Albuquerque (*Albuquerque Journal*, 26 May 1958:21). She also gave talks to interested groups about the Archaeological Mobile Camp Program, and in 1957 was honored with GSUSA's "Thanks" award at a luncheon in Albuquerque for her work on behalf of so many young women.

Bert continued to advise the Chaparral Girl Scout Council after it became responsible for Scouting in the eight northern New Mexico counties plus parts of the adjacent Navajo Reservation in Arizona. Vorsila Bohrer was working for the Council in 1960, and she enlisted Bert's help in planning some aspects of summer archaeological camps for local Scouts at Chaparral's Camp Eliza Seligman in the Jemez Mountains. These camps were patterned after Bert's model, but with a local emphasis.[4] Bohrer (1963) also assembled Chaparral's *Council Resource Guide,* a substantial task, and enlisted Bert as advisor and reviewer.[5]

In 1963, Bert led a tour for National GSUSA representatives (including a group of Senior Girl Scouts) to look for a potential site in northern New Mexico for the 1965 Senior Roundup. She arranged for them to tour the Galisteo Basin and spent a day with them at sites on private property, including the site of Las Madres, which she had just finished excavating (see below), as well as explaining to them the purpose and importance of the region and anthropology (Agnes E. Jones to Dutton, August 27, 1963, 99BPD.xx). Her goal was to illustrate some of what New Mexico had to offer if the state were selected for the Roundup, but apparently it was not.

Dutton also continued to stay in touch with many former Diggers throughout the late 1950s and thereafter. When in the area, the women (some now with families) continued to visit and sometimes stay with her at the Rancho, signing the guest book she kept in readiness. She likewise maintained friendships with former Mobile Camp staff members, especially those who lived near Santa Fe (Margaret Buck, Penny [Elizabeth] Parker, Marie Nourse, and others).

Pueblo Largo Again: "All-Girl Archaeology," 1957-1961

In the late 1950s, working on archaeological sites in the Galisteo Basin was becoming more difficult. Most of the area was in private rather in public hands, and several of the large ranches contained the major Ancestral Puebloan sites that Nels Nelson had visited in 1912. To complicate matters, properties were being sold and divided, and several of the new owners had fenced their lands to contain their cattle and keep out trespassers. Gates were locked, and permissions had to be secured separately to enter each piece and certainly to do any collecting or digging. There were absentee owners and managers for whom contact information was not readily available. San Cristobal Ranch, where Pueblo Largo was located, was among those that changed hands during this period. It had been owned by the Sawyer Cattle Company of San Angelo, Texas, with whom the MNM had its original excavation agreement. The new owner, a "Senator from Texas," balked at allowing any continuation of MNM activities there (Dutton 1985). Access issues frustrated Bert, the MNM, and other archaeologists interested in the area, and especially those pursuing larger questions like evidence for migrations. In order to begin to answer such questions, they needed comparative data based on broad-based surveys and more thorough excavations. A few landowners were sympathetic to the need for work on their lands, but by no means all. The Galisteo Basin was becoming "locked up," and the archaeologists, including Bert, were being "locked out." Bert could no longer travel off-road to many places in the Basin, as had been her habit in her Model T since the 1930s.[6]

Although the issue of access loomed large, Bert continued to press forward with sorting and analysis of the Pueblo Largo collections in the MNM during the late 1950s and early 1960s, again folding the work into her expanding daily schedule. Certainly the auto accident had made initiating new field work at the site impossible for her personally for at least six months—even if she could get access. In addition, the MNM had no immediately available funds to support additional excavations at Pueblo Largo or elsewhere, as emphasis was now shifting to salvaging sites in highway right-of-ways and other construction sites in the region.[7] Her plan to involve former select Scout Diggers in additional work was likely not very viable either, as nearly all of those she would have invited to participate were now involved in advanced undergraduate or graduate training or otherwise moving forward with their lives (13ARM.001 [Christmas letters, 1958, 1959, 1960, 1961]; 99BPD:xx; 1960b).

But Bert did accomplish some tasks on the Pueblo Largo project from 1956 to 1961. After the close of the excavation camp in 1956 and during the fall of 1957, she sorted and set aside those artifacts and other materials from the Pueblo Largo collections at the MNM that needed to be analyzed by specialists. Then she delivered or sent them to those who agreed to be involved. They included: Erik Reed, physical anthropologist, who would look at the human remains from the site to characterize their physical features and compare them with human remains recovered from other Puebloan areas;[8] Thomas Mathews, who would identify mammal bones, including species used to manufacture bone tools; Lyndon Hargrave, who would identify the bird bones and artifacts made from them; David Brugge, who would work on the maize cobs and kernels; Kenneth Honea, who would characterize the flaked stone artifacts; and people at the University of Arizona Laboratory of Tree-Ring Research, who would date any of the remaining wood samples that had not been sent previously (Chapter 5).[9] All of these individuals and institutions were considered to be "the experts" or certainly highly knowledgeable of their specialties at the time (95PLE.005, 009: Brugge 1957; Hargrave 1961; Honea ca. 1963; Mathews 1957; Reed 1956).[10] One of the Diggers, Jeanne Ellis, then in graduate school in chemistry at the University of Arizona, also agreed to undertake chemical analyses of corn and pottery sherds to try to identify sources (Ellis to Dutton, June 19, 1957; 95PLE.005, 99BPD.xx).[11] There is no evidence that Bert obtained special funding from the MNM or other organizations for any of these studies. More likely, these individuals did the analyses out of interest in the research or friendship—not uncommon at the time. Bert also compiled a preliminary count and identification of the types of pottery from the site along with some miscellaneous notes on Pueblo Largo's architecture (Dutton ca. 1956a, ca. 1956b). All of this was necessary to better evaluate exactly what additional excavation and analysis work was needed at the site.

Another task she accomplished during this period was writing a brief outline for a report on Pueblo Largo, likely as a preliminary assessment of the site. It was to be titled "All-Girl Archaeology: Excavations at Pueblo Largo, a Prehistoric Site in the Galisteo Basin, N.M." The outline included the standard topics that site reports were expected to cover at that time: chapters on the setting and environment; a history of the work at the site (i.e., Nelson [1914], Girl Scout excavations); chapters on the architecture (village plan, masonry, construction phases); detail on specific areas within the site investigated (dwelling rooms, ceremonial chambers, plazas, refuse accumulations, other significant features); tree-ring and ceramic dating; and detailed analyses of artifact assemblages by categories. These chapters were to be followed by the sections contributed by the specialists on identifications of the bird and mammal bones and the artifacts made from them, analysis of human remains, dendrochronology (tree-ring dating), minerals, ceramics, corn and other vegetal remains, including the names of those who had agreed to write them (see above). Some reports had yet to be commissioned. The last chapters were to be the syntheses and conclusions. They were to be based on comparisons to features known ethnographically from the Pueblos as well as regional archaeological sites, with an overall stress on the "life pursuits at Pueblo Largo," population size, evidence of defense from enemy pressure, and lastly, her conclusions as to whether (or not) evidence of migrations, in or out of the area, was found, and if so, from where and by whom (emphasis in original; 95PLE.036).[12]

Bert started an introduction to the report, spelling out her orientation to archaeology and the reason for the title. The report would emphasize her view as to the place and meaning of archaeology within a "holistic anthropology." In other words, it was to be a fully integrated view, including data from the other subdisciplines (ethnology, linguistics, physical anthropology), in order to answer human-centered questions, not just identify artifacts and structures—today what would be called "anthropological archaeology." She would be stressing specifically how important ethnology was to providing explanations for how people had gone about their daily lives and years at this particular site as well as the site's overall integration into the rest of the Galisteo Basin and beyond. She also wanted to stress why the work at Pueblo Largo was a bit different than the standard—and hence the title. As she wrote in part (95PLE.036):

> What started as a program in applied anthropology, the bringing of living people (in this case Senior Girl Scouts) to the study of archaeology, resulted in bringing archaeology alive for them. The purpose of the present account is to follow that lead. Pueblo Largo, like other pueblos of the region, was occupied by human beings just as alive as the Girl Scouts. Rather than place emphasis on the things which they left behind them, endeavor was made to lay stress on the people who fabricated the things, and to show the cultural meaning of the things.

In addition to the outline, Bert provided what appears to be a work schedule for the four-month period that she estimated it would take her to write this report. It may have been her proposal to the MNM to justify the allocation of a specific block of her research time, or a leave of absence.[13] If this was its purpose, no evidence was found that she was granted the time. Rather, she continued to snatch a few hours here and there to work on the project—mainly, as it appears from her correspondence, on classifying the pottery types and their designs.

At this point, Bert's efforts to write a separate preliminary report on Pueblo Largo appear to end. She would make one additional attempt to continue work at the site and especially to delve deeper into the Mesa Verdean migration issue through another project in the Galisteo Basin (see below: Anasazi Migration Project). Her interpretation of the site, its actual features, and what she learned there towards resolving the migration issue would remain primarily as she stated them in her yearly summaries of the Mobile and Dig seasons (Chapter 5). Additional comments and syntheses concerning Pueblo Largo would be published later, after she had excavated another site in the area, Las Madres (Dutton 1964b, 1966, 1980). This additional excavation allowed her to place Pueblo Largo within a broader context and to reaffirm some of her conclusions from the earlier Largo excavations.

The Anasazi Migration Project, 1962–1963

Apparently not totally frustrated as of late 1961 by the issue of access to Pueblo Largo and other Galisteo Basin sites, Bert applied for a grant from the National Science Foundation under the title "Problems in Anasazi Migrations," to be carried out the following year (July 1962 to July 1963). This would be a final attempt to breathe life into the work begun at Pueblo Largo and especially to more systematically address the question of evidence for a Mesa Verdean migration into the area. This time she would follow a proposal, made recently by a leading Southwest Archaeologist, Emil Haury of the University of Arizona, for identifying migration versus more gradual in-situ change in archaeological sites (Figure 8.2). In a symposium on the migrations in prehistory, Haury (1958) discussed the evidence found at a site at Point of Pines in east-central Arizona. He systematically outlined evidence for a migration

Figure 8.2. Dr. Emil Haury, University of Arizona, and Dr. Bertha Dutton, enjoying each other's company at a Pecos Conference, 1960s. Photograph by Helga Teiwes. Courtesy of Arizona State Museum, University of Arizona, No. 67965.

(in this case of Ancestral [Kayenta] Puebloan people into this Mogollon region) by positing a specific set of criteria that should be identifiable in the archaeological record in a site.[14] Bert was awarded the $12,000 she was seeking—a feat in itself for a woman at the time, although a modest amount by today's standards.[15] The grant proposal and the summary report she submitted the following year indicate clearly that the original request was to involve excavations and laboratory work on known sites in the Galisteo Basin, including Pueblo Largo and at least two others (Dutton 1962a; 1963c). Bert knew full well that the six two-week sessions by the Girl Scouts at Pueblo Largo were not sufficient to answer the migration question and others about this site. She especially wanted to finish excavations in Nelson's area V (The Point), as it seemed to be the earliest part of the site and had the most potential to shed light on the migration issue. The two additional sites that she felt were key to her investigations were Colina Verde (LA309) and LA3333, also thought to be early and thus perhaps characterize the pre-migration period occupations in the area.[16]

According to the grant application, the MNM would give Bert a full salaried year for the project and would provide laboratory space and excavation equipment. However, the proposal does not indicate that the work would involve former Girl Scouts, although the funds that the GSUSA had already contributed to the Pueblo Largo excavations (largely for salaries for GS Reps) were noted as matching monies. Bert requested funds for a "field labor crew" for 40 days plus a field assistant and a laboratory assistant. She apparently abandoned the idea of hiring former Diggers to continue excavating the site, choosing to employ local Hispanic men instead—most already experienced in other excavations in the region. But she did hire DDD Sigrid "Sigi" Holien, then living in Santa Fe, as the laboratory assistant. She also asked Vorsila Bohrer to identify and evaluate the plant remains resulting from the work (Dutton 1964c).

As it turned out, even with funding in hand, Bert was unable to convince the new owner of San Cristobal Ranch to allow access to his property, including Pueblo Largo and the two other sites she wanted to evaluate.[17] She wrote in her summary report of the NSF project, "Because of this fact [lack of access], the NSF project was forced to amend its plan of procedure and to widen its contemplated survey" to look for other promising sites in the area to excavate (Dutton 1963c:3).

Following Haury's suggestions, Bert set up a series of criteria that she felt would best fit signs of a migration versus gradual in-situ change in the Galisteo Basin. After surveying where she could within the Basin, she next looked for sites to the north-west of the area, in the direction of Mesa Verde (Cuba-LaVentana area) to see if she could see features that met her criteria—with some success. She also sampled to the west as far as Zuni, New Mexico and St. Johns, Arizona and as far southwest as Ramah and as far east as White Lakes, New Mexico (north of Moriarty). She was looking for comparative data, as she felt that she could not and should not rule out possible influences or in-migrations coming from these directions. She searched for distinctive markers such as certain pottery types (Black-on-white wares, glaze wares, others), architectural characteristics (choice of building materials, architectural plans, *kiva* configurations and placement, plaza construction), choice of site locations, and more. She reasoned that "newcomer" status should be marked not only in pottery, but perhaps also in a concern for defense, as local people might be hostile to new people moving into the area, and they or the newcomers would either fortify or select new sites with that in mind (Dutton 1963c). The pottery types she used as a guide were those thought at the time to date close to the period when the Mesa Verde region lost population, perhaps to other areas (1250s to 1290s). After assessment of the materials and notes from roughly 30 surveyed sites, including those within the Galisteo Basin she could access, she settled on a promising site to excavate that she would later name Las Madres (LA25; Dutton 1963c). This site seemed to show the best possibility of having a direct Mesa Verde connection, and she was able to negotiate permission from the property owner to excavate it (Dutton 1964c; 1980:89).

Las Madres (LA25) is located less than 10 miles north of Pueblo Largo along Galisteo Creek. In 1912, Nels Nelson (1914) recorded the site as part of one he called Pueblo Galisteo, made a preliminary map of it, and excavated one room. The site is on a promontory above the creek, suggesting that it might have been built there for defensive reasons. The pottery visible on the surface was primarily Black-on-white of a local variety, but thought by some archaeologists to be linked to Mesa Verde types and styles. The site was built mostly with stone masonry making it more like Pueblo Largo, while other Galisteo Basin sites seemed to be of more mixed adobe and stone construction—adobe and stone being more typical of the region.

Between October and the end of December, 1962, Dutton and a crew of local men cleared 45 rooms, a *kiva*, and another large circular enclosure, and trenched several refuse areas (Figure 8.3). Instead of yielding exclusively or even primarily the hoped-for Mesa Verdean features, the excavations produced an assemblage of characteristics, a few of which could have been Mesa Verde related, but most of which were the same or very similar to those at other sites in the area thought to be occupied by local people over a long time span. Oral traditions linked Galisteo Basin sites to the Indigenous Tano and Keres peoples still living in Pueblos in the Rio Grande Valley to the west, and Bert's excavation results also fit with that interpretation. Construction at Las Madres was initially started in the early 1300s, and the site was expanded and likely occupied for less than 100 years. That period was one when climate in

Figure 8.3. Bertha Dutton examining metate at Las Madres, Galisteo Basin, NM, 1962. 95LME.037(b). Courtesy of MIAC/LAA.

the Basin seems to have been moister and thus more conducive to growing maize and other crops (Dutton 1964b, 1980:91). After that time, the region became dryer, and this climatic change, plus perhaps other reasons, caused the people to move on or consolidate with people in nearby locations. Following archaeological terminology of the day for the Northern Rio Grande region, the period near its founding was within the late "Coalition Period" (1200–1325) and ended in the early part of the "Classic Period" (1325–1600; Wendorf and Reed 1955). The site apparently had been abandoned before the Spanish *entrada*, although neighboring Pueblo Galisteo and a few others either survived or in some cases were reoccupied after Spanish settlement of northern New Mexico and the Galisteo Basin.

Based on evidence for subsistence as well as the quantity and quality of other material remains, Bert concluded that the people of Las Madres were never particularly well off. However, they made a sufficient living from their crops, supplemented by the game that they hunted and plant products they collected, which allowed them to remain at the site and continue its construction. They were well entrenched in and knowledgeable about their region and neighbors, as indicated by the birds and mammals they utilized, as well as trading habits with nearby communities, especially for locally made Glazeware pottery (Dutton 1964c; Hargrave 1963; Schaafsma 1995). Bert felt that, although some of their local Black-on-white pottery designs were reminiscent of those on Mesa Verde pieces, these wares differed in other ways, likely because they were local rather than imported or made by newcomers. Additional features, especially in other pottery types, suggested trade or influences from areas to the west and south, including as far west as the Little Colorado River, upper Gila-Salt rivers, and Mogollon region.[18] Bert favored these plus local linkages for Las Madres over those from Mesa Verde. She argued that these relationships seemed to have been in place over a long time, thus strengthening the overall interpretation for the site and region as one where indications were more supportive of gradual in-situ change with outside influences over a direct migration (Dutton 1964b). Based on what she had learned at Las Madres, Pueblo Largo, and the few other sites for which there were data, Bert concluded in two papers published not long after the excavations that there seemed to be no firm evidence for a direct linkage to Mesa Verde, at least in the southern Galisteo Basin (Dutton 1964b, 1966).

Dutton produced several manuscripts on the Las Madres project, including a preliminary report on the site and various drafts of a two-volume site report, most under the broader title "Prehistoric Peoples of the Galisteo Basin, New Mexico: Report on Migrations of the 13th and 14th Centuries" (Dutton 1963d, 1964c, 1964d).[19] These documents include the supplemental studies commissioned of specialists for the Pueblo Largo report, some with additions incorporating Las Madres materials but also new ones covering only materials from Las Madres (especially Dutton 1964c).[20] This seemed to have been Bert's way of incorporating these unpublished data on Pueblo Largo into a final manuscript. She attempted to get the manuscript published by the MNM over the next several years, but apparently funds were not available. Several years later she remarked that an outside donor would have been required to see the report through to print (Dutton 1990:10).

Bert continued to study collections from Pueblo Largo, Las Madres, and other Galisteo Basin sites, and to add references and marginal notes to the draft manuscript

Figure 8.4.
Suggested
reconstruction
of portions of
Roomblocks II, III,
and IV of Pueblo
Largo, by Alice
Wesche (1962).
Courtesy of MIAC/
LAA. Enhancement
by Patricia
DeBunch.

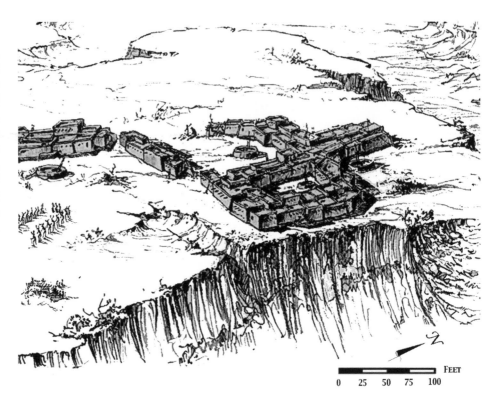

until her formal retirement from the MNM in 1965 and for several years thereafter.[21] In what was to be her final and best summary statement on Galisteo Basin archaeology, Dutton (1980) returned to data from Pueblo Largo and Las Madres, again affirming her original chronologies for the sites and evaluations of the architecture and other materials (including ceramics) as displaying local features more characteristic of slow development than rapid change. She concluded with reference to Pueblo Largo that although work there had been terminated before the site could be evaluated fully: "What we had unearthed and placed in repository at the Museum gave no evidence that Mesa Verdeans had occupied this pueblo. Architectural expressions were of Rio Grande type, as those are currently understood, and ceramics were not those of Mesa Verde. The latter merely had certain design likenesses and decoration

FEET

0   25   50   75   100

Figure 8.5. Suggested reconstruction of Roomblock V (The Point) at Pueblo Largo, by Alice Wesche (1962). Coutesy of MIAC/LAA. Enhancement by Patricia DeBunch.

"(Dutton 1980:88). And for Las Madres, she again favored local plus western and southern similarities and features over northern.

Additional work, including a review of Galisteo and regional pottery types as well as evidence from new excavations within the central and southern Galisteo Basin, seems to bear this out (Snead and Allen 2011; Wilson, ed. 2009; see also Wilson at al. 2015). However, matters hardly seem to be settled. The impact of Mesa Verdean and other migrations into northern New Mexico generally (when, where, who, and of what impact) is still very much discussed in the literature (i.e., Cordell 1995; Crown et al. 1996; Kohler 2004; Kohler et al. 2010; Ortman 2012; Snead and Allen, 2011).

Bert's published summary papers, the various drafts of the Las Madres report, the analyses of specific classes of materials by specialists for both sites, and the raw data in the notebooks and other reports by Dutton's Dirty Diggers form

an important, if uneven, archival record (see also Chapter 5). In addition, the
Laboratory of Anthropology Archives holds correspondence files, miscellaneous
notes, artifact drawings, rendered reconstructions of both sites by Alice Wesche
(Figure 8.4 and 8.5),[22] and a site map for Las Madres, but apparently not a new one
(beyond Nelson's) for Pueblo Largo (Chapter 5; but see Wilson et al. 2015). Although
Bert failed to complete a report on Pueblo Largo using the approach she had originally outlined, or see the Las Madres report through to publication, she was not
alone in these failures,[23] thus making the Galisteo Basin one of the most interesting but in many ways still one of the most poorly known archaeological areas in the
region (Blinman 2008; Snead 2011).

Fortunately, a dedicated trio took on the difficult task of reworking some of the
Dutton data on Pueblo Largo. They focused especially on the ceramic collections,
puzzled over the areas excavated, and reevaluated the data from the important tree-
ring chronologies to provide a much-needed summary for the site (Wilson et al.
2015). Their work also contained the original appendices that Dutton commissioned,
some updated to include materials from Las Madres. Their effort was not an easy
one after so many years, especially taking into account the quantity and quality of
some of the data and apparent attritions to the collections over 50+ years. However,
as they in part summarized (Wilson et al. 2015:98):

> We wish the Dirty Diggers' recording format [Chapter 5] had focused more on
> the details of the excavation and architecture of the rooms and less on enumer-
> ating every artifact, or possible artifact they found. However the Diggers' photo-
> graphic record of the experience, their obvious pleasure and excitement while
> getting filthy dirty in the heat of the Galisteo Basin summer makes it clear that
> the Largo project was not only a major contribution to Southwestern archaeol-
> ogy, it was a priceless, life-changing experience for many young women grow-
> ing up in the 1950s.

And further, with reference to Dutton's conclusions that there was no evidence
for a Mesa Verdean migration at the site: "Our purpose has been to bring Largo to
light, not to enter the ongoing debate about population growth versus migration,

but we do note that the majority of non-local ceramics throughout the site after 1300 indicate the Largo community had extensive ties and similarities with people to the north, in the Tewa Basin." In other words, as the old archaeological saying goes, "more work needs to be done."

Although not an archaeologist, I can but echo their sentiments. As indicated previously, the migration issue, its timing and influences within the region (including in the Galisteo Basin), is still being debated, and likely will be for many years to come. It is also likely that there were missteps by Dutton at Pueblo Largo, especially in not being at the site more during those very busy years for her and in perhaps trusting that her senior personnel knew more about the methods and techniques of properly excavating and recording a site than they did. Further, she may have thought that they would communicate more of what they did know to their crew members than they seem to have done.[24] But unlike an archaeological field school, where the primary goal should be teaching proper methods and techniques, this was largely a work-oriented enterprise.[25] That is not an excuse for work not done thoroughly. But we also need to remember that the methods, techniques, and standards of the 1950s were not those of today, and for many then, giving accurate placement information for significant artifacts recovered was often primary. Some of the later crew reports do talk about other details, whereas earlier reports appear to be more haphazard. It also seems clear that Dutton recognized some of these deficiencies after she reviewed the reports by the Diggers, and that she fully intended to go back to Pueblo Largo for further work. She makes this point in her letter to Yoffa about her obligations to the site and reinforces it in her letter to Claire Yeagley as quoted initially (see above). But she did not get the chance, and so the records for Pueblo Largo remain what they are. But who is to deny that the DDDs on the Pueblo Largo crews certainly learned a lot, and gained many other benefits from their experiences, over those six years?

Dutton's Final Museum Years

Bert finished her career at the Museum of New Mexico in 1965, having completed 30 years of service to the museum, SAR, the State of New Mexico, and its people

Figure 8.6. Bertha Dutton, Director, Museum of Navajo Ceremonial Art, 1966. Photograph by John Marlow. Susan S. Martin Collection.

and visitors. Upon retirement, she was immediately named Director of the Museum of Navajo Ceremonial Art (now the Wheelwright Museum of the American Indian), which is less than a mile west of the Laboratory of Anthropology—culminating her museum career at last with a directorship, something she was very proud to have attained (Figure 8.6). She was specifically recruited for the position by the MNCA's Board of Trustees.[26] The museum was started and funded by Mary Cabot Wheelwright, a wealthy Bostonian, to showcase and house her collection of sand painting tapestries, recorded ceremonial chants, and sacred stories from Hosteen Klah, prominent Navajo Singer and *Hatatlii* or Medicine Man (Armstrong 2015; Babcock and Parezo 1988:175).

Built in the shape of a traditional Navajo sacred *hogan*, the museum had been a frequent stop on the Girl Scout Mobile Camps; but by 1965, it had lost its viability as a tourist destination (there was not much to view), having been in decline since its founder's death the 1958. In her 10 years there as director, Bert brought the institution back from near financial collapse, repaired and expanded the physical plant, revitalized the exhibition and publication programs, and increased the visitor-ship and paying membership to the point of stability.

Bert also retained her affiliation with the MNM during her tenure at the MNCA, including her office in the Lab and access to the collections for continuing Galisteo Basin research (A.E. Dittert to D.N. Kolb, November 19, 1965; 89LA.061; 99BPD.xx; 13ARM.001 [Christmas Letter, 1966]). With this new administrative challenge, and now interests in Navajo history and ceremonial art, Bert had less time to devote to the Galisteo Basin and archaeology in general. After her last summary article (Dutton 1980), she moved on to topics related to Navajo culture in her remaining years.[27]

Honoring Their Mentor

Reunion and Memorial

Digger Poof Song
We will serenade our Bert, while life and love they last,
and will pass and be forgotten with the rest.
Girl Scout songsters out on a spree, digging from here to
eternity.
Lord, have mercy on such as we, following Bert.

−1954

The Reunion

In the summer of 1982, with Bert's eightieth birthday approaching the following year, Lila "Luckie" McCall, who had been on Mobile Camps in 1947 and 1948, decided that it would be an appropriate occasion to honor their mentor for all she had done by organizing and running the Girl Scout Southwest archaeological program. McCall knew that she and others had benefitted so much from the experiences and felt that it was time for as many as possible to get together again and show their appreciation in a more formal way. She contacted Bert and asked her if that would be okay, and Bert seemed pleased and enthusiastic. McCall, living in Houston, then enlisted Susan Martin (1954, 1955 Mobiles; 1955–1956 Digs), a part-time Santa Fe resident, to oversee local arrangements. Other Santa Feans were also recruited, including Caroline Kline (1954–1956 Mobiles and Digs), Gillian Wethey McHugh (1953–1954 Mobiles; 1952–1954 Digs,) and Sigrid Holien Marlow (1950–1952 Mobiles; 1951–1953 Digs, and Las Madres Laboratory Assistant).

Together they hatched a plan for a reunion of all the Dutton's Dirty Diggers, GS Reps, and staff that they could locate. They would try to get them to hold it in Santa Fe as close to Bert's birthday as possible. They networked with all those they remembered from their own years and camps, and asked them to do the same, broadening the contacts as fast and as far as they could. They pored through lists of former subscribers to *The Sipapu,* Bert's Christmas letters, applications for the camps still in Bert's files,[1] and other potentially useful documents—like Bert's guest books.

It was going to be hard work, of course, as many of the Scouts had married and changed their last names and/or had moved several times over the last 25 years. Quite a few had little connection to where they had lived when they were young—but their last known addresses were used. Thankfully, Bert and other Diggers had stayed in contact with many, especially those who had come for more than one season, and those who had visited Bert over the years at El Rancho del Cielo or written letters.

With their tentative list—nearly 200—the organizers then contacted GSUSA to enlist their help, hoping that they had some old records that might provide more information on the whereabouts of the missing. Susan Martin and Lila McCall each wrote to National for information, sending them a list of names of those they could not locate. Both stressed in their letters the pivotal role Bert and the Archaeological Mobile Camps and Digs—and scouting in general—had played in their lives and careers, and the deep feeling that they had and would always maintain for Bert and their Southwest Girl Scouting experiences. They also pointed out that the majority of the participants had excelled in their chosen fields of endeavor, especially in the scientific areas, and that this, too, reflected the success of the archaeological program and of Scouting and its principles. They suggested that if they were successful in honoring Bert and the program as they planned, they would welcome participation by GSUSA National headquarters in any way they felt appropriate (S.S. Martin to GSUSA, August 2, 1982; L.L. McCall to Jane Freeman, January 17, 1983; GSUSA Archives, Camps and Camping; All American Camps-General).

Their inquiry got attention from National headquarters, although after staff queried various offices and searched where they thought pertinent files on the program might be located, they were unable to find any more information that would be of help in contacting the missing. However, in an internal memorandum between "Jeanie" and "Margery" (Lawrence), it was agreed that Jane Freeman, then President of the GSUSA, should certainly send a letter of congratulations to Dr. Dutton; in fact a "real special letter from JCF would be JUST GREAT," wrote Lawrence. She said further that this was "indeed a remarkable group, a remarkable leader AND, in my opinion, one of our greatest Wider Opptys [Opportunities]" and should be celebrated (internal memo, Margery to Jeanie, ca. 1983; GSUSA Archives, Camps and Camping, All American Camps-General).

The celebration organizers sent out approximately 125 letters to persons on their confirmed list, inviting them to attend the Dutton's Dirty Digger reunion on Saturday, March 26, 1983. It would honor Dr. Bertha P. Dutton on the occasion of her eightieth birthday[2] and be held at the Museum of International Folk Art in Santa Fe. Over 100 women responded with cards and letters indicating whether they could attend or not, and also congratulating Bert and forwarding their best wishes. Several who could not attend updated Bert as to what had occurred in their lives since those trips to the Southwest (99BPD.xx; see below and Chapter 10).

Roughly 60 attended the reunion in person, apparently many staying at the La Fonda Hotel where a large block of rooms were set aside for them. Pre-reunion celebrations at the hotel included a no-host dinner the night before and a no-host brunch the next morning (L. McCall to Diggers, March 8, 1983; S.S. Martin copy). There were also pre- and post-reunion tours offered to the local places for nostalgia, such as Bandelier National Monument and Pecos National Historical Park, Rio Grande Pueblos that were hosting dances, and more.

According to an article published on the Dutton celebration in *New Mexico Magazine* later that spring, the reception included a "pot-shaped birthday cake which [Bert] appropriately enough, cut with an archaeologist's trowel" (Figure 9.1;

Figure 9.1. Sigrid Holien Marlow, Emily Jefferson, and Bertha Dutton at Dutton's eightieth birthday party and Digger reunion, posed with a cake decorated with a pottery design, 1983. 99BPD.xx. Courtesy of MIAC/LAA.

New Mexico Magazine, June 1983:21). Bert was driven to the reunion by Caroline "Casey" Kline in Casey's Model A Ford (like Bert's), and Bert was reported as "beaming on her arrival to multiple cheers." After a brief overview of the program and Bert's career and association with Scouting, it was time for testimonials. Individuals expressed their feelings about "Man and Nature in the Southwest" and how it had changed them. Portions of letters from those who could not attend were read to the audience. Sally Buckley Lane (Camp II, 1949), who sent regrets at not being there, said: "I will always be grateful to Bert for giving me an interest in and appreciation for all peoples and cultures, for helping me to see and enjoy the wonders of nature, from the strata in rocks to the path made by a sidewinder" (*New Mexico Magazine*, June 1983:21). Another said: "I felt that you and the camps opened so many doors for me." And yet another wrote: "You gave me a great sense of accomplishment, by showing me the pleasure of working hard and successfully with others, the interdependency we all had on one another, the importance of doing our share of *kapers*…and although I love all the creature comforts that I have accumulated through the years, because of your inspiration and teaching, I know I could adapt and survive in almost any situation, with only the barest of necessities" (99BPD. xx). A letter of congratulations and thanks from GSUSA President Jane Freeman was read to those assembled officially congratulating Bert on her role in developing so many fine young women and sending warm wishes "on behalf of millions of sister Girl Scouts…and my warm thanks for all you mean to this organization and the girls it serves" (99BPD.xx). Thus, Bertha Dutton joined a long list of other mentors who through various Girl Scout programs and activities had made a big difference in many women's young and adult lives, and the generations that followed them.

Other cards and letters from those who could not attend were presented to Bert. Nettie Kesseler Adams (Camp 1, 1950; Dig 1951–1952; and anthropologist) wrote in her note that "Bert was a very important figure in my career as she must have been to many of us, and it would surely be gratifying to her to see what the seeds she planted have become." Diana Avery Amsden (Camp 1, 1950; Dig 1951; also a PhD anthropologist) wrote: "Bert was a memorable part of my life. She made some wonderful times possible, and her own competence makes her an inspiration." And Eunice Prien, former Region IX Director (plus Camp 2, 1949) and now 80 years old, reminisced about learning "the hard way," as Bert said she would, about the benefits of weak tea over carbonated drinks in quenching thirst, and added: "You and the Dig are highlights of my years in the Southwest" (99BPD.xx).

Bert also received a booklet giving the names and addresses of all in attendance, as well as a hand-lettered scroll that the organizing group had devised on behalf of all assembled. It read as follows (99BPD.xx):

Bertha Dutton, Doctor of Philosophy, anthropologist, museum director, author, teacher, field expeditions director, recipient of many fellowships, honorary degrees, nominated to rolls of honor, certificates of appreciation, and life memberships, interpreter of human and natural history, supporter and judge of first arts and crafts of the Southwest, representative of her profession to the international scientific community, chronicler and advocate of the native people of her adopted home, and friend to scores of former Girl Scouts from all parts of the United States. As we gather to celebrate the eightieth anniversary of the birth of Bertha Dutton, the alumnae of the Senior Girl Scouts Archaeological Mobile Camps and Pueblo Largo field seasons, held from 1947 to 1957, who forever call themselves Dutton's Dirty Diggers, stand in grateful appreciation of the youthful enthusiasm shared with us in our youth; the love of life and learning and uncompromising devotion to excellent hard work and truth that has inspired us, our daughters and granddaughters during past years and will in years to come.

As those assembled toasted Bert, they sang the *Digger-Poof Song*, "with their tea-cups raised on high"—actually souvenir glasses labeled "Dutton's Dirty Diggers, 1983"—as its chorus and final verse rang out.

The party lasted several hours, with more songs, visiting, catching up on each other's lives, work, children, grandchildren, and a host of other topics. Bert enjoyed it all immensely and, with characteristic modesty, summed up her thoughts as follows: "It was quite an honor to have about 60 women from around the country gather here in Santa Fe, and to know that I touched their lives in some way" (*New Mexico Magazine*, June 1983:21). Just as in the old days when the girls, now mature women, departed at the end of the Mobile Camps and Digs, more than a few tears were shed and promises made to keep in touch with each other, and especially with their mentor, Bert. Several local Diggers honored Bert again on her eighty-eighth birthday in a smaller, private party in 1991, held at the home of Susan Martin in Santa Fe.

Postretirement

In her postretirement years, Bert remained active by serving on several local and national boards, foundations, and other organizations, and accumulating more honors and awards than the dozens she had already received (see Bohrer 1979, Morris and Olin 1997 for partial lists). In 1985, on the occasion of its fiftieth anniversary, the Society of American Archaeology named her among the important figures in the history of the discipline. Also in 1985, she was interviewed over a two-day period in preparation for a special conference to be held the following year titled "Daughters of the Desert: Women Anthropologists and the Native American Southwest, 1880–1980." The conference, along with an accompanying exhibition and catalog, was developed by Barbara Babcock and Nancy Parezo of the University of Arizona to celebrate the lives and achievements of the Southwest's pioneering women archaeologists, ethnographers, and linguists. Bert attended the two-day conference in Tucson in the spring of 1986, along with several other honorees, where they all "shared their lives and focused on what it was like to work in the Southwest" in those early years (Parezo 1993a:xvi). In the follow-up volume to that conference, plus another where scholars and discussants reviewed and synthesized what had been learned from both the interviews and previous research into the lives of these pioneering women, Bert is profiled and quoted several times, including her work with the Girl Scouts (Parezo, ed. 1993; see also Morris and Olin 1997:656). The exhibition, along with a video-documentary, toured national, state, and local museums and other institutions for three years (Babcock and Parezo 1988; Parezo 1993a:xvi).[3] As a result of the exhibition being shown at UNM's Maxwell Museum of Anthropology, the Governor named the New Mexico women profiled (including Bert) official "State Treasures." In 1987, Bert also was declared a "Santa Fe Living Treasure," another distinctive honor. On that occasion she was interviewed again about favorite parts of her life, speaking once more about the personal importance of her 11 years with the Senior Girl Scout Archaeological Mobile Camp Program and all of the wonderful young women she had met and who remained in her life (Dutton 1987:10). She was also cited on that occasion for her "participation in the life, heart, and spirit" of the Santa Fe community (Morris and Olin 1997:655). At her induction ceremony, a tree was planted in her honor, and it still grows in Santa Fe's Larragoite Park.

Memorial Celebration

Bertha Pauline Dutton passed away on September 11, 1994, in Santa Fe. Two obituaries appeared in the local paper. Both listed several of her accomplishments, but neither could begin to adequately cover the many in her long and fruitful career.

George Ewing, former director of the Museum of New Mexico, was quoted as saying: "She was quite a remarkable person—a widely beloved character. She had a continuous string of publications, archaeological site reports and other information about the Indians of New Mexico" (Van Eyck 1994a). The other notice added that: "From 1946–1957 [sic: 1947] she carried on a series of archaeological Mobil[e] camps for Senior Girl Scouts, educational trips in nature, archaeological excavations, museum visits, contributing to the understanding of man and nature in the Southwest; with these girls she established an important lasting and loving relationship" (Van Eyck 1994b). Her survivors are listed as including: longtime friend and colleague, Dr. Caroline Olin; the John McHugh and John A. Dillon families; and her archaeological "Dirty Diggers." Organized by former Scouts and Santa Fe friends and professionals, the celebration was "to be cheerful and upbeat."

The Memorial Celebration was held in St. Francis Auditorium, Museum of Fine Arts (now New Mexico Museum of Art), October 22, 1994, 10 a.m.–12 p.m., and indeed was upbeat as advertised. After a musical prelude, played appropriately by Gillian Wethey McHugh, speakers included several of Dutton's Dirty Diggers: Susan Martin, Elizabeth Galligan, Claire [Yeagley] Harrison, Gillian McHugh, Lila McCall, and Caroline Kline. They spoke of her career, Girl Scout memories, and the many influences Bert had on their lives. Colleagues from the Museum of New Mexico and Museum of Navajo Ceremonial Art (now the Wheelwright Museum of the American Indian)—including Marjorie Lambert, Stewart Peckham, Susan McGreevy, and Harry Walters—all added tributes and reminiscences, as did special friends John McHugh, John Dillon, Ellie Pratt, David Brugge, and Elizabeth Ann Morris. Others in the audience also spoke, including more Dirty Diggers. In typical Scout fashion, the event was punctuated with Digger songs, and Diggers served as ushers.

After the memorial, there was a reception in the sculpture garden of the museum, and later in the day, additional gatherings in private homes to visit further and reminisce, and share condolences. It was a fitting celebration of a great career of one who meant so much to so many.

10

Bertha Dutton's Legacy

"I Have Over 200 Daughters"

Tune: *Tennashay alla ee*
Dirty Diggers are we, traveling the Southwest to see
The ruins, the *kivas*, the Pueblos, the dances,
Enjoying the deserts so free.

Zuni, Hopi, and Navaho, ancient cultures as well as new.
Zuni, Hopi, and Navaho, ancient cultures as well as new.

Friends forever we'll be, though scattered from sea to sea
Though time may pass, I'll never forget you
But cherish this memory.

—1954-1957

Bertha Pauline Dutton remains in the minds of those who knew her a unique individual, in a region of the country that has known its share of unique personalities and especially women. She created a unique program, the Senior Girl Scout Archaeological Mobile (and Excavation) Camp Program, and it had a major impact on a number of young women at a critical time in their lives, and in a period when paths to the future for women were uncertain and not nearly as varied as they are today. Our purpose in telling this story—hers, theirs, and ours—has not been to assess Bert's rich life and career as an anthropologist, but to better place her and the program in the context in which it functioned. We also wanted to emphasize its significance for both her and the Senior Girl Scouts who were privileged to participate in it with her. Their legacies and hers remain forever intertwined.

Bertha Dutton, Dirty Digger Mentor

It was a fortuitous day in 1946 when Sue Little met with Bertha Dutton in her office at the Museum of New Mexico, and they immediately began planning the first Senior Girl Scout Archaeological Mobile Camp. What happened that day certainly left its mark on Bert, many of the 292+ young women involved, and perhaps during the 11 years of its operation, on the Senior Girl Scout camping program. Something special occurred between 1947 and 1957 in the Southwest for Senior Girl Scouts, and it continues to be important today.

Bert often reflected on those years with enthusiasm, in her annual summaries of the trips at the end of the season, her posts to the anthropological newsletter *Teocentli*, and in the oral interviews she gave in her later years (Dutton 1983; 1985; 1987; 1990). Once she started her annual Christmas letters in 1966, she continued to refer to the girls (now women) and former staff members she had seen or heard from during the year. She kept in touch with others on a more personal basis. Although the program always took a great deal of work each year, and ultimately became too taxing for her to continue, she would not have traded the chance it gave her to work with the girls and young women, and in later years, to stay connected to them and their families as they moved through life. Several she saw frequently, especially those living in Santa Fe and northern New Mexico, including Gillian Wethey McHugh, Pat Hart, Caroline Kline, Sigrid Holien Marlow, Susan Martin, Vorsila Bohrer, and Elizabeth Galligan, and former staff members Margaret Buck, Elizabeth Parker Overton, and Marie Nourse. She stayed in touch with others at a greater distance through their periodic visits and correspondence, including Anne Rushmer McClelland, Virginia Franklin, Lila "Luckie" McCall, Martha Harlan,

Claire Yeagley Harrison, Joan Treher, Pat Sowers, Evelyn Stobie, and Nettie Kesseler Adams. More dropped by if in Santa Fe, or wrote notes to her on special occasions, or saw and spoke with her at other venues.[1] She was always happy to see or hear from her Dirty Diggers no matter how infrequently. Somehow we felt that she cared about us individually as much as all of us collectively. Roughly 60 DDDs came to her eightieth birthday/reunion in 1983, several (locals) to her smaller eighty-eighth birthday party, and others to her memorial service in 1994. As she often stated, she never felt that she had sacrificed in not having a family, because, after all, she "had over 200 daughters" (Kessinger ca. 1980). They, their spouses, children, and friends, were her family, along with her anthropology colleagues and her many other local and nonlocal friends.

Bert often denied that she influenced her Digger daughters and their lives, although there is no doubt that she did. She was a positive role model for many, whether she realized it or not. She was seen as accomplished and successful, a woman who had earned an advanced degree and had a satisfying career, obviously extremely knowledgeable and engaged with her subject matter, respected by her peers, determined and firm, yet also fun-loving and happy. We all felt that she could make her way anywhere. She also introduced us to a subject matter that we knew little about, or some of us didn't even knew existed—anthropology, including especially its subfields of archaeology and ethnology. But she also stressed the importance of other disciplines that were more familiar: history, biology, geology, geography, agriculture, forestry, art, dance, and more. Most of these we had at least heard of through school and/or Girl Scouting, but she presented a chance to see these abstract ideas put into practice, in the hands of people who were devoting their lives to them and were passionate about promoting them. What she and others taught us about the Southwest, its long and rich history, the beauty and complexity of the its landscape, the diversity of its people and their lives, their arts, and much more, created a deeper understanding of a complex place—certainly most of which we did not fully grasp then, but at least we had a fine introduction. It made some of us into permanent fans of the region with a desire to stay connected to this place—even if only in memory. Many began their own collections of Southwest art—if not specifically Native American Art—from the region as continual reminders and because it engaged them esthetically.

Dutton's Dirty Digger Daughters (DDDD)

Bert took particular pride in those who went on to higher education, the many DDDDs who earned undergraduate and graduate degrees, and moved into various professions. But she was equally proud of those who married out of high school or after a short stay in college and raised families. And there were those who did it all, again showing that they were capable of managing multiple roles at the same time. She was also happy when her girls stayed connected with Girl Scouting into adulthood, as she did after the Mobile and Dig Camps were over, hoping that they would make a difference for the next generation of girls and young women, as she felt Scouting had for her and her Digger daughters. And she was happy to hear that those who stayed in contact with other DDDs—even if not with her—had bonded as a result of their trips. Certainly the camps created friendships and a certain kinship among the girls that lasted. Staying with Scouting through one's Senior Scout years was an important bond. But a special bond existed among DDDDs and, in many ways, still does.[2]

Those Diggers whom we have been able to track, largely because they stayed in contact with Bert, us, or each other, are too numerous to mention by name, but some examples will suffice to illustrate some of the impacts of Bert and the program.[3] We start with one of the DDDs who stayed connected with Bert perhaps the longest: Vorsila Bohrer. Bohrer was a veteran of three Mobile Camps and leader of one, plus a participant in one Dig Camp and a volunteer at others. She earned her BA in anthropology and Botany at the University of Arizona, as well as an MS in botany with an anthropology minor from the University of Michigan. She worked at the MNM for Bert periodically (employee and volunteer) and led archaeological survey and excavation camps for Senior Scouts at the northern New Mexico Chaparral Council's Eliza Seligman Camp in the Jemez Mountains in the early 1960s. And she was Chaparral's district representative for the western Navajo Reservation before returning to school to finish her doctorate at the University of Arizona in botany and geochronology. Bohrer became the leading Southwest paleobotanist[4] of her generation, doing innovative research throughout her career at many Southwest archaeological sites and elsewhere. She also mentored other paleobotanists through individual training and consultantships from her base in Portales, New Mexico. In

1997, she received the Fryxell Award, a prestigious honor given by the Society for American Archaeology for interdisciplinary contributions to archaeological theories, methods, and interpretations. Her list of publications is very long.

Five other Diggers earned advanced degrees in anthropology, did additional fieldwork in archaeology and/or ethnology, and went on to successful careers in academic or related posts. They include: Nettie Kesseler Adams, Mary Anne Stein, Ernestine Green, Diana Avery Amsden, and Catherine (Kay Sweeney) Fowler. All were veterans of one or more Mobile and/or Dig Camps.

Nettie Adams majored in anthropology at the University of Arizona, where she met fellow student and future husband archaeologist/ethnologist William Y. Adams. They worked together as archaeologists for the Museum of Northern Arizona on the Glen Canyon Archaeological Salvage Project, a multidisciplinary and multi-institutional effort to document anthropological and environmental knowledge and concerns in and around the Glen Canyon of the Colorado River before it was inundated by the Glen Canyon Dam. Later, from their base at the University of Kentucky, the Adamses excavated and analyzed materials in Egypt and the Sudan endangered by another dam, the Aswan High Dam on the Nile. They coauthored major publications on their studies there as well as elsewhere in the region. Nettie Adams became especially well-known as an archaeological textile analysist.

Mary Anne Stein earned her BA and MA in anthropology from the University of Oklahoma. She worked for the Museum of Northern Arizona on the Glen Canyon Archaeological Salvage Project, and then in 1964–1965 as laboratory supervisor on the University of Arizona's multiyear excavations at Snaketown, a large Hohokam village near Chandler, Arizona. She then worked for the National Park Service at Bandelier National Monument, and after attending the NPS's Albright Training Center, as Park Archaeologist at Walnut Canyon National Monument. She then earned her PhD in anthropology at Southern Methodist University and a second doctorate in law (JD) at the UNM's Center for Wildlife Law. She held positions for several years as a lawyer in defense of western conservation issues.

Ernestine Green, also a PhD anthropologist, spent most of her career as an archaeologist and manager with the US Forest Service in Montana and elsewhere. She is best known for essays on archaeological ethics, a very relevant topic today.

Diana Avery Amsden, who came from a family of archaeologists in New Mexico,[5] earned her PhD in anthropology at the University of New Mexico, as well as other advanced degrees elsewhere. She participated in major digs in several areas of the Southwest and also worked as a research anthropologist for private businesses, including for the film and television industries where she authored several production scripts. An independent thinker and writer, she remains interested in anthropology, archaeology, architecture, and art history (Amsden 2017).

Elizabeth Galligan majored in anthropology as an undergraduate at the University of New Mexico for her BA. Like Stein, she worked for the Museum of Northern Arizona on the Glen Canyon Archaeological Salvage Project. She earned an MA at UCLA and later returned to UNM, finishing her PhD in American Studies. She became an educator in her home state of New Mexico, and also a mystery writer.

I (Kay Sweeney Fowler) first worked as an ethnologist on the Glen Canyon Archaeological Salvage Project while a student at the University of Utah—a cooperating institution with the Museum of Northern Arizona in that large project. My task was to find Southern Paiute archaeological sites through Southern Paiute consultant-directed fieldwork in southeastern Utah. I met and later married Don Fowler while there and, after finishing my BA, followed him to the University of Pittsburgh where I earned an MA and we both finished doctorates in anthropology. I spent my career teaching at the University of Nevada, Reno, specializing in ethnographic, ethnoarchaeological, ethnobiological, and linguistic research among Great Basin Indigenous peoples. I was elected to the National Academy of Sciences and the American Academy of Arts and Sciences in 2011.

Other DDDDs went into different fields, also earning graduate degrees. (Bert always told us to follow our passions.) Susan Martin finished her PhD at the University of California, Santa Cruz, in biochemistry/biology. She spent most of her career as a research biochemist at the United States Department of Agriculture's Agricultural Research Service at Colorado State University. Jo Tice Bloom earned her PhD in American History from the University of Wisconsin-Madison in 1967 and taught in colleges and universities in various states, plus Afghanistan, ending her teaching career at New Mexico State University. She married John Bloom, also an educator, and son of Lansing Bloom, an early mentor of Bert's at UNM. She remained active in Girl Scout activities as a council member and camp volunteer during most of her life, and especially in the Las Cruces, New Mexico, region. Like Bloom, Merideth Medler Grover earned her PhD in history and became a professor of history at St. Cloud State University, Minnesota.

There is less information available on some of the other Diggers, although a few additional sources (beyond personal knowledge) exist. As noted earlier, between 1951 and 1954 Bert wrote a column in the DDD newsletter, *The Sipapu*, cataloging graduations, engagements, marriages, and births of children. She also actively corresponded with Anne Rushmer McClelland from 1948 to 1954, often updating her on DDD activities (99BPD.xx). Dutton also referred to Digger activities in her annual Christmas letters from 1966 to 1988, unfortunately not always by the person's full name (13ARM.001). Most recent and useful are the cards and notes that Diggers wrote to Bert on the occasion of her eightieth birthday in 1983 (99BPD.xx). From these sources, combined with what is known from some who kept in touch with each other, we learn something about the later activities of roughly 60 of the participants—a small but useful sample. Some examples are detailed below.

At least 20 beyond those already named earned at minimum undergraduate degrees, and became grade school and high school teachers in a variety of subjects from health and physical education to mathematics and other sciences (biology, chemistry, etc.). Examples include: Patricia Sowers who, by 1983, had taught for 17 years at Keams Canyon in Hopi country. In that same year, two others were also teaching in reservation or other schools in Arizona: Stella Schultz Weakes and Bertha Talahytewa. Caroline Kline (MA, History) taught at St. Michael's High School in Santa Fe, earning the New Mexico junior high school teacher of the year award in 1997 (Morris and Olin 1997:655). Helen Gaskill Trautter taught school in Albuquerque, and Saudi Arabia (for Saudi Aramco) for five years and went on to work at a women's crisis center in Oregon. Jean Webber graduated from Purdue as a teacher, received two MA degrees, earned a EdD from Brigham Young University, and in 1983 was a high school principal in California.

At least nine DDDDs became nurses. Some, like Cyndy Tice, combined nursing with teaching. Tice graduated from nursing school and joined the Peace Corps, serving in Bangladesh. Later in her career she joined CARE, taught nursing, and helped during medical crises in Asia and Africa, finishing her long career in Saipan (Jo Tice Bloom, personal communication, 2010). Several others were still actively working as nurses in 1983, including Ruth Salter, Katheryn Wollan, Reita Stuart, and Judith Lohr.

Four DDDDs became physical/mental health therapists or other health professionals. Eloise Moore received her MSW (Masters of Social Work) and was working in a mental health center in Texas in 1983. Also by 1983, Dian Milam Wadley had retired as coordinator of the work therapy department at an Oklahoma state mental hospital.

At least five DDDDs received BAs in anthropology but then chose other career paths. Of these, two become journalists: Martha Harlan and Sigrid Holien Marlow. Nancy Skiles, who double-majored in anthropology and government, worked in Africa. She married Irven DeVore, a well-known Harvard anthropologist and specialist in human evolutionary biology, and accompanied him on several expeditions to Africa for field studies among hunter-gatherer societies as well for detailed observations on the social lives of nonhuman primates. With him, she cofounded and managed the nonprofit photographic archive Anthro-Photo which specializes in providing photographs in anthropology and behavioral biology. Jeanne Ellis earned an MS in chemistry at Kansas State and by the early 1960s had entered the PhD program at the University of Arizona. She spent two summers working in the Anthropology Department at the Museum of Northern Arizona analyzing the composition of archaeological pottery sherds, and hoped to be a ceramics technologist in the Southwest. She also was solicited to work on the chemistry of the corn and the pottery recovered from Pueblo Largo at Bert's request (LAA 95PLE.004). Claire Yeagley Harrison earned a BA in anthropology from the University of Arizona and entered the graduate program in anthropology at University of Texas, Austin. When contacted in 1983, she was affiliated with the Horace M. Albright Training Center, National Park Service, Grand Canyon, Arizona.

Several other DDDDs chose other career paths. At least one in addition to Mary Anne Stein became a lawyer: D'ette Looney Foulkes. Rebecca Adams Mills, who graduated from Swarthmore with a BA in history, joined the National Park Service in mid-career, and served as superintendent of Great Basin National Park from 1995 to 2002—one of the few women to gain such a position in the NPS at the time. She is presently on the Board of Directors of the Great Basin Observatory located near Great Basin National Park. In 1983, four former DDDDs were employed in business and industry: Barbara Henderson with Bell Telephone Laboratory and another with PanAm, although their positions were not known. Two botany graduates worked for nursery and landscape companies. At least one DDD had joined the military (Women in the Air Force [WAF]) by the 1960s, and two had become missionaries or otherwise followed a religious calling. One co-operated a large cattle ranch with her husband in Texas.

Three DDDs are known to have been actively involved in the arts. Gillian Wethey McHugh, as previously noted, taught piano and voice to many Santa Feans and was a patron of the arts there. Henri DeStefano was much involved with Little Theater in her Texas community, including in productions as well as fundraising. Nancy Reed Miller became a musician and also went to business college. For Sylvia Shipley Warder, both a potter and weaver, artistic achievements were not only hers but her children's. She married Navajo painter Narciso Abeyta, and three of their children became well-known artists: clay sculptors Elizabeth and Pablita Abeyta, and painter Tony Abeyta—an artistic second generation.

At least three other women received either MA or PhD degrees according to Bert's various records, but their college majors are unknown: Evelyn Stobie, Gwenyth Morris, and Evelyn Harvey. Several others who sent notes to Bert in 1983 for her birthday celebration wrote they had not lost their interest in anthropology, ecology, and the history of the Southwest, and had gone on to cultivate additional knowledge of these subjects locally and in other areas of the world. Some said that they had visited archaeological sites in other regions of the United States, Mexico, and South America, as well as in England and Italy based on what they carried forward from their DDD days. Bert was always very eager—and proud—to hear about their family lives, their husbands, their children, and all their achievements. The totality of their lives mattered to her.

As undoubtedly had their parents, Scout leaders, and other mentors, Bert had attempted to instill in all of her Scouts a curiosity and a willingness to take a chance on a career. Several took a chance and followed less traditional paths than were the norm at the time. Above all, she wanted her Diggers to follow their hearts, use their minds, be individuals, and persevere in whatever they chose—but always with an option if their first choice did not work out. "Do something constructive with your lives," she often said. In 1985, when asked whether she felt that she had had any influence on all these young women, Bert was characteristically modest, replying that it was more likely "just as a friend... just by being me, that's what I say. I guess I gave some guidance... or just as a friend" (Dutton 1985:19–20).

The Legacy for the Girl Scouts

Bert and the Girl Scouts fit well together from the beginning as they shared similar values and goals. Through their programs both wanted to prepare girls and young women to be good leaders for their families, communities, and country; hold solid values; and have a set of life skills that would serve them well in the future. Their programs thus oriented their activities to achieve good citizenship, honesty, self-sufficiency, and feelings of self-worth, but also the ability to work well together toward a common goal. An essential outcome was to be the feeling that they could do and be whatever they wanted. Bert's chosen field and achievements in it seemed to demonstrate these values to the participants as well as a certain boldness, as has been noted before.

Although Bert and the GSUSA did not always fully agree on the exact means needed to achieve these various goals, neither faltered in their overall orientations. In the end, the girls and young women, in particular, were the beneficiaries. From her personal perspective, Bert also wanted to foster in the girls and young women a genuine appreciation of cultural differences and achievements derived from accurate knowledge about other people and their histories, so as to promote a deeper and more sincere cross-cultural understanding. This was her message from anthropology. Certainly an unexpected legacy of her effort was the number of veteran Diggers who returned again and again to Southwest, having been captured by the environment, scenery, cultural-historical-ethnic diversity, arts, and many other aspects of the region that had so captivated Bert during her undergraduate and graduate years at UNM.

Certainly the legacy of Bert's program for Scouting is seen in the number of Diggers who continued to be involved in GSUSA activities well into their adult years. Using the same sources cited above, again an admittedly small sample, we learn that many DDDs who stayed in contact with Bert were also eager to update her on their Scouting ventures after their Southwest trips. As noted previously (Chapter 7), 13 DDDs, plus three former DDD staff, attended the first 1956 National Girl Scout "Roundup" in Michigan and hoped to get together and reminisce about their Southwest trips. Some of the same plus others went to *All States* and on additional "Wider Opps," including to camps in Europe and Mexico and to other events. Several also served in local camps all over the USA during and after attending Digger camps. They became camp counselors, swimming instructors, camp naturalists, and more, some continuing with positions well into adulthood. Several earned at least their 10-year pins and Gold Bar awards while still in high school, and at least one (Vorsila Bohrer) worked as an employee for a regional council.

Based on other notes and cards sent to Bert in 1983, at least 25 former Diggers retained their memberships in the GSUSA well into adulthood and/or took up leadership positions for their home areas. They reported having served or were still serving as local troop leaders and on GS councils and boards, chairing the yearly district cookie sales, and filling other administrative posts. Helen Garcia Tahbo, went into Scouting professionally for a time and directed a Girl Scout camp in Oregon for at least two years. Likely several of these women remained actively involved in Scouting well beyond that time. Undoubtedly this count would be much higher if our information were more complete.

It is less certain whether the Senior Girl Scout Archaeological Mobile Camp program had any larger impact on Girl Scouting in general. There is no indication that an "archaeology badge" ever was instituted, as Gretchen Yoffa had suggested in the mid-1950s, although there may have been another local archaeological opportunity during that same time.[6] The GSUSA and Region IX did award Bert a "Thanks" award in 1957 for all she had done to further the aims of Scouting with her service. And there was the letter sent by then GSUSA president, Jane Freeman, to Bert on her eightieth birthday (Chapter 9). Although it seems that she and the program are now largely forgotten at National headquarters, in 1983 at the time of her birthday, when asked for help in locating "lost" Diggers for Bert's reunion, at least some employees at the offices in New York City remembered enough about it to remark that it had been one of their best "Wider Opps," if not the best (Chapter 9). The Southwest camps were important enough in the 1950s to earn a place on the National rather than Regional roster of summer camping opportunities, along with All States, Roundup, and a few others.

Ed Ferdon, Bert's colleague at the Museum of New Mexico and the person who actually had the original idea to offer such an opportunity for his Boy Scout troop, remarked in 1985 that he and Bert used to laugh when his requests for field trips for boys on the unimproved roads of the Navajo Reservation were turned down by Boy Scout authorities, while hers were approved by the Girl Scouts. Either Regional or National Girl Scout authorities did not know the actual conditions or were forward-thinking enough at the time to see the value the camps could have over time (we hope the latter). Yes, the program was ultimately overwhelmed by bureaucracy and liability issues, as well as perhaps being "too much of a good thing" for one person to handle beyond 11 years (even a person with the stamina and drive of a Bertha Dutton). However, those eventualities do not detract from its overall worth and value. As noted above, several of Dutton's Dirty Diggers remained active in Scouting in their adult years and were eager to share the fact with Bert. The women undoubtedly recognized their debt to Girl Scouting and also to Bert and Senior Girl Scout Archaeological Mobile Camp Program in the Southwest.

In the end, those of us who were and are still proud that we "followed Bert" wherever she was willing to lead us salute her and all she stands for in our lives. Upon hearing of her death, Susan Martin wrote the following heartfelt tribute to Bert and her value to all who were and are part of the Dutton's Dirty Digger sisterhood. Martin read it at the memorial service on October 22, 1994:

Bertha Pauline Dutton
Blithe spirit, roaming the Southwest, leading by example, role model unknowing...a pixie whose disarming smile disguised an iron will.
We followed—swinging wildly between eager anticipation, understanding beyond our years and girlish silliness (how that must have irritated her!)

Afterward, as years passed, she continued her interest in our diverse pathways
to careers and families until finally we understood,
we were as important to her as she was to us.
A doer, a liver of life who took happiness from small pleasures.
A thoughtful scholar who loved to tend her raspberries.
A writer of serious papers and books who zipped around town in her Model A,
beret set jauntily atop her head.
A private, reserved person who reveled in the companionship of her dear friend
Caroline...a leader who gave of herself and her knowledge
when it would have been easier to withdraw.
Friend but not confidante, mentor but not counselor.
Gone, but not forgotten by those who are as always,
following Bert.

Epilogue

Pueblo Largo, 50 Years Later

In 2009, and again in 2011, three Dutton's Dirty Diggers were privileged to visit Pueblo Largo through arrangements made by the New Mexico Office of Archaeological Studies (OAS), and with the kind permission of the present owners of the San Cristobal Ranch where the site is located. The first occasion was a private tour that included Susan Martin, Mary Anne Stein, Kay (Sweeney) Fowler, Diane Bird (MIAC/LA Archivist), and Melissa Powell (Curator of Archaeology, MIAC/LA). H. Wolcott Toll (OAS) drove us to the site on a bright, clear New Mexico summer morning, where we walked the area, looking at the different parts of the Pueblo and other features, including where the tent camp and kitchen had been. We also enjoyed the spectacular view of Estacado Creek below the mesa, the Sangre de Cristo Mountains to the north, and the Pueblo Colorado cliffs to the south.

Former Dig crew members Martin and Stein remarked on changes that had occurred over the 50+ years since they were teenagers working on the crews in 1955 and 1956. They spent two weeks each year digging in the sun, sheltering from the wind, and trying to dry out from the rain, as well as having a grand time laughing, singing and building lasting friendships with their Dig mates. Although they had worked primarily in Section V (The Point), they immediately recognized the layout of the site as a whole. We visited several other room blocks, including areas excavated by previous DDD crews, such as the large *kiva* in the plaza in the southern section (see Chapter 5; Figure 5.3). They identified areas where the camp was located (although noting that the individual pup tents and wall tents were not always in exactly the same places each year), the kitchen (with its small rock fireplace still

Figure E.1. Jo
Tice (Bloom), Kay
Fowler, Wolky Toll,
Susan Martin, and
Mary Ann Stein
at "Chiles and
Sherds" gathering,
Pueblo Largo,
2011.

largely intact), and other features. Their observations added knowledge to the OAS assessment of the 1950s activities, which are now part of the site's historic archaeology and thus eligible for preservation. At the different room blocks, they commented as at how nature had changed the site over time, including areas now partially filled in with sediment and vegetation, plus what appeared to be a more extensive regrowth and expansion of cholla cactus—always a threat to unwary Diggers.

Sue and Mary Anne and all spent a fine morning reminiscing about past times, and especially the Mobile and Dig camps. It was particularly meaningful for them to see the site again, and for the rest of us to share that time to better relate to the place and what had occurred there during those special summers. They were also gratified to see that Pueblo Largo remained largely as they remembered it and is being preserved with care by the present landowners.

In 2011, the OAS arranged to hold its annual fundraiser ("Chiles and Sherds") at Pueblo Largo, again with the kind permission of the landowners. Susan, Mary Anne, and I were privileged to attend, and we were joined by Jo Tice Bloom and her sister Cyndy Tice (Figure E.1). Stein prepared a poster with color photographs of the 1955 and 1956 excavation camps, and Leslie Cohen, Carole Gardner, and Gordon Wilson a poster on the work they had been doing in analyzing the Pueblo Largo collection (Wilson et al. 2015; see also Chapter 8). Again, there were chances to walk around the site, to reminiscence, and to learn yet more about those Digger days. The large group in attendance enjoyed the chance to see this impressive site and to hear about Dutton's early excavations there, especially from those who had been on the crews in the mid-1950s. A few of the people in attendance also knew Bertha Dutton personally or knew of her and of her work, including with the Girl Scouts. Others did not know about either and were pleased to learn of Bert's dedication to regional archaeology and the education of young women.

Galisteo Basin Preservation Efforts

Since Bert's time, there have been significant developments in her favorite New Mexico research area, the Galisteo Basin. On January 20, 2004, President George W. Bush signed into law the Galisteo Basin Archaeological Sites Protection Act (GBASPA, PL 108-208), creating a congressionally approved federal-state-private partnership designed to protect significant archaeological properties within the Basin. The Act recognizes that the Galisteo Basin contains unique archaeological resources significant to the heritage of the region's (and nation's) Native American and Spanish Colonial heritage, and thus provides for the maintenance and protection of its sites—something that Bert would have heartily supported. The Act covers 24 presently known Ancestral Pueblo archaeological sites (including Pueblo Largo and Las Madres), significant rock art localities, and Spanish Colonial sites on federal, state, and private lands, but also leaves open that future archaeological research may result in the incorporation of more sites and boundary changes for existing ones. Presently known sites cover some 541 acres. For sites on federal lands (largely Bureau of Land Management), the Act authorizes the application of federal laws governing archaeological protection, including the Archaeological Resources Protection Act (ARPA) of 1979 (16 U.S.C. 470aa, et seq.), Native American Graves Protection and Repatriation Act of 1990 (NAGPRA 25 U.S.C. 3001 et seq.), and others, but does not extend their application to private property. For private lands, the Secretary of Interior has entered into discretionary cooperative agreements with the landowners to allow their specific listing for the purpose of protection, preservation, and maintenance (Stewart 2005; GBASPA 2016).

GBASPA specifically directs the Secretary of the Interior to consult with various federal, state, private, and other parties to develop a preservation plan, especially for the 17 named properties within the northern half of the Basin. Las Madres is within this section. For seven additional named properties, largely in the central section of the Basin and including Pueblo Largo and others explored by Nels Nelson and Bert, the present landowners have agreed to cooperate in preservation efforts, to allow limited access, and to inform the GBASPA Working Group of any changes in their status. The Working Group meets regularly to provide input, support efforts to protect and preserve all of the sites, and help secure funding for these efforts. It includes federal, state, county (Santa Fe County), and tribal (Pueblo) representatives, area residents, professional archaeologists, and others (GBASPA 2016).

The northern section of the Galisteo Basin also contains another public-private partnership area, the Galisteo Basin Preserve. The Galisteo Basin Preserve is a land conservation and community development initiative of Commonweal Conservancy, a nonprofit organization that has been stewarding the development of a large open space, with plans for extensive public recreation trails, private conservation properties, and a residential community. GBP covers 13,522 acres, and works in cooperation with federal, state, and Santa Fe County agencies in maintaining public access to these additional lands (galisteobasinpreserve.com). The Archaeological Conservancy (AC), another national nonprofit organization that identifies, acquires, and preserves significant archaeological sites in the U.S., is also involved in the Galisteo Basin. They acquired a portion of Pueblo San Marcos in the northern section in 1981 as their first major property in partnership with the State of New Mexico, and with additional private and federal funds, and contributions from Cochiti Pueblo and the site's landowners at the time. They sponsored research projects there by the University of New Mexico and the American Museum of Natural History in New York. And they have supported a site steward who is both a guardian and often a guide to approved tours of the site. In addition, the AC has had help with acquisition and preservation efforts at other sites within the Basin (Archaeological Conservancy, 2020; Stewart 2005; Baxter 2005). Additional archaeological work has been done in the northern region, including by James Snead and Mark Allen at Burnt Corn Pueblo and other sites nearby, and others have added to the knowledge of the extensive rock art in the region (Snead 2005; Snead 2011; Snead and Allen 2011). Writer and Basin resident Lucy Lippard provides an excellent summary and guide to what is known about the early and colonial history of the region in *Down Country: The Tano of the Galisteo Basin, 1250–1783*. It contains stunning photographs by Edward Ranney and an extensive reference list (Lippard and Ranney 2010). This volume further emphasizes both the unique history and the visual beauty of this region, and why all parties have worked diligently to preserve it for the future.

Thus, on the occasions reviewed earlier, a few DDDs were able to come full circle to the Galisteo Basin and pleased to know that others are actively involved in understanding its long history and especially promoting its preservation for the future. We can but imagine that Bert also would be pleased to know that the region and sites where she spent so many hours, roaming alone on foot or in her trusty Model A, and in the company of colleagues as well as young Girl Scouts, is still being guarded by those committed to its preservation and access.

The Girl Scouts of the United States of America

As they have for more than 100 years, the GSUSA, and their many local and regional councils, remain steadfast in their goals to enrich girls' lives and to encourage them to become responsible citizens as well as tomorrow's leaders. Although popular perceptions may still associate Girl Scouts primarily with cookies, crafts, and camping, they have always been much more than that. As during Bert's day, some local groups, where primary control of programming still rests, are more progressive and well-informed than others. But nationally and locally, an amazing number of women who have achieved high leadership positions and other prominence are former Girl Scouts—U.S. Congresswomen, local and state politicians, business owners and leaders, educators, and more. Today many more former Girl Scouts are also professors, engineers, scientists of many different kinds, medical professionals, and even astronauts. These women have achieved more than was thought possible in the 1950s, although a long way remains to achieve true parity with male counterparts in job opportunities, positions, and pay. And, of course, many former Scouts are also successful mothers, raising their children as best they can to follow their passions and succeed, even if it still requires overcoming barriers and multitasking.

In the past few years, the GSUSA, including its regional and local councils, have become increasingly committed to furthering STEM educational opportunities for girls and young women, starting with the youngest grade entry level—Daisies—and continuing through high school to Seniors and Ambassadors (GSUSA 2017a). That initiative was recently enhanced by the appointment of Sylvia Acevedo as CEO of the GSUSA (May, 2016). Acevedo, who grew up in Las Cruces, New Mexico, holds a BA in industrial engineering from New Mexico State University as well as an MS from Stanford University, also in engineering. She is a former employee of NASA (like Mary Jackson and others several decades earlier [Shetterly 2016]), in this case at the Jet Propulsion Laboratory where she worked on the Voyager 2 project. She also has worked for IBM, Apple, and Dell. A lifelong Girl Scout, she credits her local troop leader with encouraging her interest in astronomy when other teachers at her school discouraged her attempt to "reach for the stars" (GSUSA 2017b). She is quoted as saying "My troop leader looked at me and saw me looking at the stars, and she taught me that there were constellations, she taught me there were systems and patterns to the stars.... Because I got my science badge, I developed that courage and that confidence to study science and math at a time when girls like me weren't studying science and math. Girls like me, statistically weren't even finishing high school" (Italie 2017). In another interview, she added: "Throughout my career I have been deeply committed to helping girls cultivate the skills they need to excel in life. I firmly believe they can change the world, that at this decisive moment in time, we need their courage, confidence, and character more than ever" (GSUSA 2017b). She pledged to continue the trend recently set by the GSUSA to vigorously recruit more girls, young women, and adults by offering even more STEM choices than presently available—as well as all of the other newly revised and additional badge choices in life skills, entrepreneurship, and outdoors.

This STEM emphasis by the GSUSA was also profiled in a guest editorial authored by Nevada Senator Catherine Cortez Masto and Sylvia Acevedo toward helping to produce the next generation of women leaders in technology and other fields (Masto and Acevedo 2019:6E). With this, and under the GSUSA's new registered trademark G.I.R.L. (Go-getter, Innovator, Risk-taker, Leader™), we wish them continued success.

Bertha Dutton and the Dutton's Dirty Diggers are also receiving additional attention. The GSUSA and the National Park Service are partnering in a program to provide middle school girls with an introduction to archaeology. The program, titled "Teaching with Archaeology," and subtitled "Crashing the Gates," outlines a set of lessons focused on early women archaeologists who worked with the National Park Service. Bertha Dutton is included in the first set of lessons for her work in Chaco Canyon at the site of Łeyit Kin, and also for her archaeological Mobile Camps and Digs. She and her program are profiled, and exercises and resources on her work and that of archaeology in general are provided (NPS 2018).

The NPS and the GSUSA are also partnered in a Girl Scout Ranger Program which includes a variety of activities designed to get girls out into National Parks, experiencing the environment and learning to care for it in the future. Through work with NPS rangers in a variety of learning activities (plant and animal identification), action-oriented tasks (trail care, identifying invasive species), and many other types of activities, they can develop an ethic of environmental custodianship, be introduced to new career opportunities, and earn badges at the same time (NPS 2019).

Bertha Dutton would have been pleased on all counts.

Roster of Dutton's Dirty Diggers and Staff, Archaeological Mobile Camps and Excavation Camps, 1947–1957

Compiled by Susan S. Martin

Mobile Camps, 1947–1957[1]

Name	Camp #	Nickname	Home State
Adams, Patricia	53:1	Pat	CA
Adams, Rebecca	56:2	Becky	CA
Adams, Susan Ann	56:1		CA
Allender, Inez	49:2		MO
Altematt, Judy	56:2	Judy	CA
Amsden, Diana	50:1		NM
Anderson, Emilita	57:1	Emy	CA
Anderson, Judy	56:1		MI

Name	Camp #	Nickname	Home State
Ard, Marion	51:1		FL
Ausmus, Bobby D.	55:3	Bobby	AL
Bahlinger, Kathleen M.	55:2		
Bailey, Pat	50:1, 51:2	Pat	NM
Barns, Mickey	50:1	Mickey	NM
Beall, Andrea	56:2		GA
Bebb, Sally	48	Sally	OK
Belcher, De Ann	55:3		TX
Bele, Linda May	57:1		DC
Bell, Gwenie	55:2		CA
Bell, Maurine	51:2	Speedy	TX
Berry, Jeanie	56:1, 57:1 (?)	Jeanie	TX
Black, Gail S.	52:2		TX
Bobo, Marjorie	52:1	Bo	TX
Boettcher, Elaine	55:2		NE
Bohman, Sharon Lee	55:1		WI
Bohrer, Vorsila	47, 48, 49:2	Rambler	IL
Boyd, Kathleen	57:1		CA
Borges, Dian Mildred	55:1	Diggie	NV
Brown, Barbara	55:3, 56:1		WI
Brown, Cindy	57:1		OH
Brown, Harriet Joyce	55:1		LA
Buck, Margaret	49:2	Yazzi	MO
Buckley, Sally	49:2		TX
Buckner, Marsha	56:1		WV
Burns, Isabel	52:1, 53:1	Dusty	IL
Bush, Jan	52:1		

Name	Camp #	Nickname	Home State
Bussolati, Jackie	53:1		
Calloway, Penny	57:1		MO
Campbell, Ellen P.	56:1		CA
Charmichael, Joann	49:2	Jody	TX
Cata, Louise	49:2		NM
Chevis, Celeste	57:1		MS
Chicado, Claudette	53:1		NM
Clark, Kaye	50:1, 52:2		TX
Clark, Mary Jean	54:1		TX
Clark, Minta Lee	54:1		TX
Clark, Sue	52:2		TX
Collier, Barbara	56:2		TX
Conover, Joann	55:2		OH
Cooper, Nancy	51:1	Pinky	NM
Crane, Joyce	51:1		NM
Crow, Jane Ellen	56:1		KS
Cruz, Antonia	50:2	Tony, Queenie	NM
Cunningham, Katheryn J.	57:1		LA
Dando, Marion Lois	55:1	Nobie	NY
Danforth, Linda	55:3, 56:1	Danny	MO
Davis, Ann	49:1, 50:1	Topsy	NM
Destine, Jill	53:2		PA
Devlin, Patricia Ann	55:2		NY
Dinkel, Elise	56:1		NE
Edson, Evelyn E.	57:2		VA
Eldred, Kay	57:1		CA
Ellis, Jeanne	50:2, 52:2, 53:2		MO

Name	Camp #	Nickname	Home State
Ellisor, Elizabeth	52:2	Liz	TX
Elvin, Eunice	49:1	Kelly	NM
Emery, Martha Ann	52:1, 53:1	Marti, Bubbles	TX
Englert, Betty	49:2		OK
Evans, Barbara	47		NM
Faulkner, Roberta	50:2		TX
Faulkner, Rogene	50:2		TX
Feuerhelm, Barbra	53:2	Cal	CA
Finfrock, Ada Sue	55:1		FL
Franke, Carolyn	57:2		CA
Franklin, Judith	52:1, 53:1	Jeff	MI
Frantz, Janet	54:1		TX
Fritsche, Carla Denali	54:2		MN
Fuller, Dorothy	57:2		NY
Galligan, Elizabeth Ann	55:2, 56:2, 57:1	Bets	NM
Garcia, Emily	54:1		NM
Garcia, Helen	55:1		NM
Gaskill, Harriet	49:2	Buzz	TX
Gaskill, Helen	49:2, 50:2		TX
Gatchell, Jean	48		OK
Gerber, Martha Jean	52:1, 53:2; 53:3	Chili	OH
Gillespie, Mary E.	56:1		CA
Gilley, Twila	56:2		TX
Gleason, Jane	49:1		NM
Golladay, Nancy	52:2	Nan	CA
Gough, Betty Jane	56:2	Bird Woman	IN
Gover, Jeanne	49:2	Pow-wow	OK

Name	Camp #	Nickname	Home State
Gratz, Donna Francine	57:1		PA
Gray, Caroline	54:1, 55:3	Cholla	CA
Green, Elizabeth	53:2	Eli	IL
Green, Ernestine (?)	57:1		TX
Guyette, Susan M.	56:1		
Hack, Jacquelyn	48		NJ
Hammer, Carol	55:2, 56:2	Thistle	MT
Hamon, Orinda	56:2		ID
Hankins, Joyce	48	Jo	OK
Hannawald, Martha Ann	54:2	Hanny	KS
Happoldt, Mary Lou	54:2	Georgia	GA
Harlan, Martha	49:1, 50:2	Marty	TX
Harrington, Barbara	56:1, 57:1		NM
Hart, Pat	48, 49:1	Pat	NM
Hart, Penny	57:1		IL
Harvey, Evelyn	54:2	Evie	MO
Hatch, Jean E.	56:1		LA
Heiss, Cheryl	55:2		ID
Henderson, Barbara	48, 49:1	Bobby	NJ
Hendrix, Judith Lee	56:2	Pete	IA
Herman, Barbara	50:1	Doc	NY
Hester, Sybil	54:2	Syb	MS
Higley, Mary Abbie	54:1	Bunny	KS
Higley, Karen	57:1		CO
Hintze, Nancy	48		OK
Hodge, Sue Layne	55:3		MI
Holien, Sigrid	50:1, 51:2, 52:2	Sigi	NM

Name	Camp #	Nickname	Home State
Holm, Janice	52:2	Jan	VA
Hopkins, Sally	56:1		MO
Hosman, Carole Rene	55:1	Green Girl	ID
Hunt, Ann	50:2		TX
Iriate, Marcia	57:2		CA
Jacobson, Regina M.	56:1		IA
Jefferson, Emily	49:1	Jeff	TX
Jenkins, Ann	50:2	Sloadie	TX
Jensen, Marilyn	57:1		ME
Jessup, Nancy	50:2		TX
Johnson, Elaine	56:1		MT
Johnson, Elsa	51:2		NM
Johnson, Faye	50:2		TX
Johnson, Gwendolyn	57:2		PA
Johnson, Myra	50:2	Boopie	TX
Jones, Marilyn	54:2		WY
Jones, Sara Frances	54:1		NE
Karakas, Kathleen	56:2		MI
Keele, Nancy	57:2		CA
Kendall, Janice Marie	54:1	Southern Belle	KY
Keniston, Patsy	49:1, 50:1		TX
Kesseler, Nettie	50:1	Rocky	OK
Klenck, Kathleen	56:1		CA
Kline, Caroline	54:1, 55:2, 56:2	Casey	NJ
Knapp, Joan Elizabeth	54:2		NY
Kofman, Sherry	51:2, 52:2		PA
Lancaster, Teresa	51:2	Terry	TX

Name	Camp #	Nickname	Home State
Larson, Ann	54:2		CA
Lee, Nancy Isabel	56:2		NM
Lewis, Roberta	52:1	Bobbie	CA
Lohr, Judith	54:1		WI
Long, Beverly Ann	57:1		CA
Looney, D'Ette	55:1		TX
Lopez, Lucianita	54:2, 55:1	Lucy	NM
Losh, Sue Ann	56:2		IN
Luckie, Lila	47, 48	Luckie	TX
Lucy, Barbara	53:2		NM
Lynch, Catherine M.	56:2		PA
MacArt, Judith	55:1	Sammie	NJ
Mantle, Janice	52:1	Frosty	MO
Martin, Joyce Ellen	56:2		MT
Martin, Susan	54:2, 55:3	Skip; Skipper	KY
Mattocks, Ann	51:1, 52:1	Looney	OK
Mayhugh, Catherine E.	57:2		CO
McClinton, Betty Jean	49:1		TX
McDermott, Delphean	57:1		NE
McDonald, Evangeline	50:2	Vangie	TX
McDowell, Mary Firth	49:2	Firth	NM
McIntyre, Gail	51:1		AZ
McNamera, Ann	47	Mac	TX
McRae, Martha	49:1		TX
Medler, Meridith Ann	56:2	Merry	WI
Miguel, Suzan	57:2		AZ
Milam, Dian	52:1	Chelsea	OK

Name	Camp #	Nickname	Home State
Miller, Kathryn M.	53:1	Kay	ND
Milliken, Constance	55:3, 57:2	Hurricane	TN
Mills, Melba	53:1	Noisy	WA
Moe, Marie	50:1	Moe	CO
Moore, Betsy	57:1		CO
Moore, Eloise	48, 49:1, 50:1	Patches	TX
Morgan, Jo Ann Elizabeth	54:1		KY
Moriarty, Mickey	50:2		TX
Morris, Barbara E.	54:2	Bobbie	IN
Morris, Gwenyth	51:1, 52:2, 53:2	Que	IN
Mudge, Barbara	53:2	Pidge	IL
Myers, Donna Lee	54:2, 55:2,	Donna	CO
Myers, Pat	52:1		OK
Nash, Beth	55:2		CA
Nestle, Lois Ann	57:2		IL
Nicely, Jeanne	51:1		NM
Nichols, Margaret	49:2		NM
Nixon, Bernadine	50:1, 52:2	Schatzie	TX
O'Boyle, Barbara	47		NM
O'Grady, Shirley	57:2		CO
Ohman, Mary Ann	53:3		MI
Olney, Lavern	51:1	Stinky	TX
Ossian, Barbara Jean	57:1		KS
Owen, Hope	55:3	Hopi	NY
Pachlhofer, Paula	55:2	Junior	KS
Parke, Penny	56:2		TX
Patrick, Alta Mae	51:1	Pat	NM

Name	Camp #	Nickname	Home State
Pearce, Phyllis	52:2		KS
Phillips, Sandra	54:1		WA
Potts, Patsy	50:1	Pottsy	TX
Price, Louzelle	56:1		TX
Price, Monica	57:2		MO
Randels, Judith	57:1		NY
Ratcliff, Betty Jeanne	50:2		NM
Ratiff, Betty	50:2	Johnnie	NM
Reardon, Jean	51:1, 52:1	Jay	NM
Reed, Nancy	51:1		NM
Reimers, Sandra	52:2, 53:2	Sandy	NE
Reyna, Mary	52:1		NM (Taos Pueblo)
Reynolds, Skipper	47	Skip	AZ
Rhoda, Sharon	53:1		NM
Rich, Kristina	54:1		NV
Richard, Lois	56:2		OH
Rieley, Karen	55:3, 56:2		CA
Rivkin, Marjorie	56:2		NY
Romero, Terecita	57:1		NM (Taos Pueblo)
Rushmer, Anne	47, 48, 49:1		OK
Ruth, Joveta	57:2		KS
Salter, Ruth	53:1	Salty	MI
Sandoval, Rosita	52:2, 53:2	Rose	NM (San Felipe)
Scharmann, Patricia	57:1		NE
Schultz, Barbara	48	Bobbie	TX
Schultz, Stella S.	57:2		KY
Schwantje, Sally	53:1		NE

Name	Camp #	Nickname	Home State
Seberhagen, Sandra	55:3, 57:2	Sandy	NY
Secor, Cynthia	55:2		IL
Seldrick, Janet	54:2		OH
Shook, Billie Ruth	53:2	Cookie	TX
Sippel, Ellen F.	56:1		
Skidmore, Marilyn	53:2	Skid	CA
Skiles, Nancy	50:1, 51:2		TX
Slomer, Ruth	51:1	Rusty	NM
Sowers, Patricia	55:1, 56:2	Pat	CA
Stamps, Betty Jean	54:2	BJ	VA
Standley, Jo Ellen	55:1		MO
Stein, Mary Anne	55:2	Dennis	TX
Stetser, Janet	54:1	Stets	PA
Stevenson, Mary Anne	53:2	Mimi	NJ
Stickler, Phyllis	49:1	Phyl	IL
Stobie, Evelyn	48, 49:1, 50:1, 51:2, 52:2	Les	MO
Storm, Mary Elizabeth	57:2		MD
Stuart, Reita	52:1, 53:2	Jackie	OK
Sunbarger, Elizabeth	53:1	Sunny	TX
Sutton, Alice Ann	54:2	Ann	ID
Sweeney, Catherine	56:1, 57:1	Kay	UT
Talahytewa, Bertha Mae	55:2	Bert	AZ (Navajo)
Taylor, Kathleen	57:1		TX
Tice, Cynthia	53:1	Cyndy	IL
Tice, Nancy Jo	48	Jo	IL
Tomme, Marilyn	52:1		TX

Name	Camp #	Nickname	Home State
Trachsel, Phyllis Ann	57:2		IL
Treher, Joan Dodds	55:2		CA
Trujillo, Martha	55:3		NM (San Juan)
Trulilla, Patsy	52:1		NM
Vance, Bess	50:1	Louie	CA
Vaughan, Phyllis	51:1	Phyl	NM
Veatch, Charlotte	51:1, 52:2	Sharky	TX
Vicinus, Martha	56:2	Vic	KY
Villarreal, Dolores	55:1		KS
Vonderlage, Kay	54:2		NE
Warder, Sylvia Ann	51:1		NM
Ware, Linda Ann	57:2		OH
Warren, Jane	49:2		TX
Watts, Sandra	56:1		TX
Wax, Sandra Rae	52:2	Waxi	VA
Webb, Alice	55:2		NY
Weeks, Carolyn	53:1		CT
Wehrli, Joan	49:1, 51:2		TX
White, Priscilla Alden	56:1	Prissy	TX
White, Susan Helen	55:3		WA
Wilcomb, Carol Louise	56:1		ID
Wildman, Harriet	56:2	Harry	OK
Williams, Judy	54:1		IN
Williams, Sandra	53:2		NM
Willitts, Joan	48, 49:1	Willie	NJ
Wohlers, Beth	51:1		NM
Wollan, Katheryn	52:2		TN

Name	Camp #	Nickname	Home State
Wood, Betty Lou	54:1		NY
Wood, Genie Sue	53:3		TX
Woody, Betty	53:2		CA
Wyatt, Beth E.	57:2		TN
Yeagley, Claire	52:2	Squeaky	TX
Young, Helen	55:1		NY
Young, Nelly Bly	57:2		CA
Zeiler, Iva H.	57:1		MD

Excavation Camps, 1951–1956

1951: Amsden, Diana; Barns, Mickey; Bohrer, Vorsila; Faulkner, Roberta; Faulkner, Rogene; Harlan, Martha; Holien, Sigrid; Hunt, Ann; Kesseler, Nettie; Moore, Eloise; Stobie, Evelyn; Vance, Bess; Wehrli, Joan.

1952: Holien, Sigrid; Hunt, Ann; Kesseler, Nettie; Morris, Gwenyth; Pearce, Phyllis; Reardon, Jean; Reed, Nancy; Stobie, Evelyn; Wethey, Gillian; Whitburn, Shirley; Wohlers, Beth.

1953: Ellis, Jeanne; Harlan, Martha; Holien, Sigrid; Matlocks, Ann; Morris, Gwenyth; Mudge, Barbara; Reed, Nancy; Reimers, Sandra; Rhoda, Sharon; Stobie, Evelyn; Wethey, Gillian; Yeagley, Claire.

1954: Emery, Martha Ann; Franklin, Judith; Fritsche, Carla; Hester, Sybil; Kline, Caroline; Morris, Barbara E.; Morris, Gwenyth; Myers, Donna Lee; Reimers, Sandra; Salter, Ruth; Sandoval, Rosita; Shook, Billie Ruth; Skidmore, Marilyn; Stobie, Evelyn; Wethey, Gillian.

1955: Burns, Isabel; Emery-Kissinger, Martha; Gray, Caroline; Hannawald, Martha Ann; Happoldt, Mary Lou; Harvey, Evelyn; Higley, Mary Abbie; Kendall, Janice Marie; Kline, Caroline; Martin, Susan; Morris, Barbara E.; Morris, Gwenyth; Owen, Hope; Reimers, Sandra; Sheldrick, Janet; Stein, Mary Anne; Whitburn, Shirley (ill; left); Yeagley, Claire.

1956:   Altermatt, Judy; Belcher, De Ann; Fritsche, Carla Denali; Galligan, Elizabeth Ann; Golladay, Nancy; Hammer, Carol; Hannawald, Martha Ann; Harvey, Evelyn; Higley, Mary Abbie; Kline, Caroline; Martin, Susan; Nash, Beth; Pachlhofer, Paula; Sowers, Patricia; Standley, Jo Ellen; Stein, Mary Anne; Treher, Joan Dodds; Villareal, Dolores; Wildman, Harriet; Yeagley, Claire.

Staff (All Camps): 1947–1957

1947:   Dutton, Bertha (Bert), Director, NM; Harvey, Nyla, GS Rep, CA; Little, Ursula (Sue), GS Rep., TX; Whipple, Velma (Whip), Naturalist, IL; Malone, Vic (Vic), Transportation, NM.

1948:   Dutton, Bertha (Bert), Director, NM; Kendrick, Pearl (Pearl), Cook, NM; Harris, Josephine (Jo), GS Rep, NM(?); Peterson, Dorothy (Pete), Driver, MO; Whipple, Velma (Whip), Naturalist, IL; Stacy, Jack, Transportation, NM.

1949:   Camp 1: Dutton, Bertha (Bert), Director, NM; Kendrick, Pearl (Pearl), Cook, NM; Harris, Josephine (Jo), GS Rep, Driver, NM(?); Burghardt, Mildred, Naturalist, NM; Stacy, Jack, Transportation, NM.
        Camp 2: Dutton, Bertha (Bert), Director, NM; Kendrick, Pearl (Pearl), Cook, NM; Prien, Eunice, GS Rep, TX; Whipple, Velma (Whip), Naturalist, NM; Stacy, Jack, Transportation, NM.

1950:   Camp 1: Dutton, Bertha (Bert), Director, NM; Kendrick, Pearl (Pearl), Cook, NM; Harris, Josephine (Jo), GS Rep, NM(?); Whipple, Velma (Whip), Naturalist/Driver, NM; Stacy, Jack, Transportation, NM.
        Camp 2: Dutton, Bertha (Bert), Director, NM; Kendrick, Pearl (Pearl), Cook, NM; Harris, Josephine (Jo), Driver, NM(?); Gaskill, Harriet, GS Rep, TX; Stacy, Jack, Transportation, NM.

1951:   Camp 1: Dutton, Bertha (Bert), Director, NM; Nichols, Alta, Cook, NM; Yoffa, Gretchen, GS Rep., NY; Gaskill, Harriet, Driver, TX; Stacy, Jack, Transportation, NM.
        Camp 2: Dutton, Bertha (Bert), Director, NM; Nichols, Alta, Cook, NM; Thompson, Helmi, GS Rep., ?; Stacy, Jack, Transportation, NM.

Camp 3 (Excavation): Dutton, Bertha (Bert), Director, NM; Sims, Agnes (Aggie), Associate, NM; Lovato, Ted, Cook, NM; Yoffa, Gretchen, GS Rep., NY.

1952:   Camp 1: Dutton, Bertha (Bert), Director, NM; Kendrick, Pearl (Pearl), Cook, NM; Buck, Margaret (Yazzi), Driver, NM; Whipple, Velma (Whip), GS Rep/Naturalist, NM; Stacy, Jack, Transportation, NM.

Camp 2: Dutton, Bertha (Bert), Director, NM; Woodward, Elizabeth, Cook, NM; Ilfeld, Bertha, Naturalist, Driver, NM; Burgess, Virginia, GS Rep; Stacy, Jack, Transportation, NM.

Camp 3 (Excavation): Dutton, Bertha (Bert), Director, NM; Parker, Elizabeth, Cook, CO; Yoffa, Gretchen, GS Rep., NY; Lucy, Esther, Shuttle/Asst. Cook, NM.

1953   Camp 1: Bertha Dutton (Bert), Director, NM; Lund, Betty, Cook; Buck, Margaret (Yazzi), Driver, NM; Wethey, Gillian (Gill), First Aid and GS Rep, England; Stacy, Jack, Transportation, NM.

Camp 2: Bertha Dutton (Bert), Director, NM; Woodward, Elizabeth, Cook, NM; Stobie, Evelyn (Les), Driver; Swift, Kate, GS Rep, NY; Stacy, Jack, Transportation, NM.

Camp 3 (Excavation): Bertha Dutton (Bert), Director, NM; Lucy, Ester, Cook, NM; Swift, Kate, GS Rep, Shuttler, NY.

1954   Camp 1: Bertha Dutton (Bert), Director, NM; Corkery, Lois I. (Corky), Cook, NM; Mosher, Joyce, Driver; Wethey, Gillian (Gill), GS Rep, NM; Stacy, Jack, Transportation, NM.

Camp 2: Bertha Dutton (Bert), Director, NM; Woodward, Elizabeth (Woody), Cook, NM; Myers, Anita, GS Rep; Stacy, Jack, Transportation, NM.

Camp 3 (Excavation): Bertha Dutton (Bert), Director, NM; Corkery, Lois I. (Corky), Cook, NM; Myers, Anita, GS Rep; Martin, Justine (Tiney), GS Rep/Shuttler.

1955   Camp 1: Bertha Dutton (Bert), Director, NM; Nourse, Marie C. (Cookie), NM; Mosher, Joyce, Driver; Fleming, Jan, GS Rep, IN; Stacy, Jack, Transportation, NM.

Camp 2: Bertha Dutton (Bert), Director, NM; Nourse, Marie C. (Cookie), NM; Bohrer, Vorsila (Rambler), Driver, Naturalist, AZ; Good, Dorothy (Cricket), GS Rep; Stacy, Jack, Transportation, NM.

Camp 3: Bohrer, Vorsila (Rambler), Asst. Director and Leader, AZ; Woodward, Elizabeth (Woody), Cook, NM; Buck, Margaret (Yazzi), Driver, NM; Good, Dorothy (Cricket), GS Rep; Stacy, Jack, Transportation, NM.

Camp 4 (Excavation): Bertha Dutton (Bert), Director, NM; Nourse, Marie C. (Cookie), NM; Martin, Justine (Tiney), GS Rep; Lourie, Dorothy, Asst. Cook/ Shuttler.

1956:   Camp 1: Bertha Dutton (Bert), Director, NM; Buck, Margaret (Yazzi), Driver, NM; Mosher, Joyce, Driver; Hoffman, Anna, GS Rep; Stacy, Jack, Transportation, NM.

Camp 2: Bertha Dutton (Bert), Director, NM; Webb, Luella (Lou), Cook, NM; Woyski, Margaret (Marge), Driver; Young, Virginia (Ginny), Driver; Fleming, Jan, GS Rep., IN; Stacy, Jack, Transportation, NM.

Camp 3 (Excavation): Bertha Dutton (Bert), Director, NM; Fleming, Jan, GS Rep., IN; Beltz, Patricia (Pat), Cook, NY; Beltz, Paul (Paul), Cook/Shuttler, NY.

1957:   Camp 1: Bertha Dutton (Bert), Director, NM; Ward, Idamae (Cookie), Cook; Fleming, Jan, GS Rep/Driver, IN; Buck, Margaret (Yazzi), Driver, NM; Stacy, Jack (Jack), Transportation, NM.

Camp 2: Fleming, Jan, Asst. Director/Leader, IN; Ward, Idamae (Cookie), Cook; Buck, Margaret (Yazzi), Driver, NM; Stacy, Jack (Jack), Transportation, NM.

Appendix B

Basic Qualifications (GSUSA) for National Camping Events and Personal Equipment List, Senior Girl Scout Archaeological Mobile Camps

Basic Qualifications for National Camping Events for Girls (GSUSA 1954d)

1. At the time the candidate's application is filed with her council she must be an active registered Senior Girl Scout who has completed the five point program. She must have been an active member of a Girl Scout Troup (Intermediate or Senior) for at least two years.

2. At the time the candidate's application is filed with her council she must be at least 15 years of age but must not have had her eighteenth birthday.

3. She must be endorsed wholeheartedly by her leader and the members of her troop as representative of the finest Girl Scout traditions. Her attitude should be such as to make her a fine ambassador from her community. She must have a sincere interest in and understanding of other people.

4. She should be in excellent physical condition, as evidenced by a medical examination recorded on a form to be furnished by the National Girl Scout

Organization; know how to take care of her health while in camp; and enjoy living in the out-of-doors regardless of the weather.

5. She must have had experience in camping and must have met the following requirements:

a. <u>Fires</u>. Build a basic fire and keep it going for: reflector, trench, bean-hole; in all kinds of weather: wind, rain, fair, cold. Select appropriate fuel, locate fireplace, and know type of fire necessary for cooking menu planned. Know forest fire precautions.

b. <u>Cooking</u>. Know basic types of cooking. Have ability to plan and pre-pare three meals a day for 15 people, including beverages, cereals, stews, salads, desserts—by boiling, toasting, broiling, or baking. Know how to make and use cooking devices, such as cranes, pot hooks.

c. <u>Clean-up.</u> Know methods of clean-up, including incinerators, grease pits, garbage disposal, dishwashing.

d. <u>Camp site.</u> Know how to establish a camp site with caches, latrine, beds, sleeping quarters, cooking and dining area, lashing gadgets.

e. <u>Toolcraft.</u> Be skilled in use and care of knife, hatchet and axe, buck-saw and digging tools. Know safety rules.

f. <u>Campcraft.</u> Know lashing and how to use it for making a comfortable camp site.

Know how to tie a square knot, bowline, clove hitch, sheet bend, slip knot, timber hitch. Know how to whip the end of a rope and how to splice.

Know how to take care of health, equipment, and camp. Know how to purify drinking water. Know simple first aid. Know proper clothing to wear in all kinds of weather.

Know how to pack a knapsack for back packing, including per-sonal equipment, sleeping bag, tools, and food weighing a total of 20 to 25 pounds.

g. <u>Personal qualifications.</u> A real love of camping. An ability to rec-ognize what needs to be done and willingness to assume her share. Personal skills that will increase her contribution to group fun, such as dancing, singing, and games. Knowledge of how to take care of herself and her personal belongings.

6. She must have participated actively in community service projects. She must show evidence of having participated as a member of a Senior planning board and/or have had experience in discussion leadership, reporting, participation in a Senior Girl Scout conference or in meetings or conferences of other community agencies.

7. She should be able to teach other girls program activities characteristic of the Girl Scout program, i.e., songs, dances, simple crafts, flag ceremonies, and campcrafts.

8. She must have an understanding of her own community, religion, and country—their geography, industries, history, and cultural background.

9. She should be expected to continue an interest in Girl Scouting for at least two years, and should be responsible for taking back reports of the encampment to Senior troops and conferences. She should be willing to use her knowledge and skills in camping to promote and stimulate interest in this type of camp project among other Senior Girl Scouts in her region.

The Trail Blazer Program, a year-round outdoor program described in <u>Senior Girl Scouting</u> (Cat. No. 20-107, $1), is excellent training for girls taking part in national camping events and looking forward to all international events.

<u>All Senior Girl Scouts attending national camping events</u> must fulfill the above qualifications. Special qualifications sometimes are added to this list according to the kind of national camping event to be held. These additional qualifications are made known at the time the event is announced.

<u>Special qualifications for All-States Encampment and for Senior Girl Scout— Museum of New Mexico Archaeological Mobile Camps</u>

1. Know how to sharpen, pack, carry, care for, and store tools.
2. Know how to waterproof matches and prepare emergency tinder, such as trench candles.

3. Know how to use basic dehydrated foods such as dried soups, fruit, vegetables, meats, powdered eggs, beverages, milk.
4. Know four types of lashing.
5. Know how to pitch, trench, and strike tents, such as pup tents or canvas tarps that are used as lean-tos and A-tents.
6. Know precautions to take when hiking at altitude 7,000 to 12,500 feet.
7. Know how to use a compass with a topographical map.
8. <u>Special qualifications for Archaeological Excavation Camp: All of the above plus previous successful experience in one or more of the Archaeological Mobile Camps,</u> and demonstrated aptitude for scientific research.

*Girls over 18 who are registered with the Girl Scouts of U.S.A. will be accepted for the Senior Girl Scout-Museum of New Mexico Archaeological Mobile Camps and the Excavation. They must be endorsed by their council or lone troop committee.

C[amping] D[ivision] 8/54

GSUSA, New York, NY

WHAT TO BRING (Application Packet; GSUSA 1950)

A duffle bag which contains your sleeping bag* <u>and all other gear</u>; should not exceed 50 lbs. There is no room for extra baggage. A flour sack or two will serve to keep clothing, shoes, etc. separate from your bedroll, accessible, and easy to manage.

Ground sheet or poncho	Chapstick
Sleeping bag	Kotex if needed
Sweater	Kleenex or handkerchiefs
Warm jacket (light weight)	2 or 3 pairs Levis or
Raincoat with hood or rain hat	Equivalent (no 3/4 length, shorts)
Light weight rubbers	3–4 shirts (type needing no ironing; at least 2 with long sleeves recommended).
Sun hat (secure in breeze; small brim)	2 pairs <u>stout comfortable</u> shoes

Dark glasses	3–6 pairs sox (heavy recommended)
Pocket knife	3–4 sets of underwear
Flashlight, extra batteries	2 pajamas (one light, one flannel recommended)
Canteen with strap or hook	2 washcloths
Writing paper, envelopes,	2 medium-sized bath towels
stamps	Toothbrush, paste, and folding cup
Sunburn lotion	Laundry soap
Comb and metal mirror if desired	Pocket notebook and pencils
Safety pins, needle and thread	

If you bring a camera, provide a reasonable amount of film. (Color film is desirable if you work in that medium.) Have a bag for them, your notebook and pencils, and such accessories as you will require during the day.

Mark Things Plainly with Your Name

*It is strongly recommended that you have a modern, light weight sleeping bag if possible. This eliminates the need for blankets and cuts down car load. With sleeping bags a sheet dyed khaki is practical. If you use a bedroll, three all-wool blankets are necessary in the high, cold altitude.

**For items you need to add to your present equipment do check the Spring Girl Scout Equipment Catalog.

If you need to send duffle in advance allow seven days or more, and ship prepaid in care of Dr. Bertha Dutton, Museum of New Mexico, Santa Fe.

If you bring a duffle and change transportation en route, be sure to check transfer of your baggage each time!

Appendix C

The Singing Diggers

Compiled by Jo Tice Bloom, Mary Anne Stein,
and Susan Martin

The following collections of songs (and a few rhymes) are from various Mobile and Dig Camps, some dated and some not, and some with known authors or those who taught them to others. Many songs were transmitted from camp to camp and year to year, and the dates for these do not mean that they were exclusive to the years indicated. In addition, given the significance of singing to Girl Scout life, many additional songs were sung around campfires, and while traveling in the caravans on Mobiles and while digging at Pueblo Largo (the latter marked as either Camp III or Camp IV).

Set 1: Dutton's Dirty Digger Songs (Compiled by Jo Tice Bloom from the Bertha P. Dutton Collection, MIAC/LAA 2008)

1948 (Camp I) Our Song

Oh, we're so glad we took this trip
In the land where there aren't any chiggers

We hunt for potsherds all day long

For we're Dutton's Dirty Diggers.

1950 (Camp I) The Dirty Diggers' Song

We are the Diggers, the dirty little Diggers

We take a bath once a week, once a week

We visit all the ruins, and never miss a doings

And at every little Pueblo take a peek.

We come from o'er the nation, and cross the reservation

To drink warm tea that is weak…that is weak

We travel in three cars that are late for many hours

And sleep in pup tents that all leak.

Bert is our leader, Pearl is the feeder

Jack is the one who fixes cars, fixes cars

Jo of the Scouts, keeps in line the sprouts

And Whip tells us all about the stars.

We are the Diggers, the dirty little Diggers

Archaeology is our aim, is our aim

We go from cliff to cave, so everybody save

So we can come back and dig again.

1951 (Camp III) The Old Rocky Road Tune: The Old Rugged Cross

On a hill far away

Stands an old rocky room

The emblem of suffering and pain

Still I love that old room

With its boulders and rocks

We'll dig 'til we hit that old floor.

(Chorus:)

Oh I'll cherish the old rocky room

'til my shovel at last I lay down

I will cling to the old pick and trowel

And exchange them one day for a bed.
On the hill far away
We just dig night and day
In hopes of discovering that floor
While the pick hits rocks
And the trowel hits the stones
We still have not found that old floor.

1951 (Camp III) Tune: *This Old Hammer*

This old pickax rings like silver,
This old pickax rings like silver'
This old pickax rings like silver,
Feels like lead, girls, feels like lead.
Ain't no pickax in this *kiva*
Ain't no pickax in this *kiva*
Ain't no pickax in this *kiva*,
Weighs like mine, girls, weighs like mine.

Take this pickax—take it Aggie
Take this pickax—take it Aggie
Take this pickax—take it Aggie
Tell her I'm tired, girls, tell 'er I'm tired.

1951 (Camp III) Tune: *Tell Me Why*

Tell me why the walls do fall
Tell me why the boulders aren't small
Tell me why the dirt's so hard,
And I will tell you just why we're IV-F2.
Because the walls were so darned tall
Because the boulders the Indians did haul
Because the rain packs the dirt so hard
Because Bert loves us, where still IV-F2.

Sometimes I think that Dr. Bert,
Tries to get even with us with work
And picks us out from all the rest
To be the ones who work in IV-F2.

1951 (Camp III) Tune: *Down In the Valley*

Down in the valley
To Pueblo Largo
Came Gretchen Yoffa.
It was quite a show.
She brought "minimum standards"
And rules galore,
"Now let's all wear Scout socks
So our feet won't get sore."
And then there were crew hats
For the photos to log
"Have you written home lately"
And "wear your Scout togs."
But Bert to the rescue.
We all gave a cheer
"To hell with the rules
Things are different out here."

1951 (Camp III) Mailbox Reminder

Would you write a friendly letter?
Do it now.
It perchance may drive a shadow
from the brow.
Of one who will receive it
and may tend
To bring kinder, happier feelings
to a friend.

1954 (Camp 1) The Saga of Tripalong Placidly (Nancy Reed)

Once there was a girl, Beth was her given name.

Until she went a swimming. Now Tripalong is the same.

To swim in Oak Creek Canyon, for days she was waitin'.

She swore that none would stop her, not even devil Satan.

Finally she arrived, and in she jumped right quick.

In her two-piece suit, she sure looked might slick.

But rocks were on the bottom, and some were down right sharp.

She cut her foot on one, but let out not a yarp.

She just went right on swimming, for if she was discovered,

She would have to stop her fun, while around her Gretch hovered.

The whistle then was blown. In our game they put a crimp.

The Tripalong donned her shoes. She wouldn't walk without a gimp. She walked
   around all afternoon, but finally was seen

By our little doctor, who found it wasn't clean.

She put the foot in Epsom salts. It must have really burned.

When she stuck it in, a pretty shade of red it turned.

She used some naughty words, but worse it was to hurt.

For then dear Gretch discovered the thing was filled with dirt.

Wither her little tweezers, she pecked and poked around.

She removed a hunk of wood, a splinter at a time we found.

She finally finished, and added iodine

After one last holler, Tripalong felt just fine.

1954 (Camp I, II) Tune: Girl Scouts Together (Caroline Kline and Donna Myers)

Diggers together, dirty are we

Picking up potsherds, all that we see

Drinking our milkshakes, where'ere we go

Diggers together, in every Pueblo.

Diggers together, following Bert

Changing our tires in heat and dirt

Wondering where Jack is, when not in sight
Diggers together, we're happy tonight.
Diggers together, drinking our tea
Winding the old trails, thirsty are we.
Chewing our prune pits, all the day long
Diggers together, with this as our song.

1954 (Camp II) Tune: *Missouri Waltz*

Away in Arizona, on the Muddy Mogollon
Slippin' and a-slidin' O so many miles from home.
The rain is a-falling, 'adventure is callin',
We're pushin' and tuggin' to get through the mud.

Bert's spinnin' round the middle of the road
Jack is creepin' up the hill like a Horny Toad
With Les in the middle, as fit as a fiddle,
Just cussin' the mud.

1954 (Camp II) Tune: *Life Upon the Wicked Stage*

Life upon the western plains ain't nothin' for a gentle Girl Scout
Tough and rugged you must be if you follow Bertha.
We just sit around and drink our tea, dirty archaeologists are we
Life upon the western plains ain't nothin' for a Scout.

1954 (Camp III) Tune: *Five Foot Two*

A Leader, by Judith Franklin.
Five foot two, hair steel gray
Navajo boots, eyes searching far away.
Searching for a ruin on a mesa top
She doesn't have to search for a cool place to stop.
Adopted by Laguna, tops with us she's rated.
She tells us of the calendar by which the Pueblos are dated.

About the Pueblo people, she's a walking book of knowledge
Six weeks with her is like a year in college.
"It should only take you '30' what you do in '45'."
Down an arroyo fool speed—a breathtaking dive
She'll go off without you, like she says she will
And I can't imagine her in anything with a frill.
I'd know her in the winter, washed of all the dirt
For even on Fifth Avenue, she'd still be our BERT!

1954 Camp 1 Tune: *Tennashay alla ee*

Dirty Diggers are we, traveling the Southwest to see
The ruins, the Pueblos, the *kivas*, the dances
Enjoying the desert so free.
Chorus:
Zuni, Hopi, and Navajo
Ancient cultures as well as new
Zuni, Hopi, and Navajo
Ancient cultures as well as new
Friends forever we'll be,
Tho' scattered from sea to sea
Tho' time may pass, we'll never forget you
But cherish this memory.

The following are not specifically dated:

Pearl. Tune: *Smiles*

Pearl's the cook that never fails us
She's cook that fills us full
When we're tired and feeling awfully empty
She steps in and makes us smile anew
She's the one to drive away our hunger
And her pancakes, ham, and biscuits, too

Pearl's the cook that we love so true.

Now that we all are leaving

We want it understood

Tho' she seemed to favor Flagstaff

We took her on to Cottonwood

So that she could keep on cooking

That wonderful spaghetti and salad, too

And of course we'll look for <u>Pearl</u> next year

And we hope she will want us too

The Diggers Cheer

We are the Diggers, Diggers are we

We never lose our vitality, rah, rah, rah

We have the rep and we have the pep

For we are Mobile campers, rah, rah, rah.

Where is Bert? Tune: Brother John

The Chevy's lost its way, lost its way

Where is Bert? Where is Bert?

The Cadillac has fallen back, fallen back

Where is Bert? Where is Bert?

Oh Bert!

I've a Potsherd in My Pants Tune: There is a Tavern in the Town

I have a potsherd in my pants

It is an extra nice one

But if I let Bert see it

Will she ever free it

And will I have a potsherd in my pants?

I have a potsherd in my pants

I'd like to know its history

But if I ask Dutton

She may not say nuttin'
But the potsherd won't belong to me.

Jack

First the Cadillac—bang!
Then the Chevy—pop!
Then the station wagon goes—sss!
First the tire and then the spring,
then the muffler, gosh darn thing
For every mile we have to stop
Either for fumes or a pop!
Put on the coffee, let it boil
Just to make Jack's hair coil.
Pack those duffels, pile them high
He will store them without a sigh
Coffee and beefsteak keep him strong
For the journey weary and long
Over the highways and the byways
Always ever following Bert.

Set 2: Dutton's Dirty Digger Songs as Recalled by Mary Anne Stein and Susan S. Martin. Sung from 1953–1956

1953 (Camp I, II) Sunset Crater Song Tune: *Follow Winding Trail*

Follow dusty trail, through the desert
Follow Bertha's lead, until she stops
Follow the trail up, Sunset Crater
Until you reach, the very top.

Take a step and slip, but keep on going
Ever see so much, dirt in the air?

Then down comes someone, who has reached the top

To say you're only half way there.

Pushed on to Wupatki, for a dry camp

Only dust and cinders, on the ground.

Back in an old log *Hogan*, dry and sound.

1949 (Camp I) Digger Poof Song Tune: *The Whiffenpoof Song* (transmitted to 1955, Camp I, by Caroline Kline)

From the pup tents down at Dutton's, to the place where Pueblos dwell

To the dear old mountain rocks, we love so well

Where the "Diggers" all assemble, with their tea cups raised on high

And the magic of our singing casts it spell,

Yes, the magic of our singing, of the songs we love so well

"Tell Me Why," "We Are the Diggers," and the rest.

We will serenade our Bert, while life and love they last

Then we'll pass and be forgotten with the rest.

Chorus:

We are poor little diggers, who have lost our potsherd

Boo, hoo, hoo.

We are poor little scouts, who have been led astray,

Following Bert!

Girl Scout songsters off on a spree, digging from here to eternity

Lord, have mercy on such as we,

Following Bert!

1954 (Camp III) The Cow Tank Tune: *The Ash Grove*

Down yonder dry valley

Where cattle meander

When digging is over

We wash ourselves off.
But at the high noontide
We see the cool water
Out at the big cow tank
We wish we were there.
'Tis then that we take up
Our towels for our shovels
We trudge back to dig up
Our potsherds and rocks.
Ah, then we do think of
That wash up at day's end
The cow tank at that time
Spells comfort for us.

1955 (Camp II) Ode to Cookie Tune: *Johnny Appleseed Grace by Gwenie Bell, Elaine Boettcher, Mary Anne Stein, and Paula Pachlhofer*

Oh, Cookie's been good to us
And so we thank her so
For giving us the food we eat
The tea we drink, and the government meat
Oh, Cookie's been good to us.
And we gain a few more pounds
With every meal we have
And with every meal we have
Are a few more pots and pans.
So we scour and scour
Hour after hour
Using every ounce of power!
Oh, Cookie's been good to us.

1955 (Camp II) Our Cheer [Together these letters spell the true meaning of the Mobile Camp of 1955]

M—Museums we have visited along the way

O—Opportunities to look into the past

B—Basketmakers lives who we have relived

I—Indians of the Southwest and the cultures they have given

L—for the Legends left in the ruins

E—Enchantment for the ruins of the ancients

C—Craftsmanship displayed in many arts

A—Archaeology which has made these ruins come to life

M—Mesa Verde which has revealed many of the finest stories ever told anywhere

P—Pueblos new and old have helped to enrich our lives.*

1955 (Mobile Camps) Memories Tune: Love Grows Under the Wild Oak Tree

Jack lies in the Cadillac

Reading mysteries by the stack

End of the evening finds him there

After a hard day's wear and tear.

Rambler roams the countryside

Picking up specimens far and wide

Skinks and skunks and insects too

Anything for her will do.

Cricket creeps around out of sight

Trying to keep us quiet at night

Writing in her notebook all day long

Always singing a merry song,

Now we come to our dear Bert

Trying to keep us all alert

Sharing her knowledge—all that she knows

Scenery, Indians, and Pueblos.

Chorus:

Memories, memories, of the *Sipapu*

Memories, memories, one for me and you.

Bert's Caravan Tune: *Noah's Ark (Paula and Martha to Laine and Mary Anne)*

Bert, she said, "There's gonna be a trippy, trippy"

Bert, she said, "There's gonna be a trippy, trippy"

Pack your duffel, in a jiffy, jiffy

Diggers of the mobile.

We left the ranch so early, early, early

Left the ranch so early, early, early

Even beat the little birdies, birdies

Diggers of the mobile

We traveled and traveled for 14 daysy, daysy

Traveled and traveled for 14 daysy, daysy

Nearly drove our councilors crazy, crazy

Diggers on the mobile

We camped and camped every nighty, nighty

Camped and camped every nighty, nighty

Rained and hailed and gave us a frighty, frighty

Diggers of the mobile

It all had to end some timey, timey, timey

It all had to end some timey, timey, timey

So at Dutton's we said good byedy, byedy

Diggers of the mobile

We'll all come again another yearsy, yearsy

All come again another yearsy, yearsy

And go on a digsy, digsy, digsy

Diggers on the mobile.

1955 (Camp II) Digger Farewell Song Tune: *There's a Long, Long Trail*
(Caroline Kline, Bets Galligan, Carol Hammer, Kathy Bahlinger)

> There's a long, long road a'winding
> All over mountains and plains
> And the fun we've shared together
> Will never be again.
> Digging, working, and hiking
> Singing the same old refrains
> And without us all together,
> Things will never be the same.

1955 (Camp II) Tune: *Auld Lang Syne (Elaine Boettcher, Gwenie Bell,*
Paula Pachlhofer, Mary Anne Stein, Bertha Talahytewa)

> Should all good diggers be forgot
> And never brought to mind?
> Should happy days be bygone days
> That are left far behind?
> Let's pause a moment now and then
> To think of fun we had
> The friends we made, the things we did
> That will never come again.
> We'd take a cup of tea then
> And chew a prune pit!
> And remember things we learn each day
> Never more to forget.

1956 (Camp III) Song to "Daddy D" Tune: *Cowboy's Lullaby*

> Bunch of Dirty diggers came to Santa Fe
> Never saw each other 'fore that day
> Got on Digger clothes in Daddy D's ranch shop
> Hit the road with Bert without a stop
> So, now, we sing to Daddy D

He's always very willing to do the things we need
He's there to lend a helping hand, so Daddy D
We thank you one and all.

Ode to Cookie Tune: *Johnny Appleseed*

Oh, Cookie's been good to us
And so we thank you so
For giving us the food we eat,
The tea we drink and the government meat...
Oh, cookie's been good to us.
We gain a few more pounds
With ever meal we eat
And every meal we eat
There're a few more pots and pans...
So we scour and scour
Hour after hour
Using every ounce of power...
Oh, Cookie's been good to us.

You Take the High Road Tune: *Loch Lomond*

Oh you take the fender, and I'll take the bumper,
And we'll take the oil-pan between us.
We pull out the rock, but push we still must...
OH YOU'LL NEVER GET TO HEAVEN FOLLOWING BERTHA.
Oh you take the flywheel, and I'll take the birdie.
And we'll change the tire between us.
Looking ahead, we wish that we were dead...
OH YOU'LL NEVER GET TO HEAVEN FOLLOWING BERTHA.
Oh you take the muffler, and I'll take the gas tank,
And we'll split the wheel rim between us.
We sit around for hours, identifying flowers...
OH YOU'LL NEVER GET TO HEAVEN FOLLOWING BERTHA.

Oh you take the "bleeping sag" and I'll take the "buffle dag,"

And we'll pack the trailer between us.

We get up at dawn, of why was I "bawn" [born!]...

OH YOU'LL NEVER GET TO HEAVEN FOLLOWING BERTHA.

Oh you've got the bee sting, and I've got the mosquito bite,

And we'll chew the prune pits between us.

We pump up the tire and throw tea on the fire...

OH YOU'LL NEVER GET TO HEAVEN FOLLOWING BERTHA.

Oh you take the shovel, and I'll take the T.P.,

And we'll dig a big hole between us.

And as we return, our faces will burn...

OH YOU'LL NEVER GET TO HEAVEN FOLLOWING BERTHA.

Oh you pitch a pup tent, and I'll drive a tent peg,

And we'll have the tent collapse between us.

We all pitch our tents, and then the rain relents...

OH YOU'LL NEVER GET TO HEAVEN FOLLOWING BERTHA.

Oh you build the fire, and I'll burn the steaks,

And we'll make 'em all sick between us.

And then we drink our tea, so thirsty we'll not be...

OH YOU'LL NEVER GET TO HEAVEN FOLLOWING BERTHA.

n.d. *Camping Dream* Tune: *April in Portugal*

I found my camping dream

In fair New Mexico

When I discovered mesas

And mountains capped in snow.

Where cottonwoods are green

And yucca flowers bloom

Where stars shine high above

And lovely as the moon.

I found new camping friends

And memories that glow

With Bert in fair New Mexico.

1956 Camp II Tune: *There's a Long, Long Road*

There's a long, long road a'winding

All over the mountain and the plain

And the fun we've shared together

Will never be again.

Digging, working, and hiking

Singing the same old refrain

But without us all together

Things will never seem the same.

Jettin' Thru the Desert Tune: *Comin' Round the Mountain*

(repeat three times each)

We'll be jettin' thru the desert when we come ("haa, haa").

We'll be drivin' four of Jack's cars when we come (crank, crank).

We'll meet in Santa Fe then when we come ("Hi, y'all").

We'll pitch our tents at Dutton's when we come (pound, pound).

We'll scrub the pots and scour when we come (scratch, scratch).

We'll be sorry that we're leavin' when we go (sniff, sniff).

We'll all drink Coke-a-Cola [sic] when we're gone (guzzle, guzzle).

When we all come back here next year we'll drink tea (hee, hee).

For All We Know Tune: *For All We Know*

For all we know, we may never meet again

We'll still be friends, makes no difference where or when

We won't say farewell until the last minute

We'll hold out our hands and our hearts will be in it.

When memories fail, this will only be a dream

We will still be friends, wherever we will be.

So sing out tonight, as tomorrow will soon unfold

Fond memories for you and me, for all we know.

1956 (Camp II) Many a State Tune: *Sixteen Tons (Carol Hammer, Karen Rieley, Lois Richard, Patty Sowers; submitted by Rebecca Mills)*

Chorus—sung between verses:

Twenty-four girls from many a state

Many an accent and many a shape

We've had loads of fun and we'd like to come back

By taxi cab or railroad track.

Verses:

Our strip began on a Tues. morn.

A plan for many a mile was born

But soon or chariot began to fail

And this was a lag in a well started trail.

But we weren't stopped because we're Scouts

And we came to Kuaua after long hard bouts

The moon shone on us and kept us awake

But we weren't sorry it gave us an ache (I mean a heart ache).

Chaco was once a populated place

And now it's full of ruins and space

The ruins offered much besides a snake

Kivas, rain and many little lakes.

Our dinner was delayed at Window Rock

'Cause of a knee with an insect shock

Next day we went on to Canyon de Chelly

Which made it a perfectly beautiful day.

The *Niman* dances impressed us all

Besides making very heavy raindrops fall

The early waking hours created a stir,

And made that whole durn village purr (I really mean purr).

Our next accommodations were good but wet

The cooks like the kitchen, that you can bet

The museum kept us all entranced

And surely enjoyed the songs for to dance.
The following helped make this camp a success
Jan, Ginny, Marge, Lori, and Jack, no less
We like them all a lot, they're really swell
Without them camping would surely be nill.
Bert we decided that this is enough
Thanks for the time spent on roads that were rough
We can't explain our feelings toward you
We'll remember this camp our whole life through.

Appendix D

Senior Girl Scout Archaeological Mobile Camp Routes and Itineraries, 1947–1957

Note: All place names are listed as on the itineraries, but some names have changed since the Diggers visited them. See List of Name Changes in the front section of the book.

1947 July 6–July 19 (seven campers, five staff). Sources: Bohrer 1947a, 1947b; Dutton 1947a; Region IX GSUSA mimeo circular 1947.

Sunday, July 6–Tues. July 8: Santa Fe, Hyde State Park; camp organization and orientation. July 7: regional orientation; School of American Research, National Park Service; Museum of New Mexico, Laboratory of Anthropology, Museum of Navajo Ceremonial Art. July 8: Santa Fe to Pecos National Monument, Coronado State Monument (Kuaua Ruin), to Chaco Canyon. July 9–10: Chaco ruins (Pueblo Bonito, Chetro Ketl; University of New Mexico excavations; Navajo ethnology; to Aztec National Monument. July 10: Aztec Ruins to Mesa Verde. July 11–14: Mesa Verde National Park ruins, museum, attend campfires. July 15: Mesa Verde, Ute Mountain Reservation, trading posts (Toadlena, Chinle); Ute and Navajo ethnography and arts. July 16–17: Canyon de Chelly, Canyon del Muerto, Turkey Canyon ruins. July 17: Canyon de Chelly, Gallup, trading posts, El Morro National Monument. July 18: El Morro; visit Inscription Rock and local ruins; to Enchanted Mesa. July 19: Enchanted Mesa to Acoma and Laguna Pueblos; Albuquerque to disband.

1948 July 10–24 (15 campers; six staff). Sources: Bloom 2011; Bloom 1948; Bohrer 1948a, 1948b; Dutton 1948a; Stobie 1955; Region IX GSUSA mimeo circular 1948.

July 10–12: Santa Fe, Hyde State Park. July 11: camp organization. July 12: regional orientation, Santa Fe museums, National Park Service. July 13: Santa Fe to Coronado State Monument (Kuaua Ruin) and Chaco Canyon. July 14–15: Chaco Canyon ruins. July 15: Chaco Canyon, Gallup, sites at Manuelito, AZ, Painted Desert, Petrified Forest National Monument, Slim Pickings Ranch. July 16: Meteor Crater, Walnut Canyon and Wupatki National Monuments, Museum of Northern Arizona excavations at Wupatki. July 17: Wupatki ruins, Museum of Northern Arizona. July 18: Museum of Northern Arizona, Winona Ridge Ruin, Oak Creek camp. July 19: Tuzigoot, Montezuma's Well, Montezuma's Castle. July 20: Montezuma's Castle to Sitgreaves National Forest (now Apache-Sitgreaves National Forest), Sitgreaves Ranger Station. July 21: Showlow to Kinishba, camp near Kinishba Ruins. July 22: Kinishba Ruins, Southwestern Lumber Mill at McNary, camp at Lumber Mill. July 23: McNary to Springerville, Socorro; camp at Isleta Pueblo. July 24: tour Isleta Pueblo; Albuquerque and Santa Fe, disband.

1949 Camp I: July 23–August 5 (16 campers, five staff); Camp II: August 13–26 (15 campers, five staff). Sources: Bohrer 1949; Dutton 1949a.

Camp I: July 23–24: Santa Fe, Rancho del Cielo; organization and skills practice. July 25: Santa Fe museums, National Park Service. July 26: Cerrillos turquoise mines, Paako [Paa-Ko] Ruin, Sandia Cave; camp at Paako Ruin. July 27: Hispanic villages at Escabosa, Chilili, Tajique, Manzano and Punta de Agua; Quarai State Monument; camp at Abó State Monument. July 28: Gran Quivira, Galisteo Basin; Comanche Gap petroglyphs; San Cristóbal Ruins. July 29: tour San Cristóbal Ruins; pass Santa Fe to San Juan Pueblo (Ohkay Owingeh); Abiquiú ruin, St. Rose of Lima Mission ruin; camp at Dyke, CO. July 30: Chimney Rock Ruin, Cherry Creek forest; to Mesa Verde. July 31–Aug. 1: Mesa Verde; tour Far View, Pipe Fetish House, Little Long House, Square Tower House, Cliff Palace, Balcony House, Spruce Tree House; horseback trip through

Pool Canyon and ruins; museum. Aug. 2: Cuba, Seven Springs Forest Camp; NM State Fish Hatchery; Soda Dam, Jemez Cave, Giusewa Ruin (Jemez State Monument); Jemez Pueblo for Old Pecos Dances; La Paliza Forest camp, Vallecitos Canyon; August 3: Valle Grande, Los Alamos, Frijoles Canyon; Aug. 4: Bandelier ruins, Santo Domingo Pueblo for Green Corn Dance; August 5: Santa Fe museums; disband in pm.

Camp II: Reversed the order after two days orientation to start with Green Corn Dance at Zia; Kuaua ruin; then to Aztec, Enchanted Desert, Mesa Verde, back through Durango, Pagosa Springs, Echo Amphitheater near Ghost Ranch, Arroyo Hondo, Taos, Abiquiú; San Juan Pueblo, Santa Clara Pueblo, Bandelier National Monument, Perague (ancestral site for San Ildefonso Pueblo); August 23: Pecos Conference in Santa Fe. Final three days on eastern NM frontier with same stops as Camp I.

1950 Camp I: July 1–July 15 (16 campers, five staff); Camp II (July 22–August 5 (16 campers, five staff). Central Route. Sources: Dutton 1950a; Region IX GSUSA mimeo circular 1950.

July 1–3: Rancho del Cielo; local, regional orientation. July 4: Laguna, La Mesa Entrada, Acoma, Ice Caves, to El Morro. July 5: El Morro, Zuni Pueblo; bread baking demonstration, artisans' homes; Zuni Day School camp. July 6: Petrified Forest National Monument (Wendorf excavations), Meteor Crater; Walnut Canyon. July 7: Museum of Northern Arizona; lectures. July 8: Sunset Crater; Crack-in-the-Rock, Wupatki National Monument; camp at MNA. July 9: Hopi Pueblos for Katsina dance; camp at Shungopavi Day School. July 10–11: Canyon de Chelly; Mummy Cave in Canyon del Muerto, Three Turkey and White House ruins, excavations; camp at Canyon de Chelly. July 12–13: Canyon de Chelly to Chaco Canyon; Window Rock and Navajo Tribal Headquarters, Chaco Canyon and several ruins, Pueblo del Arroyo stabilization; back country to other sites; camp at Chaco Canyon. July 14: Chaco to Santa Fe and Rancho del Cielo; Coronado State Monument (Kuaua), start equipment cleanup. July 15: Rancho del Cielo, cleanup and disband.

Camp II: Same route and routine overall.

1951 Camp I: June 30–July 14 (16 campers, five staff); Camp II: July 21–August 4 (10 girls, four staff); Camp III: August 18–September 1 (13 campers; four staff). Southern Route. Sources: Dutton 1951a; Dutton to Boaz Long, June 21, 1951, MIAC/LAA 89LA5.063; Region IX GSUSA printed circular 1951.

June 30–July 2: Rancho del Cielo; orientation, Santa Fe museums, NPS. July 3: Moriarty (Valley Irrigation Company), Mountainair; camp at Abó State Monument. July 4: Abó; San Gregorio Church (1625–1672–75); Socorro, Magdelena, Plains of San Agustin, Datil; camp, A.M. Cleaveland ranch. July 5: Quemado; Peabody Museum of Harvard excavations, guests of J.O. Brew and Watson Smith; Williams Ranch camp. July 6: Quemado to Reserve; Chicago Museum of Natural History excavations, guests of Paul Martin and John Rinaldo (Pine Lawn [Mogollon] pithouse sites); Turkey Ridge Site, guests of Elaine Bluhm; Reserve camp. July 7: Sitgreaves National Forest, AZ; tour Southwestern Lumber Mill at McNary; forest ecology, wildlife; camp at Pinetop Forest camp, AZ. July 8: Along Mogollon Rim; ecology; camp at ranger station, Long Valley. July 9: Mormon Lake, Schnebly Hill lookout, Sedona, Oak Creek camp. July 10: Walnut Canyon, Meteor Crater; Painted Desert (geology); Puerco Ruin; camp at Petrified Forest National Monument. July 11: tour area, history and culture, Navajo people; camp at U.S. Indian Service Vocational School, Fort Wingate. July 12: Cebollita Mesa; excavations of A.E. Dittert and R.J. Ruppé (Pueblo I and others); camp at Bibo Ranch. July 13: Laguna Pueblo; camp at Rancho del Cielo. July 14: clean equipment, disband.

Camp II: Same basic itinerary except visited Flagstaff and the Museum of Northern Arizona instead of Walnut Canyon; added Green Corn Dance at Santo Domingo on August 4.

1952 Camp I: July 5–19 (16 campers, five staff); Camp II: July 26–August 9 (16 campers, five staff). Northern Route. Source: Dutton 1952a; Region IX GSUSA printed circular 1952.

Camp 1: July 5–7: Rancho del Cielo; Santa Fe museums, agencies. July 8: Cochiti Pueblo, Peralta Canyon (volcanic tuff cones); Bear Springs, Jemez Pueblo; Gallina area, camp at Frank Hibben ranch. July 9: Jicarilla Apache country, El Vado Lake; camp Rio Blanco. July 10: Pagosa Springs; climbed Chimney Rock to Pueblo Parado

(1100–1300 AD), inducted into "Honorable Order of Squirrels"; Mesa Verde. July 10–12: Mesa Verde, visit cliff dwellings, including Pipe Fetish and Far View areas, Mummy Lake reservoir. July 13: Mesa Verde to Dead Horse Point, UT; new area to see [now part of Canyonlands National Park]; camp at Dead Horse Point. July 14: Arches National Monument, UT; Windows section; Parade of Elephants, Balanced Rock, Delicate Arch, Fiery Furnace, Devils Garden; camp near headquarters with swimming hole. July 15: Arches to Aztec National Monument via Cortez; camp at Aztec. July 16: Aztec ruins, Navajo country, Nacimiento Range to Jemez Mountains, Calavaras Forest camp. July 17: Seven Springs Fish Hatchery, Soda Dam, Jemez Mission, fossil beds, Valle Grande; El Rito de los Frijoles camp. July 18: El Rito de los Frijoles (Bandelier); Florence Ellis excavations at Pojoaque; MNM excavations at Cuyamungue; Santa Fe Indian School (Arts and Crafts Department), Al Packard's trading post; El Rancho del Cielo. July 19: clean, store equipment.

Camp II: Follow the same route.

1953 Camp I: June 27–July 11 (15 campers, five staff); Camp II: July 18–August 1 (16 campers, five staff). Central route, general itinerary only; some variation on stops between Camps I and II. Sources: Dutton 1953a; *The Sipapu* I:1 1954; C. Tice letters (see Chapter 3).

Rancho del Cielo, Santa Fe; museums, other agencies. Remainder of stops: Laguna, Acoma, and Zuni Pueblos; El Morro National Monument; the Painted Desert; Petrified Forest National Monument; Meteor Crater; Sunset Crater; Flagstaff (Museum of Northern Arizona); Wupatki; Hopiland (Moencopi, Old Oraibi); Canyon de Chelly (White House, Antelope House, Mummy Cave); Window Rock, Chaco Canyon (Pueblo Bonito, etc.); and Coronado State Monument.

1954 Camp 1: June 19–July 3 (16 campers, five staff); Camp II: July 10–24 (16 campers, five staff). Southern Route, general itinerary Only. Sources: Dutton 1954a; *The Sipapu* I:2, II:2 1954; Wethey 1955.

Rancho del Cielo; Paako, Quarai and Abó; Datil and Cleaveland Ranch; excavations of the Peabody Museum, Harvard University near Quemado, and the Chicago

Natural History Museum near Reserve; the Mogollon Rim country of Arizona; and Oak Creek Canyon, the Museum of Northern Arizona, and Walnut Canyon; ruins in the Manuelito area of western New Mexico; Fort Wingate; Columbia University's excavations atop El Morro; and Laguna.

1955 Camp I: June 25–July 9 (16 campers, five staff); Camp II: July 16–30 (16 campers, five staff); Camp III: July 6–20 (16 campers, five staff). Northern route. Sources: Bohrer 1956; *The Sipapu* II:2, III:1 1955; Stein 1955-1956; GSUSA Itinerary, 1955.

Camp I: June 25–27: Rancho del Cielo and Santa Fe museums, etc; June 28: Espanola, Abiquiu, Coyote; camp at Rio Puerco Camp Ground; July 29; Gallina sites, Enchanted Mesa, Jicarilla Apache Reservation, Regina, Bloomfield, Aztec National Monument; camp at monument. June 30: Farmington, La Plata, Mesa Verde National Park; visit sites and museum; camp three nights. July 3: Cortez, Dolores, Rico, Ouray, Telluride; camp at Sneffels Creek. July 4: Silverton, Durango; camp at Vallecito Campground. July 5: Bayfield, Chimney Rock, Pagosa Springs, Monte Vista; geology, rock hunting; camp at Alamosa River Campground. July 6: Antonito, Tres Piedras, Ojo Caliente, Howiri excavations; July 7–8: Bandelier National Monument; tour sites, camp at monument. July 8: Espanola, Chimayo, Cordova, Vadito, Mora, Las Vegas, Pecos, Santa Fe.

   Camps II and III, roughly the same.

1956 Camp I: June 30–July 14 (23? campers, four staff); Camp II: July 21–August 4 (24 campers, six staff). Central Route. Sources: GSUSA Itinerary, 1956 (see Chapter 4).

Camp I: June 30–July 2–3: Santa Fe, Rancho del Cielo; museums, NPS. July 3–4: Coronado State Monument, Chaco Canyon; camp at Chaco Canyon, tour sites. July 5: Chaco to Gallup, Window Rock, AZ (Navajo Indians, arts and crafts); camp at Window Rock. July 6: Canyon de Chelly, archaeological sites, Navajo Indian culture, products; camp at Chinle or Hotevilla. July 7: Keams Canyon, Hopi Indian villages and their arts and crafts; camp at Toreva Day School. July 8: Hopiland for Katsina dances; camp at Toreva Day School. July 9: Wupatki National Monument and Flagstaff; camp at Museum of Northern Arizona. July 10: Walnut Canyon (Sinagua archaeological culture), Winona Ruin, Meteor Crater, trading post, Petrified Forest National Monument; camp. July 11: Sanders, AZ, Zuni Pueblo, NM, (Zuni Indians and their arts and crafts); camp at Zuni Day School. July 12: Zuni ruin sites and El Morro National Monument (archaeology and excavations); camp. July 13; El Morro region, Grants lava flow; Albuquerque and Santa Fe; camp at Rancho del Cielo. July 14: Close camp and cleanup.

Camp II: roughly the same.

1957: Camp I: June 29–July 13 (24 campers, six staff); Camp II: July 20–August 3 (24 campers, six staff; Jan Fleming, leader). Northern and central routes combined. Sources: GSUSA Itinerary, 1957; Chapter 4.

Camp I: June 29: Rancho del Cielo. June 30–July 1: Santa Fe museums, other institutions. July 2: Isleta Pueblo; Pottery Mound; camp at Datil (Cleaveland Ranch). July 3–5: Springerville to Vernon, AZ; visit Chicago [Field] Museum of Natural History excavations, other sites; camp at Vernon. July 6: Sanders, AZ and St. Johns; stop at sites; Navajo Reservation, Window Rock, Ganado (Hubbell Trading Post). July 7: Canyon de Chelly, south rim to Spider Rock overlook; Shiprock, NM to Mesa Verde; July 8–9: Mesa Verde; Cliff Palace, Spruce Tree House, Far View Ruin, Sun Temple, Balcony House, etc. July 10: Durango, Aztec National Monument; camp. July 11: Cuba to Bandelier; visit major sites; camp at Bandelier. July 12: Rio Grande Pueblos, camp at El Rancho del Cielo. July 13: Cleanup and close camp.

Camp II: same route.

Appendix E

Senior Girl Scout Archaeological Mobile Camp and Dig Camp Speakers List, 1947–1957

Sources

Dutton 1947a, 1948b, 1949a, 1950a, 1951a, 1952a, 1953a, 1955a; Chapters 3, 4.

1947

Sylvanus Griswold Morley, Acting Director, MNM, archaeology of Four Corners area; Marjorie Tichy, Palace of the Governors, archaeology and history; Bertha Dutton, tour Hall of Ethnology. Glen Burroughs, US Soil Conservation Service, Southwest soils, conservation. Dale King, NPS, Park Service activities, Parks vs. Monuments, specific sites they would see; Natt Dodge, NPS, overview of Southwest environments. Kenneth Chapman, LA, Indian arts and crafts; tour of collections. Ranger? Newnham, USFS, Southwest forests and conservation. John Sinclair, custodian, Coronado State Mon., Kuaua Ruin, *kiva* murals, Rio Grande archaeology. William Kelly, Harvard University, Navajo Ethnology; NPS Ranger William Guillet, Chaco Canyon, Pueblo Bonito, tour of petroglyphs, talus ruins; Gordon Vivian, stabilization work at Chetro Ketl; J. B. Kuykendall, UNM's excavations. NPS Ranger Bob Walker, Aztec Ruins National Monument, site tour. Deric O'Bryan, Mesa Verde National Park, Developmental Pueblo ruins; NPS Ranger Jim Hall, Mesa Verde ruins; NPS Ranger Don Watson, campfire talks. NPS Custodian Meredith Guillet and Ranger Scotty Benson, Canyon de Chelly, Canyon del Muerto, Three Turkey Canyon. Sallie Lippincott, Wide Ruins Trading Post. Custodian Bates Wilson and Ranger Bill Scott, tours of El Morro National Monument. Evon Z. Vogt, Institute of Human Relations, Harvard University, applied anthropology, Navajo culture change.

1948

S.G. Morley, Marjorie Tichy, Bertha Dutton, tours of MNM halls. Kenneth Chapman, LA. Natt Dodge, NPS, Southwest environments; Charlie Steen, NPS, Parks and Monuments. John Sinclair, Coronado State Monument, custodian, museum, Kuaua Ruin, Painted *Kiva*. Chaco Canyon National Monument Custodian Irving McNeil, Chacoan archaeology; Gordon Vivian, tours of Chetro Ketl, Hungo Pavi, Una Vida, Wijiji, Shabik'eschee (BM III); Bertha Dutton, Łeyit Kin. Wesley Hull, *Gallup Independent* [newspaper], Manuelito sites. Ranger Harold Broderick, Petrified Forest National Monument, museum, site tour. H.H. Nininger, American Meteorite Museum, Meteor Crater; Wupatki National Monument, Watson Smith, Museum of Northern Arizona excavations. Davy Jones, Custodian, Citadel, Wupatki, and Wukoki Ruins, Navajo *Hogan* and summer camp, Sunset Crater; Harold S. Colton, Director, Museum of Northern Arizona, regional archaeology (Cohonina, Kayenta, and Sinagua). Ranger Roland Richart, Tuzigoot National Monument, excavation and museum (Sinagua site). Custodians Homer Hastings and Albert Schroeder, tours of Montezuma Castle, Montezuma Well, cavate lodges in cliffs bordering the valley of Clear Creek, Mogollon Rim. F.M. Hodgin, Acting Supervisor, Sitgreaves NF, forest and animals, birds

1949

Boaz Long, Director, MNM, Marjorie Tichy, Palace of the Governors, Bertha P. Dutton, Hall of Ethnology. NPS, Dale King and Natt Dodge; Kenneth Chapman, LA, Indian arts of Southwest; Dr. (?) Howe, Aztec National Monument, plus a ranger, tour of sites. Mesa Verde National Park Assistant Superintendent Jean Pinkley, tour of all major and some minor sites over three days; Ranger Don Watson on Hopi Snake Dance, discovery of Mesa Verde campfire talks. Josefite Garcia, pottery of San Juan Pueblo. Severa Tafoya, pottery of Santa Clara. Mr. Brooks, Los Alamos Laboratory, history of the laboratory. Unnamed NPS Ranger, Bandelier National Monument, site tour of Tyuonyi and cavate dwellings. Bruce Sewell, Turquoise Post, turquoise mines at Cerrillos. Unnamed rangers at Salinas Pueblos, missions; also U.S, Forest Service, NM Fish and Game speakers.

1950

NPS Ranger Ed Ladd, El Morro National Monument, plus Harvard graduate students working at Ramah (Munro Edmonson, Richard Kluckhohn, Don Michaels, Bob Rappaport). Harold S. Colton and staff, Museum of Northern Arizona, Gladys Reichard, Navajo Ethnology (Camp 1); Katherine Bartlett, Indians of Arizona (Camp II). William Bowen, Superintendent, Wupatki National Monument, and rangers led groups through Wupatki Ruin, etc. Mr. and Mrs. John Connolly, teachers at Sipaulovi Day School, Hopi lifeways. Fred Wendorf, Museum of Northern Arizona, Petrified Forest National Monument excavation. Robert W. Young, Window Rock, linguistics, and Navajo language. Gordon Vivian, Chaco Canyon, ruins stabilization; John Sinclair, Coronado State Monument, Kuaua Ruin.

1951

"Each camp, 20 to 30 individuals as specialists are enlisted to speak with Senior Girl Scouts: teachers, administrators, traders, museum people, specialists in archaeology, ethnology, cultural anthropology, art, linguistics, history, geology, botany, zoology, forestry, and various industries and different kinds of work" (Dutton 1951a:355). Among them, Erik Reed; Natt Dodge; Dale King; Charlie Steen; Sallie Brewer, NPS; Boaz Long, MNM; Kenneth Chapman; Bruce Inverarity, Museum of International Folk Arts (opening, 1952); Mrs. Charles Shook, Moriarty, Valley Irrigation Company on agriculture/hay, livestock; Agnes Morley Cleaveland, history of ranch and ranch life; J. O. Brew and Watson Smith, Harvard's Peabody Museum, Quemado excavations; Paul S. Martin and John B. Rinaldo, Chicago [Field] Museum of Natural History, archaeology of Reserve, AZ (Camp I); Camp II, same but at Pine Lawn excavations; Elaine Bluhm, Turkey Ridge Site, AZ; Nathan Snyder, USFS, Pinetop in Sitgreaves NF, fire and lumbering, staff at MMA, exhibit on Awatovi Murals; A.E. Dittert and R. J. Ruppé, past and current excavations near Grants; Camp III (Dig), Marjorie Lambert of MNM, Galisteo Basin ceramics; Charles Lange, University of Texas, Pueblo ethnology; Huston Thompson of Washington D.C. and Henry Dendahl, Santa Fe.

1952

Florence Hawley Ellis, UNM, Tri-cultures of NM, Camp I; Fred Wendorf, MNM, Camp II, Southwestern Archaeology; Kenneth M. Chapman, Lab, Indian arts and crafts; NPS: L.P. Arnberger, Tom Onstatt, natural history, archeology of areas to be seen (Camp I); Natt Dodge and A.L. Schroeder (Camp II); Boaz Long, Director, MNM, and affiliated organizations, welcome; Marjorie Lambert, Southwestern archaeology and history; Bertha Dutton, ethnology; Ramon Herrera, Governor, Cochiti [Pueblo], welcome and courtesy of picture taking; Mr. and Mrs. Al Pecos, furniture; Mr. and Mrs. Eufrasio Suina, drum; Mr. and Mrs. Alfred Herrera, jewelry, etc.; Mrs. Manuelita P. Chavez, *horno* bread baking; Frank C. Hibben, UNM, Gallina Culture; James C. Griffin, University of Michigan, archaeology of Mississippi Valley, comparison with Southwest; unnamed Forest Service, Ranger, Chimney Rock (induction into "Ancient and Honorable Order of Squirrels"); Jean Pinkley, Leland Abel, lectures, Mesa Verde National Park; Al Lancaster, Pipe Fetish and Far View Pueblo areas, Mummy Lake; Bates Wilson, Superintendent, Arches National Monument, tour of sites and areas; Fred Wendorf, review of pottery at Cuyamungue excavations; Al Packard, his trading post.

1953

Only Pueblo Largo in Dutton's (1953a); see Chapter 4 for some accounts.

1954

Richard Woodbury and Nathalie F. Woodbury, tour site on top of Inscription Rock.

1955

Stein (1955-56): Fred Wendorf, Southwest archaeology and prehistory; Mr. Latham, role of the Museum of Int'l Folk Art; Bruce Ellis, LA, Pueblo art, primarily pottery; Charlie Steen, NPS, Southwest vegetation; and early uses as food; Albert Ely, history of MNM, SAR; Marjorie Lambert, Palace of the Governors tour and summary of exhibits and Pueblo/Hispanic history; Charles McNitt, highway excavations near Tesuque by F. Wendorf; Governor of Tesuque Pueblo, welcome and canes of authority (1873 A. Lincoln; Mexican or Spanish).

1956

Sweeney (1956): Fred Wendorf, MNM, North American and Southwest Prehistory; Mr. Lippincott, Museum of International Folk Art; Bruce Ellis, Laboratory of Anthropology, Southwest Pueblo pottery, then and now; NPS: Natt Dodge, wildlife, especially birds, vegetation, and what to avoid (rattlers, scorpions, flash floods); Erik Reed, NPS, early Pueblo history, organization; Boaz Long, MNM, early Santa Fe history; Marjorie Lambert, "how she became interested in archaeology," plus current exhibits on Spanish/Pueblo Influences, Early Man in the Southwest, Bandelier community, Pueblo/Spanish history; Bertha Dutton, ethnology, *katsina* exhibit; branches of anthropology; John Sinclair, Coronado State Monument, Kuaua ruin; Harold Colton, Museum of Northern Arizona; Jimmy Kewanwytewa, *katsina* carving; Mr. Matsen, El Morro National Monument; Richard and Nathalie Woodbury, at site above Inscription Rock, + unnamed others.

1957

Sweeney (1957): Repeat of MNM, NPS, LA, Folk Art Museum, speakers from 1956; Fred Wendorf; Paul S. Martin, Vernon excavations; Marie Nourse, Cleaveland Ranch,

Datil. No others specifically named. After 1952, there were no yearly summaries of the Mobile Camp trips that would have included speakers.

Job Descriptions, Archaeological Mobile Camp for Senior Girl Scouts, 1955 (MIAC/LAA 99BPD.xx)

Director's Responsibilities

Pre-Camp:

- Year-round publicity—talks and articles
- Works closely with GSUSA on all phases of planning, finances, dates, staff, publicity, transportation, etc. and receives copies of applications.
- Plans itinerary, scouts it for mileage, mail stops, doctors, campsites, churches, food stores, water, specialists, permits, etc.
- Works with cook on initial food order, menus on which based, and delivery.
- Arranges for permanent, stored equipment to be at the campsite when staff and campers arrive.
- Clears arrangements for meeting campers, their hostessing by Santa Fe Council, and for their transportation to ranch campsite.
- Acquaints new staff members with ranch campsite, equipment, water supply, latrines, wood supply, etc. so that they may line up first day orientation.
- Discusses general plans with staff and reviews responsibilities so that each understands her area of responsibility and authority.

- Provides necessary transportation to Assistant Director for official Girl Scout business.

During Camp:
- Generally keeps a watchful eye on everything and is the overall leader and-coordinator, working with and through the Assistant Director (Girl Scout representative).
- Drives lead car; responsible for daily route, mileage and time schedules.
- Sees that drivers have route plan.
- Teaches archaeology and related subjects and supplements the specialists; shares camp skills as needed; group meetings, campfires, etc. as they fit into travel schedule.
- On last day gets campers off on designated transportation by 2 p.m., except for emergencies requiring special handling for campers' safety.
- Checks total mileage records with Assistant Director to authorize her signing of bill. Receives all records from Assistant Director on last day.

Last Day & Post Camp:
- Arranges for storage of equipment.
- Sends Girl Scouts of the United States of America all finance records, health cards, recommendations, etc. within four weeks of the close of the season.
- Assists with follow-up evaluation, if any.
- Excavation Site, Special Arrangement: Arranges for use of excavation site and sees that all equipment is in readiness.
- Sees that State health Department gives certificate of approval for water and water trailer.
- Takes staff to excavation site for orientation the day preceding the opening of the camp.
- Arranges for excavation permit and sees that all arrangements are ready at camp by the time campers arrive.

Assistant Director Administrative Responsibilities

Pre-camp:

1. Arrival: Lodging in Santa Fe will be provided for one night in advance as required in order to assure availability at least one full day in advance of opening day of session. Please make own reservation in advance. Suggest the Santa Fe Indian School Employees Club, El Rey Motor Courts or De Vargas Hotel. For the Indian School reservation write Mrs. Lucy Ratzo, Principal's office, advising her that you are a member of the Girl Scout Mobile Camp Staff.

2. Day before camp opens: Arrange with Dr. Dutton for visit to her camp to become familiar with campsite, equipment, water, and food sources, etc. Consult with Dr. Dutton about staff and camper orientation plans, etc. See Transportation agent and sign agreement form if necessary. If mutually convenient settle in at camp with personal equipment even though spending the night elsewhere, in order to avoid delay and confusion on the opening day.

3. Opening day-morning: Arrive at Dr. Dutton's office (Museum of New Mexico) at 9:00 a.m. to check first day preparations and plans to receive all necessary data and materials.

4. Materials checklist: Duplicate of equipment inventory; camper information: health cards, arrival plans, Life Savers and First Aiders, whom to notify in emergency, etc., menus and advance food orders. Also check: Additional supplies to be purchased with the cook; plans for first meal (supper); Santa Fe Hostess plans and transportation arrangements to the camp. Talk about supply stops; review of Kaper needs, camper needs.

During Camp:

1. Checks in both staff and campers, collecting staff health cards and supplementary health statements from campers.

2. Plans first day orientation with girls, carried out with help of all staff as needed. Includes: Review of pup tent pitching, knots, axemanship, sawing; kaper discussion, and chart to be posted in appropriate place (chuck wagon); health and safety standards discussion; First Aid discussion.

3. Maintains Girl Scout camp standards with special emphasis on: Drinking water and dish water and dishwashing; swimming and horseback riding

rules; safety in climbing—staying with group; rest periods—promptness; care and use of cars and care and erection of tents.

4. <u>In case of accident notifies parent or guardian and GSUSA as soon as possible.</u>

5. Keeps record of names and addresses of people in trail camps to be thanked and for what. Records car mileage at beginning and end of trip camps in order to sign bill before it is sent to the Girl Scouts of the United States of America for payment.

6. Works with cook to facilitate shopping en route, by advance preparation of lists, and consults with her about the role of the campers in meal preparation. Notifies director of the supply needs, etc.

7. Arranges time for meetings, campfires, rest periods, etc. with director

Closing Day:

1. Sees that camp is closed by 2 p.m. and that last meal is lunch.

2. Works with cook and campers: Inventory of used supplies and return to Director (except at end of season when unused supplies returned for cash refund). Washing equipment inventory and storage of all equipment including chuck box, noting repairs and replacements needed. Sees that soiled towels, etc. are left at the laundry pick-up place and date reported to Director.

3. Works with Director: Reports any cash balance and all finance records, all health cards. Checks list of persons to be thanked and leaves with director. Checks mileage record for authorization to sign car rental bill. Leaves copy of Kaper Chart with Director.

4. Signs transportation bill for the trail camps.

5. Post Camp: Sends reports and recommendations within a month of the close of the session to the Girl Scouts of the United States of America, 1555 East 44th St., New York, N.Y.

This list is abbreviated and includes only Director's and Assistant Director's (GSUSA Rep) responsibilities. Not included: Cook-Dietitian, Transportation Agent (Stacy), Shuttle Counselor (excavation camp only; MIAC/LAA 99BPD.xx).

Manuscript Sources
and Additional Photograph Credits

All photographs cited as MIAC/LAA in captions are used with permission of the Museum of Indian Arts and Culture/Laboratory of Anthropology, Santa Fe, New Mexico.

Materials from Girl Scouts of the USA National Archive, New York:

1. *Annual Reports 1950, 1951.*

2. *"National Camping Committee" Camping Division 1946-19xx (typescripts).*

3. *Camp and Camping*
    - General to All-American Camp; file name: Camping-General; Camp and Camping History, 1956 Report, letters dated April 6, 1982 and January 17, 1983.
    - History: 1952 work plan for 1953; report by Yoffa on GSUSA taking over administration of archaeological project from Region IX.
    - Reports, Monthly (April, 1953; June, July, August, September, 1953).
    - Meeting Minutes, 1954–1958. Quotes from programs of conferences in 1948, 1952, listing Mobile Campers giving papers at conferences; Region IX awarding Dr. Bertha Dutton "Thanks Badge" at conference, Albuquerque, New Mexico, 1958.

Sources from Archives of the Museum of Indian Arts and Culture/ Laboratory of Anthropology (MIAC/LAA)

Bertha P. Dutton Collection (99BPD.xx), including Girl Scout Files, Scrapbooks, 1948, 1951, 1952, 1953 (2), 1954, 1955 (2), 1956. Donated materials by Vorsila Bohrer, Susan S. Martin, Kate Swift, Mary Anne Stein. Pueblo Largo—Dutton Excavations 1951–1956 (95PLE.001–037). Las Madres Excavations (Dutton) 1961–1962 (95LME.037, 038). "Project Accomplishments" [Las Madres, 1963] (89LA6.061). Las Madres Reports (Dutton MSs, LA.xx). MNM/LA General Correspondence (89LA5.061– 89LA5.066). Reports of Excavations at Girl Scout Camp Eliza Seligman (89LA6.115.1, 2; 08ARM.001–101). Anne Rushmer McClelland Collection. 1947, 1948 Archaeological Mobile Camps (08ARM.001–101, 13ARM.001).

Other Manuscript Sources

Vorsila L. Bohrer diaries provided by Mollie Toll, Santa Fe, New Mexico, 2016.

Mills, Rebecca Adams; letters, maps, provided by Adams, Berkeley, California, September, 2017.

Notes

Chapter 1

1. The exact count, as well as the names of all girls who attended the camps from 1947 through 1957, may not be totally accurate. These data were taken from small notebooks kept by Dutton with the names of participants for each camp in each year; but occasionally there were errors and some girls names were not entered, especially in later years. Most likely they were "alternates" chosen after the first lists were assembled and Dutton was notified of attendees. See Appendix A for names and camps attended.

2. The Senior Girl Scout Archaeological Mobile Camp Program actually had several names through the years, but is best known by this title. In 1951, a two-week excavation camp was added (at Pueblo Largo, a site in the Galisteo Basin south of Santa Fe) providing this additional experience for those who were interested (Chapter 5).

3. Shetterly (2016) provides a stirring portrayal of the struggle of African American women (especially Dorothy Vaughan, Mary Jackson, Katherine Johnson and Christine Darden) to overcome barriers in gaining educations and positions in mathematics and engineering during their years at Langley Memorial Aeronautical Laboratory and NASA in the postwar era and up through the 1950s and 1960s. Her book also reviews additional materials on the general status of women in the sciences in those years.

4. Parezo (1993b) provides an excellent account of the situation and causes for lack of women's success, especially in the academic fields like anthropology, but likely also applicable to other employment situations for women. For more information on the continuing pay gap and more see the website of the American Association of University Women (www.AAUW.org): "The Simple Truth About the Gender Pay Gap" (Vagins, 2018); "Solving the Equation: The Variables for Women's success in Engineering and Computing" (Hill 2015); "Barriers and Bias: The Status of Women in Leadership" (Hill, 2017); also "Female Education in STEM" (Wikipedia 2018b).

5. The *Girl Scout Promise* and *Girl Scout Laws* have gone through various revisions through the years, but in the late 1940s and 1950s they were as follows: *Promise:* "On my honor, I will try: To do my duty to God and my country, To help other people at

all times, To obey the Girl Scout Laws;" *Laws:* "A Girl Scout's honor is to be trusted. A Girl Scout is loyal. A Girl Scout's duty is to be useful and to help others. A Girl Scout is a friend to all and a sister to every other Girl Scout. A Girl Scout is courteous. A Girl Scout is a friend to animals. A Girl Scout obeys orders. A Girl Scout is cheerful. A Girl Scout is thrifty. A Girl Scout is clean in thought, word, and deed."

6. Examples include Mary Wheelwright, Amelia and Martha White, Natalie Curtis, Mary Austin, Willa Cather, Alice Corbin Henderson, and several others (Armstrong 2016; Babcock and Parezo 1988; Lewis and Hagan 2007). Elsewhere in northern New Mexico were Mabel Dodge Luhan and Millicent Rogers in Taos, Carol Stanley at Ghost Ranch, and Georgia O'Keeffe at Abiquiú (Babcock and Parezo 1988; Jewell and Stout 2013; Poling-Kempes 2015; Robinson 1989; Rudnick 1987).

7. Florence Hawley (Ellis) came to UNM to teach full time in 1934, a year after Bert arrived. Hawley had already participated in UNM's Chaco Canyon field schools in 1929 and 1930. Her master's thesis (University of Arizona) was on southern Arizona archaeology and her PhD dissertation (University of Chicago) on the site of Chetro Ketl in Chaco Canyon—thus making her a particularly valuable addition to the faculty (Mathien 1992:11).

8. Bert does not name the Marmon daughter who was at the University of New Mexico at that time, but it was likely Miriam Marmon (Dutton and Marmon 1936). Miriam Marmon graduated from UNM in the 1930s.

9. Joiner (1992) explains the division of the two field schools, with Jemez Canyon being for undergraduates and other interested people, a more popular approach, and Chaco Canyon for advanced undergraduates and graduate students with research aims—a good division in the eyes of many.

10. Walter was not an actual salaried employee, but a newspaper man and later banker and a good friend of Hewett's. He edited the journal from 1913 to 1958 (Chauvenet 1983).

11. Bert likely chose Columbia University through having known Duncan Strong, then Department Chair, while studying at the University of Nebraska, Lincoln—but also because of Hewett's advice. Bert learned early on her own and then from Hewett to "network": get to know many people and gain their support.

Chapter 2

1. When Hewett founded both institutions, their separate boards had several overlapping members, many of them his personal friends and people of power and influence in the region and beyond. Their story is a complex one that did not interfere with the Girl Scout program, but it did mean that given that Bert worked for both institutions, she had to ask permission of both boards for activities outside of her regular work assignments (see D. Fowler 2000, 2003; Lewis and Hagan 2007). Both

boards decided that the Girl Scout program could be part of her museum work as long as she also completed her regular duties for both institutions.

2. In the 1890s, the Fred Harvey Company, in partnership with the Santa Fe Railway, developed the popular Indian Detours. These featured motor coach travel to places of scenic and cultural interest in northern New Mexico and Arizona. Tours departed from Harvey hotels and other stops to visit national monuments with archaeological sites, Pueblo villages, and scenic wonders. Tours were led by trained "Couriers" who lectured about what the people were seeing, advised on arts and crafts purchases, and more (D. Fowler 2000:344–47; Thomas 1978). Other private companies also operated tours both before and after the Indian Detours, which were on the wane by the start of World War II.

3. There is no correspondence from this period in the Laboratory of Anthropology Archives, and nothing from the period was found by Diane Bird and Jo Tice Bloom when they visited the GSUSA Archives in 2009. Region IX was in charge, befitting local control of programs, a standing policy of the GSUSA. But GSUSA was also involved at some level, as the 1947 camp was open to other than Region IX girls. It is also not clear whether Sue Little was actually a GSUSA person detailed to Region IX for a short time, or primarily affiliated with a New Mexico council. She left Dallas the following year for California and then settled back in Albuquerque. She seems to have worked with or for the Albuquerque GS council at one time (Bohrer 1947a). Vorsila Bohrer's papers at the Arizona State Museum Library (Archive MS 47) contain an envelope related to the 1947 Mobile Camp itinerary. The envelope is marked with the Santa Fe Girl Scout Council logo and a receipt. Bohrer and Velma Whipple spent a few days before the Mobile at a Girl Scout Camp in the Jemez Mountains, likely what would become the Eliza Seligman Camp, and the receipt may be for that stay. Although Bert makes no mention of the local Santa Fe Council, they seem to have helped host GS representatives in the area for the Mobile Camps and other activities (see Chapter 3).

4. In 1948, in that Ferdon was getting nowhere with the local Boy Scout Council on sponsoring another trip, he proposed a 20-day tour for Boy Scouts to be cosponsored by MNM and the Philmont Scout Ranch near Cimarron, NM. It was considered by Philmont for a time, but then turned down. He and the MNM made additional proposals to those in charge of Philmont for a summer survey of their property and the excavation of a mammoth (or mastodon) skeleton discovered there. The boys would participate in both and learn archaeology and paleontology (89LA5.62.2 Philmont Ranch). There is no indication that this occurred either, although much later Philmont did sponsor some archaeological work at the ranch (Dennis Gilpin, personal communication, 2010).

5. Hewett had just died the year before, and perhaps Bert also wanted to honor his memory—but it likely was his philosophy that she most admired and felt that it worked. See also note 6, below.

6. Bert often stated in oral interviews that "outdoor people" were really the best people, based on her own field school experiences, and that being outdoors and observing nature was very important in teaching people how to live better lives (Dutton 1983; 1985a).

7. Applied Anthropology is a broad subfield within anthropology. Applied anthropologists attempt to point out cultural differences so that people in cross-cultural situations will better understand what appear to them to be "different" or "strange" behaviors, ideas, beliefs, and actions. Museum anthropologists do this through developing exhibits and otherwise interacting with the public; medical anthropologists help in cross-cultural health situations; and today, industry and corporations employ applied anthropologists to help company and management staff better understand not only cross-cultural situations, but also the internal dynamics of their corporate social structures.

8. Mary Anne Stein (personal communication, 2010) jokingly remarked that her notes from introductory lectures on Southwest archaeology given by Dr. Fred Wendorf to the 1955 Mobile Camp were nearly sufficient for her to pass her PhD prelims at Southern Methodist University. Vorsila Bohrer later made typescripts of her notes which are extensive and are now part of her archive in the Arizona State Museum library (Archive MS 47).

9. See Suggested Reading in the Preface and other references cited, for updates and changes to these chronologies and terminologies. The pace of archaeological and other work in the region since the 1940s and 1950s has accelerated enormously, bringing forward advances in understanding more and more about the region's human history, and especially the interrelationships of peoples and archaeological sites and cultures through time.

10. This comment was actually in the context of her complaint as to the girls' "excessive singing"—an important part of the basic Girl Scout experience, as she would come to appreciate later. But they also needed to keep quiet at times and really "listen" to the country as far as Bert was concerned!

11. According to Vorsila Bohrer (1947b; personal communication 2008), Whip was her teacher and a good friend who alerted her to the NM opportunity, and with whom she traveled that summer to New Mexico and back to Illinois. They stayed with Whip's Albuquerque family both before and after the 1947 trip and in subsequent years. Bohrer and Whip loved to identify birds and plants together, including on the trip out and back as well as during the 1947 and later camps. It was Whip who gave Bohrer her nickname "Rambler." Whip moved back to Albuquerque before long and continued to teach school there.

12. *Scouts' Own* is a meeting held in the troop or camp—usually on Sundays—during which Girl Scouts reaffirm their ideals. It is planned by the girls in cooperation with their leaders. It can include readings from books, songs, poems, or individual

recitations by the girls that all will enjoy. It is held at a place and time agreeable to all (GSUSA 1954c:45).

13. The Four Corners region includes the areas adjacent to the convergence of the states of New Mexico, Arizona, Utah, and Colorado—the northern heartland of the Pueblo Southwest (ancient and modern). Morley had participated in archaeological surveys there in 1907. He excavated Cannonball Ruins the following year (Morley 1908).

14. All route maps shown in these chapters are schematic only, given road changes in modern times, plus Bert's desire—and in many cases need—to travel unpaved back roads to sites and camps.

15. Kuaua is a large Pueblo that was first excavated as a combined project of the MNM, SAR, and UNM from 1934–1939. It was likely occupied by Tiwa-speaking people who left the site as the result of the Tiguex War with the Spanish in 1541. It may also represent a site constructed or at least occupied by peoples migrating into the region from the northern San Juan drainage in the late 1200s (Dutton 1963a; Noble 2000; Sinclair 1951).

16. This was a well-established camp for the UNM field school for several years, with permanent buildings, water, and various other amenities. It was a favorite stop for the Girl Scout Mobile Camps in later years, even after UNM finished working in the area and abandoned the site.

17. Threatening Rock was a giant multi-ton boulder that fell onto the northeastern section of Pueblo Bonito on January 22, 1941. The original builders of the Pueblo were well aware that it could fall, and had attempted to shore it up with rock and wooden underpinnings. It destroyed several rooms when it fell, and still lies atop them.

18. There is a vast literature on interpretations of these large structures, what are now referred to as Chacoan Great House sites. They occur in several areas of northwestern New Mexico, southwestern Colorado and southeastern Utah (see, for example, Cameron 2009; Reed 2008; Reed and Brown 2018).

19. Now this transition is viewed slightly differently than as a more complicated transition, with scholars questioning the function of some of the structural changes in these sites (like aboveground storage structures becoming living quarters, and pithouses becoming kivas) were really that simple or occurred roughly at the same time (Noble 2006; Wilshusen 2006).

20. All Mobile Camp groups who visited Mesa Verde were able to see these exhibits, and especially the dioramas, which were fondly remembered. They are classic examples of early museology, and remain just as popular today as they were when they were first installed.

21. According to Bohrer's (1947a; 1947b) diary, Watson gave very interesting presentations the three evenings they were there: one describing a Navajo wedding ceremony and all of the social processes and conventions involved; a second on how and when the Navajo people came into the region; and the third on what the Indian

people of the region had contributed to "civilization." All were followed by Navajo dancers and singers in various performances. Bohrer (1947b) took extensive notes on the archaeology of Mesa Verde and all of its structures—as Bert had told the girls to do. She also recorded plants new to her and especially birds.

22. Vogt's family had a ranch at Ramah where he was raised. He later earned a PhD in anthropology, using his study of veterans as his dissertation topic. He came back to the area many summers after that while a professor at Harvard University and continued to publish on Navajo ethnology and culture change.

23. She does not say whether they visited the Marmon family she had known since her first school days at UNM, but in all likelihood they did. The family had established and run the trading post there over a long period.

Chapter 3

1. Bert's primary measure of the success that year was that several girls said at the end of the trip that they would come back if there were another camp next summer. However, as Bert wrote to Anne Rushmer (Dutton to Rushmer Aug. 9, 1948), she did not hear from Region IX or National as to whether 1947 had been a success or failure. It took some prodding, but both ultimately decided that it had been a success. Some of the campers wrote to Bert after the 1948 camp, thanking her and saying that they had enjoyed the trip; but again, seemingly nothing from the staff.

2. See Dutton 1948b; 1949a; 1950a; 1951a, all *El Palacio* summaries. She also wrote shorter notes for *Teocentli* referencing each year's activities (Dutton 1949b; 1949c; 1950b, 1950c, 1951b).

3. Bert (1949a:279) referred to the role of the Dallas Office as "coordinating." By 1953, GSUSA National Headquarters was entering into formal agreements with the Museum of New Mexico (89LA.063, Yoffa to Long, February 27, 1953; see Chapter 6).

4. There seems to have been some national distribution early, but it is not clear how extensive it was. Girls from other states were already attending in 1947 and 1948, apparently learning of the camps because their mothers were directly involved in scouting or from friends who had been on a trip. By 1949 and 1950, girls were also spreading the word more widely through conference attendance, newspapers, and by other means.

5. We don't know how the budgets were handled, nor are there examples of them in the archives. Attempts to find archives for Region IX have proved futile, although the GSUSA have a few items from Region IX from later dates (see Chapters 6, 7).

6. It appears that Prien was involved in choosing at least some of the GS Reps during these years, as some of them were from California, Colorado, and other western states. But this might also signal a bigger role for National at this time period than is apparent from documentation.

7. In 1947, Sue Little was acting as Community Outreach Representative for the GSUSA and was working with Region IX. She served as GS Rep on the mobile camp that year along with Nyla Harvey. Later, others whom Bert did not know or had not met also served. Bert did not get along with some of the GS Reps, and this was sometimes a point of contention between her and Region IX.

8. Whether SAR remained an official joint sponsor is not clear; but board members did visit excavation camps in 1951 and occasionally thereafter. Bert still requested leave from both organizations, but since they had overlapping members on their boards, this was more a formality than necessity. Her salaried appointment was with the MNM, so she reported to the Director of the MNM first.

9. Based on 16 campers times $70/per camper, this yields $1,180. This was to cover food and expenses for campers plus a staff of five, or 21 people; three vehicles, at an average of 1,300 miles each (counting a few side trips for repairs, being lost, etc.). Gas prices at the time averaged roughly $0.19/gallon at 12 mi/gallon. So an approximate overall budget would be roughly $550 for transportation, $500 for food, $50 for cook's salary, and $80 for other budgeted costs (entrance fees, incidental expenses—unforeseen auto repairs) would equal roughly $1,180. Tight, but adequate.

10. Several girls started what turned into impressive Southwest Native art collections on these trips and always appreciated Bert's advice so as to where to acquire quality pieces and if the asking prices were fair.

11. According to M.A. Stein's diary from 1955, in which Bert reviewed the first year, she actually considered not continuing for a second year—as she was uncertain if the effort could be sustained. It was quite clear that something had to be done about the vehicle situation and cooking duties—especially if more girls and adults would be traveling on the trips.

12. These notes are taken from an introductory lecture on the history of the program that Bert gave to the 1955 Archaeological Mobile Camp II, as entered by camper M.A. Stein in her diary (Stein 1955).

13. Anasazi, Mogollon, and Hohokam were then the names of the largest agriculturally-focused archaeological traditions in the Southwest region. Each was characterized by different set of ceramic traditions, architectural constructions, and artistic emphases, and each occupied different overall environments. The Anasazi (now Ancestral Pueblo) were in the north, centered in the Four Corners or Colorado Plateau area; the Mogollon in the central Arizona-New Mexico highlands; and the Hohokam in the hot deserts of southern Arizona. In those years maps typically showed "boundary" lines around each, although even recognizing at the time that these marked more generalities than firm separations. Today the situation is viewed as even more complex, and the tendency to think much more of mutual influences at different points in the past. Other agricultural traditions were known then (Sinagua, Cohonina, Fremont) and are

still recognized today with the same caveat—the Sinagua and Cohonina centered in northwestern Arizona, and the Fremont in Utah.

14. There is no indication that GS Reps or the drivers were paid; if they were, it apparently was not out of Bert's budget.

15. Although there is no direct evidence in the records, it is likely that insurance was handled through the GSUSA. In a 1985 interview, Bert said that she doubted that "the Girl Scout executives were well enough informed… Parents had to sign releases before they [daughters] could come on these expeditions, and the things they were signing didn't cover everything that we were doing [likely a very generic form]. We were climbing cliffs and getting into far back country" (Dutton 1985a:8).

16. Chronologies are more complex than this. But at least Tice was repeating some of the basic ideas (see Chapter 2, footnote 9 for the approximate chronology current in the 1950s).

17. This is an oversimplification of the situation at that time. Although the pottery traditions of some of the Pueblos had been altered considerably through the years, as some potters turned to smaller "souvenir" pottery pieces for the tourist market, others continued with older vessels, and yet others were revitalizing their art and taking it in new directions.

18. The wives of both Dodge and Steen were Girl Scout leaders in the area, and this may have made their husbands even more willing to speak to Bert's Girl Scouts. They both continued to do so in most of the following years.

19. This may have been the *hogan* and summer camp of the Peshlakai Etsidi family, long resident in the Wupatki area. Members of the family continued to be involved with the Monument, including Clyde Peshlakai, son of Peshlakai Etsidi, who was an acting superintendent and frequent guide to visitors to the site (Roberts 2014).

20. Bert lectured the girls on being flexible in career choices and to have alternatives in mind. She had found herself unhappy in her first choice (secretarial, banking), but fortunately was able to pursue an alternative—archaeology (Chapter 1).

21. One was Vorsila Bohrer, who entered the University of Arizona, in Tucson; but the identity of the second is not clear. She apparently entered UNM. Nettie Kesseler would follow Bohrer at the U of A in two years.

22. But it wasn't an open invitation to stay on for any length of time. Bert had other duties and her job to attend to.

23. Chimney Rock and its Companion Rock are two pinnacles that rise roughly 300 feet (91 m) above the surrounding area. They are associated with Ancestral Pueblo sites, including a "Great House" and "Great Kiva" of Chacoan style masonry as well as other sites. Little archaeological work had been done there when the Girl Scouts visited, but beginning in the 1960s and continuing until recently, additional excavations have suggested that the site was largely ceremonial and related to the "lunar standstills" which can be observed there 18.6 years apart. During these events, the moon rises between the two rock columns for approximately 18 months. Although

the area was occupied prior to Great House construction, the Chacoan Great House and Great Kiva seem to have been constructed for ceremonies involving the observance of this phenomenon.

24. Cleaveland was much remembered by all the girls who met her. Her personal reflections on the history of her family's west-central New Mexico ranch (also portrayed in her book) were fascinating to the girls. She was also a cousin of MNM director Sylvanus Griswold Morley (Miller 2010). Marie Nourse, who served as cook in 1955 and was another friend of Bert's, was also related to Cleaveland.

Chapter 4

1. For example, Anne Rushmer McClelland's personal letters received from Bert and her collection of Bert's Christmas letters are in the Laboratory of Anthropology Archives as part of the Bertha Pauline Dutton Collection (99BPD.xx). More letters from DDDs are in other files in the Dutton Collection.
2. There may have been an earlier newsletter, as Bert refers to an attempt in a letter to Anne Rushmer. If so, no copies have been found to date.
3. This figure may not be accurate as the states of origin are not indicated for campers for all years (Appendix A).
4. Bert led two mobile camps that year, and Vorsila Bohrer led the third. Bohrer (1956a) wrote an article about the trip, stressing its value in teaching basic science. See also Marty Gerber's account of 1955 III, below.
5. There is only scant reference to visiting Pecos State Monument (i.e., Stein's account of the 1955 camp, below). There is a large Pueblo (founded in roughly AD 1100) and Spanish church (built in 1619) there. It is highly likely that several trips stopped there as it is so close to Santa Fe. It is also of interest as the Pueblo was occupied until 1838, when the few remaining survivors left to be part of Jemez Pueblo. The site was made a State Monument in 1935, a National Monument in 1965, and Pecos National Historic Park in 1990.
6. Letters home include those by Cyndy Tice, Marty Gerber, and Mary Anne Stein. Others are from personal diary entries.
7. To enter these sacred spaces was indeed a privilege, and did not happen very often for groups of people. It reflects that both the teacher and Bert were known for their courtesy and cultural understanding of the significance of these sacred places.
8. Although dyslexic, Cyndy Tice went on to a significant career as a nurse, serving in several foreign posts in addition to hospitals in the United States (see Chapter 10). Her letters were transcribed by her sister, Jo Tice Bloom.
9. Gillian Wethey was a Girl Guide from England who was there as a sponsored camper for international experience. She had visited other camps in the US in 1952, and was also on the excavation camp that year as a guest and responsible for first aid. She also participated in Camp I in 1953 and Camp I in 1954, as well as the Dig in 1953. She

traveled with Bert to Mexico and Guatemala in 1954, and ultimately settled and married in Santa Fe where she taught piano for many years.

10. Not likely a Squaw Dance, which is more of a social occasion. This sounds like a ceremonial healing or chant, which is much more private and infrequently seen by outsiders.

11. Dr. Fred Wendorf was at the Laboratory of Anthropology at the time, later serving as its director from 1958–1964. He had an illustrious career in Southwest archaeology, later moving to a position at Southern Methodist University where he worked for many years on additional archaeological projects in the Southwest and also in Egypt. He was Mary Anne Stein's dissertation chair.

12. This was likely at Cuyamunghe, where the MNM was working that summer.

13. The Lincoln Canes are silver-tipped canes bearing the signature of A. Lincoln. They were given in 1863 to the 19 New Mexico Pueblos as symbols of the peaceful relationship between the U.S. Government and each of the Pueblos. Today they still represent the Government's commitment to honor the sovereignty of the Pueblos. They are passed down to each new Pueblo governor upon their election (SantaFe.com, 2015).

14. Areas on the eastern Navajo Reservation referred to as "checkerboard" are private lands "allotted" to Navajo families interspersed with other reservation, public, and private lands. On a map, they appear as a checkerboard.

15. Howiri (LA711) is a site located near Ojo Caliente, and is one of the many sites surveyed and either tested or excavated prior to highway construction, beginning in the 1950s. Laboratory of Anthropology archaeologists began excavating in in 1954 (Peckham et al. 1981:34).

16. This is the only specific mention of visiting Pecos ruins, although there likely were others, as it is conveniently located east of Santa Fe. It features the remains of a large mission church as well as an Ancestral Pueblo that was excavated by famous Southwestern archaeologist Alfred V. Kidder between 1915 and 1921. In 1955, Pecos Pueblo and the church were a state monument. Now they are within the broader Pecos National Historical Park.

17. I remember only two lines, and not the tune: "Casa Rinconada stands high on a hill. It stands there today, and it always will".

18. The camera was borrowed, and was 35 mm SLR, with separate light meter, etc., and I did not know how to use it properly. On my return, I returned the camera and several rolls of exposed film to be developed to the owner, but never heard back.

19. Anthropology was my alternative choice, following Bert's advice. At that time, women were discouraged from going into large animal practice (my preference). I had worked in a small animal practice during high school, and wasn't sure that was for me. Bert sat us down as a group each of the two years that I was on mobiles and discussed our future plans with us.

20. Niman, often referred to as "Home Dance," is the last Hopi *katsina* dance and ceremony of the season, after which the *katsinas* leave the villages for their home on the San Francisco Peaks. They then send the rain clouds and rain to nourish the crops and the people, and replenish the villages' water supplies.

21. Pottery Mound, southwest of Albuquerque, was excavated by UNM archaeological field schools from 1954–1958 (except 1956) under direction of Dr. Frank Hibben of UNM. The site was occupied between roughly 1350 and 1500, and so named because of the large number of beautifully painted pottery sherds and vessels recovered there. It is also noted for its numerous *kivas* decorated with murals (see P. Schaafsma 2007). The site was deeded to Isleta Pueblo in 2012.

22. This was the ranch of Agnes Morley Cleaveland, and I thought this was her. But she could not have been, as Mrs. Cleaveland had left the ranch for good in early 1956. The person may have been her friend and neighbor, and former DDD driver/cook, Marie Nourse. She would have known the stories from hearing Cleaveland, and of course, having read Cleaveland's book *No Life for a Lady* (see Miller 2010).

23. Paul S. Martin and John B. Rinaldo excavated in the Vernon, AZ area for several years, and had earlier in western New Mexico, along with Elaine Bluhm. Their results are reported in several publications, including Martin and Rinaldo (1950; 1960). These sites were then considered to represent the Mogollon archaeological tradition (see also Nelson and Hegmon 2010).

24. The miniature dioramas, now considered classics in museum exhibitions, were still on exhibit the several times I returned to the museum in subsequent years.

25. The only unique one I remember, other than the line from the Chaco song cited above, was "Dirty Diggers Are We" (see Appendix C).

Chapter 5

1. In the 1940s, Dutton purchased the site of Pueblo San Lazaro for back taxes, with the plan of excavating it. However, after a few years, the former owner successfully sued to recover the property. Dutton was repaid her purchase price, but would rather have retained the site (Dutton 1953a:340).

2. Some notes for these early years are in the MIAC/LAA (95PLE .001–.037; see especially .012, .013, .030, .031), but the coverage is spotty. The artifacts from these years are also incomplete—not too surprising after 50+ years. For their publication, Wilson and colleagues (2015:6) pulled together what records and collections (principally pottery) that could locate from the GS excavations at Pueblo Largo, then available in LAA and the Archaeological Resources Management System (ARMS) files.

3. Most of the field notebooks remaining in the Archives (95PLE.001–037) appear to be from the 1954 to 1956 seasons, with only spotty coverage before that as noted. Notebooks from these later years were collected at the end of each season. Missing

ones apparently were never turned in (S. Martin, M.A. Stein, personal communication, 2015; see 95PLE.014–029,.035).

4. Crew chiefs today are experienced excavators (often graduate students in archaeology) who are put in charge of a site or a portion thereof by the Principal Investigator. They keep track of the progress of the excavation through detailed notes, drawings, and photographs, including measurements of depths and levels and anything else of interest. Their notes concern the site's stratigraphy or other features (hearths, walls, rooms, courtyards/plazas, clusters of artifacts, human remains if encountered)—anything that might be important toward interpreting the site. They act as the primary agents of control, so that whoever ultimately reports on the site can analyze accurately not only what it contained but anything else of significance to explaining the site's overall history and significance.

5. Wilson and others (2015:6) did not find either a new site map or an updated version of Nelson's map (Figure 5.3) marking designations for newly excavated rooms or other features. Nor has one been found in the Dutton Collection as of 2018. Wilson and others (2015) did what they could to reconstruct the additional excavation units and match them to their contents.

6. Again, some of these data are missing, making it difficult after so long a time, and without full notes, to correctly place some artifacts.

7. According to Wilson and others (2015:6), for Room Block V, out of 21 rooms excavated, "Only one room's fill was screened." But according to S. Martin and M.A. Stein who were on the 1955 and 1956 Digs when most of this area was excavated, screening of the fill from at least lower levels of rooms was standard procedure. But again, this detail may be missing from the notes they reviewed.

8. This is not unusual behavior. As crew chiefs or leaders gain more experience, the person who may have the overall responsibility for the excavation has less need to oversee the total operation.

9. Nettie Kesseler Adams, personal communication, July 2009.

10. Not all artifacts encountered were given catalog numbers nor were their specific locations recorded—only those considered potentially significant to interpreting the activities at the site. A large sample of pottery was collected, but not all of these sherds would have been cataloged individually; stone flakes were not. Decorated or "worked" sherds (made into other artifacts) and all recognizable projectile points were separately numbered.

11. The Kinsey Reports of 1953 include a volume on female sexuality and another on male sexuality. There have been updates since then (Wikipedia 2019).

12. Bohrer told the Dig crew that she returned as often as she could to help because she learned so much from Bert and from the program—much more than in school, including graduate school (see also Stein Diary, 1955–56).

13. This so-called "tower" would have been a unique feature for the area, and its function still remains to be fully explained. Nelson (1914) suggested that it might have been a shrine. Dutton thought it might have been a "tower" built for defensive purposes. Richard I. Ford, an expert on northern New Mexico archaeology, visited the site when Wilson and others (2015) were examining it, and suggested that it might be a World Quarter Shrine, a specific area set aside by contemporary Rio Grande Pueblo people, thus agreeing with Nelson (Wilson et al. 2015:97). Nelson (1914) photographed another shrine south of the site that was known to Dutton and to some Dirty Diggers, but not visited by them due to its sacred nature—although they may have held a *Scouts' Own* in the vicinity on one occasion. There is also one more shrine that has been identified at the site since excavation (Wilson et al. 2015).

14. Apparently the site was not "back-filled," a procedure used by most archaeologists at the end of an excavation that involves dumping screened materials back into the site to protect it (plus people and animals). Much of the material removed from the eastern side of the site was dumped over the mesa after screening and thus no longer available to fill that portion. The decision not to back-fill any of the remainder perhaps reflected Dutton's plan to return to the site in the near future to continue the excavation. Back-filling now is standard procedure (see Chapter 8).

Chapter 6

1. This was in addition to her title as Director's (Hewett's) Assistant, which had continued until his death in 1946.

2. Daddy D. had been a widower for some years by then, as Bert's mother had passed away while she was in school at the University of New Mexico (Chapter 1).

3. Jo Tice Bloom and Diane Bird visited the GSUSA Archives, New York City, in 2009, checking for records, but could find only some memoranda and monthly reports that contained information about the archaeological program. These were dated principally from 1951–1958 and 1982–83. See Credits and References Cited for additional details. Attempts to locate independent archives for Region IX, Dallas, TX, have not been successful.

4. After all, Sue Little had originally contacted the MNM and Bert with this goal in mind (Chapter 2).

5. It is possible that Sue Little knew about this impending policy change as early as in 1947 when she approached Bert and the MNM. But if so, she apparently did not attempt to place the program in the hands of GSUSA National headquarters at that time. It remained a program of Region IX until the control shifted in 1952. Unfortunately, the paper trail on any of this is very slim in the GSUSA Archives, at least as far as Bloom and Bird could determine in 2009.

6. The exact year of these initiatives is not clear, as it is not mentioned until GSUSA reports in 1952 and 1953 as cited.

7. Rockwood was a national Girl Scout Camp near Potomac, MD. It had been donated to the GSUSA in 1939 to be used mostly by troops while visiting sites near Washington, D.C., though it is now a public park. All States continued yearly at least until 1955, when it seems to have been replaced by Girl Scout Senior Roundups, which began in 1956 and occurred at three-year intervals until 1965. These were intended to be international. Since then, other national and international events have been held irregularly (Wikipedia 2020).

8. There is no correspondence—at least with Bert—indicating that Yoffa recommended changes in operations after that first year. She did later, however.

9. Mimeographed pages were still sent to campers who were selected, however, as these likely could be produced in the national office. These included all of the necessary information that each girl needed: names and addresses of fellow campers, equipment lists, health and contact information, and more.

10. This is based on Stein's (1955–56) diary entry about how the selection process now worked. That, in turn, was based on what the girls had been told by Bert and other girls. How many brochures were printed and mailed to each council is not known. No correspondence on numbers was found in the Camping Division materials of GSUSA Archives or in Bert's papers.

11. It may have contained a first draft, but if so, that document is no longer in the files. A brief note in the GSUSA's Camping Division, Camps and Camping Reports file, for December 1952, states that "Yoffa developed a first draft of an agreement with the Museum of New Mexico" (see Note 3, above).

12. We do not know how Bert felt about this contract, particularly whether she favored this approach. But codifying some of these aspects may have been a way for her to settle some points of contention, including control over the Dig and some staffing choices.

13. Just what this equipment was is not clear, as tents, cooking gear, etc., were part of the permanent camp equipment maintained by the Museum—much of it donated by Santa Fe businesses and private parties. Official Girl Scout hats are the only obvious additions, at least as seen in some photographs of the camps and campers. Campers complained that these were not practical, either on the trail or on Digs, but agreed to wear them for "official" photographs. They wore cowboy hats or other broad-brimmed hats instead when on the trail for better sun protection and also more practical head wear when excavating.

14. Previously, Bert had at least reviewed applications for Mobiles, although Region IX had made the initial selection. She wanted to get an idea of the girls' backgrounds and why they wanted to attend.

15. The GS Reps to the Dig camps in 1953 and 1954 noted in their reports at the end of the season that there was not a great deal for them to do at the camp, especially if they did not want to dig (which they did not). They did little other than participate

in planning GS-oriented activities, such as *Scouts' Own* or other general discussions of Scouting, supervising initial orientations to camping skills and *kapers*, and setting up and taking down the camp. They recognized that the Dig camp was different—a "work" situation—but the GS Reps felt that their job needed further definition (Swift 1953; Myers 1954).

16. Apparently in part stimulated by the archaeological Dig camp program, Camp Winona, one of the Massachusetts State Camps, in cooperation with Dartmouth College, carried out a faunal survey in 1953 and was sponsoring another in 1954 (GSUSA Archives, Camping Division Report [June, July, August, September]: 2–3). There is no indication as to which animals were to be observed or counted or by what methods. By rumor, there may have been an opportunity to participate in either an archaeological survey or an excavation through the River Basin Surveys, Smithsonian Institution, in the 1950s, but efforts to verify this failed.

17. The annual Gallup Inter-Tribal Ceremonial was August 11–13 that year, and Bert thoroughly enjoyed judging it each year (Memorandum, Girl Scouts, Boas Long, May 12, 1955; 89LA5.064).

18. Although there is no indication of it in the correspondence, the MNM may have been concerned about having someone other than an actual museum employee directing one of the mobiles. There would have been no questions as to Vorsila Bohrer's qualifications, as she was well known at the MNM, having volunteered there on several occasions and having been a salaried employee for several months one year.

19. Especially with those who were not officially employees of the MNM. Although excavations during this period sometimes had volunteers, everyone was beginning to see some of the issues of liability involved when this was the case.

Chapter 7

1. There is nothing in the official correspondence of the MNM to indicate that the museum's administration was telling Bert to diminish her role in the program. But it is likely that she and Director Long had discussed it and reached that conclusion.

2. Chair was Mrs. Joe H. Luckie of Houston, TX, who was the mother of one of the veteran campers (Lila Luckie) and had been an active supporter of the archaeological camps for several years (Dutton to Wasson, May 21, 1956; 89LA5.065). It is unclear how long Bert remained on the committee, but probably at least a year or more.

3. Bert likely had already decided that the Dig camps needed to end, and thus wanted to have a larger than normal crew to accomplish what they could this last year.

4. The Roundup list that year included: Gwenie Belle, Elaine Boettcher, Martha Jean Gerber, Mary Lou Happoldt, Cheryl Heiss, Judy Hendrix, Catherine Lynch, Susan Martin, Kathryn Miller, Paula Pachlhofer, Mary Anne Stein, and Harriet Wildman, all either 1954, 1955, or 1956 Mobile Camp or Dig members. Ex-Mobile or Dig staff

included Patricia Beltz, Jan Fleming, and Gretchen Yoffa (GSUSA Memorandum, July 7, 1956). Mary Anne Stein and Susan Martin did not recall that they ever got together for a suggested reunion at Roundup 1956 although there had been talk about doing so initially.

5. Dutton (1985) also indicated that the San Cristobal Ranch where Pueblo Largo is located was changing hands at about this time, and that "the Senator from Texas" who now owned it "didn't like what the Scouts and the Museum were doing" (see Chapter 8). Thus, the project may have been in jeopardy for this reason as well.

6. Fowler remembers Fleming from at least one Mobile Camp, either in 1956 or 1957, or both. She was very athletic and a good camper and leader. Martin and Stein remember her as well from the 1956 Dig as a good camper, friendly, and efficient. None of us remember that she was particularly knowledgeable about the region's landscape, history, archaeology, or ethnology—but then Bert was the leader and did most of the talking.

7. In a card to Anne Rushmer McClelland on June 6, 1957, Bert said that she would be starting the annual reconnaissance (a week to 10 days), and then Camp I would follow on June 29, and she would direct it (Dutton to McClelland, June 6, 1957). In a card dated August 23, 1957, she writes: "It was a relief to have the final Mobile expeditions over with. Both camps this summer drew good gals for the most part. We had a Papago [Tohono O'odham] Indian girl, for a change, and she was fine" (Dutton to McClelland, Aug. 23, 1957; 99BPD.xx). Suzan Miguel, the Papago girl, was on Camp II. Bert's specific role in Camp II is not clear, but given that it started and ended at Rancho del Cielo, she would have at least met all of the campers. She also would have participated in the final evaluation report to GSUSA along with Fleming.

8. I doubt that any of us campers really realized the significance of this gift to Bert, as we were not familiar with the history of the program, how special it was, or what she had done in all of those previous years. We just remembered the gesture (Chapter 4).

9. Neither the Museum of Northern Arizona nor Hopi country qualify as "archaeological stops." There could have been a specific stop at a site at Petrified Forest, as there was one on the monument that Bert and the campers on the central route had visited in the past. But this sentence seems to indicate that Fleming was not that well informed about the region, and particularly its archaeology versus ethnology.

10. Perhaps additional research beyond 1958 would turn up something more of interest that would clarify this point.

Chapter 8

1. There likely were some volunteers from time to time who helped with day-to-day matters with the collections, and Bert refers to a student intern working on accessioning collections during the two summers of 1950 and 1951. Vorsila Bohrer also

worked as Assistant Curator of Ethnology full-time from September, 1955 to the summer of 1958—with three months leave in early 1957 for ethnobotanical research (Dutton 1951d:50; Dutton 1957c:34).

2. She was assigned to this task by MNM-SAR Director Wayne Mauzy and had it "available for use in the public observance of September 5 (Dutton 1957c). Two years later, the New Mexico Legislature severed the ties between the MNM and SAR. They determined that the intertwined governance of the MNM and the SAR (overlapping board members, authority given to a private institution's [SAR] board to appoint a State institution's director [MNM]), as instituted by E.L. Hewett in 1907, was illegal. So were some of the staff's double appointments—even though there were no double salaries (Lewis and Hagen 2007:70). After that, Bert had one less "job" to do, but she remained a supporter of SAR throughout her lifetime.

3. The Kuaua murals project involved the site of Kuaua, part of Coronado State Monument (now Coronado Historic Site). At the site, Scouts saw replicas of the multicolored and multilayered paintings discovered on the walls of one of the *kivas* during UNM/SAR excavations in the 1930s. Bert's mentor, E.L. Hewett, had suggested to Bert at that time that she interview members in nearby Pueblo communities to see what they might be willing to share about the paintings. She had done so, but had not completed the project. She was likely motivated to take up the project again by the publication of Watson Smith's (1952) book on the *kiva* murals at the Hopi site of Awatovi in Arizona. This gave her much-needed comparative materials on which to base her analysis. Bert had tried to use the Kuaua mural project as her dissertation topic in 1946–47, but her doctoral committee felt that it was too large and perhaps nebulous to be suitable. See Davis (2008) for a history of the Awatovi excavations, including work on the murals. When funds became available to the MNM at the end of 1957 for publishing, Bert took advantage of the opportunity.

4. Bohrer led two groups of Girl Scouts in surveys and test excavations in the Vallecito de los Viejos in the Jemez region in 1961 and 1962. She filed two brief summary reports on the results with the MNM, the permitting agency (Bohrher 1961–1962: 89LA6.115 1, 2). She also planned a Mobile Camp tour for girls attending the Camp Seligman in 1962 and 1963 (Chaparral Girl Scout Council 1962:14, 1963:9), but did not lead the one in 1963. They were called the "Heritage Trips" and included several of the nearby stops that had been covered by Dutton's Mobile Camps. As late as 1968, the Seligman Camp's Archaeological Unit was still looking for surveying and excavation opportunities through the MNM, a direct legacy of Dutton and Bohrer (Kathleen Murphey to Delmar Kolb, May 26, 1968; 89LA6.115.2).

5. Bohrer also served as Chaparral Council's District Advisor for the Navajo Reservation until she returned to the University of Arizona to complete her doctoral work.

6. Richard Ford (personal communication, 2007) described one of Bert's later "treks" in her specially-equipped Mercedes with its steel-plated undercarriage as going over

hills, rocks, sagebrush, and sand—no roads required. Ford said that Bert was as a "demon driver." She had the Mercedes specially equipped for off-road use, so that she could go where she used to like to go in her 1928 Model T Ford.

7. The Lab's involvement in salvage archaeology, specifically highway right-of-way operations, started in 1954 with excavations of the site of Howiri near Ojo Caliente (Peckham et al. 1981:34). It was not long before other sites were in danger from construction, and MNM budgets had to be adjusted to accommodate these needs.

8. Today's archaeologists would likely not include these materials in their site reports, as procedures are now different. Some human remains that cannot be avoided in salvage excavations would most likely be observed in the field by a physical anthropologist and then either left in place and covered, or removed and turned over to the appropriate Native American tribe or community for reburial. Remains from past excavations on federal lands also fall under the Native American Graves Protection and Repatriation Act of 1990. Rules governing private lands do not necessarily apply, although some landowners today voluntarily reinter remains newly encountered. As of 2018, human remains from Pueblo Largo had not been repatriated and reinterred as the site is on private land.

9. Dr. Erik Reed worked for the National Park Service, Santa Fe; Thomas Mathews and Lyndon Hargrave were affiliated with the Southwest Archaeological Center in Globe, AZ; David Brugge was then at the University of New Mexico; Kenneth Honea was apparently in the Santa Fe area, but his affiliation is unknown. He may have started on his analysis during this early period, or he may have been commissioned in 1962 after Bert had finished excavating Las Madres (LA25), as his report covers materials from both sites. See also individual citations.

10. These and other reports are now published as appendices in the reanalysis of the pottery, architecture, and tree-ring chronology of Pueblo Largo by Wilson and others (2015).

11. There is no further information in the Dutton Collection as to whether Ellis completed the work, and no evidence of a finished report.

12. This outline is not dated, but based on internal evidence as to which specialists she was having write various sections, and the resulting dates of those sections that were completed and are in the Archives, it was between 1957 and 1960.

13. Directorship of the MNM (and SAR) changed hands in 1955, when Boas Long retired. He stayed for an additional year, but then turned the reins over to Wayne Mauzy as new director in late 1956. Mauzy was not an anthropologist, and may have needed this information in order to approve of Bert's leave. The request is not formalized, so perhaps Mauzy suggested that Bert apply for outside monies for the project—which she did in 1962 (see below).

14. Haury's (1958:1) conditions for identifying a migration were as follows: "(1) if there suddenly appears in a cultural continuum a constellation of traits readily identifiable

as new, and without local prototypes, and (2) if the products of the immigrant group not only reflect borrowed elements from the host group, but also as a lingering effect, preserve unmistakable elements from their own pattern." Further, he added that "The probability that the phenomena outlined above do indeed represent a migration, rather than some other force that induces culture change, is increased: (1) if identification of an area is possible in which this constellation of traits was the normal pattern, and (2) if a rough time equivalency between the 'at home' and the displaced expressions of the similar complexes can be established."

15. This award was very important at the time, as very few women archaeologists received any independent funding from the National Science Foundation or from other major granting agencies. This indicates that Dutton was held in high esteem by her archaeological peers who worked in the region—almost all males at the time.

16. These two had been tested or partially excavated by MNM colleagues. Colina Verde (LA309), in particular, seemed to show promise "because it appears that a Mesa Verde community may have been re-established intact" (Dutton 1963c). It was also of the right age according to 42 tree-ring dates (1270–1272) and had Black-on-white ceramics identified as of Mesa Verde type (Dutton 1962a:3). LA3333 was similar, and perhaps even earlier, as it might have shown some key phases to argue for the significance of in-situ development.

17. As she said later in an interview, the owner was "just a little man, more interested in money than anything else" (Dutton 1985a:21).

18. These arguments based on ceramics are quite technical. Those interested in more details should see the publications by Dutton (1964b, 1966, 1980; Schaafsma 1995; Wilson et al. 2015).

19. There are several partial or full typescripts of these volumes (titles slightly varying), plus one Xerox copy that appears to be from yet another source than these currently in the Laboratory of Anthropology Archives. The mostly complete set (two volumes) includes original photographs clipped to the pages. All of the typescript volumes contain marginal editorial notes and bibliographic entries in Dutton's hand, likely added at various times over several years, at least into the mid-1980s. It obviously remained a work in progress given lack of funds to publish it. Curtis Schaafsma, former Director of the Lab, indicated that he had the manuscripts at one time in his Lab office (personal communication, August, 2017), but that Bert asked for them back and had them until just before she passed away (see note in bibliography under Dutton 1964d).

20. These include: Kenneth Honea (ca. 1963) on flaked stone from Pueblo Largo and Las Madres, also printed in Wilson et al. 2015 as Appendix C; Hugh Cutler on corn from Las Madres (See also LA 95PLE.000). Dutton also listed other special studies to be done for which there are no manuscripts.

21. The manuscript includes bibliographic entries and marginalia in Bert's hand in pencil through the mid-1980s. She and Curtis Schaafsma worked on ceramic analysis projects for Las Madres at least until the mid-1980s.

22. Reconstructions of this type can leave the false impression that the entire site was constructed and occupied at the same time—unlikely given the data recovered at Pueblo Largo that show that certain areas, such as portions of Room Block V, seem to built and occupied first, and that the other sections of the site followed, but likely at different times (see also Wilson et al. 2015).

23. Nels Nelson also intended to finish larger and more complete site reports on his work in 1912 in the area (Dutton 1980, 1989).

24. Stein, in particular, felt that the crews were not getting full information about excavation techniques nor the overall plan for excavating the site.

25. Some archaeological field schools at the time, as well as now, are also better than others at teaching students methods and techniques.

26. She was recruited to take on this position by the MNCA's board of directors, who were attempting to stabilize the institution after the death of Ms. Wheelwright and the general downward slide of the institution on nearly all fronts.

27. Bert published several works with Caroline Olin, the artist and art historian she met through their mutual interest in Navajo sand painting. In the early 1970s, Olin began renting the small house at El Rancho del Cielo that had been Daddy D's as a studio and part-time residence while in New Mexico. Olin ultimately retired there a few years later, and she and Bert focused on writing popular books of Navajo and Pueblo stories and related topics, especially for children. They remained close until Bert's death in 1994.

Chapter 9

1. As noted earlier, not all names of camp attendees were represented in Bert's notebooks or files, especially after GSUSA took over processing of the applications in 1953. Some names that do not appear on the Bert's lists were likely "alternates," chosen as replacements after an accepted participant had to back out.

2. Her birthdate was actually March 29, 1903 (Bohrer 1979).

3. The exhibition toured nationally under the auspices of the Smithsonian Institution's Touring Exhibitions program (SITES) and was seen by thousands of people.

Chapter 10

1. In 1964, when I was about to present my first paper at a professional anthropology meeting, I (Fowler) remember seeing Bert walking toward the venue. I asked her which paper she was going to hear (the program offered choices), and she remarked,

"Of course I'm going to hear yours." I was so proud I could hardly contain myself, that *she*, as well-known as she was, would come to listen to *me*, then a lowly graduate student. I saw her at many subsequent professional meetings as well, but that first one stayed with me.

2. Discovering that another person was a DDD somehow makes them an instant friend, and someone you want to remain in your life if at all possible. It is a special sisterhood.

3. Tracking former DDDs later in life becomes difficult, for the same reasons that it was hard to contact them to alert them to Bert's eightieth birthday party (Chapter 9). Many were no longer at the same addresses, or even in the same towns or states where they grew up; the parents of some were now deceased, thus further breaking the chain; many had changed their names upon marriage(s); and some have undoubtedly passed away over the last 60–70 years.

4. Paleobotanists identify plant remains, including seeds, leaves, stems, flowers, and sometimes pollen from archaeological sites. They compare these to the local flora growing near the site at present, and often, from well-dated samples, can reconstruct past environments at various points through time. They help the archaeologists to suggest reciprocal interrelationships that took place between resident populations and their environments. Always interested in plants, birds, and archaeology from an early age, Bohrer learned of the specialty field of "ethnobotany/paleobotany" from Jean Pinkley of the NPS at Mesa Verde on the 1949 Dutton Mobile Camp. Pinkley advised her to specialize if she wanted to be an archaeologist and, given her interests, that ethnobotany would be an excellent specialty (Bohrer 1949). She took that advice.

5. Diana Avery Amsden's father was an artist on excavations in Arizona and New Mexico; one uncle worked on several excavations in Mesoamerica, and yet another uncle was a curator of the Southwest Museum of the American Indian in Los Angeles, CA.

6. I have been unable to trace the other archaeological opportunity rumored to have been available in the 1950s Midwest, and can only suggest that it might have been with the Smithsonian's Missouri River Basin Surveys or with a local college or university.

Appendix A

1. See also lists of "Excavation Camps" for additional camps attended by the Senior Girl Scouts listed here.

Bibliography

Albuquerque Journal
  1958   Forty Years of Growing. *Albuquerque Journal,* 26 May: 21. Albuquerque, New
          Mexico.
Amsden, Diana Avery
  2017   Diana Avery Amsden, PhD, Accomplishments, http://dianaaveryamsden.
          webs.com/accomplishments.htm/, accessed June 11, 2017.
Archaeological Conservancy
  2020   The Archaeological Conservancy. http://archaeologicalconservancy.org,
          accessed February 29, 2020.
Armstrong, Leatrice A.
  2016   *Mary Wheelwright: Her Book.* Wheelwright Museum of the American Indian,
          Santa Fe, New Mexico.
Babcock, Barbara A., Jennifer Fox, and Nancy Parezo (compilers)
  1986   Women Anthropologists in the Southwest: Reflections and Reminiscences.
          Handout for conference "Daughters of the Desert: Women Anthropologists
          in the Southwest 1880–1980," March 14, 1986. Wenner-Gren Foundation for
          Anthropological Research, New York.
Babcock, Barbara A. and Nancy J. Parezo
  1988   *Daughters of the Desert: Women Anthropologists and the Native American
          Southwest 1880–1980: An Illustrated Catalogue.* University of New Mexico
          Press, Albuquerque.
Baxter, Bill
  2005   Site Stewardship at Pueblo San Marcus. *Archaeology Southwest* 19(4):15.
Blinman, Eric
  2008   Perspective. Galisteo Basin: Centuries of Collaboration and Conflict [inter-
          view with]. *El Palacio* 113(3):55–61.
Bloom, Jo Tice
  1948   Scrapbook of 1948 Archaeological Mobile Camp. On file, Bertha P. Dutton
          Collection, Museum of Indian Arts and Culture/Laboratory of Anthropology
          Archives, Santa Fe, New Mexico.
  2007   Dr. Bertha Dutton and Her Dirty Diggers. *La Crónica de Nuevo México* 73:1–3.
  2011   Bertha Dutton, Mentor. In *Words and Sherds: In Papers in Honor of Meliha
          S. Duran & David T. Kirkpatrick,* edited by Emily J. Brown, Carol J. Condie,

and Helen K. Crotty, pp. 79–83. Papers of the Archaeological Society of New Mexico No. 37. Albuquerque.

2012   Dr. Bertha Dutton and her Dirty Diggers. In *Sunshine and Shadows in New Mexico's Past. The Statehood Period, 1912–Present,* edited by Richard Melzer, pp. 395–404. Rio Grande Books/Historical Society of New Mexico, Santa Fe.

Bohrer, Vorsila L.

1947a   Unpublished Diary, Girl Scout Archaeological Mobile Camp, June 26 to July 19, 1947 [in author's hand]. In possession of C.S. Fowler; to be added to the Vorsila Bohrer Papers, Arizona State Museum Archives No. 47. Tucson.

1947b   Unpublished Diary, Girl Scout Archaeological Mobile Camp, July 26–July 19, 1947, [typescript by V. Bohrer]. In possession of C.S. Fowler; to be added to the Vorsila Bohrer Papers, Arizona State Museum Archives No. 47. Tucson.

1948a   Unpublished Diary, Girl Scout Archaeological Mobile Camp, July 10–24, 1948 [in author's hand]. In possession of C.S. Fowler; to be added to the Vorsila Bohrer Papers, Arizona State Museum Archives No. 47. Tucson.

1948b   Unpublished Notes on People and Places, Girl Scout Archaeological Mobile Camp, 1948. In possession of C.S. Fowler; to be added to the Vorsila Bohrer Papers, Arizona State Museum Archives No. 47, Arizona State Museum Archives No. 47. Tucson.

1949   Unpublished Diary, Girl Scout Archaeological Mobile Camp, 1949, with hand-drawn map of route and typescript notes appended. In possession of C.S. Fowler; to be added to the Vorsila Bohrer Papers, Arizona State Museum Archives No. 47, Arizona State Museum Archives No. 47. Tucson.

1954   Back in 1947. *The Sipapu* 1:2:1–4. Bertha P. Dutton Collection, Museum of Indian Arts and Culture/Laboratory of Anthropology Archives, Santa Fe, New Mexico.

1956   Mountain Ranges: Their Museum Walls. *Pacific Discovery* IX(1):27–29. California Academy of Sciences, San Francisco.

1961–   Archaeological Site Survey and Test Excavation Reports, Camp Eliza
1962   Seligman, NM—Site 5917. Includes miscellany, 1964 to 1968. Bertha P. Dutton Collection, Museum of Indian Arts and Culture/Laboratory of Anthropology Archives, Santa Fe, New Mexico.

1963   *Council Resource Guide.* Chaparral Girl Scout Council, Albuquerque, New Mexico.

1979   Bertha Pauline Dutton: A Biography. In *Collected Papers in Honor of Bertha Pauline Dutton,* edited by Albert H. Schroeder, pp. 1–32. Papers of the Archaeological Society of New Mexico 4. Albuquerque Archaeological Society Press, Albuquerque.

Brugge, David

1957   Maize of Pueblo Largo. Manuscript on file, Museum of Indian Arts and Culture/Laboratory of Anthropology Archives, Santa Fe, New Mexico.

Cameron, Catherine M.

2009 *Chaco and After in the Northern San Juan Region: Excavations at the Bluff Great House.* University of Arizona Press, Tucson.

Chaparral Girl Scout Council

1962 50 Years of Scouting, 1912–1962: Camping, 1962. Chaparral Girl Scout Council, Albuquerque, New Mexico.

1963 Camping, 1963. Chaparral Girl Scout Council, Albuquerque, New Mexico.

1964 Camping, 1964. Chaparral Girl Scout Council, Albuquerque, New Mexico.

Chauvenet, Beatrice

1983 *Hewett and Friends: A Biography of Santa Fe's Vibrant Era.* Museum of New Mexico Press, Santa Fe.

Clark, Jeffery J., and Barbara J. Mills

2018 Chacoan Archaeology at the 21st Century: New Questions and Ongoing Revelations. *Archaeology Magazine* 32(2–3):3–5.

Cleaveland, Agnes Morley

1941 *No Life for a Lady.* Houghton Mifflin, Boston, Massachusetts.

Cohen, Leslie

2006 Dutton's Dirty Diggers: "She Taught Us to be Bold." *El Palacio* 111(2):34–35.

Colton, Harold S.

1939 Three Turkey Houses. *Plateau,* 12(2):26–31.

Cordell, Linda S.

1995 Tracing Migration Pathways from the Receiving End. *Journal of Anthropological Archaeology* 14(2):203–211.

Cordery, Stacy A.

2012 *The Remarkable Founder of the Girl Scouts: Juliette Gordon Low.* Viking, New York.

Crown, Patricia L., Janet D. Orcutt, and Timothy A. Kohler

1996 Pueblo Cultures in Transition: The Northern Rio Grande. In *The Prehistoric Pueblo World, A.D. 1150–1350,* edited by Michael D. Adler, pp. 188–204. University of Arizona Press, Tucson.

Crown, Patricia, Keriann Marden, and Hannah V. Mattson

2016 Foot Notes: The Social Implications of Polydactyly and Foot-Related Imagery at Pueblo Bonito, Chaco Canyon. *American Antiquity* 81:456–448.

Culmer, Marjorie M.

1962 Forward into the Future. *Girl Scout Leader (Fiftieth Anniversary Issue)* 39(3):7–9. Girl Scouts of the U.S.A., New York.

Davis, Hester A.

2008 *Remembering Awatovi: The Story of an Archaeological Expedition in Northern Arizona, 1935–1939.* Harvard University, Peabody Museum Press, Cambridge, Massachusetts.

Downum, Christian E., (editor).
   2012   *Hisat'sinom: Ancient Peoples in the Land without Water*. School for Advanced Research Press, Santa Fe, New Mexico.
Downum, Christian E., Ellen Brennan, and James F. Holmlund
   2012   Red House in Black Sand. In *Hisat'sinom: Ancient Peoples in a Land Without Water*, pp.79–86. School for Advanced Research Press, Santa Fe, New Mexico.
Dunmire, William W.
   2013   *New Mexico's Spanish Livestock Heritage: Four Centuries of Animals, Land and People*. University of New Mexico Press, Albuquerque.
Dutton, Bertha P.
   1938   *Łeyit Kin, a Small House Ruin, Chaco Canyon, New Mexico*. University of New Mexico and School of American Research Monograph Series Vol. 1(5). University of New Mexico Press, Albuquerque.
   1939   Excavations in Guatemala, Tajumulco—A Sacred Precinct. *El Palacio* 46(5):99–107.
   1941   The New Hall of Ethnology. *El Palacio* 48(8):178–188.
   1947a   Girl Scout Archaeological Expedition. *El Palacio* 54(12):294–95.
   1947b   Letter [reconnaissance, 1947/start of Mobile]. *Teocentli* 43(June):4–5.
   1947c   Letter [trip account]. *Teocentli* 44(December):6–7.
   1948a   Girl Scout Archaeological Expedition. *El Palacio* 55(7):200.
   1948b   Senior Scout Mobile Camp of 1948. *El Palacio* 55(8):252–256.
   1949a   Senior Girl Scout Archaeological Camps of 1949. *El Palacio* 56(9):278–285.
   1949b   Letter [1948 Mobile]. *Teocentli* 47(June):4–5.
   1949c   Letter [1949 Mobile]. *Teocentli* 49(December):6.
   1950a   Archaeological Mobile Camps, Senior Girl Scouts, 1950. *El Palacio* 57:366–71.
   1950b   Letter [1950 Mobile, itinerary]. *Teocentli* 49(June):4–5.
   1950c   Letter [1950 Mobile, summary]. *Teocentli* 50(December):7.
   1951a   The Diggers Complete Their Fifth Season of Senior Girl Scout Archaeological Mobile Camps. *El Palacio* 58(11):354–369.
   1951b   Letter [1951, plans]. *Teocentli* 51(June):5.
   1951c   Pueblo, Navaho Census Shows Population Increase. *El Palacio* 58(5):150–51.
   1951d   Ethnology. In *School of American Research, Annual Report* 1951:47–51. Santa Fe, New Mexico.
   1952a   Senior Girl Scout-Museum Archaeological Program of 1952. *El Palacio* 60:342–52.
   1952b   Letter (1952, plans). *Teocentli* 53 (June):3.
   1952c   Letter (1952, results). *Teocentli* 54 (December):7.
   1952d   The Toltecs and Their Influence on the Culture of Chichen Itza. PhD dissertation, Department of Anthropology, Columbia University, New York.
   1953a   Galisteo Basin Again Scene of Archaeological Research. *El Palacio* 60(10):339–351.
   1953b   Letter (1953, beam dates at Pueblo Largo] *Teocentli* 55(June):6–7.

1954a   Letter (1954, Mexico]. *Teocentli*, 57(June):4–5.

1954b   Letter (1954, Mobile/Dig]. *Teocentli* 58(November):6.

1955a   Report on Senior Girl Scout Archaeological Mobile Camp. *Southwestern Lore* 21(3):35–41.

1955b   Tula of the Toltecs. *El Palacio* 62(7-8):195–249.

1956   A Brief Discussion of Chichen Itza. *El Palacio* 63(7-8):202–232.

ca. 1956a Unpublished notes on pottery types from Pueblo Largo. Manuscript on file, Bertha P. Dutton Collection, Museum of Indian Arts and Culture/Laboratory of Anthropology Archives, Santa Fe, New Mexico.

ca. 1956b Unpublished notes on architecture, Pueblo Largo. Manuscript on file, Bertha P. Dutton Collection, Museum of Indian Arts and Culture/Laboratory of Anthropology Archives, Santa Fe, New Mexico.

1957a   The School of American Research: At the Half Century. Manuscript on file, School of Advanced Research, Santa Fe, New Mexico.

1957b   Letter (termination, Mobile/Dig program]. *Teocentli* 61(Dec.):7.

1957c   Hall of Ethnology [Museum of New Mexico]. In *Annual Report*, 1957, pp. 34–35. School of American Research of the Archaeological Institute of America, Santa Fe, New Mexico.

1958   Studies in Ancient Soconusco. *Archaeology* 11(1)48–54.

1960a   *Indians of the Southwest*. Southwest Association of Indian Affairs, Santa Fe, New Mexico.

1960b   Letter (year's activities]. *Teocentli* 62:199.

1961a   Chiapas-Guatemala Relationships. In *Los Mayas del Sur y sus Relaciones con los Nahual Meridionales*, pp. 111–14. VIII Mesa Redonda, San Christóbal Las Casas, Chiapas. Sociedad Mexicana de Antropología, Mexico City.

1961b   *Navaho Weaving Today*. Museum of New Mexico Press, Santa Fe.

1962a   Problems in Anasazi Migration: An Application to the National Science Foundation for a Grant-in-Aid for Research for the Period 1 July 1962 to 1 July 1963. Ditto copy, appended to Las Madres Report (Dutton 1963d). Bertha P. Dutton Collection, Museum of Indian Arts and Culture/Laboratory of Anthropology Archives, Santa Fe, New Mexico.

1962b   *Happy People: The Huichol Indians*. Museum of New Mexico Press, Santa Fe.

1963a   *Sun Father's Way: The Kiva Murals of Kuaua, a Pueblo Ruin, Coronado State Monument, New Mexico*. University of New Mexico Press, Albuquerque, School of American Research, Santa Fe, and the Museum of New Mexico Press, Santa Fe.

1963b   *Friendly People: The Zuni Indians*. Museum of New Mexico Press, Santa Fe.

1963c   Problems of Anasazi Migration: Project Accomplishments. Ditto copy. Manuscript on file, Bertha P. Dutton Collection, Museum of Indian Arts and Culture/Laboratory of Anthropology Archives, Santa Fe, New Mexico.

1963d   Las Madres, LA25, First Draft, Vol. 1. Typescript. Manuscript on file, Bertha P. Dutton Collection, Museum of Indian Arts and Culture/Laboratory of Anthropology Archives, Santa Fe, New Mexico.

1964a   Mesoamerican Culture Traits Which Appear in the American Southwest. In *XXXV Congreso Internacional de Americanistas*, pp. 481–492. *Actas y Memorias* I. Mexico City.

1964b   Las Madres in the Light of Anasazi Migrations. *American Antiquity* 29:449–454.

1964c   Preliminary Report on Prehistoric Peoples in the Galisteo Basin, New Mexico (Two typescript volumes, photographs clipped in; marginal corrections in Bert's hand). Manuscript on file, Bertha P. Dutton Collection, Museum of Indian Arts and Culture/Laboratory of Anthropology Archives, Santa Fe, New Mexico.

1964d   Las Madres (LA 25): Prehistoric Peoples in the Galisteo Basin, New Mexico, Vol. 1, First Draft. Margin notes in Dutton's hand. Manuscript on file, Bertha P. Dutton Collection, Museum of Indian Arts and Culture/Laboratory of Anthropology Archives, Santa Fe, New Mexico.

1966   Prehistoric Migrations into the Galisteo Basin, New Mexico. *XXXVI Congresso Internacional de Americanistas* Vol. 1:287–300. Seville, Spain.

1975   *Indians of the American Southwest.* Prentice-Hall, Englewood Cliffs, New Jersey.

1980   An Overview of the Galisteo Archaeology. *Transactions* 72(4):86–96.

1981   Excavation Tests at the Pueblo Ruins of Abó. In *Collected Papers in Honor of Erik Kellerman Reed*, edited by Albert H. Schroeder, pp. 177–195. Papers of the Archaeological Society of New Mexico 6. Albuquerque Archaeological Society Press, Albuquerque, New Mexico.

1983   Video Interview with Dr. Bertha P. Dutton, by Tom McCarthy, Museum of New Mexico. On file, Bertha P. Dutton Collection, Museum of Indian Arts and Culture/Laboratory of Anthropology Archives, Santa Fe, New Mexico.

1985   Audio Tape Interview with Dr. Bertha Dutton. Jennifer Fox, interviewer; Nancy J. Parezo, transcriber. Recorded for *Daughters of the Desert: Women Anthropologists and the Native American Southwest, 1880–1980* (Project Directors: Barbara Babcock and Nancy J. Parezo). Wenner-Green Foundation, New York.

1987   Interview with Dr. Bertha P. Dutton. Living Treasures transcripts, AC338, Recording #15, 10/1987; and #27, 09/1991 [120 minutes]. Fray Angélico Chávez History Library, Santa Fe, New Mexico.

1989   Nels C. Nelson and the Galisteo Basin. In *From Chaco to Chaco: Papers in Honor of Robert H. Lister and Florence C. Lister*, edited by M. S. Duran and D. T. Kirkpatrick, pp. 99–71. *Papers of the Archaeological Society of New Mexico* 15.

1990   Oral Interview of Bertha Dutton, by Shelby Tisdale. Typescript Manuscript on file in C.S. Fowler's possession, Reno, Nevada.

Dutton, Bertha P. (editor)

1948   *New Mexico Indians Pocket Handbook.* New Mexico Association on Indian Affairs, Santa Fe.

Dutton, Bertha P., and Hulda Hobbs

1943   *Excavations at Tahumulco, Guatemala.* Monograph No. 9. School of American
         Research, Santa Fe, New Mexico.

Dutton, Bertha P., and Miriam A. Marmon

1936   The Laguna Calendar. *Bulletin, University of New Mexico, Anthropological
         Series,* 1:2. Albuquerque.

Fish, Suzanne K. and Paul R. Fish (editors)

2007   *The Hohokam Millennium.* School for Advanced Research Press, Santa Fe,
         New Mexico.

Fowler, Catherine S.

2004   Bertha P. Dutton and the Girl Scouts in the Southwest. Paper presented
         at the 69th Annual Meeting of the Society for American Archaeology, in
         "Unconventional Scholars: Making Archaeology Happen" Symposium,
         Montreal, Canada.

2010   Bertha P. Dutton and the Girl Scouts in the Southwest, 1947–1957. In *Threads,
         Tints and Edification: Papers in Honor of Glenna Dean,* edited by Emily J.
         Brown, Karen Armstrong, David M. Brugge, and Carol J. Condie, pp. 61–71.
         Papers of the Archaeological Society of New Mexico 16. Albuquerque.

Fowler, Don D.

2003   E.L. Hewett, J.F. Zimmerman, and the Beginnings of Anthropology at the
         University of New Mexico, 1927–1946. *Journal of Anthropological Research*
         59(3):305–327.

2010   *A Laboratory for Anthropology: Science and Romanticism in the American
         Southwest, 1846–1930.* Reprinted. The University of Utah Press, Salt
         Lake City. Originally Published 2000, University of New Mexico Press,
         Albuquerque.

Franklin, Judy, and Martha Emory (as Jeff and Marty)

1954   Excavation '54. *The Sipapu* II(1):1–3. Bertha P. Dutton Collection, Museum of
         Indian Arts and Culture/Laboratory of Anthropology Archives, Santa Fe, New
         Mexico.

Galisteo Basin Archaeological Sites Protection Act (GBASPA)

2016   Electronic document, http://galisteo.nmarchaeology.org, accessed August
         20, 2016.

Gifford, Carol A. and Elizabeth A. Morris

1985   Digging for Credit: Early Archaeological Field Schools in the American
         Southwest. *American Antiquity* 50(2)395–411.

Girl Scouts, Inc.

1925   *Scouting for Girls: Official Handbook of the Girl Scouts.* 6th ed. Girl Scouts,
         Inc., New York.

Girl Scouts of the USA (GSUSA)

1950   Personal Equipment List, Archaeological Mobile Camp Program. In
         Application Packet on file, Bertha P. Dutton Collection, Museum of Indian Arts
         and Culture/Laboratory of Anthropology Archives, Santa Fe, New Mexico.

1951   Monthly Report, September–October. National Camping Committee Camping Division, 1946-19xx., GSUSA National Archive, New York.

1952a   Monthly Report, January–February. National Camping Committee, Camping Division 1946-19xx. GSUSA National Archive, New York.

1952b   Monthly Report, June–July. National Camping Committee, Camping Division 1946-19xx. GSUSA National Archive, New York.

1952c   Report, Camps and Camping, 11/24–25. Camp and Camping—Camp—History. GSUSA National Archive, New York.

1953a   Camping Division Report, June, July, August, September 1953. National Camp Committee Camping Division 1946-19xx. GSUSA National Archive, New York.

1953b   Report to Camping Division by Gretchen Yoffa, October–November. Camping Division Records. GSUSA Archives, New York.

1954a   Camping Division Meeting, June 8, 1954. Camping Division, Camp and Camping, Meeting Minutes. GSUSA National Archive, New York.

1954b   Minutes from Camping Division Staff Meeting, September 30, 1954: Subject—1955 Plans—Confirmation and Changes. Camp and Camping, Meeting Minutes. GSUSA National Archive, New York.

1954c   *Girl Scout Handbook: Intermediate Program.* 5th ed. Girl Scouts of the USA, New York.

1954d   Basic Qualifications for National Camping Events for Girls. On file, Bertha P. Dutton Collection, Museum of Indian Arts and Culture/Laboratory of Anthropology Archives, Santa Fe, New Mexico.

1956   Meeting on Special Events, September 24, 1956. Camp and Camping Minutes, 1956. Camp and Camping Division, GSUSA National Archive, New York.

1958   Camp and Camping, Meetings and Minutes 1958. Region IX Box, Camp and Camping Box— Meetings and Minutes, March 25, p. 2. New York.

1962   Rear-View Mirror. *Girl Scout Leader*, 50th anniversary issue. 39:2:27-28, 30-35.

2017a   Girl Scouts and Stem: Changing the World with Science, Technology, Engineering, and Math. Electronic document, https://www.girlscouts.org/en/about-girl-scouts/girl-scouts-and-stem.html, accessed November 12, 2017.

2017b   Sylvia Acevedo Named Next Chief Executive Officer of the Girl Scouts of the USA. Press release, May 17, 2017, https://www.girlscouts.org/en/press-room/press-room/news-releases/2017/sylvia-acevedo-named-GSUSA-CEO.html, accessed November 12, 2017.

2020   Timeline: Girl Scouts in History. Electronic document, https://www.girlscouts.org/en/about-girl-scouts/our-history/timeline.html, accessed February 29, 2020.

Hannum, Alberta

1945   *Spin a Silver Dollar, with Paintings in full color by Beatien Yazz.* Viking, New York.

Hargrave, Lyndon L.

1961   The Identification of Bird Bone Artifacts from Pueblo Largo (LA 183), New Mexico. Manuscript on file, Museum of Indian Arts and Culture/Laboratory of Anthropology Archives, Santa Fe, New Mexico.

1963   The Identification of Bird Bones from Las Madres (LA25), New Mexico. In
        Las Madres (LA 25): Prehistoric Peoples in the Galisteo Basin, New Mexico,
        Vol. 1, First Draft, edited by Bertha Dutton. Manuscript on file, Museum of
        Indian Arts and Culture/Laboratory of Anthropology Archives, Santa Fe, New
        Mexico.

Harlan, Martha
1952   The Dig. *The American Girl* (May):7–10.
1953   Harlan Reports on Camp III. *The Sipapu* I(1):1–3. Bertha P. Dutton Collection,
        Museum of Indian Arts and Culture/Laboratory of Anthropology Archives,
        Santa Fe, New Mexico.

Haury, Emil
1958   Evidence at Point of Pines for a Prehistoric Migration from Northern Arizona.
        In *Migrations in New World Culture History,* edited by Raymond H. Thompson,
        pp. 1–8. Social Science Bulletin No. 27. University of Arizona, Tucson.

Hewett, Edgar Lee
1933   Field School in Jemez Canyon. *El Palacio* 34:56–62.

Holien, Sigrid
1953   Report on Kiva A. Scrapbook on file, Bertha P. Dutton Collection, Museum of
        Indian Arts and Culture/Laboratory of Anthropology Archives, Santa Fe, New
        Mexico.

Hill, Catherine
2015   Solving the Equation: The Variables for Women's success in Engineering and
        Computing. American Association of University Women, Washington D.C.
        Electronic document, https://www.aauw.org/research/solving-the-equation/,
        accessed February 29, 2020
2017   Barriers and Bias: The Status of Women in Leadership. American Association
        of University Women, Washington D.C. Electronic document, https://www.
        aauw.org/research/barriers-and-bias/, accessed February 29, 2020.

Honea, Kenneth
ca. 1963 Flaked Stone Artifacts: Pueblo Largo LA183 and Las Madres LA 25.
        Manuscript on file, Museum of Indian Arts and Culture/Laboratory of
        Anthropology Archives, Santa Fe, New Mexico.

Italie, Leanne
2017   Robots, race cars and weather: Girl Scouts offer new badges. *Associated
        Press*, July 25, 2017, https://apnews.com/51424f354eb546e0ae32f-
        d2a027cb166/Robots,-race-cars-and-weather:-Girl-Scouts-offer-new-badges,
        accessed February 21, 2020.

Joiner, Carol
1992   The Boys and Girls of Summer: The University of New Mexico Archeological
        Field School in Chaco Canyon. *Journal of Anthropological Research*
        48(1):49–66.

Jewell, Andrew and Janis Stout, eds.
2013   *The Selected Letters of Willa Cather.* Knopf Publishing, New York.

Kessinger, Christine
   ca. 1980 Digging Up Bones: Dr. Bertha Dutton, Archaeologist. In "People of the Rio
            Grande," *The Santa Fe New Mexican* (newspaper). Nancy J. Parezo files,
            "Daughters of the Desert," University of Arizona, Tucson.
Kohler, Timothy A. (editor)
   2004   *Archeology of Bandelier National Monument: Village Formation on the
            Pajarito Plateau, New Mexico.* University of New Mexico Press, Albuquerque.
Kohler, Timothy A, Mark D. Varian, and Arron M. Wright (editors)
   2010   *Leaving Mesa Verde: Peril and Change in the Thirteenth-Century Southwest.*
            University of Arizona Press, Tucson.
Lekson, Stephen
   1999   *The Chaco Meridian: One Thousand Years of Political Power in the Ancient
   [2015]   Southwest.* Rowman and Littlefield, Lanham, Maryland.
   2014   Architecture: The Central Matter of Chaco Canyon. In *Living the Ancient
            Southwest,* edited by David Grant Noble, pp. 45–53. School for Advanced
            Research Press, Santa Fe, New Mexico.
Lewis, Nancy Owen, and Kay Leigh Hagan
   2007   *A Peculiar Alchemy: A Centennial History of SAR 1907–2007* School for
            Advanced Research Press, Santa Fe, New Mexico.
Lippard, Lucy, with Photographs by Edward Ranney)
   2010   *Down Country: The Tano of the Galisteo Basin, 1250–1782.* Museum of New
            Mexico Press, Santa Fe.
Lister, Florence C.
   2018   Aztec West's Great Kiva. In *Aztec, Salmon, and the Puebloan Heartland of
            the Middle San Juan,* edited by Paul F. Reed and Gary M. Brown, pp. 45–52.
            School for American Research, Santa Fe, and University of New Mexico
            Press, Albuquerque.
Lister, Robert H., and Florence C. Lister
   1981   *Chaco Canyon: Archaeology and Archaeologists.* University of New Mexico
            Press, Albuquerque.
Martin, Paul S., and John B. Rinaldo
   1950   *Sites of the Reserve Phase, Pine Lawn Valley, Western New Mexico.* Fieldiana:
            Anthropology 38(3). Field Museum of Natural History, Chicago, Illinois.
   1960   *Excavations in the Upper Little Colorado Drainage, Eastern Arizona.* Fieldiana:
            Anthropology 51(1). Field Museum of Natural History, Chicago, Illinois.
Martin, Susan
   1956   The Dig—1955 Style. *The Sipapu* III(2):1–2. Bertha P. Dutton Collection,
            Museum of Indian Arts and Culture/Laboratory of Anthropology Archives,
            Santa Fe, New Mexico.
Masto, Catherine Cortez and Sylvia Acevedo.
   2019   Girls are key to powering America's STEM future. *Reno Gazette Journal* 24
            January:6E.

Mathien, Frances Joan

1992   Women of Chaco: Then and Now. In *Rediscovering Our Past: Essays on the History of American Archaeology,* edited by Jonathan E. Reyman, pp. 103–130. Avebury Press, Albershot, United Kingdom.

2003   Lucy L. Wilson, Ph.D. An Eastern Educator and the Southwestern Pueblos. In *Philadelphia and the Development of Americanist Archaeology,* edited by Don D. Fowler and David R. Wilcox, pp. 134–155. The University of Alabama Press, Tuscaloosa, Alabama

Mathews, Thomas

1957   Faunal Identification of Bone Artifacts: Mammals, Pueblo Largo (LA-183), New Mexico. Manuscript on file, Museum of Indian Arts and Culture/ Laboratory of Anthropology Archives, Santa Fe, New Mexico.

Miller, Darlis A.

2010   *Open Range: The Life of Agnes Morley Cleaveland.* University of Oklahoma Press, Norman.

Mills, Barbara J.

2005   Curricular Matters: The Impact of Field Schools. In *Southwest Archaeology in the Twentieth Century,* edited by Linda S. Cordell and Don D. Fowler, pp. 60–80. University of Utah Press, Salt Lake City.

Morley, Sylvanus G.

1908   Excavations at Cannonball Ruin in Southwest Colorado. *American Anthropologist* 10:598–610.

Morris, Elizabeth Ann and Caroline B. Olin

1997   Obituary: Bertha Pauline Dutton 1903–1994. *American Antiquity* 62(4):652–658.

Myers, Anita

1954   Archaeological Mobile Camp III—1954: Report—Assistant Director. Bertha P. Dutton Collection, Museum of Indian Arts and Culture/Laboratory of Anthropology Archives, Santa Fe, New Mexico.

Nash, Beth

1955   Personal Report on Archaeological Mobile Camp II, July 16–July 30, 1955. Bertha P. Dutton Collection, Museum of Indian Arts and Culture/Laboratory of Anthropology Archives, Santa Fe, New Mexico.

National Park Service

2018   Crashing the Gates: Female Archaeologists in the National Parks. Lesson Plan 2: Scouts with Shovels: Bertha Dutton. Electronic document, https://www.nps.gov/teachers/classrooms/scouts-shovels-bertha-dutton.htm, accessed February 29, 2020.

2019   Girl Scout Ranger Program. Electronic document, https://www.nps.gov/subjects/youthprograms/girlscoutranger.htm, accessed February 18, 2019.

Nelson, Margaret C. and Michelle Hegmon (editors)

2010   *Mimbres Lives and Landscapes.* School for Advanced Research Press, Santa Fe, New Mexico.

Nelson, Nels

1914   *Pueblo Ruins of the Galisteo Basin, New Mexico.* American Museum of
         Natural History Anthropological Papers 13(1):1–124.

New Mexico Magazine

1983   Dutton's Dirty Diggers. June:21.

Noble, David Grant (editor)

2000   *Ancient Ruins of the Southwest: An Archaeological Guide.* Northland
         Publishing, Flagstaff, Arizona.

2004   *In Search of Chaco: New Approaches to an Archaeological Enigma.* School of
         American Research Press, Santa Fe, New Mexico.

2006   *The Mesa Verde World: Explorations in Ancestral Pueblo Archaeology.* School
         of American Research Press, Santa Fe, New Mexico.

2008   *Santa Fe: History of an Ancient City.* Revised and Expanded Ed. School for
         Advanced Research Press, Santa Fe, New Mexico.

2014   *Living the Ancient Southwest.* School for Advanced Research Press, Santa Fe,
         New Mexico.

Ortman, Scott G.

2012   *Winds Out of the North: Tewa Origins and Historical Anthropology.* University
         of Utah Press, Salt Lake City.

Parezo, Nancy J.

1993a   Preface. In *Hidden Scholars: Women Anthropologists and the Native American
         Southwest*, edited by Nancy J. Parezo, pp. xi–xix. University of New Mexico
         Press, Albuquerque.

1993b   Anthropology: The Welcoming Science. In *Hidden Scholars: Women
         Anthropologists and the Native American Southwest*, edited by Nancy J.
         Parezo, pp. 3–37. University of New Mexico Press, Albuquerque.

Parezo, Nancy J. (editor)

1993   *Hidden Scholars: Women Anthropologists and the Native American Southwest.*
         University of New Mexico Press, Albuquerque.

Peckham, Steward, Nancy Fox, and Marjorie Lambert

1981   The Laboratory in the Modern Era: 1947–1981. *El Palacio* 87(3):32–44.

Poling-Kempes, Leslie

2015   *Ladies of the Canyons: A League of Extraordinary Women and Their
         Adventures in the American Southwest.* University of Arizona Press, Tucson.

Powers, Robert P. (editor)

2005   *The Peopling of Bandelier: New Insights from the Archaeology of the Pajarito
         Plateau.* School of American Research Press, Santa Fe, New Mexico.

Reed, Erik K.

1956   The 14th Century Populations of the Galisteo Basin: Skeletal Remains and
         Burial Methods. Manuscript on file, Museum of Indian Arts and Culture/
         Laboratory of Anthropology Archives, Santa Fe, New Mexico.

Reed, Paul F. (editor)

2008   *Chaco's Northern Prodigies: Salmon, Aztec, and the Ancient Anasazi of the Middle San Juan Region after 1100 AD.* University of Utah Press, Salt Lake City.

Reed, Paul F., and Gary M. Brown (editors)

2018   *Aztec, Salmon, and the Puebloan Heartland of the Middle San Juan.* University of New Mexico Press, Albuquerque.

Reimers, Sandra

1955   Pueblo Largo—1955: Plaza V. Manuscript on file, Museum of Indian Arts and Culture/Laboratory of Anthropology Archives, Santa Fe, New Mexico.

Reyman, Johnathan E.

1999   Women in Southwestern Anthropology: 1895–1945. In *Assembling the Past: Studies in the Professionalization of Archaeology,* edited by Alice B. Kehoe and Mary Beth Emmerichs, pp. 213–228. University of New Mexico Press, Albuquerque.

Roberts, Alice

2014   The Wupatki Navajos. In *Living the Ancient Southwest,* edited by David Grant Noble, pp. 89–95. School for Advanced Research Press, Santa Fe, New Mexico.

Robinson, Roxana

1989   *Georgia O'Keeffe: A Life.* Harper Collins, New York.

Rossiter, Margaret W.

1982   *Women Scientists in America: Struggles and Strategies to 1940.* The Johns Hopkins University Press, Baltimore, Maryland.

Rudnick, Lois Palken

1987   *Mabel Dodge Luhan: New Woman, New Worlds.* University of New Mexico Press, Albuquerque.

Salomon, Julian Harris

1928   *The Book of Indian Crafts and Indian Lore.* Harper and Brothers, New York.

SantaFe.com

2015   Treasured Lincoln Canes a Living Spirit of New Mexico's Tribes. Electronic document, http://santafe.com/article/treasured-lincoln-canes-a-living-spirit-of-new-mexicos-tribes, accessed February 29, 2020.

Schaafsma, Curtis F.

1967   Pueblo Largo Metates; Plus Stone Tools Other than Manos and Metates. Manuscript on file, including drafts, Museum of Indian Arts and Culture/Laboratory of Anthropology Archives, Santa Fe, New Mexico.

1995   The Chronology of Las Madres Pueblo (LA 25). In *Of Pots and Rocks: Papers in Honor of A. Helene Warren,* edited by Meliha S. Duran and David T. Kirkpatrick, pp. 155–165. The Archaeological Society of New Mexico: 21. Albuquerque.

Schaafsma, Polly (editor)

2007   *New Perspectives on Pottery Mound Pueblo.* University of New Mexico Press, Albuquerque

Shetterly, Margot L.

2016   *Hidden Figures: The American Dream and the Untold Story of the Black Women Mathematicians Who Helped Win the Space Race.* HarperCollins Publishers, New York.

Simmons, Leo W. (editor)

1942   *Sun Chief: The Autobiography of a Hopi Indian.* Yale University Press, New Haven, Connecticut.

Sinclair, John

1951   The Story of Kuaua. *Papers of the School of American Research* 45. Santa Fe, New Mexico.

Skidmore, Marilyn

1954   Pueblo Largo, July 26–August 9, 1954: Notes. Exploratory Trench B2 (with Annex A; Refuse Mound B1). Manuscript on file, Museum of Indian Arts and Culture/Laboratory of Anthropology Archives, Santa Fe, New Mexico.

Smith, Watson

1952   *Kiva Mural Decorations at Awatovi and Kwaika-a, with a Survey of Other Wall Paintings in the Pueblo Southwest.* Peabody Museum of American Archaeology and Ethnology, Harvard University, Papers, Vol. XXX–VII. Reports of the Awatovi Expedition, No. 5. Cambridge, Massachusetts.

Snead, James E.

2005   Burnt Corn Pueblo and the Tano Origins Project. *Archaeology Southwest* 19:4:6–7.

2011   Burnt Corn Pueblo and the Archaeology of the Galisteo Basin. In *Burnt Corn Pueblo: Conflict and Conflagration in the Galisteo Basin A.D. 1250–1325*, edited by James E. Snead and Mark W. Allen, pp. 1–11. Anthropological Papers of the University of Arizona No. 74. Tucson.

Snead, James A., and Mark Allen (editors)

2011   *Burnt Corn Pueblo: Conflict and Conflagration in the Galisteo Basin A.D. 1250–1325.* Anthropological Papers of the University of Arizona No. 74. Tucson.

Stein, Mary Anne

1955–56 Diaries and Letters Home, Archaeological Mobile Camp, 1955, and Dig, 1955–1956. Manuscript on loan to C.S. Fowler, 2017–19.

1956   Scrapbook, 1955 Mobile Camp; Dig Camp 1956. Bertha P. Dutton Collection, Museum of Indian Arts and Culture/Laboratory of Anthropology Archives, Santa Fe, New Mexico.

2008a   Excerpted Letters Home, 1956 Dig. Manuscript in possession of C.S. Fowler.

2008b   Excerpted Diary Entries, 1955 Archaeological Mobile Camp. Manuscript in possession of C.S. Fowler.

Stewart, Tamara J.

2005   Preservation Efforts in the Galisteo Basin. *Archaeology Southwest* 19(4):14.

Stobie, Evelyn

  1955   The Diggings in '48. *The Sipapu* II(2):3–4. Bertha P. Dutton Collection, Museum of Indian Arts and Culture/Laboratory of Anthropology Archives, Santa Fe, New Mexico.

Sweeney, Catherine (Kay)

  1957   Scrapbook of Southwest Archaeological Mobile Camp, 1957. In possession of C.S. Fowler.

Swift, Kate

  1953   Girl Scout Archaeological Excavation Camp, 1953. Bertha P. Dutton Collection, Museum of Indian Arts and Culture/Laboratory of Anthropology, Santa Fe, New Mexico.

Theil, A. Paul

  1953a   Digging for a Hobby—The Story of "Dutton's Dirty Diggers. *Straight* (formerly *Boys' Life*) LX 28 (April 12):6–7.

  1953b   Junior Archaeologists. *New Mexico* (April):22–23, 45.

Thomas, Diane D.

  1978   *The Southwest Indian Detours.* Hunter Publishers, Phoenix, Arizona.

Vagins, Deborah J.

  2018   The Simple Truth About the Gender Pay Gap. Electronic document, American Association of University Women, Washington, D.C. http://aauw.org/research/the-simple-truth-about-the-gender-pay-gap/, accessed February 29, 2020.

Van Dyke, Ruth M.

  2007   *The Chaco Experience: Landscape and Ideology at the Center Place.* School for Advanced Research Press, Santa Fe, New Mexico.

Van Eyck, Zack

  1994a   Renowned Archaeologist, Museum Director Dies. *The Santa Fe New Mexican.* 12 September:A7, A9.

  1994b   Memorial Service for Bertha Dutton. *The Santa Fe New Mexican.* 13 September:A11.

Varien, Mark D.

  2010   Depopulation of the Northern San Juan Region: Historical Review and Archaeological Context. In Timothy A. Kohler, Mark. D. Varien, and Aaron M. Wright, editors, *Leaving Mesa Verde: Peril and Change in the Thirteenth-Century Southwest*, pp. 1–33. University of Arizona Press, Tucson

Wadsworth, Ginger

  2012   *First Girl Scout, the Life of Juliette Gordon Low.* Clarion Books, New York.

Wagner, Sallie

  1997   *Wide Ruins: Memories of a Navajo Trading Post.* University of New Mexico Press, Albuquerque.

Watkins, Frances E.

  1928   Letter to Dr. Edgar L. Hewett, October 24, 1928, and Newspaper Clipping. AC15.08, School of American Research Miscellaneous Records. School for Advanced Research, Santa Fe, New Mexico.

Wendorf, Fred and Erik K. Reed

1955   An Alternative Reconstruction of Northern Rio Grande Prehistory. *El Palacio* 62(5-6):131–173.

Wethey, Gillian H.

1953   Camp I: An International View. *The Sipapu* I(1):4–6. Bertha P. Dutton Collection, Museum of Indian Arts and Culture/Laboratory of Anthropology Archives, Santa Fe, New Mexico.

1955   Girl Scouts Southwestern Trek. *Arizona Highways* 31(6):14–17.

Wikipedia

2018a   Girl Scouts of the United States of America. Electronic document, http://en.wikipedia.org/wiki/Girl_Scouts_of_the_USA, accessed October 20, 2018.

2018b   Female Education in STEM. Electronic document, http://en.wikipedia.org/wiki/Female_education_in_STEM, accessed October 28, 2018.

2019   Kinsey Reports. Electronic document, https://en.wikipedia.org/wiki/Kinsey_Reports, accessed February 14, 2019.

2020   Girl Scout Senior Roundup. Electronic document, https://en.wikipedia.org/wiki/Girl_Scout_Senior_Roundup, accessed March 6, 2020.

Wilson, Gordon P. (editor)

2009   Guide to Ceramic Identification: Northern Rio Grande Valley and Galisteo Basin to AD 1700. *Laboratory of Anthropology Technical Series Bulletin* No. 12. Laboratory of Anthropology, Museum of Indian Arts and Culture/Laboratory of Anthropology, Santa Fe, New Mexico.

Wilson, Gordon P., Leslie G. Cohen, and Carole Gardner, with Stuart Patterson, Database Manager

2015   *Pueblo Largo (LA283), Including the Excavations of Bertha Dutton, 1951–1956, and Unpublished Manuscripts from David M. Brugge, Lyndon L. Hargrave, Richard Honea, Thomas W. Mathews, and Erik P. Reed*. Maxwell Museum Technical Series No. 23. University of New Mexico, Albuquerque.

Wilshusen, Richard H.

2006   The Genesis of Pueblos: Innovations between 500 and 900 CE. In *The Mesa Verde World: Explorations in Ancestral Pueblo Archaeology*, edited by David Grant Noble, pp. 19–27. School of American Research Press, Santa Fe, New Mexico.

Woodbury, Richard B.

1993   *Sixty Years of Southwestern Archaeology: A History of the Pecos Conference*. University of New Mexico Press, Albuquerque.